THE GUARDIAN BOOK
OF THE COUNTRYSIDE

THE GUARDIAN BOOK OF THE COUNTRYSIDE

SELECTED BY RUTH PETRIE

INTRODUCTIONS BY MARTIN WAINWRIGHT

guardianbooks

Published by Guardian Books 2008

2 4 6 8 10 9 7 5 3 1

First published in Great Britain in 2008 by
Guardian Books
119 Farringdon Road
London EC1R 3ER

www.guardianbooks.co.uk

A CIP catalogue record for this book
is available from the British Library

ISBN 978-0-85265-109-4

Designed by Two Associates
Typeset by seagulls.net

Printed and bound in Germany by
GGP Media GmbH, Pößneck

❧ CONTENTS ❧

❧ INTRODUCTION ❧

In very recent times, the *Guardian* was something of a rarity in many parts of the English countryside. A copy or two in the village store would be overshadowed by a pile of the shires' apparently preferred choice of reading, the *Daily Telegraph*. That has changed, not in the sense that the newspaper is necessarily sweeping all before it, but because the people who live in rural Britain have also changed. A small fraction of them now earn their living from farming and related, traditional rural trades. Tourism, telecottaging, commuting and retirement each account for a much bigger share.

Readers do not buy an international newspaper, by and large, to learn about their own patch of the planet. But if a *Guardian* is left lying about in the village pub or the church hall, a curious newcomer to the paper who picks it up and scans through may be surprised by the sheer amount of writing they discover which deals with the countryside, conservation and generally 'green' affairs. If they go one step further and access the new digital archive, which puts 187 years of *Guardian* journalism within a mouseclick's reach, they will also find that this has always been the case.

Some of the most famous names in the countryside's literary roll of honour have written for the newspaper, from Richard Jefferies to Richard Mabey. John Masefield was actually on the full-time staff. The leading voices on either side of the many debates which have engulfed the countryside since 1821 are also represented, at length. And Merrie England is here too, in all its vivid, bucolic fun.

More than 170 pieces are interspersed with brief introductory essays which pick out a number of other rural themes, some touched on in the main selection, others not. Enjoyment is the main, simple aim, but we hope that you will also find a series of signposts to further reading or web-browsing, like those throughout the British countryside which were famously removed in 1939 to ensure that invaders would be baffled by the dense web of drunkenly rolling English roads and serpentine lanes.

There is so much more to discover. The British countryside has been fought over, brutalised and exploited from humanity's first arrival, and our means of changing things are today so devastating that the threat of irreversible damage to landscape, flora and fauna is real. But park the car, open the kiss-gate, take the track, and soon, almost anywhere outside the country's towns, you can be immersed in what Andrew Marvell called 'a green thought in a green shade'. We hope that in the comfort of your armchair, or on a picnic rug in the countryside itself, this book has the same effect.

The editors would like to thank Eric Hilaire and the *Guardian* and *Observer*'s Newsroom for their help with pictures. Thanks also to Lisa Darnell and Sara Montgomery at Guardian Books, and especially to Helen Brooks and Poppy Hughes for their attentive and careful help in transforming archive material into print.

❧ CHAPTER ONE ❧

Green fields, battlefields
1840–1920s

The *Manchester Guardian* was born on the day that Napoleon died, May 5 1821, and its founding fathers were famously influenced by the Peterloo Massacre, which took place in their city two years earlier. The two events are connected and both are profoundly linked to the British countryside, whose gentle sweetness is all too often a sham when it comes to mankind's business rather than Nature's.

The 10 Mancunians and one American who founded the *Guardian* (all of them textile entrepreneurs) were not driven primarily by altruism, even though it played a part. They were businessmen as well as (for the most part) Unitarians and believers in social improvement, justice and fair dealing. Like all the 'haves' of their time, they were frightened of the 'have nots' and the roots of their fear lay in the French Revolution.

They saw the seeds of something similar in the slums of their own city, but not only there. We have become so urban that we naturally but mistakenly think that great political movements must have city roots. The Paris guillotine, like the distant but still terrifying ex-emperor on St Helena, became the lasting symbol of overthrow and mayhem. But in Britain in the 1820s the most gruesome stories still circulating about the French Revolution concerned the butchery of landlords and their families on their country estates.

Riding out from Manchester, the cottonmen-turned-journalists were at once in a countryside similarly afflicted by depression, poor farming and rotten wages, which drove anyone with any hopes of self-improvement into the burgeoning industrial towns. The ruling aristocracy, whose powerbase was almost entirely rural, were in a state approaching siege. Two months after the first *Manchester Guardian* appeared, the much older *Macclesfield Courier* announced a self-defence organisation set up by local landowners, the Leekfrith Association for the Prosecution of Felons, whose list of offences gives an idea of what was going on. Here they are:

Burglary, highway or footpad robbery. Wilful arson of a dwelling, barn, stable building, ricks, corn, grain or hay. The maiming of horses, bulls, oxen, etc., sheep, pigs. Stealing corn, grain, hay, clover out of buildings, ricks or stocks. Stealing cocks or turkeys, geese, ducks, hens, chickens, turnips, potatoes, carrots, cabbages or grass, wagons, implements of husbandry. Robbing any garden, milking any cow or purchasing or receiving stolen goods. Stealing doors, windows, gates, stiles, pens, freaks, rails, posts, hedges, hedge wood fuel of any sort, lime, iron, wood – growing or fallen. Cutting, chopping down, breaking, destroying or carrying away timber trees, fruit trees, plants, underwood, gorse, furze or heath. Damaging wagons, carts, plows, harrows. Taking any fish in any pond, brook or water belonging to us.

It is a list not only of what you might term 'survival offences' – by which the grindingly poor got by in the manner of Robin Hood poaching the King's deer – but more significantly of vengeful attacks on authority. Within five years the embers evident in Leekfrith were fanned in other parts of the country into organised violence and outrage: the rick-burning and wrecking of machinery led by shadowy figures using a shared nom-de-plume on their threatening letters to landowners: 'Captain Swing'.

The letters and the name with its reference to the gallows were intended to be frightening. A typical one to a village parson in Wiltshire read: *Sir, Your name is down amongst the Black Hearts in the Black Book and this is to advise you and the like of you to make your wills. Ye have been the Blackguard Enemies of the People* ... But the conditions which prompted rural mobs to wreck threshing machines and burn barns were nothing less than destitution. In 1826 (four years before the first Swing letter) William Cobbett visited Pewsey and the river Avon valley and recorded the misery in trenchant terms in his famous, and influential, *Rural Rides*:

I have to express my deep shame, as an Englishman, at beholding the general extreme poverty of those who cause this vale to produce such quantities of food and raiment. This is, I verily believe it, the worst used labouring people upon the face of the earth. Dogs and hogs and horses are treated with more civility; and as to food and lodging, how gladly would the labourers change with them! This state of things never can continue many years! By some means or other there must be an end to it; and my firm belief is, that the end will be dreadful.

Cobbett lived in order to broadcast his exposures and remedies, and the same was naturally true of the initial *Manchester Guardian* team. The first editor and eventual outright owner, John Edward Taylor, had been directed towards journalism by a printer friend from Suffolk, John Childs, a radical like Cobbett who told him: 'It is plain you have the elements of public work in you. Why don't you start a newspaper?'

This was typical of what we might call the enlightened response to the sufferings and consequent unruliness of the poor. The other was the authoritarian approach, which initially swept all before it in the countryside. There was no police force and instead the Justices of the Peace, drawn exclusively from the gentry, called out the yeomanry in the shires as their urban counterparts had in St Peter's Field on August 16 1819. By December 1830 more than 2,000 men and women were in custody in the southern counties of England, awaiting trial for rural rioting. Nineteen of them were in due course executed, 600 were jailed for more than a year and 500 were transported to Australia as convicts for terms of between seven years and life.

Gradually, however, the enlightened response gained ground, especially through attempts to spread knowledge and improve the education of the poor. Although struggling against the government's punitive 'taxes on knowledge', which were designed to suppress mass-circulation newspapers, the *Manchester Guardian* challenged reaction successfully from the start. Taylor and his colleagues had to pay 4d out of each 7d cover price to the Treasury, along with 3d duty per pound of paper purchased, and 3s 6d on every advertisement published. In modern values, these sums are respectively £1.17, £2.04, 88p and £12.26, which gives an idea of the size of the burden. But the newspaper thrived, along with such initiatives as Lord Brougham's new Society for the Diffusion of Useful Knowledge, founded in 1825. The poet Robert Southey was among those who witnessed the spread and influence of the press in the countryside. There might only be one paper in a village, he observed, but that was enough: 'One reader serves a taproom of open-mouthed listeners.'

The best evidence of effectiveness, as always, came from opponents. If this goes on, complained the magazine *John Bull* in 1823, the rural poor will all become well-educated and 'who then will sweep the chimneys and kill the pigs?' A tract by A Country Gentleman took the same line, forecasting 'French' government and predicting: 'We are to have our fields ploughed by philosophers.' These were the sort of responses which encouraged the men and women of the 19th century *Manchester Guardian* to report on the countryside as well as the town, to sell copies well beyond their native city and to hold to a reforming, liberal course.

ANTI-CORN-LAW MEETING AT KNUTSFORD

September 27 1843

On Monday last, Mr Cobden, MP, and Mr Bright, MP, met the farmers and others by appointment, at Knutsford, to address them on the present condition of the country, with reference to the corn-law. A concourse of upwards of 1,100 persons, including many farmers – but not nearly so many as might have been expected, for reasons hinted at by the speakers – and a considerable number of farm labourers and respectable inhabitants of the district, assembled on the race course; the stand No.9, and the adjacent ones on each side, being filled with the friends of Mr Cobden, Mr Bright and the influential free-traders of the neighbourhood. From that stand, as from a hustings, the speakers addressed the meeting.

About 11 o'clock, Mr Cobden, Mr Bright, and numerous friends, came upon the hustings, amidst loud cheers. About the same time, there was a procession with flags, band of music, &c., which approached the front of the stand, and took up their station inside the course. They came, we believe, from Wilmslow; on their banners were inscribed various anti-corn-law mottoes, such as 'No sliding-scale', 'No fixed duty', &c., and on one we saw 'Queen Victoria'.

Shortly after 11 o'clock, on the motion of Mr John Howard of Brereton, seconded by Mr Poynton, E. D. Davenport, Esq, was unanimously called to the chair; in taking which, he said he had a bad cold and weak eyes, and must therefore apologise for any deficiency, especially as he came only as a listener, and it was only five minutes since the honour of occupying the chair had been proposed to him. He came there simply as the advocate of free trade, a doctrine, he apprehended, which now needed no apology – (hear! and applause) – indeed the apology ought to come rather from the opposite side for he regarded the meaning of the words to be, the seconding of the benevolent dispensation of Providence, which had endowed different countries with various productions, with the intention that they should interchange them, for the general advantage. (Applause; Mr Cobden observing 'that is the whole bible of free trade'.) If this was true as to freedom of trade in general how much more so of the trade in the great article of human existence? If there was any article on earth in which a free trade was required it was in food – a proposition, he thought, consistent both with reason and religion. But he knew not how it came to pass that many who possessed and called themselves Christians were the greatest opponents of this doctrine. (Hear!) He saw there not many of the landowners of the neighbourhood, and none of the clergy. What was the reason? ('They don't like it!') Why if this had been a meeting for the purpose of running down some poor clergyman for doing a great service to the public, for exposing abuses and performing his duties in an exemplary manner, then indeed, there would have been a muster of a very different kind. (Laughter and applause.) He saw no one present of the same class as himself (the landowners) and doubtless he should be considered by some a very weak and foolish man for advocating the doctrines he did; but when a man came to his time of life there were other considerations besides personal interest which ought to govern him in the interests of the community at large; and considering them, he was prepared to contend, that there ought to be no tax or duty upon corn. (Great applause.)

Mr Bright, MP, then came forward amidst great cheering and said that the deputation of the league (Mr Cobden and himself) at whose request this meeting was held, had no party object to serve and no merely political purpose to advance. The league knew nothing of politics, except as regards the question of free trade, and nearly every one of its active members had consented to lay by his politics upon other questions, until the great question of free trade could be settled. (Hear!) Great Britain was pre-eminently the country in the world most dependent on trade, the monuments of which were everywhere around us; with a dense and rapidly increasing population, which, for a long time past, the land had not supplied, and who must come, in a great measure to pauperism and destitution if trade should ever fail us. (Hear!)

They were there within 15 miles of the seat of the most important trade carried on in the whole world; within two hours' ride of that portion of the civilised world containing the largest number of people in the square mile or acre; they were close upon a county, for which were existing, in prosperous times (and would in all times, if the laws did not interfere with the industry of the people) – (hear!) – a population the most dense, most industrious, and most willing to obtain their living honestly; brought together from all parts of the kingdom and the world, there being 300,000 persons in Lancashire who were not born in that county, and who had been attracted there solely by the extraordinary development of its manufacturing industry. (Hear!)

Dwelling so near this population, the deputation thought themselves justified in calling the attention of the farmers of Cheshire, to a law which was most detrimental to the interests of both counties, as well as of every other in the kingdom. Lancashire was dependent almost entirely on trade and some farmers in Cheshire might suppose that that county was dependent upon the land, but he thought he could convince them that they were quite as dependent upon the people of Lancashire as upon their own county; that although the Mersey separated one county from the other, there was no difference of interest between the people on its northern and its southern banks. The landowners, in labouring to teach the farmers that these interests were different, were inculcating most injurious notions, from the effect of which the farmers were now suffering. (Applause.)

He (Mr Bright) as a Lancashire manufacturer, employed capital and the labour of many hands in producing clothing; and the Cheshire farmers, if they farmed as they ought to do, employed some capital and the labour of the peasantry in producing food. Where was the great difference between them? They both employed the same means of producing what they had to sell, and they both sold to precisely the same people; and it required industry, skill, enterprise, perseverance and the blessing of Providence upon both the one and the other, and prosperity among their customers to enable either to prosper.

In Lancashire they complained of being badly off, because trade was crippled and confined, that with an increasing number of people there was no corresponding increase in the demand for labour and for the employment of capital; and the profits of capital and the wages of labour had consequently declined. They inferred, then, that little trade was bad for Lancashire, and he was there to argue that little trade was just as bad for Cheshire; and that the corn-law, which the Cheshire farmers had supported, was a law every day crippling the trade of this great commercial country, to the injury not only of the manufacturers and artisans of Lancashire, but also of the farmers and farm labourers of Cheshire. (Hear!)

How did the corn-law limit trade? We were a population of 27 million. We made three times as many cotton goods as the people of this country chose to buy, even at the present low prices; far more woollen goods were made in Yorkshire than were consumed in this country; the Sheffield people made twice as much cutlery, and the Birmingham people far more hardware of every description than they could sell at home; the potters of Staffordshire made at least twice as much earthenware &c. as they dispose of in England, and so with the linen, the silk and many other trades. Were we then to sit down and make only just as much as the landowner, the clergy, the farmer and the labourer, and the rest of the community in England could buy? If so, then there could be no employment for all the people. If that were the case, then some would be entirely without employment, and consequently without wages, and many of those employed would only have partial employment, and at very low wages. What were we to do with this surplus? Why, wherever in the world man had emerged but one step from the rudest barbarism, there was a market for the production and manufactures of our people – (hear!) – and they all had something they could give in exchange. We asked merely that no man or body of men here should stand up and separate us, and make us as foes and aliens to each other. (Hear! and applause.) But permit us to fulfil the beneficent designs of Providence, and look upon all mankind as our brethren. (Applause.)

ASHTON-UNDER-LYNE: CHARGE OF IMPURIFYING A STREAM OF WATER
June 12 1856

At the county sessions yesterday, Samuel Fitton was summoned at the instance of Mr Paul Cooper, cotton spinner, Hurst Brooks for throwing nightsoil in the brook which runs into his reservoir, on the 31 ult, and thereby damaging 200 gallons of water.

Mr Cooper stated that on the day in question he caught the defendant wheeling nightsoil and ashes into the brook. He had suffered considerable injury in consequence of this practice, which had been carried on by the defendant for many years, and the nuisance had become so great that Mr Higgs, when inspector of nuisances, had served him with a notice under the Sanitary Act. The defendant was a servant under Mr Fletcher, a collector or sub-agent for the property from which the nightsoil came, and he had often cautioned the defendant and remonstrated with him, but he paid no regard to him.

Mr Brooks, solicitor, who appeared for Mr Fitton, contended that the case did not come under the act relating to malicious injury to property; and that the magistrates had no jurisdiction, as the act expressly provided that it should not extend to a party trespassing who acted under a fair and reasonable supposition that he had a right to do the act complained of. The magistrates inflicted a fine of 5s, and costs.

THE SECRETS OF ANGLING*
August 15 1865

Mr Moffat tells us that he was born on the banks of a lovely and crystal stream, that his childhood was happy as the waters to which he listened and by which he played, and that with a contemplative disposition and a sensitive mind he became a worshipper of nature from habit and association. Parental indulgence permitted a roving life, and thus the boy grew into a sportsman. He speedily 'contracted almost amphibious habits; and from being at first only a babbling dreamer by locks and streams, became eventually a confirmed angler, and an occasional otter hunter'. His hunting notes have already been published, and he gives to the world in the book before us the results of much piscatorial experience.

Anglers will ever constitute a minority of outdoor pleasure seekers. Nature

---

* *The Secrets of Angling* by A. S. Moffat, author of *Reminiscences of Otter Hunting &c.* (Edinburgh: Adam and Charles Black, 1865)

dispenses sparingly an instinct for fishing; even were she more generous, there seems to be a visible and definite limit to the opportunities and employments of disciples of Izaak Walton. Any considerable increase in their number would probably destroy the sport, viewed, we mean, as a solitary but artistic and exciting pursuit of game. Too many rods in a stream would be more than an intolerable nuisance, they would be fatal to angling, and when we reckon the hours, or rather days, spent in the capture of a small creel of fish we are convinced that to the few and happily circumstanced the art will for the most part be confined.

It is amusing to note the enthusiasm of your genuine angler. Everything is superlative. His descriptions are all magical, his enjoyments all but ineffable. He is 'serenely happy' in following his 'craft', 'internally at peace with himself, the world and all mankind'; all nature wears 'the same sunny smile that gilds his own happy reflections'. His prayer is that all ordinary avocations, dealings and pursuits were productive of 'such blessed results' as angling.

Who, then, would not be fishers? They must be the happiest, and being so, the most amiable and charitable of men. But practice, we fear, does not bear out the promise of theory. There are indications in Mr Moffat's revelations, little suggestive hints, which show that fishermen are only like the rest of us, fond of pleasure, inclined to be selfish and, we fancy, testy and ill-tempered when hindered, interfered with or opposed. Why Mr Moffat should call his book *The Secrets of Angling* we do not understand. To the uninitiated his facts are certainly revelations. None but anglers care about baits, rods, lines, throwing, spinning, trolling and striking, and probably none but they will care to join him in inquiries as to the times and seasons of all the 'flies' suitable for fishing purposes – the varieties of worms, grubs, maggots, and minnow employed in ensnaring the finny tribes.

Secrets or not, however, this volume makes public a mass of information which must be acceptable to anglers of every degree of experience. A key to the 'secrets' faces the reader before he turns the title page, and he may speedily learn where in the book the special knowledge he desires is to be found. Rod, reels, lines, artificial and natural flies, minnows, worms, cad-bait, floats and trimmers are minutely dealt with. Bait for every day – indeed for every hour of every day – is carefully analysed, explained, recommended or rejected, and if enthusiasm can keep a man, rod in hand, through the ghostly hours as well as during daylight, he may know how, where and what for to fish through the 'live-long night'. Indeed, from our own perusal of Mr Moffat's opinions we are inclined to think that Toby Tosspot's method of procedure will answer the best in fishing, which is to sacrifice one's 'moderate estate of sun' and borrow 'more largely of the moon'.

The discussion of trout fishing occupies two thirds of the 'secrets'; but salmon, eriox and whittling receive due attention in the remaining third. Mr Moffat writes clearly and intelligently. Tyroes in the art may accept him as a teacher, adepts will sympathise with his enthusiasm, while they profit by his experiences and enjoy his anecdotes.

FARMING FOR LADIES
July 24 1889

The devout student of Dickens will find at Lynn, in Norfolk, much to remind him of his favourite author. In the smoking-room of his inn he will probably, to his infinite delight, meet a group of ancient cronies, each with his churchwarden pipe reserved religiously for his special use, which he puffs audibly, like the ticking of a somewhat wheezy clock. Here, to be sure are Mr John Willett and his Maypole friends, still alive and in the full enjoyment of tobacco and warmth. Then, again, he will hear girls addressed as 'mawther', and will be glad to learn that the snail, as in Mr Peggotty's vocabulary, is still known as a 'dodman'.

The country round will, I regret to add, recall the countesses who repulsed Mr Mantalini in having no outline – not even the 'demd outline' possessed by the Duchess. It is one dreary flat, unrelieved by any object of beauty or interest – except, indeed, the glorious cathedral-like churches which are the pride of the fen country. But this plain, unpicturesque as it may be, contains some of the best agricultural land in England. Hence at Lynn you soon discover that agriculture is the one absorbing topic of conversation, and also that 'high farming' is the universal aim. The talk is all of oilcake, silo-pits, nitrates, guano, pedigree cattle and so forth.

Those who utter their opinions on these subjects are typical Englishmen. In the market place of Lynn on market day you would find very few men indeed whose chest measurements are less than 40 inches and whose waist measurements suggest pessimist views as to agricultural depression. One old gentleman I saw might have walked straight out of the pages of Fielding or Smollett. He wore a low-crowned hat; a vast rotundity of body was clothed in a green coat with brass buttons and a scarlet waistcoat; a pair of spindle legs, tightly gaitered, ended in two enormous boots. I did not know, before I saw this charming figure that such garments – especially such hats – had been manufactured or could have been procured any time during the last half century. Then again, if you watch the landlord carving at the market ordinary;

if you observe the magnificent sweeps of his knife, the prodigious helpings he gives and his generosity with the gravy; if, moreover, you notice the artistic way in which his manipulations suggest the juiciness of the lean and the richness of the fat – any misgivings you may have entertained as to the degeneracy of country-bred Englishmen disappear for ever.

The rural labourers are equally satisfactory. Their peculiar twang, their heartiness of manner, their method of shaking hands as if they were working a pump handle, and their tendency to be doubled up with laughter at exceedingly feeble jokes – all these things combined have relieved me from a serious mistake. I had always imagined that the stage rustic was a product of the stage and did not exist in nature; I now find that he comes from the northern parts of Norfolk.

The object of my visit to this agricultural community was to inquire into an exceedingly interesting experiment in farming. I had heard that two ladies by birth and breeding – and very cultured women to boot – were themselves farming a small farm and in short had voluntarily subjected themselves to the perilous conditions of modern agriculture. On the way I conjectured much and felt greatly puzzled. Surely these ladies would not understand when the ploughing was rightly done, when the cattle were properly fed and when and how the crops should be sown and gathered. Unless they employed a bailiff to superintend everything they would be at the mercy of their labourers. So also they could not be expected to do much work themselves. They might see that the dairy was kept clean and they might feed the poultry in a superior Dresden china sort of way. But they would have to pay for the doing of many things which a small farmer does with his own hands. How could such an experiment be economically successful?

Such was my reasoning and, as will be seen, the reasoning may have been right, but the premises were altogether wrong; in fact, it was difficult to guess the truth beforehand. Most of us, indeed, have read the works of Miss Wetherall, in which the experiences of ladies on American farms are given. Their life, as described by the accomplished novelist, seems to have been simple and luxurious: first they cried, then they quoted texts, then they had a comforting meal of pork, corn cake, pickles and tea, then they cried again, and so on ad infinitum. But such idyllic methods will not answer in these days of fierce competition. I must, however, give the story of the Home Cloister Farm without further preface.

Some years ago Miss Pung was in partnership with her brother, who farmed on a very large scale. Their farming did not prosper and Miss Pung retired from the partnership after suffering considerable losses. Under such circumstances any other lady would have betaken herself to town life, would have cultivated any tendencies she might have in the way of tea drinkings, gossip, curate worship and nervous headaches, and would have lived tolerably happy on her straitened means. Not so Miss Pung. She was fond of the country and of active work, and did not like to give up the battle which the agricultural producer has nowadays to fight. A small freehold farm had come to her by inheritance and here she settled down with Miss Dodds, who had the like tastes and the like determination of character.

These two ladies at once overcame the difficulties which I had imagined for them by doing (with the slight exceptions which I shall mention) the whole work of the farm themselves. They began by mastering the theory and practice of agriculture. They read all the best books on the subject, noticed what went on around them and turned every blunder into a useful lesson. No physical labour possible to women was shirked; no task, however disagreeable, was evaded. The result with regard to their health was remarkable. Headaches and other ailments vanished out of memory and they are now two as sturdily healthy women as one would wish to see. Moreover, they have achieved the triumph of making their farming, even in these bad times, actually successful. In other words, they are earning from it a sufficient income.

This story was told me in a pretty little library containing at least a thousand volumes. It was quite clear that Miss Pung and Miss Dodds do not allow their hard physical work to interfere with their intellectual life. Indeed, they study science in and through their farming operations. At the time of my visit they were, for instance, reading Mr Charles Plowright's *Monograph of the British Uredineae and Ustilagineae.* These appalling words have, I believe, some reference to blight or mildew. Then they have applied themselves to entomology, and Miss Dodds has a shelf of veterinary works, for she courageously avails (chiefly by dieting) any diseases that occur on the farm, and has already attained considerable local repute as an animal doctor. The library opens into a small conservatory, where there is a vine which is Miss Pung's special care and yields, I was told, excellent profits.

After taking all this in I went over the farm with Miss Dodds. There is a large pasture field of six acres, a small croft of an acre and a half and, deducting the garden and the house and farm buildings, the rest is arable. They have one field of boulder clay, the best possible soil for wheat, but otherwise their land is a free loam, brown, fragrant and nutty, and with just enough consistency to prevent the waste of manure. In short, as the ploughman observed, 'It's the finest land as ever crow lit on.' Moreover, the good soil is of uncommon depth and I was shown parsnips which, burrowing downwards and finding still fresh nutriment, elongated themselves to absurd dimensions.

When the two partners first began farming they started a herd of pedigree Kerry cows. But the breed is not popular in that neighbourhood and they found a difficulty in disposing of the calves. So they sold off their herd and took to pigs, thereby following the advice of Arthur Young who (in his *Itinerary of Ireland*, published in the last century) recommended pigs as paying best on a small farm. They have now 53 pigs, all of pedigree breeds, selected particularly for the production of bacon. This they cure themselves, smoking it in their kitchen chimney in the smoke of oak sawdust. The pig-army has turned up much of the pasture-field, but this, Miss Dodds explained, was 'not bad farming', because the pasture wanted renewing and in the spring they would take advantage of the amateur ploughing done by the pigs to sow fresh grass seed.

Beside the pigs they have a horse, which does the carting and takes Miss Pung to market, and a cow named Rosebud, which supplies them with milk and butter. Rosebud is half shorthorn and half Alderney, and of pedigree breed on both sides. Her Alderney parent was from the Prince of Wales's herd and here I must interpose the remark that the Prince's country neighbours are most grateful for his kindness in helping the farmers to improve the breed of their cattle. Miss Pung makes the butter and is a famous hand at the work. Even when Rosebud feeds chiefly on turnips there is no turnip taste in the butter. This is partly due to skill in the making, but still more to the preparation of the turnips for Rosebud's consumption.

On the field, which consists of 'boulder clay', the partners grow wheat. They find it best to treat this field with artificial manure in order to save the expense of carting. On the rest of their farm, enriched with pig manure, they grow white turnips, mangolds, swedes, carrots, cabbages, lettuces and prickly comfrey. The lettuces are consumed in great quantities by the pigs. One thing these ladies have learned by experience: it is most economical to get the best possible seed from the best seed merchants. Miss Dodds showed me a strip of swedes. These had been grown partly from seed supplies by a crack seedsman and partly from seed sold by a local merchant. In the former case the swedes were twice or three times larger than in the latter. Here is a lesson which many farmers, especially in Ireland, are very slow to learn.

And now I come to the important question of labour. As I have, already said, the two ladies do much of the work themselves. They mill, make butter, feed the pigs and help in drilling and sowing and gathering the crops. Laughingly, they assured me that when they had their thick boots on and their common clothes, and were plentifully adorned with soil and mud, they had often been mistaken for labouring women. Again, the task of superintendence is not light. Minute attention to detail is the rule on Home Cloister Farm, so that from the best stock and the best materials the best results may be attained by the best means. Miss Dodds, for example, has every ounce of food for the cow or the pigs prepared under her own eyes. The regular labourers on the farm are two apple-cheeked Norfolk lads, who receive 8s and 6s a week, respectively. For the ploughing a man with a team of two horses is engaged. He charges 10s a day and ought to plough an acre in that time. If he does his work wrongly or badly Miss Dodds is quite able and ready to correct him. The partners, I must add, have no household servant, and only employ a charwoman occasionally.

It will now have been seen under what conditions the partners have been able to make their farming a success. They work like labouring women and sometimes, indeed, like labouring men, and they have learnt their business so thoroughly that they are able to give efficient superintendence to the extra labour they need. Thus in these respects they are on an equality with the ordinary male farmer, and in other respects they beat him all round. Their methods are scientific; they aim at the highest possible excellence; and they have the special feminine power of bestowing unceasing attention on small details. Again, they do not allow themselves to remain in a groove. They watch the markets carefully and at once drop any kind of farming – for instance, they have dropped poultry farming – if they learn that another kind is more profitable. Their experiment therefore demonstrates the possibility of ladies farming with good results to pocket, health and happiness; but, to my thinking, it also demonstrates that not one lady in a hundred has the physical and mental energies which such a life requires.

SHOOTING AND FISHING

April 9 1896

Before Easter grouse moors of moderate extent were fairly in demand, but the higher-priced shootings, equally with deer forests, have not been letting freely. Whether the cause be scarcity of the wherewithal to pay for them, as suggested by some, it is none the less singular that tenants are few in a season which promises exceptionally well. Stalking red deer in Highland forests is scarcely so fashionable a sport as it was some years ago. American millionaires no longer rent vast tracts of deer ground – not always to the benefit of its occupants – and for one man who devotes himself to the arduous, uncertain pursuit of stags, a dozen prefer to walk the heather after grouse. Moreover, the acquisition of a good forest demands a long purse.

As a rule mild, open winters are not followed by good breeding seasons, because winters of this description are usually wet. But that of 1895–6 has proved an exception in this respect. Birds are healthy, well plumaged and forward in condition. Heather burning, which had been delayed by unsuitable weather, is now in full swing and prospects could scarcely be more favourable at this season. The great frost 14 months ago sadly reduced the breeding stock on some shootings, and in consequence these were lightly shot or left altogether untouched last year. The number of grouse on the great majority of moors is fully up to the average this spring. From north Wales I hear excellent accounts of the grouse, and the smoke of the burning heather may be seen from many a hill too.

Although spring salmon fishing has been somewhat interfered with by unfavourable conditions of weather and water – rivers too low at one time and latterly unsettled by constant rains – it has none the less been a success this year, comparing very favourably with the results last season. The heaviest fish so far must be credited to the Shannon, where quite a number of salmon exceeding 40lb have been killed, while a couple each scaling 45lb have been landed from the Killaloe and Castleconnell sections respectively. Angling on the Tay has been disappointing, but as regards weight the great Perthshire river runs the Shannon close with a 42-pounder. The Aberdeenshire Dee is affording grand sport; the river is teeming with salmon and a dozen fish to one rod in a day is no uncommon record.

It is satisfactory to note that the Tweed has given better results than for several years past. In north Wales rivers are on the low side, but trout fishers have been busy and some fair baskets have rewarded their efforts. The male and female March browns, February red, blue, iron and grey duns should kill well at this season, and the latter will be found most deadly without wings, especially in fine water. The Dee at Corwen and Llangollen, the Tryweryn at Bala, the Clwyd at St Asaph, and the Elwy at Llanfair Talhaearn may be mentioned as some favourite angling resorts on rivers, while lakes innumerable afford good sport. April and May are the best months for trouting in north Wales; as the summer advances the fish are slow to take a fly, except on the lakes.

STRAY GATHERINGS IN THE SHOW
June 29 1897
An agricultural show in Manchester is like a foreign body in our midst, recalling one of those streaks or 'faults' of earlier rock which have thrust their way in to the heart of the newer formations. We are so completely taken up with manufacture that

we are almost in danger of forgetting that the largest portion of the nation is concerned with agricultural pursuits, and spends its time in raising crops and in rearing cattle, in making butter and cheese; that fowls are to many a prime object of interest, and that even pigs have their devotees; that the horizon of one section of the population is bounded by the occupations of a farm.

Yet one has only to visit the Royal Agricultural Show to see that this is so, and that there is a point of view from which those connected with the display are as interesting a subject of study as the exhibits. It is so keenly written on the faces of the men who move about among the sheep and cattle that their minds are wholly absorbed in the livestock under their charge, and that they neither know nor care about anything beyond.

They hardly seem to see the crowds who wander about from stall to stall. Their way of life, so different from ours, produces its own quaint philosophy of things, a philosophy born of close communion with one aspect of nature's forces. Their experiences have been chiefly concerned with the courses of life and death and the recurring changes of the seasons, and it is possible that the adoption of machinery in farming operations brought on so rapidly, may do more, by the introduction of a new factor, to change their modes of thought than a most elaborately devised system of elementary or mechanical education. Until the advent of machinery – 'the devil's own team,' as an enraged landowner once termed it – the link with the past had not been broken, and the farmer and his labourers carried on, in not dissimilar fashion, the occupations which have been the chief concern of mankind since the dawn of history.

With the occupations there lingered, too, something of the thoughts and feelings, the habits of mind, and a few of the customs and superstitions of early times. The student of folklore is well aware that information of the highest value with regard to remote periods of civilisation is still to be gathered in conservative English villages, while from some of the more backward countries of the continent there emerges every now and then some fact which shows with startling clearness that the mental characteristics of early periods are as yet far from having ceased to exercise their influence upon the actions of mankind.

These, however, are matters which are chiefly interesting to the student, and agricultural shows are designed primarily for the practical man. After all, the person for whom all the ingenuity is set in motion, all this display arranged, is ultimately the consumer. And perhaps it may be admissible to consider the show for a few minutes from the point of view of what we may call the 'intelligent consumer'. The community at large has undoubtedly benefited enormously by the foreign competition which has proved so fierce a trial to the British farmer. We are better fed, have a more generous, a more varied, and more wholesome diet than our fathers. Take the fruit supply of Manchester, for example. Bananas, once a rarity, are to be had all the year round, oranges are at this moment on every stall, though a few years ago June would have been reckoned three months out of date, and in the cherry and strawberry season the railway stations are encumbered with huge piles of baskets, full in the morning, empty at night. We may grumble at eating New Zealand mutton or American beef under the name of English; but all the same we have better meat and a more varied supply than our fathers had, and if it were not for foreign meat there would have been a famine long ago, or we would have seen ourselves compelled to accept any inferior article that the home producer thought fit to thrust upon us. But, in spite of such improvements as have been indicated, the consumer, if he is not among those who, as the French waiter tersely put it, 'do not distinguish what they eat,' has some grievances against the newer order of things. Though the general level of food commodities has improved, the standard reached is not that of the best under the old regime, and some of the excellences of former days have either disappeared altogether or have become inaccessible to persons of relative means by reason of scarcity or dearness. Take butter for example. Formerly we made up for the heavily salted butter of the winter months by delicious unsalted butter in summer; now the average household is appeased with Danish butter of fair or moderate quality all year round, but real fresh butter is beyond the purse of the multitude. The flavour of good fresh butter – now called 'farm' butter – is almost unknown to the majority of middle-class townsmen and their families.

In such particulars the agricultural show is a source of bewilderment to the lay mind. There is a magnificent display of poultry, the fowls exhibited are gorgeous creatures and their vocal powers, at any rate, are of the most pronounced but why, after all this careful breeding, are eggs so scarce? To judge from shop windows, eggs would seem to be stale from the laying, the disproportion between the stale and the fresh is so great. One wonders how the piles of cooking eggs have had time to pass into staleness before being eaten by a populace greedy of fresh eggs. No doubt there is a want of quick communication with districts such as the west of Ireland which ought to supply fresh eggs: but these are points for the caterer and the agriculturist to settle; the irate consumer only knows that he not infrequently sends his egg in haste from the breakfast table with what are deemed suitable objections.

The jam-maker has struggled so courageously and on the whole so successfully that it would be harsh to disparage his person and it may be that factory methods are in danger of rivalling the homely and domestic preserving pan filled with fresh-gathered fruit and tended by loving hands. Some of the pickles and preserves which our grandmothers used to make with so much care are almost unrecognisable in their present form of shop-bought goods, which must be unpalatable to those who remember the old flavour. What, for example, are the pickled cabbages sold in the shops compared to the ancient home-made variety? The making of them was almost a religious ritual and it was a marked day in the yearly calendar when the walnuts, each carefully chosen, and generally of enormous size were laid out on the grass in the sun to undergo the first part of the process. These and other well remembered produce have disappeared, a sacrifice to the new methods which have rendered possible a much wider range of commodities and a greater variety. While thankfully recognising the benefits conferred, however, the intelligent consumer may be forced to query as he wanders round the Royal Show and notes the keen energy displayed in every department, whether these exhibitions will end by restoring to us the most important at any rate of our lost excellences.

FARM NOTES

September 9 1897

Is high farming a mistake? This is a question which has repeatedly arisen, and which is discussed on the basis of the evidence of several of the witnesses in the report of the Royal Commission. While on the one hand it is urged that the more highly a man farms the more he loses, it is shown on the other hand that low farming is a mistake, while some of those – and among them Sir John Lawes – who are not favourable to high farming in the ordinary acceptation of the word, admit that it is possible to farm low with bad results and that a line must be drawn.

It would appear, upon examination of the question, that the term 'high farming' has been often misapplied. In days gone by, farmers and others with money in their pockets to spend took great delight in cultivating their land, in maintaining their stock and their buildings in what may be termed show condition. The fields were as clean as gardens, the land heavily manured and splendidly cultivated, and the crops magnificent. When prizes were offered by the Royal Agricultural Society for the best cultivated farms there were many cases – and I speak from repeated inspection of many of these farms – in which money was lavishly spent for the purpose of winning the prize. This was high farming in one sense of the word, but it is misapplication of the term. In a common sense view of the question, high farming should mean good farming and cultivation, including the employment of sufficient manure and labour to secure a satisfactory crop. Let it be remarked that it is possible to manure at a loss; in other words, it is possible to increase the crop by the application of manure to such an extent that every extra bushel of corn grown or hundredweight of grass mown costs more than it is worth, and it is here that high farming should cease, the object being to obtain as large a crop as possible, not altogether at a minimum expenditure, but at an expenditure which is warranted by the return.

I recently had an opportunity of inspecting a farm, a portion of which had been damaged by the inroad of a neighbour's cattle. The wheat was a lamentable sight, the plant being extremely thin, promising not more than three sacks to the acre, nature having filled up the vacant places with the worst of weeds, while the mangold crop adjoining, if not equally thin, was poor in the extreme, not so much because of the poverty of the soil – which is naturally excellent – but of a bad plant. Adjoining this was a piece of oats, which was the poorest and foulest that I ever remember to have seen, docks and thistles, among other weeds, absolutely choking the poor plant and already commencing to shed their seed. The tenant made a bitter complaint, followed by a claim, which it was the object of himself and his neighbour to settle. It was remarked that some portions of the crops were not worth the labour of saving and that the necessity of cutting the foulest in order to prevent the seeding of the land scarcely existed any longer, the weeds having become too ripe. The reply was that prices were so bad that it did not pay to farm well, and this was practically the excuse for the condition of the fields, which would assuredly have shamed 99 farmers in every hundred.

This is, however, a sample of many cases which I have known, and of many more in which the state of affairs was not quite so bad. It must surely follow that if a crop is not worth harvesting it is not worth sowing. Whatever crops a farmer intends to produce, a certain amount of labour is entailed. If nothing is expended in manure, there is the cost of ploughing, harrowing, rolling and seeding, and the sum expended for each item is no larger when the crop is large than when it is small or worthless. If, therefore, the initial expenditure on a crop is £4 an acre and the produce is worth only £3 then there is a definite and serious loss upon every acre cultivated. If, however, the cost is increased by higher farming to £6 an acre with the result that the produce is only worth an equivalent sum of money, no loss is entailed upon the crop, while the land is left in good condition for future years. The result is that if there is no immediate profit the expenditure, which must follow in the next process of cultivation, is diminished rather than – as in such a case as we have mentioned – enormously increased. Comparisons of this kind can be multiplied freely, but the principle involved will always be found the same. It seems to me to follow that there is a certain amount of labour which is absolutely necessary in connection with every crop, and that if this is diminished in the vain hope that money will be saved a farmer is deluding himself, for he is only saving a pound today to spend £2 tomorrow.

Let us take the root crop as another example of the importance of labour. A good result cannot be achieved unless the land is in practically perfect condition. There should be a deep tilth and the soil, as far as the tilth goes, should be fine and rich. Tilth depends first of all upon early ploughing, before winter, followed by frosts and consequent pulverising; this, in its turn, is followed by two or perhaps three ploughings if the land requires it. Exceptional instances are, of course, omitted from this calculation. Nevertheless, I have repeatedly seen roots drilled upon soil which is hard beneath or which is lumpy at the surface, with the result that there has either been a failure of plant altogether or less than a quarter of a crop. Some farmers argue that a root crop is necessarily a losing crop, that it is costly and a mere preparation for grain and seeds, but this not correct. It is probable that where roots are carefully grown and thoughtfully used they are the most – or one of the most – profitable crops on the farm.

Ordinarily the yield of a crop of mangolds or of swedes – and the remark applies equally to potatoes – depends upon the labour employed and the manure used. It is possible to spend money in both departments carelessly and to reap little or no result in consequence. But just as a skilled gardener knows that in potting particular kinds of plants he will fail unless he mixes the soil as experience dictates, so it is that the root grower fails if the mechanical condition of the soil is imperfect and its quality is not enriched by the employment of manure. Again a root plant may be secured and nevertheless spoiled or immensely diminished in value by defective cultivation. Singling should be carried out early and the horse hoe kept continuously at work, not merely cutting off the weeds as they grow between the rows but stirring the soil – one of the most important features in root cultivation. Whether the hand hoe or the horse hoe is used, the work performed is almost as beneficial to the plant, by the moving of the soil as by the killing of the weeds with the ulterior object of cleaning the soil and preventing the future distribution of seeds, which would assuredly damage if not destroy the crop of the following year.

There is no doubt that in the past large sums of money have been expended in the purchase of manure which were in no sense of the word justified: but English farmers are men of great liberality when they have money to spend, and in many instances there is much personal pride and satisfaction in making liberal purchase of artificial fertilisers and of feeding cakes in the public market. If these purchases are followed with commensurate result the action of the farmer is justified, and his judgment and liberality is praised: but if, as has often happened, the results have not been commensurate with the expenditure, then it follows, in the majority of cases at least, that his knowledge of the requirements of the soil is defective or that liberal manuring has not been accompanied by thorough cultivation.

THE CENTRAL SPINE OF ALL ENGLAND
December 26 1903

Of all the four Bank Holidays in the year, today is the one we townsmen have least learnt to use. At Easter, Whitsuntide and the beginning of August everyone now goes out of doors to kiss his mother earth and be strong again. At Christmas there still lurks undispelled in us the dread of early man for his still unbaffled adversaries, cold and rain. We stick by the fire as if in the first flush of our forefathers' joy at learning to light one; we make as prime an aim of keeping dry as if we had only just caulked the roof of the cave. Affection and repletion reinforce primitive instinct; of all Bank Holidays it is the one on which most friends are seen again, and on the eve of which the truths enforced by Mr Barrie have been least regarded.

Still there are some – and every year there are more – who take to the open for their Boxing Day, even though there be no ice to skate on, no snow to toboggan and no road shallow enough in mud for a bicycle to wade. They lift up their eyes to the hills; they make, if they can, for the mountains of Wales or the Lakes; if not, they turn due east if they be Manchester men, and at the end of a morning's walk from a suburban station – Glossop, Crowden, Greenfield or any one of half-a-dozen others – they eat their sandwiches on the tip of the ridge of the Pennine, sitting on the central spine of all England and seeing the whole country fall away below their feet, eastwards and westwards towards the sea and southwards to the great central English plain where our northern and western crust of stone, with all its incidents of stonewalled fields, grey cottages and black pit-heads, dips down under the broad level sea of sands and clays that bear the wheat and hedges and brickfields.

Standing on Stanedge or Langsett Moor, you can almost see with your eyes how Cobden came to be, and why Mr Chaplin is unlike him; walking from Oldham to Holmfirth on a soft day, you may suddenly find all the separate industrial history of Lancashire and Yorkshire conveyed to you compactly in a slackening of the rain as you work past Dead Head Moss and leave behind the steep, drenched western slopes on which the ruling wind has dropped most of its takings from the Atlantic, to enter on the drier, brighter eastern slant. On these heights – to which a Manchester cyclist can ride after luncheon and be back for tea – there stick out the raw ends of half the forces that have shaped England's life. You get your country's history poured in at your five senses, not merely read of in a book, but seen in the contrast of two landscapes viewed at once, or heard in the several qualities of the sound of moorland streams, or perhaps felt in the goodness or badness of the holds on a wayside rock that you stop to climb, or in the changing intervals between the drops that fall from a soaked cap to your nose as you cross a wide upland.

Of course the Pennine is no Alps. Still, it is genuine mountain. South of Whernside, Ingleborough, and Pen-y-Gent it does not achieve 2,200 feet, and the Peak, its last dying effort to be high, rises but little over 2,000 feet. Still, it has a flora that runs to the Arctic Circle; when Manchester was under ice the Pennine rose superior to the general misfortune; it stood out and kept its ancient grit and limestone unreddened by the rising tide of geological modernisms all the time that a continuous sea was washing over Cheshire and all the southern English plain, making a strait at the gap where the London-to-Holyhead railway picks its way between the Peak and the Welsh hills, and laying down the red sand from which Chester Cathedral was to be made and Fallowfield Station in the fullness of time to be scooped.

The heights that come into view from the top of the tram as the Denton cars cross the canal bridge close to Hyde Road Station rose high above the level of Roman occupation and civilisation in Britain; they and the range of which they are part have a climate of their own that stands out as an island of comparative cold and sunlessness on the climatic maps of Great Britain; against its southern buttress, the Derbyshire Peak, stream after stream of racial movement and conquest, warlike and peaceful, broke and parted like water at the pier of a bridge; the Celts and Romans and English all took distinctly to the left when, on their outward way from Kent and London, they struck on the desert of rock and forest that culminates in Kinder Scout. From the western slopes of the Peak you look towards the Welsh hills across a level gap along the floor of which Romano-Celtic Christianity and Anglo-Saxon paganism and the Christianity of Augustine flowed out to the Atlantic seaboard as naturally as the waters did that left their brine at Northwich or as the trains of the North Western Railway do today. So, though the Pennine be not high, it has had a respectable career. A break in it has shaped the history of Ireland; the crumpling of its strata has shaped at least the industrial history of England; a type of life peculiar to it made the Brontës – which is more than the Alps themselves have ever done for letters.

Of course, to draw these joys from our suburban mountain range you must exercise a little historic imagination. But even the most literal man can get from it authentic mountain thrill. If you put out of your head everything but what you actually see and hear, it feels very much the same to have lost your way in a big snowstorm on the top of Kinder Scout and on the Grand Plateau of Mont Blanc. The Downfall, well curtained with ice, yields quite as engaging a 'pitch' as the glazed garden wall of rude construction over which you get at the peak of the Zermatt Rothorn. The Alport Stone, the Black Rocks Crack, and the Boulder climb at Robin Hood Stride give short climbs that the wise compare seriously with at least the Gable Needle and some of the hard ways up the Pillar Rock and Scawfell Pinnacle. The climber who would rather climb the other way about and in the dark, as the great masters play chess, can climb down some apparently delectable deep holes, by which you 'visit', like Lycidas, 'the bottom of the monstrous world'.

A Pennine enthusiast, Mr E. A. Baker, has just made a book, which Mr John Heywood has published (*Moors, Crags and Caves of the High Peak and Neighbourhood*), out of accounts of good Pennine walks and climbs. So many of these accounts appeared in our own columns that propriety forbids us to do more than warmly to commend the others. Much more than anyone has written yet might be said of the piquancy of scrambling in such places as the Wharncliffe Crags. They seem designed for a climber's gymnasium. If Paley had been a climber – however, the piquancy of the game at Wharncliffe lies in its accessories. The player, resting midway in a charmingly smooth and square-cut 'chimney', sees below him among the bracken the twisted, notchy roots still left of a famous 'chase' that was itself preserved from the time when inhabited England from end to end was covered with forest and roamed by droves of swine, like rural Servia today. From 200 yards below, across an intervening quarry, there comes all day the whistling of engines busy in a siding, and every few minutes a Great Central train comes grunting up or sliding down the main highway between the two halves of the industrial north.

From beyond the railway you hear the broken water of the Don, whose pace was the fortune of Sheffield's grindstones. The whole prospect epitomises the England of the north-west – its juxtaposition of a more primeval landscape with less primeval types of human labour than those of the south, its greater closeness to bare rock and its more universal use of steam. But, of course, rock-climbing is not the only mountain pleasure to be had by us here for a sixpenny return ticket. On a Saturday afternoon we can stand after rain on heights commanding mountain valley-heads and watch a whole river system in miniature, the tapering tips of the upper tributaries twisting and groping up under the very rim of this moorland basin as the roots of a hyacinth growing in water grope and search in the recesses of the jar. Or we can trace pairs of famous eastward and westward flowing rivers to their first rivalry in one square foot of sodden peat on some soaked sponge of a moorland moss, where both compete for the oozings of the overgorged tissues of the same hummock of bog. If you care to you can see the absolute birth of large rivers – the single drop lipping over from a flooded outer cell of the bog through a nick in the peaty trash of its edge and trickling down a few inches till its route approaches that of another, and they rush together like two raindrops on a pane, repeating these coalitions till there are enough to make an infinitesimal plash, the first cry of an infant river. Sentiment, of course – but quite as good as the sentiment of the fat pastoral Cheshire flats to which all of us flee on our bicycles on every fine Saturday.

PITY THE POOR ANGLER

July 2 1904

Pity the poor angler on these bright sunny days that we have been having. He is in a minority as compared with the great majority of sun-worshippers, but it is a substantial enough minority – as the early Sunday trains witness – fretting for the cloud that, though no bigger than a man's hand, it can still trust. To these men with their humble sport the brazen sky offers a poor prospect; the reports from all the accessible places is the same – there is too much sun, too little water, and therefore the fish will not bite. Possibly few of us appreciate the size and thrills of this patient, noiseless pastime, and yet one has only to travel on any of the earlier Sunday trains that carry the town dwellers just beyond the suburbs to note that something is doing.

And it is a serious business. Wherever a suitable stretch of canal or less formal stream offers, one may come upon 30, 40 or even 50 silent, intent figures with their rods at regular intervals. This is some angling association fishing for some shield or championship. There is concentration and excitement here – grim sport and rivalry by the rules – none of your Cleopatra's merry wagering lost to Antony in that her diver 'Did hang a salt fish on his hook, which he / With fervency drew up'. As many as three-fifths of a 'field' have been known to catch fish, and by the reports – pitiless comments on the notorious fishing story – a first prize has been won by a catch of 7 ozs 5 drs. When one recalls the traditional wisdom, the reticent, philosophic temperament of the angler, it is reassuring to think that most of these men have votes.

A COUNTRY LOVER'S DIARY

August 9 1905

Holidaymakers who today must return to town may be excused if they grumble a little. The sun was shining brightly when trainloads of people were hurrying back to work. The farmer as well as the holidaymaker found the heavy rain of yesterday a little trying. Much of his corn was already badly laid and the heavy thunder showers beat it down still more. In Cheshire many fields of oats have been cut early, but there are many more untouched; it makes one sad to look at the ripening wheat, flat as if a roller had passed over it; the promised early harvest will be a laborious one. Sparrows are holding high festival in the corn, for them it is a time of riot and feasting. Some are still feeding young in the nest, and we hope feeding them on noxious grubs, but large numbers have deserted for a time the habitations of man, only, however, to take their young to his cultivated fields. I saw a boy walking round one field with old-fashioned clappers. When he approached the sparrows rose in a cloud and flew; but they departed from the edge of the field to drop near the middle, so the clapper was not much use.

THOMAS COWARD

NUT-DANCING: CURIOUS ROSSENDALE CUSTOM

March 30 1907

The traveller through Rossendale yesterday found the village of Tunstead gleaming in the spring sunshine much more brilliantly than its neighbours by reason of the coloured streamers and bunting with which it had bedecked itself. If he happened to approach the right spot at the right moment, his ears were assailed with clicking and 'thwacking' sounds only a little less clamorous than the sounds of the falling mill which so stirred the fighting blood of Don Quixote with suggestions of clashing arms and armour. Between the sights and the sounds there was a direct connection. Tunstead had arrayed itself in bright colours in celebration of the jubilee of the 'nutters', 'nutcrackers' or 'coconut dancers', as they are variously called. The sounds were produced by the 'nutters' in the performance of their self-imposed task.

The appearance of the dancers is more grotesque than picturesque. Black jerseys, black velvet knickerbockers, white stockings and curiously pointed clogs is the proper attire, but it is not complete without a good coat of burnt cork on the face. The 'nutters', thus equipped, go round the streets and by-ways of Rossendale performing an unusual kind of morris dance. The effect which the ordinary morris dancers produce by the jingling of small sleigh bells is got by the Tunstead men by the knocking together of nuts. They have nuts attached to their knees and sides, and as they dance they strike these rhythmically with other nuts held in their hand.

Every Easter during 50 years these men and their predecessors have, with no small amount of physical exertion, kept alive one of those old-world forms of merriment which have in most places been suffocated by the lethal influences of industrial civilisation. The energy of the Tunstead nut-dancers is splendid. They are not content with the field offered by their own village or the neighbouring town. On Good Friday and Saturday they cover the whole of Rossendale from Rawenstall to Bacup, taking in not only the main roads but the more important of the byways. The mileage alone, estimated at about 30 miles, is as much as most people care to traverse in the orthodox mode of progression, but when the dancing is taken into account it is seen that these men do a feat of physical endurance worthy of recognition. There will be apparently no lack of nut-dancers in Rossendale for many years to come.

The youngsters of the valley have an ambition to emulate this stalwart company. Predatory bands of them were encountered yesterday by the dozen. They had blackened their faces more or less effectively and attired themselves in mysterious garments, and they made a noise with tambourines, drums and other fear-inspiring instruments. But they were not moved to these exertions by a desire to give pleasure to their fellow creatures. The principal interest of each band centred in the collecting box, which was never hidden from the eyes of passers-by. It is sad to reflect that perhaps in this particular also the children are only copying their elders.

IN THE HIGHLANDS: THREE RIVER VALLEYS AND MOORLAND
June 10 1907
The road that runs through the valley of the Dee from Ballater past Balmoral Castle and on to Braemar is tolerably well known. You reach Ballater by train from Aberdeen, and there the railway ends. The Aberdeenshire highlands lie before you, lifting themselves above a river that races along so strongly that the salmon make small rainbows in the spray as they leap for a moment into the sunshine. All the way the scene from the road at this season of the year is wonderful. The high hills are clothed

at their feet with birches pale-green in leaf; there are innumerable dark firs, some of them tipped with red blossom, and there is an abundance of larch with lissom boughs drooping and waving like tossed colours in the wind.

The firs spread so far up into the high land that the eye is lost in the endeavour to trace the edge of the forest. This is the scene for miles until Balmoral and then Braemar are reached, with dark Lochnagar standing on the left high above all, a white cloud circling round the head of the mountain and coming down presently to flood the valley with rain. The Don valley is less known or less travelled over than Deeside, but it has scarcely less natural romance. Returning from Ballater in the direction of Aberdeen, you leave the course of the railway eight miles lower down and begin a ride up to the moors that conveys you through fine loch and forest scenery, and then downward again for 10 miles to the Forbes country, cultivated richly in the lowland, and so onward to the Gordon country, as wild in parts as anything in the Highlands. A road hewn from the side of the mountain goes to Tomintoul, a quaint village with low Scottish houses and a green where the Highlander still enjoys Highland games. From Tomintoul and the Don it is a long ride further northward to the Spey, a noble river, broad, swift and strong. Across the mountains the track passes miles of peat moor, here and there dug yards deep. A few crofter cottages or huts are scattered about, from whose doors bare-legged children stare with some astonishment as the strangers go by. Two or three acres of the land around these cottages is cleared and cultivated, and the grass and garden soil are curiously unlike the moor. But every now and then a roofless cottage is to be seen, the walls crumbling away and the cultivated croft going back to the condition of waste land. A grey hare starts out of the small ruin and is lost in the heat here. 'The crofters are going,' your Aberdeenshire companion says. 'They cannot live on their bits of farm; it means sport on the mountains and work in the towns.' So you come to Ballindalloch, by the river, and are free to take a train to any of the near towns.

This is the highly interesting and, indeed, romantic country that is this summer being opened out to public travel by the Great North of Scotland Railway Company through a combined use of the train and, for the first time, of the motor car. It is not a small service of the motor that it will now enable one to obtain even a passing glimpse of so much mountain, valley and clear, abundant stream. The company call their new enterprise 'The Three Rivers Tour', but, as any map of the eastern Highlands will show, it is much more than that. Aberdeen is, of course, the starting point. The city need not be described; there are guide books in plenty, they are almost the first thing one sees at the station, and then every Aberdonian is not only ready to lead you anywhere about the city but is full of Highland lore.

The distance by rail to Ballater is over 40 miles, almost wholly by the side of the Dee and always with long stretches of forest scenery in view, and occasionally past a Scottish castle, like Drum and Crathes, on to Lumphanan – where Macbeth made his last great fight – and so by Banchory, Aboyne, and Glentana (names of Scottish song) to Dinnet, a village of small houses and great gardens. At Dinnet one can leave the train and take the motor car for the long ride over Strathdon to Tomintoul, if time does not allow of the journey on to Balmoral and Braemar. The longer ride is, however, the better, as one then travels all through the higher reaches of the Dee and is able to continue the journey right up to the Linn Falls and on to where the road merges into the forest and is lost. Besides the associations of Queen Victoria with this country, there are others of greater age. You see the memorial stone set up to mark the place where the aged queen sat and watched the kilted Gordons march by at the beginning of what to many of them would be their last footmark upon Scottish soil, and then the castle hard by the place where the Earl of Mar raised his unhappy standard. The country all around Braemar is as gloriously wild as anything that can be raised in the imagination.

Besides the old and some modern Scottish seats, the ancient towns that are scattered about Aberdeenshire, Moray and Banff are full of interest. The journey can be made to include Grantown, an old burgh of scarcely more than one street, but such a street as can hardly be matched elsewhere – it is so full of character. From the Great North station hard by the Spey it is approached by a road cut through a wood of birch, larch and lime in full leaf, while on the ground there is an almost complete carpet of anemones and wood violets. Grantown Street is very broad, with houses and shops intermingled pleasantly, and frequently a piece of lawn and branching lime tree in front of them. Castle Grant, a strange piece of architecture, once the home of the Comyns, stands in its park two or three miles further on. The castle, outwardly, is as stiff and flat and plain as any building could be, four storeys high, with sets of square windows in broad woodwork, built one directly above the other like the windows of a toy house; but inside it is roomy and well arranged, and has some remarkable paintings. The park reaches to the river and in the distance away to the west are the Cairngorms, their hollows still patched with snow. Or there is Elgin, where with pride the townsfolk show their desolated cathedral, once the glory of northern Scotland, but now scarcely more than bare walls, with a beautiful western porch and towers.

Then there are the fishing towns along the Moray Firth, Lossiemouth and Banff and Cullen, full of quaint human character. Inland among the moors, again, the country is being well developed along the river valleys. Around Castle Newe, in

Donside, another Scottish home full of Scots' memorials, Sir Charles Forbes, a most hospitable host, is lending his best energies to this purpose, and when one sees the splendid open character of the country it is obvious that this immense tract of open mountain will not long remain unvisited now that it can be reached and gone through so readily. The opening up of this part of the heart of Scotland is due largely to the energy of Sir David Stewart, the chairman of the Great North of Scotland Company, and the arrangements made for travel are admirable. It is well to enlarge the English outlook into these broad vistas. One would like to see new crofters' homes rising on the borders of the moors, replenished with families and providing green herb for the service of men.

BRAINS ON THE FARM

August 31 1907

The notion still prevails that farming does not need brains. It is a complete delusion. If brains are needed to succeed in trade – to buy and sell profitably – how much more is this the case in farming, where skill in both operations is the least of the chief requisites of success? The handicraft of the farm – to fodder and milk, to plough and harrow, to sow with care and accuracy, to mow and reap, to repair hedges and ditches – the simplest ploughboy learns in time. But the farmer has much more to do than this; he has, for example, to judge what his land will produce best. The farmer himself knows very well that he has to use his head as well as his hands. What he is slow to learn is to use his brains for the best purpose. Too seldom does he realise that for that he needs scientific knowledge.

Take an instance or two. A heavy crop depends on seed which is pure, which possesses high germination power, which has, in fact, been bred for quantity and quality. It depends also on the soil being suited to the crop and being treated with the right kind of fertiliser, whether natural or artificial. The crop and the stock are beset by hosts of enemies – weeds, fungi, insects – which the farmer cannot combat without a knowledge that no mother-wit will supply. It is true that even the poorest farmer learns a rough and ready practice in such matters. But how many do more than their forefathers did to eradicate the greatest thieves that ever robbed the farmer – the fungi and the weeds and the insects? Charlock may be killed as effectually as the rat, yet it still reigns the queen of weeds. How many farmers of the second rank test and select their seed, and better it by continuous selection?

Yet there is no other way to real success. How many test their soil and learn thereby what are its requirements? How many are there who even consult the farm physician – the man of long experience and training, and thereby reap a score of times the cost of the advice obtained? Our farmers in general appreciate manures so well that while they tread their straw into 'muck' (misnamed 'manure') – often, it is true, because the lease forbids its sale, – this country uses the smallest quantity of artificial manure per acre of any leading agricultural country, Belgium and Holland included.

It is not that the English farming class lacks brains. The farmer sells his corn but once a year, his cattle go to market only occasionally, his purchases of food or tools are few: yet in these occasional transactions, dealing with men of much wider experience than his own, he usually makes a pretty good bargain. But the farming class must learn to use their brains to better advantage. On their brains mainly they must rely to meet foreign competition. It is true that in lands where there are no rent and no tithes and where rates are nominal there is a margin far beyond the difference between the prices of home and foreign produce. That margin, which tempts men to the colonies, also tends to prevent the development of their best effort, by means of which they could undersell us even more than they do. But in the United States, in Canada, and in Australia men already employ brains in agriculture to very good purpose, and they will do so more and more. A short time ago I received a long and interesting letter from a young Englishman of high intelligence now farming in America. He is a practical man, but he follows every scientific advance with close attention and applies it to his own system of cultivation – and in this, as we know, he is helped by the government of the country. In research and the furnishing of helpful knowledge to their farmers the Federal and State governments of the United States have made great development, and this has been proceeding side by side with comparative inactivity on the part of the recent governments in Great Britain. However, though years have been wasted our Board of Agriculture is following the example of the American Department so far as its means permit.

Let our English farmers, then, be as eager to profit by advances in knowledge as their fellows over the water. It is essential from first to last that every operation on the farm should be governed by principles, and these science has explained so simply that every farmer should master them and teach the son who will succeed him that he may do the same. Nor does this apply only to the big farmer. In no case is the aid of science more necessary than in farming second-class land. The struggling class of farmers who have to put up with inferior farms must cease trusting to luck to make them pay. The application to his business of a keen brain well stored by science will raise the farmer to a higher plane; he will be not only a richer man but a more finished man – in a word, a master of a difficult vocation.

JAMES LONG

A COUNTRY DIARY: CHESHIRE
December 2 1907

What has become of the Canada geese? A dozen together is quite a large flock this year, but it was not so a year or two ago; then 50 or 100 birds on the borders or waters of the Cheshire meres was no unusual sight. Apparently, these semi-wild geese have almost deserted some of their favourite waters; the meres look lonely without any geese, even if they are half-tame. Can it be that the wet spring was fatal to the goslings? Strange though it seems, a wet season is often a bad one for young water as well as land birds. This is a more reasonable explanation than that the birds have been ruthlessly shot down; though a few are killed by farmers and sportsmen every year, it is very unlikely that so many more have been destroyed than usual that the difference in numbers should be noticeable. Nor is it probable that the birds have suddenly reverted to the habits of their ancestors on the other side of the Atlantic and migrated; the domestication of the Canada goose seems to have destroyed its migratory instinct.

WOMEN AND THE LAND: SOME SUITABLE OCCUPATIONS DISCUSSED
July 7 1910

Only one of the papers read at the Women's Congress today, when it again met at the Japan-British Exhibition, dealt with women as general farmers, the others being confined to the consideration of smaller branches of agriculture which, according to the majority of the speakers, offered more scope and quicker returns to women who wished to make a living out of the land. The need of cooperation, especially with regard to the selling of produce, was again insisted upon, but while no undue encouragement was given to women to look upon farming as a lucrative occupation, there was a more hopeful tone about today's discussion than was noticeable yesterday when women gardeners were being considered.

Mr E. O. Greening, expressing the views of Lady Mount Stephen – who was in the chair but who beyond ringing down the speakers when they reached their time limit left the duties of the office entirely to her deputy – said that the new entry of women into agriculture arose largely from a desire to combat the evils resulting from the aggregation of people in crowded towns, and to preserve a balance between town and country by encouraging the revival of rural industries. Women had not perhaps the physical strength of men, but they had greater alacrity of mind and deftness of finger, qualities which enabled them to deal more successfully than men with those lesser branches of agriculture upon which the whole success of farming so much depended.

Bee-Keeping

Miss Bertha de la Mothe, in her paper on bee-keeping, held that the advantages of this branch of agricultural history far outbalanced the disadvantages, which indeed could be summed up in the one fact that bees had stings; and this was in reality an advantage, enabling the bee-keeper to leave her hives for the whole winter in perfect safety without a caretaker. It was an occupation suited to all climates and all ages, was a source of profit, an interesting hobby, and also a means of doing good, if the qualified bee expert were to form a cooperative bee-keepers association, as was sometimes done, among the cottagers who kept bees in her own neighbourhood. Bee-keeping was especially suited to delicate people, as it entailed no heavy work, and no work at all in bad weather. The original outlay need not be large, as a new hive could be bought for £2 or at the most £3 and second-hand bees for less.

Pony-Breeding

A good deal of practical information was to be obtained from Miss Colmady-Hamlyn's account of her experience as a breeder of polo ponies. There was plenty of scope, she maintained, for more women breeders of ponies of all kinds. A woman who took up this work must be strong, as it entailed hard work in all weathers. And she must be possessed of infinite patience. The hardest thing for a woman to learn, perhaps, was not to allow sentiment to interfere with business when it became necessary to sell a failure. She herself never gave a long price for a mare, but having noticed one at some great show used it as a dressmaker uses a Paris model and visited farms and country shows until she found its counterpart, and bought it at a much lower price. But this method, naturally, demanded knowledge and experience. Her own branch of the industry, the breeding of polo ponies, was not the best for women, as a rule, to take up, because the schooling of the ponies must necessarily be left to men, and this meant that the old ponies must be sold as young as four years old and therefore at a lower price than when mature. Also the severity of competition was greater, polo being the game of the rich, and there was the further difficulty of breeding to size. Nevertheless, she had managed to make good profits and strongly recommended women to follow her example.

Farming

Practical experience was also the note of Miss V. Courtauld's paper on lady farmers. She had worked her own farm for 20 years and had made a success of it, but had seen so many failures that she advised both men and women to consider the matter seriously before entering upon it as a means of livelihood. She placed experience before a scientific training; recommending two years of the former on a farm as essential, and one year at an agricultural college, if possible, as a useful adjunct to the practical work. At least £10 per acre should be put down as capital and it was advisable to work a large farm, one of more than a hundred acres, rather than a smaller one. In her opinion only a man who had been brought up on the land could make a small farm pay. Such a man would work harder for his own profit than for wages and his standard of living would be no higher than that of a labourer. But for a woman this was not to be recommended for a moment. A large farm demanded the exercise of more brain than muscle, and therefore a woman could do it as well as a man, provided she was a countrywoman used to the life and not inclined to view the country as a summer holiday resort. Before obtaining her training she should decide on the kind of farm she meant to work. There were many kinds, dairy farming being at the moment the most profitable. Personally, the speaker preferred a mixed farm, because it offered more resources when one branch of it failed – 'Up horn, down corn,' as an old country proverb expressed it.

Dairy Farming

Miss M. Brown (Lancashire County Council) expressing her inability to deal in 10 minutes with dairying as an occupation for women – in view of the large number of branches of this work that might be touched upon – proceeded to narrow down her paper to a consideration of the less well-known branches as being likely to be of more use to her audience. She considered dairy farming a more suitable career for women, whether in its practical aspect or as a means of imparting knowledge to others, and instanced six of the ways in which it could be carried on. Soft cheese making, for instance, was a lucrative branch that demanded originality and close attention to detail but no great physical strength. Hard cheesemaking, on the other hand, required real muscular power and was besides more uncertain in its results, these being largely affected by outside conditions of weather, &c., especially during the ripening and mellowing process. Buttermaking, where a good supply of milk and a good train service were assured, could be made very profitable, and women managers of home dairies had been proved successful at this part of the work. Miss Brown's hearers seemed most interested in that part of her paper dealing with three of the newer developments of dairy farming – manufacturing invalid produce, such as fermented bottled milk, the management of municipal milk depots, and the sterilisation of milk in town dairies. She also made an interesting point when mentioning various training colleges, among which was the Lancashire County Council Dairy College, near Preston. She added that travel was a real advantage to women who wished to become dairy farmers, as other countries had many hints to offer on the subject.

Fruit Preserving

Miss Edith Bradley described the process of fruit sterilising; and uttered a strong plea for encouraging fruit growing and fruit-preserving in country districts in order to add interest to rural life, and also to keep the trade of bottled fruits in this country. She also reiterated the need for cooperation, pointing out that if one person did all the fruit bottling only one set of appliances would be needed, the expense could be minimised and competition with foreign bottled fruits would be successful.

August 16 1912

Only her intimate friends knew that Octavia Hill, who seemed so strong and full of life till this last illness, was likely so soon to pass away. All that was generally known was that she was in failing health and very busily engaged in planning and delegating her many activities and public service to the capable fellow-workers whom she had trained. It was known also that she was facing with absolute calm the fact that she could never hope to take up work again. The weakness of body which had suddenly come upon her had left her with a clear brain and she gained infinite comfort from the thought that such work as the management of the tenement houses in Westminster, Southwark and Lambeth, which had been trusted to her care by the Ecclesiastical Commissioners, was all definitely arranged for and would be carried on in the same wise way by high-minded practical women who were her disciples in method and organisation.

Nor could she forget in this last illness that one of the objects dear to her heart was the raising of the £560 needed for the completion of the purchase of 14 additional acres at Mariner's Hill. In 1904 and 1908 two gifts of land on this beautiful viewpoint over the Weald of Kent had been acquired by the National Trust through Miss Octavia Hill's exertions. Early in this spring 14 additional acres, which would round off the property and permanently secure it from disfigurement, were offered her for £1,500, and her last appeal, a few weeks ago, was for the £500 still necessary to ensure its purchase. Two days before her death news came to her of a gift which would enable her to obtain the wish of her heart, and Mariner's Hill will to all time be a monument not only to her interest in the work of the National Trust, but of her love for the people pent up in the bewildering city, who, escaping for half a day from their roaring prison-house, may find silence and sweet sunshine and the large prospect of the blue weald in the gorse-land and flower-land of Mariner's Hill.

THE USES OF THE AGRICULTURAL SHOW
July 31 1913

There are between two and three hundred agricultural shows held in England every year. They vary in importance according to whether they are the shows of a parish or of a group of parishes or of a county or of a whole collection of counties. You may find the simplest form of agricultural show on a hillside in Rossendale. The treasurer takes his stand at an ordinary field gate, collects shillings and sixpences on a kitchen table borrowed from a neighbouring cottage, and the visitors pass into a field where horses and cattle are haltered to a rail running by the hedgeside. At the other end of the scale you have great gatherings of things agricultural like the Royal Lancashire Show, extending over several days, involving much elaborate and costly preparation, with prize lists running into thousands of pounds and turnstiles that are expected to click off tens of thousands of visitors.

All these shows, little or big, make famous holidays. The larger exhibitions, for a brief spell, create 'an agricultural atmosphere' in the centres of industrial population; the smaller enliven the countryside and tempt the dwellers of the towns to those simple pleasures that men rejoiced in before South Lancashire became a forest of chimneys. For the agricultural show is an institution of mature years and had its beginning in those far-off days when men ploughed with oxen and competed for prizes both as ploughmen and as breeders of the beasts of burden. But it is a disparagement of the agricultural show to regard it merely as an occasion for a holiday. Your unheeding townsman does that – the man to whom a cow is just any animal with horns and a tail and a horse a not very interesting creature unless somebody is making it jump. To him the agricultural show is a diversion. For others it is an affair of bread and butter. For a great class of people it is a source of education and suggestion and encouragement in their life's work. For many it is an intensely interesting manifestation of the progressive achievements that are still possible in various branches of the most ancient of industries.

Recently I asked a north-country agriculturist whether he thought the great expenditure of effort in promoting so many shows in Lancashire was justified by any appreciable gain to agriculture. He answered me with emphasis. Two kinds of shows do incalculable good – the very small show and the very large show. The small show is a great stimulus to the small farmer; he has an inducement to compete with his neighbour in the matter of utility stock; the annual event is unconsciously a disciplinary check on slovenly farming. The larger show helps another class of farmer. It gives him a chance to see good representative specimens of livestock; it educates his judgment of the particular breeds in which he is interested. Competition at the smaller shows has helped enormously to improve the quality and milk yield of the cattle on Lancashire and Cheshire pastures. The larger shows serve agriculture in its highest farms. They keep a spirit of agricultural enterprise alive amongst men who can afford to approach farming as experimentalists and investigators. They bring together the finest specimens of pedigree animals the country possesses. The growing demand, in recent years, for first-class animals for exportation to the colonies and to foreign countries has greatly increased the value of pedigree stock, and so sound an authority as Lord Northbrook claims for the Royal and other important shows (like the Royal Lancashire) the credit for this most satisfactory state of things, because it is by these shows that the breeding of high-class stock has been encouraged.

And the large shows have another advantageous side: they afford farmers a very welcome opportunity for seeing the latest implements and the most improved farming machinery and accessories. A showground is not a place where the average farmer buys stock; he goes there to get knowledge of stock and you see his delight in the game when he turns aside the cloth and passes a skilled hand over level backs and deep quarters – but he can and does go there to buy machinery, and he gets much better served than in the old days, when often he had to buy just what the implement maker in his market town had to sell.

There are people who hold that the agricultural show as an educational institution is of less importance today because of the steady development of agricultural education in other directions, particularly by the establishment of county farm schools. But this opinion is founded on a wrong view of the manner in which the influence of the agricultural show is exercised. The farm schools are meant to equip the young agriculturist with some knowledge of the science of his occupation: they cannot do more than supply him with a good foundation on which to build as he acquires experience and nothing will help him more, after he leaves the farm school, than the bracing atmosphere of the show yard. Besides, there has been built up in connection with our larger agricultural shows a department of education and of educational stimulus in the smaller branches of agriculture that no development of farm schools could supply.

The farmer only was thought of when the Royal Society held its first show in 1839. He was offered prizes for horses, cattle, sheep and pigs and for red and white wheat, and his provider of implements was also invited to enter the lists. Today all the larger agricultural shows have two main features – livestock and implements. Those are still the farmers' interests. But nowadays the agricultural show provides encouragement for all who live in rural ways. The dairy, the poultry yard, the beehives and the garden have their interests recognised: the blacksmith who shoes the horses and mends the coulter, the hedger, the thatcher, the ploughman, the shepherd – all are provided for in the arrangements of the up-to-date show prize list.

Here, at any rate, eagerness for prizes works no mischief. A man or woman can only excel in agricultural competitions by constant practice, and in whatever they excel they benefit the community. For in agriculture more than in many industries the worker wins his harvest without disadvantaging his fellow. You may teach him much, but the greatest thing is to teach him how to learn, and there is no school for the like of that equal to the competition corner of an agricultural show yard.

A criticism sometimes levelled at the larger agricultural shows is that they tend to encourage the breeding of 'fancy' stock – in other words, stock that is 'improved' for appearance's sake rather than for practical farm purposes. By way of illustration the case of the Berkshire pig may be mentioned. The Berkshire has been improved three or four times in living recollection, and not always for the best. First he was a long, deep-sided pig with well-developed large head and light jowls, fine in the back and skin, with hair of a black, white or sandy, spotted colour. The 'improvers' set to work to secure earlier maturity and to get a more uniform colour – black with white markings. They did it, but with a loss of size, length and lean flesh. The Berkshire became short, thick, heavy on the neck and shoulders, short in the snout, with hanging jowls. For a time in this guise he was a very fashionable fellow, but when fashion forsook him and the buyer of bacon insisted on less fat the breeders had to set to work again to 'improve' him back into a more marketable commodity.

The same kind of experience has happened with other stock, but in the end 'fancy' has always to give way to market requirements, and the only sure line of 'improvement' is found to be that which ignores 'fancy' and pays regard to what the public want. It is not an inherent fault of the agricultural show that these things happen; it is rather a freakish turn which wealthy amateurs create and stimulate by the agency of the shows. But these fancies have their little day and real agricultural interests are not seriously jeopardised by them. Behind all the agricultural shows that are held in Lancashire and Cheshire there is a purposeful determination to make the exhibitions of solid use and practical value to farming folk, and the Federation of Agricultural Societies of the two counties is doing great service to the that end.

E. W. R.

A COUNTRY DIARY

October 16 1917

This morning the sun rose with rain falling heavily and a grey, dull mist hanging over the dense foliage, giving a very autumnal appearance, but soon the atmosphere cleared and at any rate we have had a fine day, though those who have still fruit to gather wished for sunshine and, of all things, a drying wind. The call of the nation to all who could help to produce food in greater quantity this season has met with such gratifying success from both professional and amateur cultivators that we may look with confidence to a still further development in the coming year. Already, profiting by the lessons gained in their first effort, many are hard at work and in many cases are taking up more land. With butter at 4s a pound and milk at the high prices now asked everywhere, it seems incredible that more cannot be done to increase the supply of both. One would again call the attention of those who have the time to attend to them to the keeping of goats. There is a large area of poor pasture even in this district of South Lancashire and North Cheshire that would support a large number of these useful little animals. I may assure those who have had no experience of it that goat's milk is of the best.

T. A. C.

UNEMPLOYED LAND GIRLS

May 21 1919

At Ormskirk War Agricultural Committee yesterday A. W. Whiteman said there was a considerable number of skilled land girls receiving the unemployment pay of 25s a week because farmers had not applied to the Labour Exchange for them. The girls were not only too willing to work on the land, but could not get employment despite the farmer's continual complaint of the scarcity of labour.

LAND GIRLS' FAREWELL: PRINCESS MARY DISTRIBUTES MEDALS

November 28 1919

Nothing could have been prettier or more glittering than the scene in the Drapers' Hall this evening when Princess Mary, who was to make her first public speech and to be entertained at her first public dinner, presented to 55 land girls the Distinguished Service Bar for deeds of special bravery or devotion. Along both sides of the main corridor, very smart in their white smocked uniforms, stood the girls who were to receive the medals, each holding upright a green wand decorated with brilliantly coloured roses and chrysanthemums. The great hall, magnificent with its oak and marble, its gilded gallery, its silver plate, its great hanging lamps, pictures, statuary and painted ceiling, was filled with land girls, and down the centre aisle stood more girls with garlanded wands.

Miss Talbot, the head of the Women's Branch of the Board of Agriculture, stood beside the Princess and read a brief statement of the reason for which the medal was awarded. They were wonderful stories and what one liked best was the knowledge that where 55 girls were receiving medals, probably thousands of girls had earned them, not all perhaps by shining deeds of heroism, but by pluck, endurance and devotion displayed through long months of trial. When a girl marched up to be honoured for her skill with the tractor or with pedigree cattle or sheep, the girls in the audience could reflect that they, too, had been praised by their employers for just such work. Before the company left the hall for the smaller halls, where dinner was provided by their hosts – the warden and members of the Drapers' Company – several farewell speeches were made. Lord Ernie, who when president of the Board of Agriculture brought the Women's Land Army into being, spoke with pride of the way in which it had won through prejudice, ridicule, hardship, fatigue and real privation to a grateful recognition on the part of all the nation.

Much of its success was due to Miss Talbot's leadership. What he had to say about the usefulness of the new Land Women's Association was echoed by the present head of the Board, Lord Lee. Lord Lee sincerely believed that there would always be a demand for women specialists in land work. He appealed to his hearers to stay on: 'I cannot be reconciled to the thought that the country is going to lose your services.'

Princess Mary, who has an excellent voice for public speaking – a curiously mellow voice – made a graceful little speech appreciative of the war-work of the women and girls of Great Britain, which will always be gratefully remembered by their King and country, and of the 'skill and courage of the Land Army'.

❧ CHAPTER TWO ❧

Coming of age
1920–1939

As the *Guardian* grew, it accumulated trophies on its liberal mantelpiece, especially under the illustrious guidance of Charles Prestwich Scott, who was editor for 57 years between 1872 and 1929. His journalists exposed injustices in the Ottoman Empire's Balkan lands and the British Empire's Ireland as well as the mistreatment of Boer War prisoners in centres which gave the world the term 'concentration camp'. Scott and his high command moved in an urban and highly political world; the editor combined his job with a less successful career as a Liberal MP for 11 years between 1895 and 1906 and was an influential, informal adviser to prime ministers Herbert Asquith and David Lloyd George.

But he was also a man to be seen on his customised bicycle whirring about the Lancashire lanes, and on holiday in the Lake District. He was not from Manchester, although he came to epitomise the city as no one apart perhaps from Sir Matt Busby has done. His first nine years were spent in sleepy Bath, never far from green fields, and when the family moved to London their house in Cornwall Terrace overlooked the vast urban 'garden' of Regent's Park. Teenage ill health led to a period enjoying the supposedly better health of the Isle of Wight where he was prepared for Oxford by a private tutor, again amidst green fields. When he accepted an invitation at the age of 25 to join the *Manchester Guardian* from his cousin John Taylor (the son of the paper's first editor and owner), he included 'an afternoon ramble once or twice a week' in the diary of his typical working day as a journalist, which he sent to his brother in April 1871.

Scott was therefore as tenacious a defender of countryside articles in the *Manchester Guardian* as he was of political exposés and financial analysis. He also assembled a team of lieutenants who shared his interest in rural matters. When Haslam Mills, the chief reporter for many years, published a memoir of life on the paper, he chose the title *Grey Pastures*, which neatly combined the north of

England's town and countryside in a smoky-sounding metaphor. Even more influential was W. T. Arnold, a nephew of Matthew Arnold and grandson of Thomas Arnold of Rugby school. He is described by the *Guardian*'s historian David Ayerst as having 'a sapper's eye for the structure of the landscape and a poacher's eye for the lie of the land; and he could communicate in words the excitement with which he saw. This love of the country overflowed into the pages of the *Manchester Guardian*.'

In the single year of 1882, when British troops sized Egypt, Jesse James was shot dead in Missouri and British women were at last allowed to own property, the newspaper found room for long series on 'Rare Birds of Lancashire', 'Past Fauna of Lancashire and Cheshire' and 'Northern Birds of Prey'. Readers were taken on a multi-part journey down the river Irwell and introduced to such specialised subjects as 'Sea Birds of Walney Island' and 'A Westmorland Haunt of Seabirds'. Encouraged by Arnold, Scott also recruited the great Victorian writer on the countryside, Richard Jefferies, to write for the paper. He brought to its columns a marvellous ability to transform the British rural doorstep into wonderland. As Walter Besant wrote on first reading Jefferies: 'Why, we must have been blind all our lives; here were the most wonderful things possible going on under our very noses, but we saw them not.'

It was in this spirit that in 1904 Scott agreed to budget 30 shillings a week (£150 today) for a noted Cheshire ornithologist, Thomas Coward, to 'contribute daily one or two articles on country life'. Thus began one of the *Guardian*'s best-loved columns, the Country Diary. The paper's owner, John Taylor, ageing and retired to a mansion in Kensington Palace Gardens but still actively interested in day-to-day *Guardian* affairs, wrote to Scott doubting that the countryside would provide enough material to keep the item going all year round. More than a century – and over 35,000 Country Diaries – later he is still wrong. Other doubters were also seen off by Scott, including on one occasion a Country Diary writer himself. The literary critic Basil de Selincourt was asked by the editor why he chose the solitary initial 'S' as the signature of his weekly diary during the First World War. De Selincourt, who sent in beautifully observed paragraphs on wildlife and farming in Oxfordshire, replied that he had felt uneasy, because 'it seemed in these days – or might seem – a little trivial to be watching insects or enjoying the countryside'. But he added that after thinking further about the matter he had decided that in grim times 'reminders of what is normal and sweet in life are more than ever necessary'. In terms of media coverage of the countryside, that has held, and still holds good.

But the diaries and other countryside articles in Scott's *Guardian* were not remotely, exclusively 'reminders of what is sweet and normal'. In 1879 the Irish potato crop failed, raising fears that the terrible famine of 1847 would be repeated. The editor summoned Arnold from his Manchester-based routines, which always included a weekend train outing to beautiful havens such as the Peak and Lake Districts, and asked him to spend two months travelling through the Irish countryside. Arnold served him well. In 13 long articles, closely argued and full of descriptive detail, he sent some 35,000 words back to the paper's Cross Street headquarters. His love of the countryside was matched by an understanding of its economy and of the dismal effect of hundreds of absentee landlords.

Not long after De Selincourt's exchange with Scott, the *Manchester Guardian* published another authoritative series on a fundamental rural problem. Led by the economist and historian J. L. Hammond, the paper exposed poor wages and harsh conditions among farm labourers, and particularly the way in which 20 shires had suspended the Education Act to close schools during harvest, so that children could replace enlisted men in the fields. The sustained campaign by the newspaper played a part in the establishment of the Agricultural Wages Board in 1917. *The Labourer* by Hammond and his wife Barbara is a monumental study and a book well worth reading.

The *Guardian*'s coverage also benefited from an international breadth of knowledge. When Hammond went to Versailles in 1919 to cover the peace negotiations which set the unhappy pattern for post-war Europe, he was accompanied by a scholarly new colleague, David Mitrany, a Romanian exile from the collapsed Austro-Hungarian empire. Mitrany was an academic expert on the peasantry of central Europe – a form of countryside knowledge which further expanded *Guardian* readers' horizons. It also helped the gradual expansion of the paper's sales to creep out more widely from its northern base. Necessary loyalty to Manchester meant that space had to be found for detailed coverage of the city's affairs and especially the fluctuations of prices for cotton and other local materials on the Manchester Exchange. But these were an obvious deterrent for others. As late as 1900 W. H. Smith's in Cambridge gave up stocking the newspaper and circulation in outer London was only maintained by a team of bicycle delivery boys working overtime from their normal jobs with the capital's own newspapers. Articles on 'The Wildlife of Wimbledon Common' or 'The Future of Richmond Park' made their employment worthwhile.

September 2 1921

The changes in the cropping of English farm land, during the period of the war and in the seasons since the Armistice, as they are revealed in the latest returns of the Ministry of Agriculture, were discussed in these columns a fortnight ago. To complete the stocktaking then described it is necessary to set out the comparison between the numbers of farm animals in stock in 1901, 1911 and 1914, and the seven following years. So far as crop changes were concerned it was deduced from the trend of the figures that crops were being largely adjusted to pre-war conditions. No great wheat or cereal extension was foreshadowed – farming, rather than aiming at the production of bread, was more and more aiming at the production of meat and dairy produce, and consequently the crops on which animals live.

A War Record in Cattle

The returns are taken in the first week in June and we get summarised early results in August for England and Wales. Taking cattle first, as first in importance, the figures may seem surprising. The first fact to appear is that the total number of cattle on the farms of England and Wales in the war years was bigger than in 1901 or in 1911, and that the total declined again in 1921. Credit is hardly given to British agriculture for this. Yet again the warning must be given that these figures are relative rather than absolute. It may be imagined that they were more scrupulously taken in the war years. Be that as it may, they are creditable.

Today the number of cattle is 3,515,600, but from 1915 right away to 1919 the numbers were kept well above six million head, and in 1917 reached over six and a quarter million. It may have been partly due to Irish and Scottish imports, but not wholly. The figures of these authorities are not available simultaneously with the English. The increase in cattle in England in the war period really marked the highest record reached. In 1901 the total was just over five and a half million, or almost exactly the figure recorded last June (1921). The numbers increased to 5,914,247 by 1911, and then stood still, despite the hardening tendency in meat prices the world over. Dearer meat was well on the way before the returns were collated in June 1914, but the numbers of cattle fell. Yet that year's 5,877,000 was the highest figure since 1911, and when, in 1913, the returns showed 6,064,000 – it was the largest number that had been recorded. That figure was beaten in each of the four subsequent years, and in 1917 the return of 6,227,150 was the highest since the returns were first taken.

The Promise of the Young Stock

The total remained above six million until 1920, when the sins of control had found us out and the action of the various controllers put 'out of action' tens of thousands of calves by encouraging their slaughter. By 1920 we were below the figures of 20 years ago. To be exact, in June 1920 the total number of cattle in England and Wales was 5,446,800, as against 5,334,613 in 1901. There are signs now of a real recovery if herds can be kept free of the more serious contagious diseases. The number of cattle returned this year was 70,000 more than in 1920, and it will be much higher next year.

The most serious feature of 1920 was the great falling off in young stock. In that year only 907,000 'under one year' cattle were returned, which was the least number since 1901. The result was that this year the number of cattle between one year and two years was under 900,000 – the lowest on record. But it is significant that this year the stock 'under one year' show a substantial increase, so that really there are more yearling stock in the country in 1921 than there were in 1901, and almost as many as 10 years ago. We reached the nadir point in cattle in 1920, for a comparison of the numbers of all the classes of stock in the 10 years under notice shows that in that year were recorded the fewest cows and heifers in milk, the fewest cows in calf, the fewest heifers in calf and the fewest cattle under one year.

It is interesting to learn from a calculation made for each of the years – adding together the numbers in the different categories – that this year's total of 2,501,300 of cows and of heifers in milk and in calf is much higher than that of 20 years ago, of 10 years ago, and of 1914. It is a little below the totals of 1918 (the highest on record) and of 1919, but the trend again is upward, and we look like attaining the same stock records in 1922. At any rate, it is something to say that after four years of war and three of its aftermath we have today in England and Wales nearly half a million more cows and heifers in milk and breeding than we had in 1901.

The Neglect of Sheep Farming

The tale is not so encouraging with regard to sheep. The only consolation is that the figures are in the aggregate a little better than those of 1920. The total of sheep in England and Wales in June last was under 14 million. In 1901 we had 19 million and in 1911 19.33 million. In 1909 we had 20.25 million. There are now six million sheep fewer than in 1911. When the figures dropped in 1913 to 17.12 million it was the lowest figure recorded. But ever since then the numbers have dwindled till today they are only 13.8 million. A recovery of 206,000 in the number of ewes kept for breeding, which was 5.10 million last year, should improve next year's aggregate, but sheep farming means arable farming, and arable farming is not developing. Prices of foods, manures, and materials and labour have been against it, yet acre for acre arable land well-farmed can carry more stock than can grassland and, above all, than the untended, neglected grassland of England. There cannot be much recovery in our sheep population in the current agricultural year, which begins with September, because the supplies of winter forage are not abundant. Milk production has hit mutton and wool-growing hard, and there are thousands of farmers today who know little about sheep breeding or feeding, and cannot manage a flock of any kind. A most remunerative branch of agriculture is now largely neglected. Many educated and practical agriculturists agree that the worship of milk production is becoming harmful to the best agricultural practice of the country.

Where Do the Pigs Go?
The pig is a mystery. There has not been an agricultural show in the country this year at which the exhibits of pigs have not outnumbered all previous records. There are now half a dozen new and flourishing herd books and so on, and pork is 2s 6d a pound in the shops (when there is any at all), while good bacon is still higher. Annual figures taken in June do not reveal much of the facts; the pig population is quickly changed and the seasons affect it. As far as the returns go, there were more than half a million more pigs in England and Wales in June last than in June 1920, viz., 2,505,000, against 1,993,900. This is nearly three-quarters of a million more than in 1918; and the prices of pig products are no lower. The mystery of today is 'Where do the pigs go to?' The figures are the highest recorded since 1911, and are also half a million above those of 1901.

Confidence in the Heavy Horse
When they come to deal with horses, the figures of the return are not a census of the horse population, but only a record of horses used in agriculture and those on the farms of the country and on all holdings above an acre. The figures show no decrease of horses and no increasing disuse of them. There were 19,000 more returned this year and the figures for 1921 are higher than those of 1901, 1915, 1916, 1917, 1918 and 1920. Under the heading of 'agricultural horses', as apart from young horses and foals, the number returned is 822,500, and that is higher than in any year since 1912, when 906,000 were returned. In 1912 the numbers were 936,749, and they were about the same in 1901. It is a drop of 12,000 or 13,000 in 21 years, but the figures are improving and increased confidence in the future of the heavy horse is shown by the renewed activity in the breeding of pedigree horses: Shires, Clydes and

Suffolks. The story of stock on the farm in 1921 is not at all an unfavourable one. Only in the case of sheep does stock breeding and rearing seem to be on the down grade.

SCOLT HEAD

June 16 1924

Scolt Head is an island, though not the remote and isolated land that certain published accounts suggest. The creek or channel that separates it from the Norfolk mainland never dries; in this it differs from Lindisfarne or Holy Island, where...

> *with the flow and ebb, its stile*
> *Varies from continent to isle.*

True, at low tide the creek can be forded, but not dry-shod, o'er sands twice every day. The distance from the shore is less than at Lindisfarne, but the crossing is always difficult, wet and very muddy. The island lies off the Norfolk coast between Hunstanton and Wells, and comprises 1,000 acres of marram-clad dunes and tide-washed saltings, the latter intersected by a maze of creeks and gutters. At high tide the sea frontage extends for three and a half miles. Rabbits and bird in immense numbers populate the unreclaimed, untilled land, but the marshes are visited by cockle gatherers, the shore by fishermen, and until the Norfolk and Norwich Naturalists' Society had secured the island the birds were at the mercy of unauthorised gunners. The Earl of Leicester, anxious to protect birds, sold the island at a low figure to the Society, who in June last year handed the deeds to Lord Ullswater as representative of the National Trust. Scolt is now, for all time, the nation's property; and a sanctuary for rare birds, insects and plants.

A watchers' hut had been erected – the only dwelling on the reserve; Miss E. L. Turner, volunteer watcher, is its present occupant. After a run through intricate channels and a tramp across marsh, shingle and sand, we joined our hostess and took possession of the two-bunk cabin allotted for visitors. Miss Turner, who has been described as the 'Woman Crusoe' and 'the loneliest woman in England', is here not only to protect the birds from molestation but to study the ornithological possibilities of the reserve. For 20 years she has lived amongst Norfolk birds, studied and watched them; they are her friends. She has helped in that protection which has met with such signal success – the reinstating of the bittern, bearded tit and ruff; constantly in touch with those landowners who have converted their estates into private sanctuaries, she has helped with expert advice and sympathy. The Society is fortunate in securing an experienced ornithologist as a watcher. The passing spoonbill, black-tailed godwit and black tern can find in Norfolk safe resting places; perhaps some day they may remain to nest, as they did in days gone by: Savi's warbler may not have vanished for ever.

In a few months we shall know how the large tern colony at Scolt has fared. The birds were arriving daily, courting and preparing to nest, when we paid our visit in the spring, but the first eggs were laid just after we left. On the neighbouring National Trust reserve at Blakeney Point four species nest regularly in large numbers and a fifth, the graceful Roseate tern, was certainly present last year, but I failed to identify a nest. The handsome Sandwich tern, a recent addition to the Norfolk mist as a nesting species, was abundant at Scolt and Salthouse last year and many were performing quaint nuptial antics at Scolt in early May, preparatory to settling down to the serious domestic duties. Ringed plovers, 'sandrunners' the fishermen call them, were in full strength, very anxious round the simple scrapes in which they place their four-colour, protected eggs. The observer must walk the shingle with caution, eyes upon the ground, or an unwary foot may annihilate a family.

A lovely sight at Scolt especially in the early morning – for the watcher must rise early – is the gathering of the shield-ducks, perhaps the most handsome of all British wildfowl. The royal stock at Sandringham, so noticeable at Wolferton and on the Warren, was recruited from Scolt many years ago. Hudson wrote sympathetically, almost affectionately, of 'the strange and beautiful Sheldrake' and at Scolt all the quaint habits of this individualistic bird may be watched, for it nests in the burrows close to the hut and meets its fellows on the marsh below for exercise, courtship, play and what looks and sounds uncommonly like parliamentary discussions.

To some of us Scolt as a migration observatory was especially interesting. Great numbers of passage migrants use the Norfolk coast as a highway, and at Scolt the spring birds travel west towards Lincolnshire on their northward journey. The Head, the highest sandhill in Britain, it is said, must be a landmark for day migrants; for over a fortnight a thin but continuous stream of swifts, swallows, martins, yellow wagtails and other birds passed by or over the Head. In one hour 300 birds passed and at times the numbers were greater. In one half-hour 148 swifts, as well as many swallows and martins, passed; and at noon one day 164 swifts passed in 25 minutes. Others, not included in this count, travelled over nearer to the mainland. An average of 300 swifts and swallows to the hour is a low estimate, and this passage lasted daily from 5 a.m. to 9 p.m. at least. It continued in sun or storm for at least 10 consecutive days, and fully half the number were swallows. Who dare say that the swallow is in danger of extinction?

Short-eared owls, harriers, stockdoves, warblers of various kinds, chats and other passerine birds came by in varying numbers; gannets, terns and gulls trailed west and north over the sea. Weary individuals remained for rest and refreshment and then vanished in the night; the suaeda bushes and the marram sheltered them during their halt. There was no huge rush of birds, nothing to compare with those great autumnal immigrations during bad weather, but a steady northward trek. Scolt is a good observatory as well as a sanctuary for birds which remain to rest.

The Norfolk and Norwich Society has done well in securing Scolt as a reserve; it has done better in putting the area under the National Trust. But the nation merely accepts the Trust, it does not provide funds; the taxpayer is presented with the property without demands on his pocket. The various reserves are supported by voluntary subscriptions to the watchers' fund. Even when the watcher gives his or her services there are expenses, for at Scolt food and water – unfortunately no good drinking water has been found on the island – has to be brought daily from Brancaster Staithe, and the equipment of the hut is expensive. On other reserves the watchers are paid and the fund needs help.

T. A. C.

PRESERVING THE LAKE DISTRICT: A DERWENTWATER BEAUTY SPOT
August 24 1925
The public has entered into possession of yet another portion of the margin of incomparable Derwentwater. This afternoon Sir John and Lady Randles handed over to the National Trust, to be held by the Trust in the name of the community, the deeds of 81 acres of woodland and meadow at the north-east corner of the lake, including Crow Park, Cockshot Wood and Castle Head. A magnificent gift indeed!

The importance of some of this property, if Derwentwater is to remain unspoiled, is out of all proportion to its acreage. Crow Park consists of 20 acres of pasture, sloping gently down to the brink of Derwentwater, immediately to the north of the landing stage. This part of the lake's margin is the closest of all to the town of Keswick. The town has gradually been coming nearer, and Crow Park might have been submerged by a housing scheme of the town council if Sir John and Lady Randles had not stepped decisively between, buying the property for the express purpose of making it a national possession. Crow Park still has a tenant, and the public therefore cannot wander over it at will.

Immediately to the west of Crow Park are the Isthmus Meadows, low-lying and liable to flood. These are a part of the gift to the National Trust, and so is the Town Cass, a bit of woodland that makes an effective screen to the north. Cockshot Wood, which is separated from Crow Park by no more than the width of a road, was in immediate danger from the woodcutters. There are also included in the gift two fields lying between Cockshot Wood and the entrance to Friar's Crag, which is already in the safe hands of the National Trust. The wooded height of Castle Head is one of the most famous viewpoints of the Lake District. From its summit the sight commands the whole of Derwentwater. The public has previously enjoyed the right of entrance to Cockshot Wood and Castle Head, but it has been only a permissive right. They are now dedicated to the public use for ever, and the footpath connecting the two properties is at the same time similarly secured.

A Proof of Affection

Today's formalities were carried out in Crow Park under steady rain. Skiddaw was wearing a bulging grey wig. Perhaps it was the sight of it that impelled Lord Ullswater, constrained by the downpour to put on his hat in the middle of his speech, to jest about the wig that he wore for so many sessions as Speaker of the House of Commons. The audience sat on a roped-off ring of chairs or stood on the fringe of the circle. For nearly an hour they listened and the speakers spoke – some of them – from under trickling umbrellas. There could have been no more thoroughgoing proof that in proclaiming himself a lover of Derwentwater in any weather – even in this! – Lord Ullswater spoke also for the rest of the nine or 10 speakers and the two or three hundred souls who heard and applauded them.

THE SUFFRAGETTE IN RETIREMENT

June 11 1924

I found her in a neat brown house on the hillside, a house that attracted instantly by its straight, plain curtains – that hallmark of intellectual domesticity – by its wide-open windows and the glimpses you caught of books in the rooms beyond; and by its general air of comfortable simplicity. It was emphatically the right house to build on a hillside, if a house must be built there at all; and it made you want to know at once who lived in it. Inquiry having elicited the owner's name, this took one back instantly to other and stormier days, days that seem a hundred years ago now, full of battles and renunciations, of big failures and bigger successes, but days, all the same, without which a certain amending Franchise Bill would not have passed last week through Committee A of the House of Commons.

For the very frail and gentle white-haired lady who opened the door to her visitor had been one of many women, never in the limelight, who gave the best years of their life to fighting in what they were told at the time was a lost cause – and to winning the first great victory of it in 1918. Of course, she did not look like a suffragette – no suffragette ever did! – though a certain kind of conversation with a certain kind of visitor will always reveal the disconcerting fact that she has a warlike eye. But the sight of her called up a whole mass of reminiscences in which she figured, in common with many another woman who would far sooner have been getting on with the world's work than merely earning the right to get on with it. And here she was, having won rest at last, and – what a great historic rebel always longed for in the heat of battle – a hillside and a few sheep.

Making a Women's Institute

But only metaphorically, of course, or she would not have been a genuine suffragist in the past. Whether the goat grazing nearby represented her 'few sheep' or not, they certainly did not bound the limits of her endeavour. She had every inducement, as she had every justification, for staying in her attractive and cleverly construed little house, with its petrol engine for generating electricity, its anthracite stove for cooking and for heating passages and water supply, its beautifully shaped hall and rooms, and its exquisite views from every window. But she did not stay in it. She had only been 18 months in the place and already, in the little village she overlooked from her stronghold of peace, she had set going a flourishing Women's Institute. Older residents, people who knew, told her it could not be done. These things were possible in other villages, no doubt. But here the women were so ignorant, so unawakened, so apathetic. There is one advantage in having, as a wag at an open-air meeting once put it, 'graduated in Holloway Gaol'. It has at least taught one that there is no apathy or prejudice too great to be overcome and, farther, that you should never believe what you hear about women's incapacity. Hence the fact that a suffragette in a neat brown house on the hillside meant a Women's Institute in the village below, where for the first time someone had taken the trouble, or possessed the vision, to recognise the human needs of the women who were the wives and mothers of the community.

It seems to be a peculiarity of village life that reading rooms are always masculine and institutes are always feminine. Perhaps the new equality in the electorate may eventually obliterate the distinction. Meanwhile, in the suffragette's village, temporary union has been achieved of necessity, since the older-established reading room has to be lent to the women until they can afford to build their own hall. So, instead of the lazy talk over old times I had anticipated when I knocked at the oaken door of the house on the hillside, I found myself precipitated within half an hour into the midst of a millinery class in the reading room, where some 20 Institute members were learning to make or trim their own hats. It was quite in keeping with suffrage discipline that within another 10 minutes I, who can do nothing with my fingers, was myself meekly manufacturing a raffia daisy – they kindly called it a daisy – under the directions of a competent county council instructor. I had no difficulty after that in understanding how the apathy of the village women had been overcome.

Leaving the Cradle to Rock Itself

The Institute has made just that difference to life in the suffragette's village that similar enterprises have already wrought in other villages. Tired and harassed women, who never before thought it possible that they could have any outside interests apart from those occasionally encouraged by church or chapel, have emerged from their cramped and insufficient homes – for housing is no better here than elsewhere, and most of the new cottages have been snapped up by tenants able to pay a higher rent than those who perhaps needed them more; they listen to lectures on all kinds of subjects, from birds to Soviet Russia; they go to Wembley for the day, as perfectly organised as for a suffrage procession. They have interesting competitions in arts and crafts, domestic or otherwise, and they are working up for a fete of their own in the vicarage garden, at which the Oxford Players will perform. The same kind of thing, one knows well, is going on in most villages today, it marks the most striking difference between pre-war and post-war rural England. It is only natural that a suffragette in retirement should be also in the forefront of this later 'women's movement'.

'Do you know all the people about here?' I asked her, as we walked back across sloping fields of young green wheat and fragrant beans. Yes, she knew all, but had no time to go about paying calls. Her friends were the women in the cottages whom she had been the first to make friends with. Once a suffragette always a suffragette, I suppose; and when I left her the words of a speaker at one of the 'victory meetings' in 1918 came into my mind: 'There's never going to be any rest in this world for us women.' Well, some of us are in Parliament, others in local government; some are in public and others in private work. But even if we live in retirement in a perfect house on a perfect hillside, I doubt if, in an imperfect world like ours, any of us are, or ever will be, 'at rest'.

EVELYN SHARP

ROD AND LINE: FISHERMEN'S PATIENCE

August 20 1926

Nothing is more trying to the patience of fishermen than the remark so often made to them by the profane: 'I have not patience enough for fishing.' It is not so much the remark itself (showing a complete and forgivable ignorance of angling as it does) that is annoying as the manner in which it is said, the kindly condescending manner in which Ulysses might tell Penelope that he had not patience for needlework. What are they, these dashing, impatient sparks? Are they D'Artagnans all, roughriders, playboys of the western world, wild, desperate fellows who look for a spice of danger in their pleasures? Not a bit of it. They hit a ball backwards and forwards over a net or submit to the patient trudgery of golf, a laborious form of open-air patience in which you hit a ball, walk earnestly after it, and hit it again.

These devotees of monotonous artificial pleasures who say that fishing is too slow a game for them seem to imagine that fishing is a sedentary occupation. Let them put on waders and fish up a full river, and then walk down it, on a hot summer day. Let them combine for an afternoon the arts of the Red Indian and the mountaineer, and in the intervals of crawling through brambles and clambering over boulders, keep cool enough to fill a basket with the upstream worm. Let them discover that they have to take their coats off when salmon-fishing on a day when the line freezes in the rings. Let them spin for a pike in February or trout in August. They will find that they get exercise enough.

Some forms of fishing are sedentary in the purely physical sense in that after a man has baited a spot for carp or roach or anchored a boat for perch he keeps still. But he has not attained a sort of Nirvana, like a crystal-gazer isolating himself from nature by concentration on a miserable ball. His mind is not dulled but lively with expectation. Of all kinds of fishing only one requires patience, and that is trailing a bait after a boat when someone else is doing the rowing. Even in these forms of fishing, which do not mean moving about, it never occurs to an angler to pride himself on his patience. Self-control, if you like, but not the most leisurely of all the virtues. There would be patience needed in watching a float which (there being no fish in the water) you knew would never budge, but there is none in watching a float that may on the instant make a demand for action.

What other people mistake for patience in anglers is really nothing of the sort, but a capacity for prolonged eagerness, an unquenchable gusto in relishing an infinite series of exciting and promising moments, any one of which may yield a sudden crisis with its climax of triumph or disaster. Something rather like patience would be required by the kind of fisherman who casts a fly mechanically and uniformly and is jerked into consciousness only by some extraordinarily altruistic little trout who, in a passion of benevolence, hangs himself on the end of an undeserving line. But such fishermen seldom persist and, if they do persist, learn to fish in a different manner.

Fishing, properly so called, is conducted under continuous tension. The mere putting of fly or bait in or on the water is an action needing skill, an action that can be done well or ill, and consequently a source of pleasure. Many an angler returns with an empty basket after a day made delightful by the knowledge that he was putting his float exactly where he wanted it, casting his fly a little better than usual or dropping his spinner with less splash at greater distances. The mere athletics of casting give the fishermen all the golfer's pleasure in good driving or putting. But (and here is the point) there is no red flag to show the angler in what direction he should aim, to take from him all initiative, to put him, as it were, in blinkers. His free will is limited only by his skill in execution.

If he is a trout-fisher he is watching the river for a rise, for a boil, for the slight swirl in the water that betrays a fish feeding, below, for the roll in the surface made by a submerged stone above which may be a motionless pocket, below which may be a minute eddy, either a fit place for a trout to lie in wait for his dinner. Now and again, if the river is new to him, he will find a hole in what he had thought was continuous shallow, and will tell himself to remember next time to fish that spot before he comes to it. All the time he is watching for cover, and will use the very hole that he kicked himself for not seeing before he came to it to keep low and out of sight while he casts to another likely spot above. He marks where the water runs slow under the banks. At the hang of a pool he tries to put his flies at once just where the fish is likeliest to be. He knows that a mistake is all but irrevocable, that a first cast has a better chance than a second, and a second a much better chance than a third. His day is a succession of crises, each with its demand on his presence of mind.

Even in float fishing so much depends on observation, on watercraft, on the reading of barely perceptible signs, that those who imagine that a good fisherman can watch his float and think of something else besides his fishing are very much mistaken. So completely does fishing occupy a man that if a good angler had murdered one of those people who prate about patience and were allowed to spend his last day at the river instead of in the condemned cell, he would forget the rope.

The ultimate test is one of time; patience is a virtue required when time goes slowly. In fishing time goes too fast. Fishermen's wives are unanimous in deploring the hopeless unpunctuality of their husbands at the fag end of the day. Fishermen rarely have time to eat all the sandwiches provided for their luncheons. If, on occasion, they do eat in leisure at the waterside it is with the peculiar relish that accompanies stolen fruit. They run a race with the sun and are always finding that it has beaten them, and is casting their shadow on the water long before they had expected to have to cross the river. The only time that seems to the fisherman longer than it is is that in which he is playing a big fish. Then, indeed, his drawn-out anxiety makes him apt to think he spent an hour in landing a salmon which was actually on the bank in 15 minutes. But no one will suggest that those minutes were so dull that they needed to be patiently borne.

Until the 16th the Lune was low and there was nothing much to be done with trout until the evening. The rains have now put the river in trim again and brought more salmon up. The Ribble is also in better condition after a week of poor sport, in which the trout, perhaps knowing that rain was to come, were extremely unresponsive though showing freely. There is little news from the Lakes, except that of a continuous run of good pike-fishing in Bassenthwaite. Last week Mr Howard had 15 pike; Mr Book three eight-pounders; Mr Humber four pike and three trout; Mr Southwell a few trout and four pike, including a 15-pounder. There has been a good spate down all the Lake rivers and the larger fish are moving, though fly fishing in daylight is still very poor.

ARTHUR RANSOME

THE ENGLISH FARM WORKER: AN OLD FARMER'S VIEWS
October 7 1926

An English farmer friend, now an old man, opened his mind to me. For years he has been paying, as many other intelligent farmers up and down the country have been paying, more than the local wages rate. He has also, for a quarter of a century 'divided something among his men'. His plan is this: 'I set down what I should pay in rent if I had not had to buy my farm. Then I add 5 per cent on my working capital, and to that, by way of wages for myself, a sum of £250, which I regard as the value of my house, free milk, butter, eggs and poultry, fruit for my family and friends, and the cost of an old man. When all this and the farm outgoings are subtracted from sales, I give my men 25 per cent of the balance.'

'But,' I said, 'how if there is no balance?'

'There has always been a balance,' he replied.

'Can't Afford Not to Farm Well'

'As to cottages, I have built half a dozen since I bought my holding, and my young fellows know that when any of them want to get married I am ready to build more. All my cottages are occupied by decent men, who, I imagine, are content. It's a comfort to farm when you have men working along with you to make a profit. In all, there are 13 cottages on my farm of 200 acres. I shall never have better men. They mostly give me of their best, I think, and they feel that they get something for what they do.

'I am sorry to say that as a young man I saw things only from the master's point of view. Nothing else entered my mind but that some men were born to be labourers, some to be masters and some to enjoy themselves as landlords. Now when I have come to see things differently a better way seems the right way after all. How can you farm well without good men? To turn out the best work in a factory you would want the best men. To do the best farming you want the best men. What can a shilling or two in wages matter one way or another in the accounts if you get more efficient service? The few shillings more I have paid have brought to me the best men, in addition to those bred on the farm, who, it stands to reason, must be the most useful of all.'

I found that my friend's wage rates were 38s for ordinary workers, 40s for more skilful men, and from 42s to 46s, with house, wood and bonus, for waggoners. The minimum rates in his county are 32s, 6d for ordinary workers and 33s for special men.

Primitive Farming

'Good wages,' said my friend, 'are unquestionably a matter of good farming. Farm well and you will have no difficulty in paying good wages. If I were a labourer I wouldn't work for a farmer who was not farming well. How could I do my best? How could he pay me for my best?

'I have no patience with the men who are for farming poorly in what they call bad times. Farm well and you will always have something to sell, if not one thing then another. Can you point out to me a single farmer who knows his business who farms too well to get a profit? The most successful farmers are those who are doing the land best. Some people abuse farmers for not keeping close accounts. If I had been able to keep strict accounts when I started the business I should have frightened myself with what I spent on feeding stuffs and artificials. You can't afford not to do your land well and if you farm intensively you have got to employ labour, and the men who are worth good money are the cheapest.

'There's no use pretending that some farmers understand their work as well as they would have people believe they do. Or that they are as good at it as they think they are. A lot of the farming one sees is primitive. We have splendid farmers in this country, but I would go as far as to say that the majority of farmers are below the level of what they ought to be. They get no effective criticism from people whose opinion carries weight with them. Most farmers believe that they farm in the best possible way. Take only the capital side of the matter – how can men farm well who are in debt? Why, too, pretend to be blind to the fact that some farmers lose money in other ways than farming? But one of the worst things is that many farmers take more land than they can do well. One of the quickest cures for bad farming would be to cut down many farmers' area of land. Not that I am against large farming if done well, even joint-stock farming in the future. There would be with it continuity of experience. At present the young man coming into a farm makes mistakes with the land, and the man who is going out of a farm lets it down. Continuous good farming would mean continuous employment of the best workers.

'If we are going to deal fairly with the labourer – and we've got to – good farmers should be free to do anything with the land but impoverish it. To do our best with the land the first of all essentials is security of tenure. With complete security of tenure and freedom to farm as he has a mind, a good farmer will take prices as they come. If one thing does not answer well, he will try another. Of course, he won't be able to pay town factory wages to his men, but he'll be able to pay more than is now paid, which will be enough to make them feel that, all things considered, they've as good a chance of putting something by as their relatives who choose to go to town, and as good a life of it and expectation of life.'

Security of Tenure the Way

'Capital and skill are essential. But how far can capital and skill carry you without security? To secure the good farmer in his holding is the best thing you can do for agricultural wages. When the master is free to do the very best he knows with the land there is a chance of his men being paid for their best work, for the master will value it.

'Friends said, when I bought my farm, that I could not do the farm better than I had been doing. "We'll see," I said. Look at these ramshackle buildings I put up as a tenant, and look at this thousand pounds' worth of pumping apparatus that I got in at once as soon as I had security. It was not till I was my own master that I could put up all the cottages that were wanted if I was to keep good men.

'The only way to content the worker and the farmer is to get their minds wholly on the job of drawing the most out of the land without impoverishing it. They can't do this if the labourer is always wondering when he's going to be able to lay a pound or two by, and if the farmer is always trotting to the agent for consent for this and that, and never getting it, unless with no prospect of compensation. You can only farm well if you feel that the land is as good as your own. But the farmer should not have to sink his capital in buying it if he doesn't want to.

'Some people abuse farmers for not putting up cottages. I begged my landlord to build cottages, and I said I would pay 5 per cent. No. I asked if I might put them up on the basis of their being taken over at a valuation if I gave up the farm. No. I asked if I might put them up on the chance of the incoming tenant taking them. No.

'The only wisdom I have got on how to give the agricultural worker his due is to get the land he works on out of the control of incompetents. I am in no way afraid of a public authority, and of inspection, and all that. The good farmer would not object. Everybody would know without any inspection who was farming well. The officials would only interfere with the farmers who wouldn't farm, and the sooner they were interfered with the better for us all.

'My father was a high Tory, but I can't for the life of me see how a good farmer hasn't everything to gain from the State taking a full responsibility for the land. There will never be a right relation between the State and the land until the State has full responsibility. And only then will the nation, the farmer and the agricultural worker get their due.'

J. W. ROBERTSON SCOTT

MORRIS DANCING 'FOR LUCK': BAMPTON'S FESTIVAL
June 9 1927

'Six fools and one morris dancer,' jested the fool as he capered in and about the Whitsun team of men that came dancing along the village street of Bampton-in-the-Bush. Neither he nor they seemed in the least conscious of being there to keep alive our last relic of an ancient nature ritual, but the merest child in the crowd of villagers who followed them about all day knew for a certainty that it would have meant bad luck for anybody to have omitted dancing the morris at Whitsuntide.

There is always a morris 'side' or set of village men at Bampton to perform this annual ceremony. Indeed, there are at the moment two sides, for the old fiddler who gave so many of his tunes to Cecil Sharp, the collector, 20 years ago has just trained a second set of younger men to carry on the tradition after him, and the two sides danced in different parts of the village this year.

But the larger crowd followed the old man and the set of six young dancers, in white ducks with their flower-trimmed hats and their gay ribbons and bells, who paused at intervals in their progress through the village to perform one or another of the dances and jigs that the folkdance revival has now made familiar in all parts of the country. Here was, however, no revival but something that had never ceased for centuries; so with the team came not only the merry fool, whose bladder scattered small boys in shrieking delight, but also a serious youth who carried the traditional spiced cake on the point of a beribboned sword and dispensed it economically to all who dropped a coin in his box and meant to sleep on their fragment of cake that night – perhaps only vaguely 'for luck', perhaps with the firm intention of invoking a dream of a sweetheart.

No better setting for the survival of a tradition could be found than this Oxfordshire village, once a clearing in a primeval forest, and later the spot whence the stone was shipped for London in barges on the Thames nearby for the building of old St Paul's. In defiance of the holiday motorists who came rushing by – or who drew up amazed to see a bronzed young fellow dancing the Broom Dance or the Bacca Pipes Jig at the side of the road – it was impossible not to feel that one was in the presence of the unchangeable here, in this collection of grey stone houses, the one place in England where the morris has never quite died out, but has been handed down from generation to generation and so preserved in the face of all change.

To the people of Bampton, however, it was all perfectly natural and commonplace. 'Now then you lazy set of rascals, altogether and one at a time in "Shepherds Hay"!' says the old musician as he strikes up the familiar tune, and the crowd closes round to watch while the dancers go through the figures, handkerchiefs in hand. With an occasional adjournment for cider the thing goes on all day now in the street, now in somebody's back yard or again in a beautiful garden. Nobody's gate is closed to the Bampton morris dancers or to the villagers who accompany them. Here it is Highland Mary that is danced, there it is Maid of the Mill or Banbury Hill, and so on and so on, while the cake bearer's box grows heavier and the crumbling cake on the sword point dwindles into shapelessness. And at sunset everything is put away of another twelvemonth, ribbons and bells and all, and the village goes home under the new moon to sleep with a scrap of magic cake under its pillow.

R. R.

CLAIM FOR DAMAGES FAILS
December 14 1927
Edward King, a mill worker, of Primrose Terrace, Mill Hill, Blackburn, claimed £43 damages at Southport County Court yesterday, from Thomas Whalley, a farmer of Halsall, in respect of injuries received at Ormskirk Agricultural Show on Whit Monday.

King stated that he was showing a mare and foal. The mares had been judged, and when King was parading his foal before the judges he alleged that Whalley's mare became restive. The man in charge of it struck it with a whip, with the result that it spun round and kicked King, who sustained a broken arm. He was taken to Ormskirk Cottage Hospital and was unable to work for nine weeks.

It was alleged, on behalf of the defendant that as King was parading his foal he was running backwards looking at the animal and he backed into the defendant's mare. Which spun around and kicked him. The animal was not struck in any way. James Horsfield said he could bring a charabanc-load of witnesses to say that the mare was struck. Judgement was given for the defendant with costs.

LAKELAND HOUND TRAILS: LEADING DOG LOSES BY STOPPING FOR A DRINK
August 20 1928
The Threlkeld (Keswick) hound trails on Saturday provided exciting finishes. In the old dogs' trail the local champion, Blencathra, led into the last field, but dropped into the beck there for a drink, and Latrigg raced ahead to pass Diamond and win narrowly, Blencathra coming in third. The puppy trail resulted in as upsetting a finish as the

old dogs' race, for Dancer, Comely and Gaily were leading in the last field but one and followed the trail round by the end of the field and over the bridge over the beck, but the cute Keswick dog Cornflake made straight across the field and through the beck to win smartly from Grimcrack, which had slipped ahead of the first three dogs.

A hound trail at Kirkbride (Cumberland) Agricultural Show on Saturday was won by Roper's Springwell (Curthwaite), with Reay's Hurry On (Cockermouth) second and Graham's Silent Lady (Bigland's) third. The puppy trail was won by Dalzell's Delver (Keswick), with Edgar's Winker (Carlisle) second and Wall's White Violet (Carlisle) third. Mr Shepherd had a double win at the Dearham hound trails on Saturday, Snowfire winning the old dogs' trail, and Snowflight the puppy stakes. This was Snowfire's 13th victory this season; and it will help him in his neck-and-neck race with Didlem for the championship.

COUNTRY DIARY: SWEET ROCKET

June 2 1928

Sweet rocket flowers, violet and white, are shining in this serene moonlight, and amongst them moths as pale as the flowers are astir. The pale columbines still show and the pale lupins and irises: iris Alcazar shows richly dark against sweet rocket and violet thalictrum, obscure like smoke, is visible still in the dusk. Now a dumble-dor zooms by, then one of those good old cockchafers. (Do you remember their fairy backs – and how they hang on with their hooky feet and will not let go until suddenly they are off on the wing again?) Now a nightjar is churring. Here in the midst of the moor we have nightjars all round us, so that sometimes their strange music weaves a criss-cross over the garden. So still it is tonight that I can't even hear the waves down at the cove or the bellbuoy in the Eastern Sea.

W. A. P.

COUNTRY DIARY: CUMBERLAND

June 4 1928

We see the adult migratory fish, the salmon and the sea trout, coming up, and at the beginning of this month we still see the young of these kind going down. Until this year I had never caught a glimpse of the descent of the two- and three-year-old smolts except at the by-passes at the weirs or in the mill lades. But last evening while I was watching the brown trout – the native trout – sucking in flies in the crystal-clear water at the tail of a pool there came a little shoal of the silvery fish that are on their way to the rich feeding-grounds of the ocean. It was quite evident that the smolts were hurrying. They stayed just a moment behind a boulder, and then off they went again on their seaward journey. Amongst them must be smolts that were bred in the hills and have passed through the Jakes holding pike and cannibal trout that each spring lie in wait for the migration. What countless dangers the smolts have yet to face before they can return as salmon in two, three or four years' time!

G. W. M

WEST RIDING ESTATE SALE: SMALL PRICES FOR BIG LOTS

June 25 1929

One of the few remaining country estates in the West Riding of Yorkshire came under the auctioneer's hammer at Rotherham yesterday when Messrs Collins and Collins of London offered the historic Thrybergh Park Estate, which had been in the hands of thane and squire since the time of the Saxons. The estate was sold about six months ago by Mr J. S. H. Fullerton, the lord of the manor, to Mr Herbert Hey of Harrogate and last night it was offered in 98 separate lots.

Before the sale, 32 lots were sold to the Rotherham Golf Club for £9,000. These lots included the Gothic mansion Thrybergh Hall, which is at present used as a clubhouse for the golf club; 116 acres of Thrybergh Hall, used as a golf course, and 15 acres of woodland building sites bordering the park.

The remaining lots comprised six farms and small holdings, nine cottages, some building sites and a number of freehold ground rents. Grange Farm, Thrybergh, containing 67 and a half acres and having a rent of £60 a year, was sold for £1,950 to Mr R. P. Marsh, solicitor of Rotherham. Mr C. A. Broadhead, a Rotherham architect, bought 17 building sites with an area of 7 and a half acres for £975. A house with buildings and land, formerly the homestead of Thrybergh deer park, with an area of 23 acres, was purchased by Mr L. Glasby of Thrybergh for £1,000.

Among the unsold lots was the Manor Farm, Thrybergh, which has been farmed by the present tenant family for over 300 years, and it was withdrawn at £2,200. A triangular enclosure of grassland was withdrawn at £75. In the middle of this latter plot stands the remains of St Leonard's Cross, an ancient stone supposed to have been the rallying point at which the Crusaders mustered before marching to the port of embarkation.

THE WHITE AND RED CLIFFS

January 6 1930

To monopolise a bit of the sea coast for oneself is not a criminal (though it may be a very selfish) act. It is done by increasing numbers of people every year, so that the red cliffs of Devon and the black rocks of Cornwall will soon be as difficult to see as the White Cliffs that are desecrated by Peacehaven. On Saturday Dr Vaughan Cornish suggested that the remedy lay in choosing as our national parks country which would include long stretches of coastline. It might be wise to take his advice and make our first national parks in Wales and Cornwall. But even so we should be only saving a bit here and a bit there; the walker would still find that, with each successive summer, a new cliff walk is obstructed and a new trudge inland is necessary if he would see his favourite bit of the shore over the shoulders, as it were, of usurping bungalows. One suggestion, not prominently urged as yet but perhaps the most practical of all methods of saving wild parts of the countryside, seems peculiarly appropriate to the problem of the coast. To acquire all the fine wild country of Great Britain for the nation by direct purchase is too long and too costly a job. But much the same or even more satisfactory results could be very simply achieved by first scheduling country which should be preserved from the builder and then passing a short Act of Parliament forbidding the owners of such country to develop it without permission. An annual rent could be paid as compensation, but as the land would in every case be wild land and no existing revenue would be confiscated the total compensation necessary would not be a large sum. Most of the landowners who now preserve our wild country and our cliff scenery would welcome the suggestion. They would know that their successors would be unable – even if they wished – to exploit that beauty which it has been their own pride to preserve.

A COUNTRY DIARY: CUMBERLAND

February 13 1930

Notes come from around Murder Wood – the big planting concealing a deep ghyll between two fells – that we have not heard since last spring. They are those of mating foxes. The shepherds say that a dog fox and a vixen fox call to each other in much the same way as a dog answers the bark of another. A huntsman tells you that he can distinguish the yap of the vixen from that of her mate. Listening the other night to the notes, we became convinced that it was not a duet but a chorus that was going on, and we were confirmed in that belief when next morning we were told that six foxes had been seen stealing about on the fell. Murder Wood is one of the favourite breeding places for vixens in the district. They may take their cubs elsewhere when they get on their legs, but the hillside dropping down to the stream in the ghyll is the place where they lay down their young and keep them while they are suckling them.

G. W. M.

MACHINERY ON THE FARM: WHAT THE 'ROYAL' HAS DONE

July 7 1930

It always comes as something of a shock to realise that only 70 years ago the corn and hay crops still fell before the sickle or scythe, that the corn was still threshed with a flail on the threshing floor, that the casting shovel still served to distinguish the light from the heavy grains and, in short, that apart from seed-drills for roots and wheat, farm machinery was virtually unknown, implements were few and simple, and farming was conducted on a basis of cheap and plentiful manual labour. Today farming is a highly mechanised industry. The smallholder sits high on his mowing machine and clatters round his one or two hayfields; on the large farms a man pilots a stuttering tractor over the arable acres with a five-furrow plough behind him.

Very occasionally someone or other mourns the passing of those old days, painting imaginary pictures of the simple joys of farm labour in those leisurely times before the great development of wheat-growing in North America, which followed the arrival of cheap and rapid sea transport. Occasionally, a few voices are lifted against the Dutch barns – 'corrugated-iron roofs on stilts', they complain – the corrugated-iron implement sheds, the bare-looking tower silos which are rising here and there. Perhaps there are farmers who would like to return to the days when the thatcher reigned supreme for covering the stacks, and roofs were patiently sliced with a hand-chopper. But farmers have to make their way of life a means of livelihood as well.

The admittedly meagre level of agricultural workers' wages is nevertheless a terribly disproportionate charge on the cost of production in relation to prices received – wages are about 100 per cent above pre-war, while produce prices average perhaps 45 per cent above the same base. Economy in manual labour, efficiency in machinery and implements, have yearly grown in importance since the last quarter of the last century, when the British farmer began to find himself in competition with the world and the struggle between intensive farming and the prairie farming of the Americas started. Today machinery is given a high place among the farmer's weapons against adversity.

Ninety per cent of the farmers who visit the Royal Show examine very closely the classes of their particular favourites in cattle or sheep or pigs, glance cursorily at the rest and spend hours among the 400-odd stands where potato-diggers raise imaginary potatoes, hay-loaders load imaginary hay, tractors travel an endless circle of minor obstacles and light stationary engines pop derisively on every side, pumping water, driving barn implements or merely showing off their own superlative quality.

Mention the 'Royal' and it is the machinery section that comes to the mind's eye of the vast majority of agriculturists. There they wander among the very latest in labour-saving devices and implement improvements. They wish they could afford this or that; they pick up a few ideas to apply to machinery or implements they already possess; they make a few tentative inquiries about implements they will shortly have to buy to replace the old. The questioning farmers among those stands always give the lie to the fond urban imagining that farmers are obstinately unprogressive and unwilling to take advantage of improved ways and improved means.

July 28 1930
The Duchess of Newcastle is staying in Harrogate and is taking the cure. She has arranged her visit to coincide with the Harrogate Agricultural Show on 8 and 9 August, when she is judging some of the dog classes. The Duchess is a typical Irishwoman in her love for dogs and horses and has judged at Harrogate for many years.

THE GROWTH OF RAMBLING: FEDERATIONS AND THEIR WORK
February 7 1931

Ramblers, wayfarers and all that happy fraternity of reputable vagabonds who tramp and climb across misty moorlands, who follow downland tracks and forest rides, who find delight on secluded fieldpaths over meadow and marsh are now banding together as ramblers' federations. Their views and aspirations and the work accomplished by the federations often pass unnoticed by the general public, though the continual growth of rambling clubs is evidence of their widening sphere. With a sound understanding of the difficulties ahead, the ramblers' federations hope to continue making the world of the rambler better than they found it. On Monday next, and on the second Monday of each month following, the Ramblers' Federations of Great Britain will contribute to the columns of the *Manchester Guardian* notes on such phases of their activities as have immediate interest for all ramblers.

Though comparatively of recent development, most ramblers' organisations were born from minor struggles in contesting the closure of useful public ways and places of scenic beauty. A long catalogue of such contests, from the days of Magna Charta, would include the verderers of the New Forest and the cottars of the Highlands. The loss of public ways and access to commons and waste lands still went on from early years until what appeared to be the culmination with the passing of Enclosure Acts. From that period there soon followed the formation of numerous footpaths societies, notably in and around the large towns and cities. About this time, too, appeared such arch-wanderers as R. L. Stevenson, W. H. Hudson, Richard Jefferies; the militant purpose which saw the birth of enthusiastic local bodies became tempered and extended with idealism.

The young rambler of this generation now makes of his pastime a veritable craft. His maps, compass and the rucksack on his back gave him far more confidence to essay the crossing of high ranges, and he finds strength and joy in battling with elements, in going out to feel the spell of conquering the unknown. It may be that Canon Rawnsley had this vision in the far-off years before the war when he said: 'The reason for preserving to the nation the ancient bridle-paths, driftways and footways will not be questioned by those who consider that with each year the number increases who need them ... appreciation of the country walk and field-side ramble grows each year ... the nation's eyes are being trained to need the country more for its intelligent pleasures ... But no one lives but can dare prophesy that it will yet become a passion with the people.'

For each open-air body in existence 20 years ago there are 20 today, and the major portion of these are rambling clubs, intensely and fiercely defending the beauty of the woods, windy heaths and open spaces, the dwindling footpaths and ridgeways, the lonely hills and rolling, field-chequered downs against the misguided despoiler.

Mechanical modern civilisation tends to eliminate the human factor in many ways, and war has taken away the finest of a generation, so it is fitting that the last decade should see the wonderful expansion of a pastime so eminently beneficial and adjustable to a population thus impoverished. A similar transformation can be seen in Germany, Holland, Austria and Scandinavia today.

The British Ramblers' Federations are drawing closer together and constantly increasing in strength. The more recent movements of national importance include the stimulation of public interest in the preservation of the countryside, which led on to national conferences. From quite a small conference at Hone, Derbyshire, there have grown the agitations against desecration of beauty spots and the requests for national parks. There is now a wide interest in what Lieutenant Commander Kenworthy names 'the Ramblers' Charter', the Access to Mountains Bill and the Rights of Way Bill. A network of hostels for ramblers is one of the present aims, and was definitely embarked on by the Liverpool, Manchester and Sheffield federations in 1929.

A. W. H.

PONY CLUB PAPERCHASE: LITTER SUMMONSES

May 10 1933

A paperchase by the North Cheshire Pony Club had a sequel at Macclesfield Police Court yesterday, when Miss Joan Adshead of Kermincham Hall, Kermincham, Cheshire, and Miss Molly Baskervyle Glegg of Withington Hall, Chelford, Cheshire, who were acting as hares for the club, of which they are members, were accused of depositing litter on the highway.

The Macclesfield County Police have been conducting an anti-litter campaign to preserve the amenities of the district and this was the second prosecution for laying paper trails. The cases were dismissed on payment of costs and a warning was issued.

Mr H. Cauldecutt of Knutsford, who defended, said it must be proved in accordance with the county by-laws that the litter was injurious to the public. If paper trails were going to be made a criminal offence then they would have to revise a lot of their old-school classics. The defendants were home on holiday from school and the club had obtained permission to hold this chase over land, but in certain places they had to cross the road.

GREAT HARWOOD SHOW

June 7 1933

The industrial depression, which has hit Great Harwood harder than almost any other cotton town, has been powerless to affect its agricultural show, although a number of the other Lancashire shows have had to be cancelled this year. Today the sun brought thousands of visitors from miles around and the number of entries for the various classes showed a substantial increase over the previous year. The entries of cattle, of heavy horses and of pigeons were all greater than last year, but the biggest increases were in rabbits and in sheep.

An Established Show

The Great Harwood Show, which is nearly three-quarters of a century old, is as indispensable a part of Lancashire's Whit Week celebrations, as are the previous day's 'walks'. On every other day of the year Great Harwood belongs as decisively to the Lancashire of mill chimneys and dismal streets as does Whalley, a mile or so farther north, to the Lancashire of villages and market towns. It is a frontier town of industrialism and seems to have as little contact with the countryside beyond as if its exits were guarded by custom-houses and passport officers. Today, however, this little market town changes its character; it becomes a meeting-ground for the two worlds. Farmers from Bowland and Pendle mingle with cotton operatives from Blackburn and Accrington. It is not only as spectators that the two Lancashires mingle at Great Harwood. They come together as competitors as well. Heavy draught-horses, cattle and sheep are brought to the showground in the same hope of winning prizes as are the delivery vans which butchers, bakers and dairymen send from all parts of industrial Lancashire.

But the strength of the Harwood show has always been in the section for dogs and it is in this department that the townspeople of Great Harwood and neighbouring places have taken most interest. It is here, too, that the industrial depression has become apparent. The entries of dogs are down this year – the only section of the show to record a decrease. It is not that the number of dogs entered is less, but that the workers who own them have only been able to afford the entrance money for one class, whereas in happier years the same dog would be sent to take its chances in several classes. The people of Lancashire have only lost the money to indulge their fancy, not the wish to do so, and it was patent today that, as far as the show proper was concerned, there was more interest in these classes than in any other section.

The Holiday Atmosphere

One says as far as the show its self is concerned, for the most popular feature of the day's proceedings was undoubtedly the light holiday relief properly added to the serious business of a Whit Week agricultural show. The evening brought whippet-racing for those with a mind to enjoy this typical industrial sport, but those who wanted the atmosphere of a fair as well as of a show had not to wait until the evening to be satisfied. In a corner one could see couples dancing on the rough grass to music broadcast from a van, whose principal purpose seemed to be to advertise patent medicines. Then at intervals in the competition ring there were highly expert displays of trick-riding by a troop of about a dozen horsemen, whose Argentinian costumes flattered the holiday desire for the picturesque without detracting from the remarkable quality of their horsemanship.

They started with the comparatively easy sports of tent-peg sticking and of picking up handkerchiefs from the ground while galloping past. They went on to jump off and on their horses, to stand on their heads, to turn somersaults and generally so to circumnavigate the galloping ponies that one was left with the impression that the horses must be stationary, so rapidly did the horsemen move. Here was a feat of dexterity which both townsmen and countrymen could admire. If it had little relevance to the stern business of an agricultural show, it had every title to form part of an engagement that is as much a holiday affair as a Whit Week show should be.

SMALL COUNTRY INNS: THEIR CONVENIENCE TO THE RAMBLER

February 3 1934

To the Editor of the *Manchester Guardian*

Sir, May we urge that more consideration should be given by licensing benches to the needs of ramblers when the closure of small inns is considered? The old modest type of inn, specially suited to the rambler, is being swept away. Between 350 and 400 licences are extinguished every year: in little more than 30 years over 25,000 houses – or one in every four – have been closed and it is generally the homely little inns that are thus abolished. A not uncommon experience among our members is to find at the end of a long walk that a little inn they have been using regularly for years has since their last visit been shut up by the local licensing bench on grounds of 'redundancy'.

Licensing magistrates when closing an inn are usually influenced chiefly by the fact it is doing only a modest trade. They tend to overlook its real usefulness as a place of rest and recreation to ramblers, whose actual refreshment needs may not go beyond a glass of beer or a cup of tea. In the hope of checking the closure of some of the more useful and attractive little country inns the association is willing to intervene in suitable cases at Brewster Sessions, and is prepared in such circumstances to give evidence and support in writing or, if possible, by personal representation on behalf of licensees catering for ramblers. We trust that in this way we may be able to help to convince magistrates that these inns are supplying a real want, felt particularly by those who like to spend their leisure time in the country, but who do not care to go to the more elaborate or expensive establishments. Yours, &c.,

George W. Moorcroft, Hon,
Catering Secretary Ramblers' Association
86 Eccleston Square, London, SW1

THE AMATEUR NATURALIST: A MODERN CULT

July 13 1934

Englishmen have always been interested in animals: our poetry from Chaucer onwards is full of references to their habits; our devotion to sport has led to a widespread knowledge of their ways. Yet it is only in recent years that the observation of animal life has become a common hobby. Its popularity is proved by the number of books on the subject published every month. There must be a reading public for such books as E. W. Hendy's *The Lure of Bird Watching* or Frances Pitt's *Animal Mind*. Clearly there are many people who wish to recognise every bird they see and who want to know something of the habits of moles or badgers or fish.

In the last century it was only the sportsman who was informed as to the way of animals, and he chiefly because he wanted to hunt or fish or shoot them, but the modern spirit is in direct opposition to the national desire to go out and kill something. The child of today, indeed, fed in infancy on Beatrix Potter, charmed by the 'Jungle Books' or the innumerable animal stories, delighting in Frances Pitt's accounts of her pets, is hardly likely to find pleasure in shooting rabbits or in hunting the fox. Animals have acquired personality and imagination has been stirred to feel the animals' point of few. The kindergarten and the infant school, too, have fostered this attitude. Children are encouraged to love and care for all sorts of animals and nature study in schools discourages the acquisition of dead specimens and inculcates the observation of their appearance and habits. We are rapidly become more humanitarian, though it may be long before hunting and shooting lose their place in our national life. The outcry against films which show the trapping or killing of wild animals is proof of this new spirit. The elderly sportsman who recounts his triumphs at stag hunting or stalking is apt to find his stories coldly received by a proportion of his younger audience whose sympathies are clearly with the stag. Children who are cruel to each other without much compunction are roused to passionate anger by any cruelty to animals.

FREDA GODFREY

HUNTING ON NATIONAL TRUST LANDS
July 18 1936
To the Editor of the *Manchester Guardian*

Sir, While anxious to further the aims of the National Trust (of which we are members) and admiring the magnificent work it has accomplished, we feel it to be only fair that public attention should be drawn to what in our opinion is the one weak spot in the Trust's management. This is its continued sanction and even encouragement of 'field sports'. Since the late T. A. Coward in 1930 attacked hunting on National Trust lands there have been many protests from naturalists and humanitarians on this score.

The position of the Trust touching sport is strangely anomalous; for one of the main purposes for which it was established is, as defined by clause 4 of the National Trust Act (1907), as regards lands 'for the benefit of the nation ... for the preservation (so far as practicable) of their natural aspect, features and animal and plant life.' Moreover, the Trust's own by-law No. 8 (1927) explicitly states that 'no unauthorised person ... shall shoot or chase or drive game or other animals ... on Trust lands.'

It may be suggested the word 'unauthorised' permits National Trust committees to give authority to local hunts. But such an idea, though it may be made to square with the act, is surely entirely foreign to its spirit and was doubtless far from the intention of those who framed it. In any case, killing for sport appears to contravene the great principle of forbidding the molestation of animals in a sanctuary, such as the National Trust should provide for wildlife which enjoys no other legal protection.

In 1930 the Trust prosecuted and obtained sentence against a labouring man for shooting eight wood pigeons on one of the largest of its estates. Yet the local committee of management of the same property, both before and after this, officially allowed foxhunting to be carried on.

In view of the growing respect for wildlife and the general desire to preserve our native fauna as part of the national heritage, we would suggest that the time has come for the National Trust to prohibit all killing for sport on lands under its entire control.

Yours, &c,

Lascelles Abercrombie, A. Ruth Fry, Dorothea Gibb, H. W. Nevinson, Noel-Buxton, Charles Oldham. G. Bernard Shaw, F. E. Weiss

London

A COUNTRY DIARY: CORNWALL

August 29 1936

There is a headland near here with a precipitous cliff to westward which looks down into a chasm full of misty blue air with a green sea floor. I ate there last evening watching two buzzards hunting. They had got the whole gulf of air to themselves to play in and powerful broad wings to enjoy it with; so they could circle up and up the opposite cliff, in and out of the hollows, scanning the steep turf, or sail out into the sky till I could see the light through their barred wings close before me, or float down idly on to a pinnacle. Then a third buzzard turned up. The sea air had another wild sound in it besides the usual noise of gulls: the mewing of the buzzards. And just as I was watching, facing the full blast from across the Atlantic, I saw a Painted Lady butterfly beside my hand. So frail a creature, but still perfect, sheltered for the moment by being a few inches below the level of the wind blowing over the headland. I could watch the gradated colours, all in a series, burning up from tawny yellow to the one perfecting flash of tawny red near the greenish fur of the body. Painted Ladies: so they manage to live even there on the precipice along with buzzards. May the gales be kind.

This is the last Country Diary I shall write. May I send my thanks to those readers who have kindly written to me 'out of the blue' about these notes during all these years I have enjoyed doing them.

W. A. F.

MOW COP: TODAY'S PRESENTATION TO NATIONAL TRUST

May 19 1937

The National Trust announces that this afternoon Mow Cop, the famous landmark surmounting the 1,000ft ridge on the Cheshire and Staffordshire boundary, will be formally handed over to the Trust.

This date is near to the anniversary of the historic open-air meeting which led to the formation of the Primitive Methodist Church at Mow Cop. For their part as leaders in the new movement at the beginning of the 19th century Hugh Bourne and William Clowes were expelled from their churches for not submitting to Wesleyan discipline. Two years later, in 1812, the Primitive Methodist Church came into being. Year after year great camp meetings were held on Mow Cop, the largest being the one celebrating the centenary of Primitive Methodism.

When, two years ago, the National Trust was offered Mow Cop, which included the Old Man and the few acres of land surrounding them, they accepted on condition that the 'ruins' surmounting the summit were made safe (they were then in a rather dangerous condition) and that all fencing was put in good order. This has now been done.

At today's ceremony the Primitive Methodists will be represented by Mr Moses Bourne and the Revd Jacob Walton. A member of the National Trust Executive Committee will represent the trust and Sir Philip Baker-Wilbraham also will attend. It was Randle Wilbraham of North Rode who erected the 'ruins' (never meant for habitation) just over 150 years ago and the land was in the possession of the Baker-Wilbraham family for many years. The last owner was Mr Joseph Lovatt of Kidsgrove, who has handed over the property to the Trust.

GUNNERY CAMP PROPOSAL

January 18 1938

A resolution demanding that a public inquiry should be held by the War Office in Blakeney, Norfolk, as soon as possible into the proposal to build an anti-aircraft camp near Stiffkey, irrespective of the War Office inquiry to be held at Wells on January 25, was carried unanimously at a protest meeting at Blakeney last night. Speakers declared that the establishment of a camp would ruin Blakeney. Several alleged that the War Office used an 1885 survey map in choosing the site and that Blakeney Point, the National Trust bird sanctuary, had moved over a mile westward since then and was now included in the suggested firing angle. The meeting also decided to ask every householder in the village to sign a petition pointing out that Blakeney depended for its livelihood on the summer visitors, whose chief recreations were sailing and fishing and the free amenities of Blakeney Point for bird watching, bathing and picnics. 'Keep these visitors away by the effects of gunfire and ruin awaits all of us,' the petition claims.

A COUNTRY DIARY: LANCASHIRE

November 29 1939

They are ploughing up the undulating field beside the wood. As I watch from my window the bulky form of the tractor looms into view over a rise and comes humming down the next slope. Yesterday they had horses drawing the plough and I do not find it easy to decide which I prefer. Admittedly ploughman and horses coming into view over the top of a slope is one of the best of country sights, but to my mind the silence which accompanies them leaves the scene incomplete. There is something very satisfying about the hum of a tractor, especially when heard from a distance. Like the throbbing hum of a threshing machine it is a peaceful, unobtrusive sound entirely in keeping with its surroundings.

I go out to the edge of the wood to watch the ploughing. Down, along, up and round go ploughman, tractor and plough, driving a slightly less straight furrow than the horse-drawn plough had done. Slowly the green recedes and the dark brown of newly turned furrows increases. A solitary gull comes floating idly over the field and drops down, as if to alight, but changes its mind at the last moment, rises again and flies off. A robin hops about among the furrows near the edge of the wood, picking to right and left, but retires to the shelter of a hedge at the approach of the tractor. A wren, which has all the time been threading its way backwards and forwards among the tangles at the foot of the hedge, pays no attention to the tractor or to me, but hops up on to an outside twig a couple of yards from where I am standing and bursts into song.

J. K. A.

A WORD FOR THE WALL

August 12 1939

One of Derbyshire's annual events is a competition of drystone-walling – that is, of building a wall of loose, unmortared material so soundly that it will last well-nigh for ever. The trick of it, which the August visitors to the Buxton area may watch in action, is in the deft assortment, arranging and handling of the stones so that they overlap to the best advantage: there must be unfilled crannies between them, but as long as these do not unite there is no weakness. In shepherd's country there have to be at intervals large removable stones on the ground level of the wall, big enough to admit the passage of a flock of sheep, one by one, when the stone is pulled out; naturally some art is needed to fit this kind of doorway, which saves the need of a wooden gate, into the loose structure of stone-walling. A dry wall can take the eye by its cunning texture, while it especially suits the farmer because of the speed and economy with which a clever hand can raise it. The mortared wall may be the more imposing because it is the finished article, but both species add to the looks as well as to the service of the countryside.

Stone walls are the very bones of some English shires, of Derbyshire not least. The grey hillsides, whether of woldy Gloucester or of millstone-gritty Pennine, are unthinkable without them, just as the countries of the plain are not to be imagined without the sprawling hedgerows that betoken lushness of ground and lazy, spendthrift farming. Can you fancy the foreign peasant allowing the songbirds these capacious and soil-consuming choirs which surround every five or six acres and exhaust fertility with their large and hungry growth? The stone walls of the naked shires are far more utilitarian. They are composed, as a rule, of stuff which had to be cleared in order that a field might be; they extort no sustenance from the soil; they need no clipping; the necessary repairs are few and can be easily made. A tumbled piece is soon put back. Even in the quarry country stone is now so expensive that it is being abandoned as material for housing and walling, with terrible results to the eye. At the new end of the old stone village are the council houses of rough-cast and brick, while the cities of stone (and therefore of a single hue), such as the great grey mass of Edinburgh, are now girdled and bedizened with cherry-ripe suburbs, sporting the scarlet tile; red brick and bogus Tudor gables of what house agents call the Cosy Palace or Little Baronial Hall. Even to surround quite a small garden (as every good garden should be surrounded) with a stone wall is almost as expensive as building a new house. For a generation the high cost of walling has been as disastrous to the looks of Britain as the high cost of living has been detrimental to the limbs and lungs of the poor and hungry. The fence of wire or of boarding is a feeble substitute for the enduring and enfolding quality of hewn rock; earth is best guarded by its fellow.

The present difficulties besetting the man who desires to have a thing so seemingly simple as a stone wall appear the more remarkable when one sees the enormous mileage of stone-walling which old England (and old Wales and Scotland no less) could afford for purposes of private vanity and grandeur. The holiday traveller who pays any sort of attention to the roadside view must be astounded by the contrast between the old and new economy of barricading and fencing. The Big House of the 18th and 19th centuries could afford magnificently built and often extremely high stone walls which ran round the parkland for mile after mile. These formidable and quite unnecessary barriers you may equally see in all their size and splendour round the Palladian mansions of England's classic style or set about the turreted baronial seats of Scotland's plutocratic Victorian conquerors. One says 'unnecessary' because the chief function of the wall is only to immure the inhabitants of the park, some cattle and tame fallow deer in most cases, herds easily restrainable by a wire fence.

But milord must have things handsomely achieved and he liked the show of privacy: his park and mansion must be concealed from the general; the stone was cheap, and cheap also, abominably cheap, was the labour of the semi-servile rural proletariat. What do these miles of carefully mortared 10-foot walling represent? The careless passer-by may take them for granted, but they are the abiding stuff of social history; the legacy of the village of Dumdrudge scored imperishably on the soil. What were the conditions of all this barricading for eternity? A 60-hour week at a 10-shilling wage? Something like it. The peasants of Britain toiled like the helots of Pharaoh or the slaves of Rome, toiled with native hands on native stone, simply in order to shut themselves out of their own countryside.

It never can happen again. There will never be that wealth on the one side, that cheapness of labour and material on the other. The ironic somersault has already been turned here and there by landlordism in its death-struggle with taxation. Another war, indeed a little more of such peace as we are now enjoying, will mean that numberless great houses will be left to rot behind their walls. In the Highlands of Scotland you may drive past mile after mile of exclusive ducal walling only to be besought by ducal placards and a ducal emissary at the lordly gateway to come inside and have a look – price, one shilling per peep per person. The old hymn verse needs sardonic amendment: we have the poor man in his castle, the tout beside his gate. The chieftain, his back to the financial wall, removes his bonnet and solicits the small silver of the motor coach. It is pride, not the stone that has fallen.

Those miles of monotonous walling which protected the nobleman's seat are absurd in their height and length and, in so far as they impede the view of pleasances within, unkindly to the passer-by. But structurally they are unquestionably sound and they can also be agreeable to the eye. There is nothing wrong with the desire for seclusion within reason: we most of us would like to build a wall. Walled gardens, those mellow enclaves of an aromatic plenty, their protective stone fruit clustered, their pathways murmurous with bees and all the rich mutter of a summer afternoon, are the proper appendage of a well-planned country house. Much craft may be expended on a hedgerow: the Tudor people played all manner of tricks with yew, as you may see at Compton Wynyates in Warwickshire, and Scotland could achieve bizarre effects with giant screens of beech hedge a hundred feet high, as you may see on the Lansdowne estate near Blairgowrie, where Lady Nairne planted on this gigantic scale nearly two centuries ago. But in the common usage of the farm and garden the wall for centuries served the Periclean ideal of Greek taste: it provided beauty with economy.

The trouble now is the cost. The beauty abides, however, and all that can be said against the wall is that it has been a destroyer in the hands of thoughtless or of desperate men. Thucydides relates how the Athenians, under Themistocles, used any material to keep the Persians out. This was dry-walling of the most rough-and-ready kind. The foundations, wrote the historian, 'are laid of stones of all kinds and in some places not wrought or fitted, but placed just in the order in which they were brought by different hands, and many columns, too, from tombs and sculptured stones were put in with the rest.'

In a similar way in our country many a noble megalithic monument has been broken up to pen in pigs and sheep. The walls of modern Avebury were the mightiest of stone sanctuaries once. But we must forgive walls for their robberies because of their good looks. The man who can still buy stone and pay for masons serves not only himself but the future with his investment.

IVOR BROWN

A COUNTRY DIARY: CUMBERLAND
October 23 1939
The good things of the earth are in abundance this autumn for bird and beast. This is an acorn year. We have never known the ground strewn so thickly with the fruit

of the oaks. The badgers, when they can tear themselves away from the rabbit snares (how differently from the foxes do they take the food left for them until the trapper comes along) gorge themselves on the little apples pattering from the trees. So do wood pigeons, of course, but not so well-known visitors are the mallard. The lake rose five inches the other day with the result that the ducks were spared a longer journey on land than they care to travel. They arrive at daybreak to feast on the acorns and afterwards, like the cormorants now hunting perch in 20 to 30 feet of water, they rest long to digest their heavy meal.

The blackbirds are doing themselves well on the laurel berries, of which there is an extraordinarily plentiful crop. An octogenarian gardener tells me that the eating of laurel berries produces a feeling of elation. It would almost seem, he says, that they are charged with alcoholic content. Starlings and wood pigeons are stripping the elders of their black grapes. Pheasants, deprived of much of the food they like by the early ploughing of the stubble, are gobbling the last of the blackberries and picking up the seeds of the dockeris. All but alone among the shrubs and trees bearing fruit to be shunned by birds is the guelder rose. The brilliantly hued wineberries find no market.

G. W. M.

CHAPTER THREE

Digging in
1940-1959

As Britain fought for her survival between 1939 and 1945 the *Guardian* found room for plenty of the small but arresting observations of the natural world which for many readers lifted morale. Among them was a discussion of the effects of the blackout on moths, which also helped to stimulate curious scientific research. Two of the country's greatest experts on the subject, Professors E. B. Ford and A. J. Harvey, persuaded the Royal Air Force to let them make a series of balloon ascents at night to gather evidence from different altitudes on the possible relationship between moths and the moon. They were jubilant to discover three moths as high as 1,000ft off the ground.

The bible for these entomologists was *The Moths of the British Isles*, published in 1907 by Richard South, three volumes with exhaustive illustrations which showed moths 'set', that is to say with their four wings stretched out in the way that collectors kept them pinned in cabinets. It was not for almost a century that this book was replaced as the standard work; in 2003 Paul Waring and Martin Townsend published a new *Field Guide to the Moths of Great Britain and Ireland* which is now in most field naturalists' packs. This book also shows all the moths in marvellously accurate paintings by Richard Lewington, but with their wings folded down their backs or very occasionally above them. This is how you will find a moth at rest in the wild or asleep in a light trap from which, after identification, it can be released unharmed.

The difference between the style of illustration tells the story in précis of natural history study during the 20th century, especially among the extraordinary army of amateurs who took part. The vast exterminations inherited from Victorian collectors – who killed thousands of insects and birds in the cause of science – gradually gave way to observation, especially as very high-quality cameras became cheaper and easier to use. This process was much encouraged and assisted by the media, from the Rolls Royce films of the BBC's Wildlife Unit to modest but practical columns such as the *Oldham Chronicle*'s weekly 'Hunting with a Camera'. This was contributed and illustrated by John Armitage, the Keeper of Natural History (1952–68) at Leeds City Museum, who also contributed nature notes to the *Daily Herald*.

The *Guardian* was quick to appreciate the value of popular natural history, both in providing news stories and for interesting and involving readers. It covered the formation of the British Ornithologists' Union in 1858 and the first meetings of the Conchological Society, for shell enthusiasts, 16 years later. *Guardian* journalists were on hand to record the early days of the British Vegetation Committee in 1904 and its change of name in 1913 to the British Ecological Society – one of the early uses of that now familiar word. The paper noted successively the arrival of national societies for frogs, toads and other amphibians in 1947, seaweeds in 1952, mammals in 1954 and lichens in 1958. This post-war burst of organised activity was significant. Like so much behaviour in the late 1940s and 1950s it developed from initiatives which had only been practicable in the pulling-together, emergency atmosphere of wartime.

Chief among these were the County Herb Committees whose job was to collect medicinal and other useful wild plants for the war effort, a job they tackled with gusto. From their heroic efforts – which saw 4,000 tonnes of rue, antimony and the like delivered to the health authorities – stemmed the huge enthusiasm which went into the plant distribution maps scheme organised between 1955 and 1959 by the Botanical Society of the British Isles. Again encouraged by friendly publicity in the *Guardian*, and elsewhere, more than 2,000 amateur botanists, including many herb-committee veterans, carried out the largest scientific survey ever undertaken by amateurs, indeed perhaps by anyone. Dividing Great Britain and Ireland into 3,500 squares, each covering some 36 square miles, the huge team trawled diligently for every plant and fern to be found in them. Full records were submitted for all but 10 and the 1,250,000 records were published in 1962 as *The Atlas of British Flora*.

On a smaller scale, similar heroics were undertaken by the bird-ringing scheme of the British Trust for Ornithology (BTO), which saw annual figures reach heights such as the 279,189 birds ringed in 1960 by more than 800 volunteers. Field studies of individual species also led to significant changes in countryside behaviour. From the 1920s to the late 1950s debates raged intermittently in the *Guardian* about whether rooks were an asset or a pest, a subject which divided the newspaper's specialist staff as much as the readers. Gradually, the birds gained the upper hand, but not as quickly as the Little Owl. A BTO investigation, given muscle by the observations of scores of amateurs, proved convincingly that the introduced bird was not a menace to game estates as had been thought, but lived on insects and small mammals, many of them classified by farmers as pests.

Similar surveys were undertaken of geese and ducks by members of the Wildfowl Trust, of the brown hare and badger by the Mammal Society, and of snakes, lizards, frogs, toads and newts by the British Herpetological Society. They produced interim reports and provided opportunities for out-and-about features which delighted *Guardian* commissioning editors looking for stories to lighten the travails of rationing, the Suez crisis or the Korean War. Perhaps the best came when the Royal Entomological Society met in Manchester and heard a paper on the story of the Manchester Moth, which proved that even in this minority and (some might reckon) obscure field of interest the famous *News of the World* slogan still applied: all human life is there.

Greed, jealousy, guile, revenge. Each was central to the story of Robert Cribb, an amateur insect collector who in 1829 found 50 specimens of a previously unknown moth on Kersal Moor, a wild park in the Irwell valley which was the scene of 18th century naked male races which were watched from a respectable distance by local women weighing up potential husbands. He asked a more experienced friend called Wood to take three of them to an expert entomologist for identification. There was a misunderstanding and the moth, which had never been found in Britain or anywhere else before, was given the scientific name *woodiella*. Deprived of his rightful fame, Cribb broke his links with Wood, abandoned collecting in a fury and set about trying to get the highest possible price for his remaining 47 moths. Unfortunately, he also left them as surety for rent arrears with his landlady. He concluded a sale, but too late to meet the rent deadline.

Furious in her turn, the landlady threw the moth collection, which she imagined to be worthless, on to the fire. It was a disaster all round, but nonetheless a good story for the *Guardian* to tell, complete with details of the three moths taken by Wood (one of which survives in the Manchester Museum). The newspaper was moved to run a leader on the episode and its resurrection by the Royal Entomological Society, which denounced a dismissive comment about industrial Manchester by the poet Tennyson. He had written: 'We are not cotton spinners all.' The *Guardian* replied: 'He might have been a bit more respectful if he had known about our eminent moth.'

A COUNTRY DIARY: CHESHIRE

January 16 1940

Out in the middle of the mere, where some 60 mallard were standing, I spotted a long-billed bird which proved surprisingly to be an oyster-catcher – of all the common waders the species least prone to wander inland in Cheshire from the coast or tidal estuary, although in the northern Pennines and Scotland it breeds in river valleys far from the coast. It flew round, piping anxiously, but always rejoined the comparatively phlegmatic duck. Comic relief was provided by a score of coots which flew to join the duck from the meadow where they were grazing. They looked like a bevy of soberly dressed old women who had just learnt to fly but were still wearing their galoshes. They had certainly not learnt how to land on ice, but crashed and slid for yards before coming to a standstill, when it was almost possible to see the look of relief on their faces. They reminded me of Mr Pickwick on the ice at Dingley Dell, with his black gaiters, his anxiety as he turned slowly round on his way down the slide, and his smile when he reached the end. Unlike the mallard, who remained entirely unmoved by this display, the coots were restless and walked about rapidly in a compact little squad. Fieldfares seem to be scarce so far this winter. Just after receiving a letter asking what had become of them I saw four in my meadow; they were the first I had seen this winter, but I have had little opportunity for regular observation; this morning quite a number were 'chack-chacking' in the fields. At roosting-time I saw a dozen reed-buntings on a hedge. Winter flocks, which, I am told, occur at times on the Pennines, are uncommon in the plain; a keen observer tells me that he has never yet seen a reed-bunting in winter within three miles of the small Cheshire town where he lives; usually I see an odd one or two by the meres and in my garden in winter, but great numbers return in early spring.

A. W. B.

WORK OF THE LAND GIRLS: MINISTER'S TESTIMONY

January 27 1941

'Farmers need have no fear of breaking the backs of the Women's Land Army. Modern women are tough and capable of giving all but the very best of the stronger sex a thoroughly good hiding.' That is what Mr R. S. Hudson, minister of agriculture, told farmers, landowners and workers at Dorchester on Saturday. He deplored as the 'height of folly and short-sightedness' the present spate of criticism of the possible usefulness of land girls. It was doing the gravest possible disservice to agriculture. The only effect at a time when the farming community required women was to discourage them from volunteering to serve on the land when farmers made it quite obvious that they considered them no good and did not want them. 'At the Ministry we have a very impressive collection of tributes from farmers to the work done by land girls. I should say if anything that women are tougher now than they were in the Victorian days.'

Assurance on Manpower

Speaking about the 'forthcoming call-up of some men from the farms', Mr Hudson said that from the number of letters in the press and resolutions passed by branches of the National Farmers' Union (NFU), one might imagine that it was proposed to denude every farm in the country of its key men. Nothing of the sort is intended. A comparatively small, I would even say a very small proportion of the total number of farms will be affected at all. He gave the assurance that the government fully realised that the agricultural industry could not give up any substantial proportion of its experienced men.

BREAD AS BAIT: ANGLER FINED

September 19 1942

At Wigan yesterday Edwin Littler of Holt Avenue, Billinge, was fined £2 with £4 3s costs for wasting bread. Mr Frank Platt, prosecuting for the Ministry of Food, explained that before the war between 800 and 900 competitors took part in the annual angling contest of the Wigan Angling Centre, and among them in two hours they used some 3,200lb of bread for bait. The Northern Angling Association took up the matter with the Ministry of Food with the result that bread was prohibited as bait, and all angling societies in the area were notified to that effect. The defendant was seen fishing in Turner's Flash near Wigan by two men, one of whom was secretary of the Pearson and Knowles Angling Club, which has the fishing rights of this water; he was using white bread for bait. It was clearly stated on his fishing permit that bread was prohibited for use as bait.

LAND GIRLS' PAY

October 23 1942

To the Editor of the *Manchester Guardian*

Sir, As a working member of the Women's Land Army (WLA) it was with great interest that I read E. M. Barraud's article in Friday's *Manchester Guardian* and the letter 'Land Girls' Pay' in Saturday's issue. My complaint is the inadequacy of pay and lack of promotion for land girls who have had some experience. When I first started on the land, nearly two years ago, I could neither milk a cow nor harness a horse. My jobs consisted of washing milk cans, sorting potatoes, sweeping the yard, &c. My wages were then 9d an hour. Today, like hundreds of other land girls, I do all the horseman's work on the farm, besides milking five cows night and morning, and can plough and sow and reap and mow either with horses or with tractor. But my pay is still only 9d an hour!

Might I suggest that for each half diamond issued twice yearly for good service, the land girls' pay should be raised by 1d per hour to a maximum of, say, 1s 2d, and that a corresponding addition should be made to overtime rates? This, I believe, would make the WLA appear far more attractive for the prospective volunteers, besides being some reward for present hard-working members. The farmers can well afford it.

Yours, &c.

W.L.A. 297

⁂

SERVANTS OF THE SOIL

November 30 1942

The hardships of the peasant's life take a great place in literature. Homer spoke of the ploughman at his heavy task, 'longing for the hour of sunset and supper', Lucretius of the insensibility to heat and cold that he gained from his stern life. In 19th-century England old age, stiff with rheumatism and often overshadowed by the workhouse, saddened those who sought delight in the peace and beauty of the country. Bridges draws in *The Testament of Beauty*,

> *an old stone-deaf labourer, lying awake*
> *O'night in his comfortless attic,*

while the rats run amuck in his thatch. Twice in the century the labourers made a combined effort to wrest from their society a life less harsh and pitiless. The first was the tragical rising in the Southern Counties of 1830, the second the Joseph Arch movement of the 70s, in which failure was all the more bitter because of its first success.

Mr Masefield, watching the wartime revolution on the fields with land girls driving tractors, has recalled the memories of his boyhood and composed a beautiful poem, 'Land Workers', on the labourers in smocks whom he remembers half a century ago. He writes of their prowess and skill with all Cobbett's admiration, but he too strikes the same sad note:

> *The pastoral those fellows played*
> *Was piped beneath no beech-tree shade,*
> *But fought by manhood grinded bare*
> *Against starvation and despair.*

His picture is as vivid and complete as his tale of 'The Widow in the Bye-Street'. He brings into it the dress of the labourers as well as their tasks changing with the seasons, their ritual for birth, wedding and death, the graces that survived from old pageants like the maypole dance, their legends and superstitions, and the scenes in the market street where they acted

> *that age-old play of Corn*
> *Cut down by Death and then re-born*

which takes the 19th-century life of his village in the West Country back to the beginnings of Greek tragedy. And in the pictures that come to his mind he sees why

> *The red line stood at Waterloo,*
> *And why all seas have felt the ploughs*
> *Of England's island-builded bows'.*

STRANGERS ON THE LAND
October 20 1944

The new hand and I were sitting under the lee of a great combine-harvester, sheltering while rain drifted across the East Anglian flats in a way that puts combine-harvesters out of action and farmers out of temper at harvest time. There was simply nothing to do but wait. I was not sorry, because after many days of satisfying the appetite of that voracious and versatile machine it was soothing to sit in the grey-green dampness, admiring a white spire which rose out of the mist a mile or so away. There was no sound but the drip, drip of rain falling from the tarpaulin to the newspaper which the new hand and I had spread over our knees.

I had thought he was a student, because the people who join us on the land for harvest tend to be students. But his opening remark showed that he was no ordinary student.

'This reminds me of Spain,' he said, and I recognised a foreign accent. I was a little surprised.

'Spain? Did you say Spain?'

'Yes, Spain, my country,' he answered. 'I have sat for hours in places like this, and worse, taking shelter from rain – and other things. I was many months in the war. And after all, we lost.' He looked out towards the white spire and I could see he was going over that losing battle. 'We began with pitchforks and shotguns, anything, but Franco was getting more planes than he wanted. We warned you that it was the beginning of a world war. You British, you deserve your victory now, but in 1939 perhaps you deserved a bit of a ... bit of a shake-up.'

Our farm being what it is, this sudden leap from the East Anglian scene into the dust and heat of world politics should not have surprised me. No one must suppose that the land has been aloof from the comedy and pathos and drama and general mix-up of a world at war. Memory moves easily and appreciatively from one oddity to another; one remembers Rudolf, for instance.

It is impossible to forget Rudolf, for how often does it happen that English labourers pick plums with a man who has responded to the applause of European opera houses; a man, moreover, who descended to the labourer's status by way of a Nazi concentration camp? The autumn sunlight came through the plum trees in golden bars on the day Rudolf left us to make his way to Palestine, and it was just before knocking-off time that he began to sing. I don't suppose he ever sang with greater effect.

We stood still under the trees, holding our baskets, while from end to end the orchard was made melancholy by an old song, 'By the waters of Babylon we sat down and wept when we remembered thee, O Zion.' It rose and fell and the quiet Cambridgeshire scene seemed to change for a scene of shame where, singing the same psalm, Rudolf's compatriots were driven to extermination at Lublin: 'If I forget thee, O Jerusalem, let my right hand forget her cunning.' The song ended, Rudolf looked round and smiled and it was a relief to be back in the orchard. When we parted at five o'clock I could only say, 'Good-bye, Rudolf. I hope that in Palestine you will find security and peace.' He bowed very courteously, and said, 'I am always happy where there are a few kind people.'

And after Rudolf one thinks of Hans: quiet, precise and the soul of courtesy. He would read Pascal's *Pensées* over his bread and cheese at lunchtime, wearing a tattered raincoat cloakwise over his shoulders – a coat that has now been changed for the white habit of the Dominican monk. Nor is that all. We have had to deal with Italian prisoners by the score. We have grown accustomed to it now, but at first the effect was terrific. They were overpoweringly friendly and insatiably curious. They would come armed with pocket dictionaries and corner you against a straw-stack, and you understood the last word only, which was the inevitable and international '*Compri?*' Weakly, you replied, 'No *Compri*.' And it all began again. Eventually you gathered that they had set their hearts on a bottle of brilliantine, a certain tube of toothpaste or a particular stick of shaving cream, and in return they would make you a ring or possibly something better. And it is a fact there is not much that an Italian cannot make, and not much that he doesn't know about catching a rabbit or cooking a hedgehog.

Well, their English is better now and Toni's fruity tenor can be heard any day in 'You are my sunshine, my only sunshine …' Most of them have 'cooperated' and lost their coloured patches, and their uniform has gone bright green, with ITALY in red on the shoulder. It is a long time since I heard an Italian dismiss the contents of an English newspaper with an apologetic but convinced, 'Plenty propaganda!' For the most part their illusions went long before their coloured patches.

Spain, Germany, Italy, Manchester (Lancashire has supplied us with land girls), it is all the same to the indifferent land and all the same to the regular land worker who watches the queer procession. One imagines him talking the oddities over in the evenings, now and in years to come: 'Do you remember Rudolf, that singer, and Hans, who went to be a monk?' One can also imagine him asking: 'What next?' Whatever the answer, he can hardly be surprised. The land can take anything now.

LAND GIRL'S LAMENT
March 9 1945
If my diary is to be trusted, my first year on the land has been a period of unmitigated suffering. Scarcely a day has passed during which I have not 'ached in every limb' or 'felt completely exhausted'. I have had 'shooting pains in the head' from stooping, 'cricks in the side' from reaching, giddiness from the heat and

paralysis from the cold. The weather has been 'absolutely ghastly' almost all the time. When I have not been 'frozen to the marrow' I have been 'soaked to the skin'. And yet I have survived.

I started off with a considerable disadvantage in being six feet from the ground. Mothers who intend their children to take up agriculture should be careful to stunt their growth and never let them get beyond the five-foot mark. Those who persist in shooting above this level should be directed into fruit-picking. As every gardener knows, it is not the bending down that presents the difficulty, but the getting up again afterwards. I used to deplore the way that country people walk about in a permanent crescent-moon shape, but now they have my full sympathy. Why take the trouble to straighten up at night when you've only got to lean over again next morning?!

After the first novelty had worn off, my entries in the diary dwindled down to a few words – sometimes simply the name of a vegetable, with a brief weather report. 'Cabbage – poured with rain' brings a vision of a grey, leaden sky, a long, depressing-looking field of wet cabbages and a group of damp, dismal land girls plodding round in deep, squelchy mud. I can almost hear the squeals of rage as they pick up a cabbage and get a stream of rainwater up their sleeves or down their Wellingtons.

In an effort to get away from mournful entries I turn to June, expecting to find some mention of frolics in the sunshine, but every day is 'wet and windy', apart from one or two which were 'not bad'. July was not much better. For St Swithin's Day there is the comment, 'Rained, of course!'

Things did liven up considerably in August. The girls came out in sunbathing tops and shorts, and we had picnic lunches under the haystack. Every day appears in the diary as 'lovely and warm' and even 'very hot'. But even here there is a snag. It was impossible to enjoy eating in the open because of the wasps. I got stung in the eye and 'suffered agonies' for days. Then the heatwave gave place to rain and I developed a 'frightful sore throat'.

There doesn't seem to have been any weather at all in September, but 'onions' figure largely. There is even one entry 'Worked overtime on onions'. It is not clear what we did with them, but if my memory serves we were pulling them up and boxing them, and the girls complained that the smell followed them home at nights.

In October we began potato-spinning, which I had been dreading because it was said to be 'the most ghastly job on the farm'. I was very much interested by the way this job was planned out, like a baseball game. All hands were mustered (even the greenhouse girls were dragged out, in spite of their complaints that it wasn't their pigeon) and placed in couples at regular intervals all round the field. Many furtive glances were cast round to see who was driving the tractor, as apparently the tractor driver could make or mar the day for everybody. An unkind driver who whizzes the spinner round and round the field without stopping keeps the girls' backs bent all day, but an easygoing driver will footle around a bit and give them a chance to straighten up now and again. I didn't find this job half so bad as I'd feared.

Far, far worse than the potato-spinning was the beet-lifting, about which no one had warned me. For this the layout was the same as for potato-spinning, except that we were placed singly round the field. Being a greenhorn, I found myself allotted the stickiest 'drift' on the field – the low-lying bit – and for a week I floundered round in the mud, getting daily weaker at the knees, while my more fortunate comrades were on the dry stretches higher up the field. To make matters worse, the boss was behind the plough, so there was no stopping for light refreshment and gossip.

Newcomers are always easily discouraged by the olds hands' yarns. In my early days, if I ventured a little moan about the vegetable we happened to be dealing with at the moment, someone would say, 'Coo! This is nothing! You wait till we start leek!' (Or marrows or swedes, according to their individual dislikes.) I have now 'done' every vegetable in the place except leeks.

Why is it, then, that in spite of wind, rain, mud, frost and snow, coughs, colds, chilblains and gnatbites land girls all love this job and wouldn't change it for any other? My personal opinion is that it is because it affords such unlimited opportunities for talking. Stuck out in the middle of a field with no distractions in the form of managers, supervisors, telephones, typewriters or factory machinery, girls can gabble to their hearts' content. And do they gabble! I have heard more heated discussions in the middle of a turnip field than anywhere else – and not, as might be imagined, about men and clothes, either. We discuss every subject under the sun except agriculture. If you begin talking about that you're liable to get hit with a swede. I mean to say, you can have too much of a good thing!

BARBARA CHILD

DRAWING TOURISTS TO SCOTLAND: ALTERNATIVES TO HAGGIS
September 26 1946
Greater use of Scotland's national assets – its lovely glens and mountains, its sport, its pipe music, Highland dancing and food – should be used to the full in expanding Scotland's tourist and holiday organisation, states the Tourist Committee of the Scottish Council on Industry in its final report, published yesterday.

'Frequently our hotel menus are a poor imitation of continental fare,' it stated. 'We are not suggesting that our visitors should be fed exclusively on haggis and brose (an oatmeal or peasemeal dish), but salmon, venison, trout, grouse, hare, Scotch broth, and well-made porridge are attractive, to say nothing of our Scottish mutton and beef. Scotland is famed for her baking. Home-made scones – girdle, drop and oven – shortbread, cakes, bannocks and cookies, heather honey, bramble jelly and Scotch marmalade should not be overlooked.'

It is suggested that visitors should be interested in concerts of Scottish music and piping, in Highland games and dancing, while films and talks would stimulate interest in Scottish history, which is full of romance and legend.

The greater part of the report is concerned with accommodation, and among the recommendations are holiday camps to be extended and others set up, at least 60 camping sites of 14–20 acres to be set up, a national organisation to establish family holiday camps and holiday hostels, and use of redundant shooting lodges.

Railways are urged to provide reduced fares for holidaymakers from England, with a graduated scale after the first 150 to 200 miles.

A COUNTRY DIARY: PENRITH

July 24 1948

Surely no 'Country Diary' would be complete without some reference to that delightful festival of village life the crowning of the Rose Queen. We attended one two days ago at Askham, a charming old-world Westmorland village, and as we sat by the beautiful river Lowther awaiting the assemblage of the procession, and contemplating the graceful serenity of the noble oaks and sycamores in the park in front of Lowther Castle, we fell into reverie. In the war years a military organisation selected this beautiful park – hallowed by the care and artistry of generations of Lowthers and their retainers – as a training ground for a tank regiment with all its attendant disruptions; and many years will pass ere the scars of that occupation are healed. Then came the procession, all the children who could walk, ride, or be conveyed on the decorated lorry being in 'fancy' dress – pretty, comic or original; the Queen-elect in white satin and her attendant maids of honour in pink. Time was when the procession was led by the local brass band conducted by old Tommy Moss (now, alas, gathered to his fathers); today we were more 'up to date' with the smart drum and bugle band of the local cadet corps, whose drum major, swinging his wand to the rhythm of the music, exuded dignity and importance from every pore. In a nearby field a local lady 'crowned' the Queen – with roses.

J. H. H.

BUS OR TRAIN?

November 20 1948

To the Editor of the *Manchester Guardian*

Sir, The address by Sir Cyril Hurcomb suggesting that the 'abandonment of unremunerative railway lines' might be accelerated raises other points besides the question of fares, to which you refer in your leader columns today.

One important aspect for rambling clubs and other large parties is that of accommodation. Where a railway service is in operation one can normally depend on getting a party – no matter what its size – on the train. Even if seats are not available, the whole party will, at least, be on its way. With bus transport, though, there is no promise that even one person will be able to board the vehicle, and anything other than a small party will certainly need to split up, with some having to wait perhaps hours for the next bus. In cold or wet weather, too, a railway station or halt has some shelter to offer, which is more than can be said of the average bus stop.

Closing of these branch lines would, in effect, put large parts of the country 'out of bounds' for rambling almost as completely as occupation by a government department! In any case the present time would be a most unfair one to make a decision of this nature. Until the full scale of cheap fares available before the war is restored, it is impossible to say what the normal traffic on a line would be.

If some closing of lines or stations is proved to be essential, one possible alternative would be to reverse the common procedure and, instead of certain stations being closed on Sundays, certain country stations and halts might open on Saturdays and Sundays only. In other cases there might be an arrangement whereby trains would stop if advance notice is given. Certainly something must be done to prevent rambling clubs and other parties from losing access to the more remote countryside, which is the part which would be cut off by these proposals. Yours, &c

Denis A. Hicks

The Ramblers' Association

20 Buckingham Street

London, WC2

A COUNTRY DIARY: PENRITH
March 19 1949

Paddy immediately recognises my voice as I call his name on approaching the field in which he has 'wintered', and ambles leisurely to the wall to receive a few slices of carrot or turnip. He is a roaned pony, about 13 hands high, and for a few years past has more than earned his keep and winter's rest with nothing to do beyond eating and meandering in a well-sheltered field below the youth hostel at the foot of the conifer wood. In the summertime he has a big reputation as a leaper in the competitions at rural sports in Cumberland and Westmorland. The cult of pony racing and jumping has developed considerably during the post-war years under the guidance of the Eden Valley Pony Club, and thousands of country people – and townspeople too – gather at these sports to watch the prowess of ponies and youthful riders. Indeed, they are almost as popular as hound trails. Apart from one or two point-to-point races in connection with the hunts there are no 'official' race meetings in the two counties, save those at Carlisle. In summer, during his 'working hours', Paddy is a great favourite with the sporting public; and no less so in winter, when he is at rest. He is a great pal of the children who parade our Beacon boulevard, and substantial portions of many sweets and sugar rations go to satisfy his appetite for tasty bits.

J. H. H.

CODE OF CONDUCT FOR THE COUNTRYSIDE
December 30 1949

The views of the owners of agricultural land upon the National Parks and Access to the Countryside Act (which received the royal assent earlier this month) were given today by the Country Landowners' Association, representing 28,000 holders of land in England and Wales. Lord Carrington, chairman of the Legal and Parliamentary Committee of the association, claimed that the first need was the early publication of the country code which must be produced under the act by the National Parks Commission. Lord Carrington does not expect that any national parks can be established by the coming summer, and indeed, he is most anxious that the code should be out – and made familiar to schoolchildren and others – before the act is fully in force. The view of the association is that if a booklet is properly produced it can have a very great effect on the relation between farmers and townspeople. 'We don't want a booklet that is a mass of by-laws,' he said. 'We want a simple booklet of what goes on in the countryside that explains what sort of thing would happen if you leave a gate open.' He suggested that it should be illustrated with amusing drawings, should offer guidance and interesting information, and should be easy to read.

Carelessness

Lord Carrington holds that most of the damage done in the countryside is the result of ignorance 'or carelessness, and not of malice'. Nothing is more irritating to the farmer than damage done by carelessness. 'The Landowners' Association,' he added, 'had never known any ramblers' or hikers' organisation cause any damage. They behave as we wish everybody would behave, but single individuals and small groups do cause damage.'

Lord Portsmouth, vice-president of the association (who will be better remembered as Lord Lymington, Conservative member for Basingstoke), said the association welcomed the act as an agreed measure. Lord Carrington, however, dealt with one or two provisions of the act to which the landowners attach special importance. The act, he said, gave no greater power to the public to roam at will over a national park area than it had at the moment – with the exception of areas designated as 'open country'. 'I say that,' he went on, 'not because we want to see people turned out but because of the damage that may be done to agriculture and forestry.'

After summarising the provisions in the act for designating as 'open country' an area that is mainly non-agricultural, Lord Carrington added: 'In open country you can roam at will, subject to a number of "don'ts" which are common sense: don't let your dog get out of control, don't light picnic fires.' He thought that some people might think of national parks in this country as being like those in the United States, where people 'can do as they will'.

Danger of the Open Gate

'In this country,' he said, 'which is so small and in which agriculture is so vital, the owner and occupier of agricultural land have the same rights as they had before.' The danger was that careless visitors to the countryside might do great damage. A gate left open, for example, might cause the ruin of a pedigree or attested herd. The act provided no compensation for loss caused in this way. The landowner had, of course, the protection of the civil law if he could catch the offender, but the association had found that in general insurance companies would not accept a risk of this kind.

Lord Portsmouth drew attention to the change in the title of the association: the Central Landowners' Association has become the Country Landowners' Association. The association had wanted to make quite certain of identifying itself with rural landowning and not urban landowning, 'which may vary widely in the extent to which it is blessed or disliked'. Many urban landowners, he suggested, applied the same standards as did rural landowners, but 'there has always been a greater impression created by certain slums, and owners of urban land were liable to be greater political targets'.

A COUNTRY DIARY: CHESHIRE
November 6 1951
A whitebeam in the garden is a wonderful sight, covered with glowing orange berries in such thousands that it looks like a tree in leaf; but these berries are fast disappearing. Early and late it is crowded with birds; rattling shellcocks and noisy bluebacks (I prefer the vernacular), redwings, throstles and blackbirds are the main raiders and bolt the fruit wholesale, but twinks (as chaffinches are known here) and tom-tits peck at a berry on the tree and follow it to the ground if it falls. Starlings, thousands of which came in from abroad last week, move from stubble and meadow to hedgerow trees and orchards, but have disregarded the whitebeam and its berries. A common sandpiper was seen on October 28 by a friend, an exceptionally late bird, although very rarely has one been found here in winter.

An American correspondent has expressed surprise that the 'Country Diary' makes little or no mention of the nightingale and wonders if it is no longer prevalent. This apparent neglect is explained by the distribution in England of the nightingale and of the Diary writers. East of a line drawn from Hull to Bristol there are nightingales, but west of it – with a few encroachments – there is virtually none, and the Pennines act as a complete bar; and so those contributors who live between Cheshire and the Border or in most of Yorkshire and confine their notes to their own districts must inevitably omit nightingales. During half a century in Cheshire I have only twice known one in the country.

A.W.B

WARNING CLIMBERS

December 20 1951

To the Editor of the *Manchester Guardian*

Sir, I fully agree with what both Mr G. A. Sutherland and Mr Wilson Hey say on broadcast warnings to climbers, but I think the best solution to both their problems is that the BBC's weather forecasts should be in terms which are much less vague than they are now.

For instance, such expressions as 'a trough of low pressure' or 'cold or rather cold' are practically meaningless to both expert and layman alike. In the former instance, surely it would take no longer to say whether it was a warm front or a cold front, as this would give a much better impression of what conditions were to be expected.

As for the temperature, it would be much less confusing if it were given as a value in degrees, particularly as the Air Ministry is always getting kicks from the public through the BBC reporting 'cold' when the air is calm at about 40 degrees Fahrenheit and 'mild' when a gale is blowing when the temperature is in the 50s.

Therefore, in the continued lamentable silence of AIRMET, my own recommendation for a more reliable weather forecast is the substitution of the rather farcical and almost entirely repetitive 'regional forecasts' by a brief description of the synoptic situation. In this way the ordinary public could hear the general forecast and such people as climbers, farmers, gardeners and yachtsmen &c. could listen to a more technical survey of the weather and draw their own conclusions. Yours &c.,

A. Thomas

Karabiner Mountaineering Club, Manchester

To the Editor of the *Manchester Guardian*

Sir, I think much of the criticism of the arrangements for broadcasting mountain danger warnings in the Lake District is due to misleading reports. It is not intended to broadcast a warning every time there is a storm over the Lake District. The sudden change of weather conditions would make this impossible and fell walkers should have sufficient sense not to start out when clouds are low.

It is the intention of the Lake District Ramblers' Association to broadcast these warnings only when snow and ice make conditions on the fells dangerous for the inexperienced climber. It is hoped that on hearing these broadcasts on a Friday night intending climbers who normally set out on a Saturday for the Lakes will postpone their visit until a later date and that innkeepers and hostel wardens will pass the warnings on to their guests who have already arrived.

There is no truth in the statement that the hotels are to fly flags when there is a danger warning: such a proposal was made and turned down by the ramblers' meeting. Yours &c.,
Roland Taylor
Honorary Secretary of the Lake District Ramblers' Association

A NATION OF SMALL FARMERS
September 1 1952

Nearly half the food we eat comes from British farms. All our liquid milk and potatoes, 80 per cent of our eggs and of our beef, more than half of our bacon, a third of our butter and lamb, and a fifth of our wheat, besides most of our fresh vegetables and a high proportion of the fruit we eat are produced on the 48m acres of agricultural land in great Britain and Northern Ireland.

The cry is for more. Dominion and foreign suppliers are consuming more of their own produce. Increase in world food production has failed to keep pace with the increase in world population. We are finding that it takes more and more manufactured goods to buy a given quantity of food. Strategic caution demands that these islands should achieve a high proportion of self-sufficiency in essential foodstuffs. No one can see, in the future, any prospect of a return to the conditions of cheap and ample food imports which were the order in the early days of this century. This may mean a lower standard of living: it certainly means more expensive food and it has wrought a minor revolution in our national economy.

A Key Industry
As these facts have gradually seeped into the consciousness of the townsman, so his interest in agriculture has begun to increase. The industry is taking its place beside coal mining, engineering and textiles as a key industry. It is intimately concerned with defence, which it touches both as an essential 'third line' and also, in an age of mechanised agriculture, as a participant in the allocation of raw materials.

So the output of British farming is being watched with ever-growing attention. Its economics are being studied with increasing closeness. People who have not the remotest interest in growth from the soil are beginning to ask questions about it and are beginning to trace the line between farm production and the quantity and price of food in the shops. Meat has become, in the public imagination, something that stands on four legs; bread something that grows in a field.

All this has led to much criticism of our farming systems and particularly of the cost-price structure which (even more since the food subsidies were reduced) ultimately determines what the housewife pays to stock her larder. Much of the criticism is serious, well-informed and constructive. But still a good deal is irresponsible and ignorant. For these critics the British farmer is a convenient target. There is a deep contradiction between the conception of farming as 'the simple life' and the extreme complexity of the agricultural industry in these lands.

Farming differs fundamentally from other industry in three ways. First, it deals not in one but in a wide range of commodities, requiring utterly different conditions and tools for their production; secondly, it is carried on in different parts of these comparatively small islands under conditions which offer so wide a range of soil and climate – particularly of rainfall – that the nature both of the work and of the product is completely dissimilar in the various regions; thirdly, it is ultimately dependent upon conditions quite outside the control of the operator.

It must always be difficult to legislate for an industry offering so great a variety of conditions, and it has become increasingly so in these days of more precise economic planning and in the full glare of public criticism. There are bound to be inequalities. It will take years of experience to smooth them out.

Guaranteed Prices
The machinery of the Agriculture Act of 1947 – certainly the most important piece of agricultural legislation since the repeal of the Corn Laws – has been the target of much criticism. It is frequently asked why the farmers should enjoy the large measure of protection which the act gives them. They enjoy security of tenure, an assured market for about 80 per cent of their produce and guaranteed prices which move up or down with the cost of production.

Because the whole period since the passing of the act has been one of rising costs, it is sometimes forgotten that guaranteed prices work both ways. If, for instance, there were to be a sudden drop in farm wages, then it would be the government who would be demanding a special review to reduce the prices paid to farmers for their produce. Nor does the act specify that farmers should be fully recouped for their increased costs, but only to such extent as to afford 'proper remuneration and living conditions for farmers and workers in agriculture and an adequate return on capital invested'. In fact, at the last three price reviews the farmers have themselves shouldered a considerable proportion of their increased costs. It remains arguable whether they might have borne more, but it is undeniable that in the past 18 months while farm wages have been going up farm incomes have been coming down.

It is, of course, perfectly easy and perfectly true to say that some farmers have made a good deal of money. In a capitalist economy it is to be expected that there should be a relationship between investment and profit. It is perhaps not generally realised that the average size of farms in England is only just over 70 acres, and in Wales it is less than 50 acres.

The Mainstay

Clearly, we could not do without the production of the small farmer, who is the mainstay of the industry. Clearly, if production ceases to be worthwhile to him, he will go out of business. Just as clearly, if his income under a guaranteed price system is going to average, say, £400 a year, the very large arable farmer in the east, with far more capital invested in his business, is going to make a good deal of money. But this state of affairs is by no means peculiar to farming. It applies equally to the small grocer and the owner of a chain of stores; to the taxi-cab driver and the owner of a fleet of motor vehicles. Farming alone cannot be denied its captains of industry.

It appears that so long as farming remains – as it must remain – a facet of a planned national economy, so machinery must be used to induce the farmer to produce those goods and in those quantities which the national larder most requires. Continuity of agricultural production along the desired lines is the chief purpose of the Agriculture Act and of guaranteed prices. This is not to say that the system is perfect or that it has not produced some glaring inequalities on both sides of the fence. But it would be folly to play ducks and drakes with an industry at once so sensitive and so long-term that a major blunder today could easily mean disaster to the nation's food for a long time to come. There is no industry which can be turned on and off at the flick of a switch.

W. H. WOODHEAD

THE VILLAGES BRING OUT THEIR FLAGS

June 3 1953

How was her Majesty greeted out of town? How did the villages celebrate; the northern villages with appropriate names like Derbyshire's Flagg or Hope, or Lancashire's Providence; or odd ones like Cheshire's Gibraltar, Shocklach Oviatt, Coole Pilate,

Tang, and Tushington–cum–Grindley? What strange festivities went on at the deserted village of Havanna?

It would be too easy to write off the rural pattern in a formal sentence: the tea, the sports, the bonfire, the old folks' treat, the distribution of Coronation mugs. The villages are conservative, true. They can also be fiercely individualistic ('Not mugs', they insisted at Hathersage: 'spoons'). A Coronation tour of Lancashire, Derbyshire, and Cheshire showed what enormous variety there can be in a dominant pattern – how many different ways there are, in short, of waving a flag.

Cheshire, of course, started out with many natural and acquired advantages. To decorate this county in early June is to pile richness on richness. The warm brick, the thatch, the glowing tiles and gleaming black and white half-timbering – of all periods or, as it is seasonable, to put it, of both Elizabeths – know how to rise to an occasion. But Cheshire is on the seemly side, and it was not here that we were likely to find the Gentlemen's Knobbly Knees Competition: that happened somewhere in wildest Worcestershire. Yet Cheshire has its Doomed Village and also – if the maps are to be believed – its Deserted Village. Finding how the Deserted Village celebrated the Coronation might have seemed a perverse sidetrack, yet it proved irresistible. The Ordnance Survey was specific: 'Havanna' (Deserted Village) it said, indicating a place a mile or two north of Congleton. No signpost that we could discover pointed to the Deserted Village, and this was no doubt as it should be. But there was a winding lane, Devon-like between tall and lavish flower-banks and narrow enough to discourage all but journalistic traffic, and soon we were in Havanna – the village that once had a cigar factory.

The Deserted Village looked in the happiest of moods. Its ghosts had not forgotten their loyal duty. The old brick frontages of the cottages were smiling with flags and bunting, and one crumbling chimney supported a television aerial. Few towns could match it for the grace and dignity of its Coronation programme. And the contents of the programme are rich and varied. After a service in the parish church the village held a grand parade, a 'Village Queen' was crowned, children sang, and the Women's Institute choir gave a concert. The maypole was 'plaited', there were sports for children and grown-ups, a tea for old folks, and at night a 'Grand Hall' in the hall of the Women's Institute.

NORMAN SHRAPNEL

BREAK-UP OF LARGE ESTATES: NFU BRANCH WANTS NATIONAL INQUIRY
September 13 1954

Stirred by the impending sale by the Duke of Devonshire of 50 farms and 4,500 acres of land in the Peak District to meet death duties, the Derbyshire branch of the National Farmers' Union (NFU) has called for a national inquiry into the breaking up of large country estates. The branch says that the disappearance of the large landowner will bring a grave risk of bankruptcy to the farming community, and asks for a national investigation into how the sales will affect tenant farmers.

Today the Duke's agents will begin making arrangements for the sales. Yesterday Mr Ivor Morten, chairman of the Derbyshire Hill Farming Committee and a member of the county executive, said: 'We think that it is a good thing for farmers to own their own land, provided they have the necessary capital. But when large estates come on the market this is what happens: the farmer either gathers together all his savings and liquid capital to buy his farm or he raises a mortgage and finds that he has to pay in interest much more than he ever paid in rent. He has no money to expand production and he may not even have enough to maintain it at its present level.

'If any depression occurs in the future these farmers will face bankruptcy on a larger scale than ever before. It is about time that all political parties realised that crippling death duties mean that large sums of capital are being withdrawn from agriculture and can never be replaced. Sales of large estates are forced on the landowners, farming loses what little security it has – and the huge sums demanded in death duties last Whitehall about 10 minutes. The landowner, the farmer and the country all lose in the end and there is no gain to anyone.'

Farmers, said Mr Morten, did not want the government to assume the role of landlord. 'Where it has been tried it has failed miserably.'

Mr P. J. B. Clive, agent for the Duke of Devonshire's Chatsworth Estate, who has arranged for representatives to call on tenant farmers at Peak Forest to give them first chance of buying their farms, said the sale had been 'forced on us by the demand for nearly £2,500,000 in death duties'.

'The Duke is anxious that the land should go to the men who understand it and will farm it properly, and therefore the tenants will have the first chance. It is the end of a happy relationship between owner and occupier and it is a tragedy which may not be appreciated until it is too late. No one is likely to buy the estate intact except "spiv" landowners – and to them the land is not for sale if we can prevent it.'

Farms at Peak Forest occupied by farmers who decide not to buy will be offered for sale next month by public auction.

A COUNTRY DIARY: PENRITH

December 31 1955

A few years ago, at the annual meeting of the Westmorland Federation of Women's Institutes, the president, a dear old lady who had reached her 90s, devoted her presidential address to the theme of looking on the bright side; and she told the story of a South Westmorland woman who complained: 'Aye, me life's bin full o' troubles, but maist o' them nivver happened.' The remark recurred to me (for I was present at the meeting in a professional capacity) when I was wondering how to end the 'Country Diary' year. I recalled how pessimistic we became in the summer when we noted week after week without rain. Everything in the garden was going to be a failure. Apples, for example, remained the size of wild crabs, and other produce was making little progress: there was similar pessimism among farmers. Corn was failing to ripen before the ears filled, and turnips and potatoes were expected to be a complete failure. But, as with the old lady's troubles, most of these forebodings failed to materialise. In the gardens the only failures were raspberries and potatoes; and on the farms all crops except potatoes were up to or above the average. As for the bumper corn crops there is still a difference of opinion whether it was due to the weather or the absence of rabbits. On the whole, therefore, 1955 has been a good year on the land.

J. H. H

PONY-TREKKING

September 19 1956

This summer we went pony-trekking through the Scottish Youth Hostels Association for £5 15s a week. Under £5 was charged for the hire of a garron (the rough, infallibly surefooted Highland pony whose ancestry goes back to the Ice Age), for the leadership of a superb horsewoman and teacher, the use of gear and the right to track over splendidly beautiful private moors near Ballater. Cooking our own food and sleeping in small dormitories, we managed the week comfortably on £7 10s each – half the price of trekking from an hotel.

Eight complete novices are enough for a leader in mountains with Indian-file tracks, bogs, places which look hair-raising from horseback, moorland mists and powerful rivers which must be plunged through. I rode Bracken, a three-year-old prize-winning grey. She was a trifle more sportive than some, being so young. Garrons work until they are 25 or so. I fell off, had my foot walked on four times and was bitten. After that I obeyed instructions to keep my feet clear of Bracken's when leading her, to offer sugar lumps from the flat palm of my hand and not between fingertips, and to stand up in the stirrups and grip with my knees when she trotted. Flo added that to sing 'John Peel' helped one to get the rhythm of when to rise and sit down in one's saddle. Only my husband had a gallop. He said it was a wonderful sensation, easier than trotting.

They say that if the ecstasy of falling in love did not fade one would die prematurely, burned up by its prolonged intensity. If the summer beauty of a Deeside moorland or glen lasted all the year it might be unbearable too. Purple beds of heath and heather rivalled earth-hugging wild thyme, which spread its neat arms like a jewelled starfish; acrid, spiky, intensely new pines in sharp blue-green brushed our horses' flanks; we smelt bog myrtle and juniper, and pointed out to each other bilberry and crowberry, cranberry and cloudberry in a leisurely botanising-on-horseback. There were long trails of antlered moss, sundew and insect-eating butterwort, rock rose and meadowsweet – the all-pervading scents made one almost delirious. Back in a small town with no characteristic smell, either pleasant or foul, I feel an emptiness and sadness at the thought of what Britain must have smelt like before industrial development and the disappearance of many wild flowers from our hedgerows.

Among animals in the glens there were wild cats, and an adder so shining, unhurried and noble that D. H. Lawrence's 'A snake came to my water-trough' came to mind. Two stags had ridiculous rabbity tails at variance with the dignity of antlers, and we saw capercaillie 2,300 feet up on a cold, mist-wreathed moor across which we found our almost trackless way by occasional white posts. We spent only two hours at base, learning horsemanship. The rest was learned on trek as the need arose. Saddling produced its jokes, such as the three-inch gap in a morning between strap and buckle which made me feel that Bracken had achieved about five months' pregnancy overnight. Girths must be hauled very tight, so that saddles did not slip in a crisis. You didn't force the bit into the horse's mouth – you persuaded her to take it in herself. The horses might kick each other, especially the mares, who seemed at times as catty with each other as women, but they did not kick you, unless you intercepted a kick meant for another horse. You took a slice of bread, that is, something large enough for the horse to see across a big field when she lifted her head at your call and came of her own accord for her bridle. You had a pocket full of lump sugar, to be doled out like a sweet at stops and after the day's trek. You could lift your horse's hooves at night to look for stones, and brush them all over, including their tails, with impunity. They loved being taken on trek, and each other's company, and Ben was as frantic as a Delacroix one day when we had to leave him behind.

From time to time we rested them and let them eat grass, ferns, bracken, wild thyme, reeds, birch and ash branches – a more aromatic and succulent diet than our own sandwiches. Had we ridden on after a hot climb they might have rolled us in the grass or doused us in the Dee when fording it. They had favourite companions and things were peaceful when every horse was behind a friend – mares seemed to like following the opposite sex, even though it was gelded.

Riding, unlike walking or motoring, is a cooperation, with you in control at one point, the horse at another, for in stony places, bogs, steep descents and in crossing rocky burns she has the surer instinct. But, unlike a driver trailing a caravan behind him or a mother carrying a baby, she thinks only of her own height and width. If her head can pass beneath the branches she doesn't care that you have to be on her neck to avoid being scraped off her back with a ruined hairdo. If fencing posts do not tear her sides she is unaware that your feet in the stirrups may be twisted by them, and she will force herself between two fat horses, squashing your feet against them. All this is more laughable than painful.

Lunchtime can be a battlefield if there is no fence to tie your horse to while you eat. Let her loose and she may lead you a 20-mile chase. Hold her and she may steal your sandwich, crush your vacuum flask in her teeth or eat your orange through a string bag. But she will eat your banana peel and solve the litter problem. Tie her to a young tree and go off to watch adders, and she may uproot it or get herself and tether into a complicated knitting pattern in the tree.

The final ecstasy was the journey up one side of the Dee among wild lupins and down the other, through an aromatic pine forest, crossing the river by wading up to our horses' bellies. I loved the sensation of being on a horse amid the waters of this great river and by now had lost all apprehension of that first deep, downward step from the bank. I would have liked to follow my week of learning with another of confident riding, but the ponies were needed for the grouse shooting, and later to carry 20-stone stags down from the moors, to be loaned, perhaps, to royalty at Balmoral or used for the harvest.

MARY MCLEAN

EBBW VALE GUARDS AN EQUINE ARISTOCRACY: KEEPING THE WELSH PONY
UNTAINTED
June 11 1957

Passionately to guard purity of the blood: to distinguish and segregate the royal strain of the elect from the pretenders and the contaminated of the common world: perhaps this is a craze which only very Protestant peoples like the Welsh can know.

Certainly, while upon the mountain above Ebbw Vale a band of steelworkers and colliers are gathering their pure Welsh pony mares into the fold and protecting them from the taint of the mongrel 'scrub' stallions which swarm on the commons, it seems natural that down among the houses there should be a vast white marquee erected by travelling evangelists, from which rise hymns and exhortations to the chosen to separate themselves from the contagion of the reprobate.

There are about 40 members of the Ebbw Vale Pony Improvement Society, two-thirds of them workers in the great steelworks and the rest colliers, tradesmen, two business men, and children. Almost never together, because so many of them are on shift work, the members climb the hillside to their ponies in all weathers. 'We never think anything of it – rain, hail or shine, we're up there all the time.' Between them they own 60 mares and five stallions registered with the Welsh Pony and Cob Society, and their ambition is to improve the stock upon the mountains around the vale until every beast is pure.

Warring against them are the 'scrub' horses which, owing to cloudiness over the manorial rights on the common hill, they cannot exclude. The Welsh Pony and Cob Society demands that all 'scrub' animals be cleared off the hill before pure ponies which run there may properly claim registration for their offspring. It is an anxious day when a mare foals: even if the foal turns out well, the next generation may uncover unsuspected sin in the grandparents in the shape of 'ears like a mule, legs like a donkey', as the secretary puts it.

No Female Members

The secretary is Mr Trevor Morgan, fitter on the steelworks tinning line. Mr Les Evans, the chairman, works in the open hearth department. The 10 or 15 members of the club who are off-shift together or who can spare the time meet in the Drysiog Inn, a quiet and friendly public house in a back street halfway up the slope of Ebbw Vale town. They refer to it as 'The Stallion's Arms': 'We don't mind where we are – it's all horses!'

An odd fact, partly but not completely explained by the fact that they meet in a public house, is that the club has no female members at all, in contrast to the 'jersey-jumping' membership of girls in an English pony club. Perhaps the effective difference is the passionate emphasis put upon blood and descent, upon discussion or silent contemplation of a beautiful animal, rather than upon the antics of a gymkhana. However, the club does a good deal of riding across the mountains to the next industrial valley or across the high plateau at the end of the vale, which stretches away towards Brecon, and in August the town council is financing a show which the club will organise.

The original colour of the Welsh mountain ponies around Ebbw Vale is said to be whiteish. Now they may be any colour except piebald or skewbald, which attach to impure blood. The ideal pony must have a 'small, neat head, eyes which are prominent and thoughtful' and a host of other physical characteristics, similarly described in the language of love. Their nature is intelligent, fiery and temperamental: they seem to pass rapidly from sulks or malice into wild rejoicings, galloping round the hillside and chasing one of the bleating solitary lambs which infest not only the slopes but the streets of Ebbw Vale itself. They were once used as pit ponies, and are still a favourite for children and for milkfloats. The Welsh Cob, a little larger, did service for the horse-drawn Army.

The Ebbw Vale Society has won plenty of prizes since its foundation in 1953. The stallion Revel Ballet Dancer, a grey pony who at 14 years old has won 10 premiums, belongs to the treasurer, Mr Ron Hawkins. Many, though none directly from Ebbw Vale, are sold abroad, mostly to the United States, which has bought 200 over the last two years for nearly £40,000, and to several European countries. The society disapproves of the wandering ponies which are allowed to gobble vegetable gardens, block main roads and clatter about the streets of Ebbw Vale to the peril of shoppers and themselves: no society pony, they claim, would be found straying and they hope to encourage the owners of the wanderers to look after them by teaching them the market value of a well-cared-for, well-descended pony. With all this care, the ponies remain tough, and even in winter a mare with a foal will often scrape away snow to eat the mountain grass rather than take bundles of hay laid out for her.

Livelihood Not Life

On a fine afternoon in Ebbw Vale men who are off-shift like to climb the slopes a little, up through the old works-housing rows where children have white faces and through the new council estates near the top of the hill where they have pink faces, to sit on the brow of the mountain in the sun looking down at their places of work far below and seeming to dismiss those distant stacks and roofs to the position of a livelihood, not of a life. Like an arm of the sea filled with ships, the narrow floor of the valley is choked with the long roofs and cranes, chimneys, furnaces and towers of the second steelworks in Europe, packed around several collieries, while the colour-washed rows of old houses lie above each other all round the walls of the valley, like tidemarks. Up here on top, the air is blue and clean, and the noises of steelmaking are only a rumour.

Mr Hawkins was shouting to his son who ran about the mountainside after his father's ponies and tried to marshal them for the photographer. Mr Hawkins is a miner: at the moment he is recovering from an accident in which his leg was dragged into the machinery of a coal conveyer and badly twisted: he walks about the hill with the aid of a walking stick whose handle is carved into a dragon's head with yellow eyes. 'I say they're mine,' he said, pointing to the ponies as they galloped past a heap of wrestling schoolchildren on the hillside, his 'own boy toiling after'. But then the boys would say: 'And what about us? Don't we come into it?'

A flock of racing pigeons burst out of a roof somewhere below and soared over the black wheels and chimneys. Pigeons, children and horses are emblems of liberty, love and courage; things which the people of Ebbw Vale find by leaving their streets and climbing upon the green mountain.

A COUNTRY DIARY: CHESHIRE

July 29 1958

Although modern transport has made our villages much less self-contained than they were half a century ago, these communities still maintain their identity and pride in being different from their neighbours. This feeling of unity in a village is well shown at local fetes, three of which took place recently within two miles of one another. At Antrobus, races for young and old were the main attraction. One youngster showed astonishing dash in the sack race and some schoolgirls a remarkable turn of speed.

At Great Budworth for the fourth year running the purpose was to raise money for the rehabilitation of our beautiful old church, which still needs a good sum before it is completed. I do not care to call this the restoration, for that calls to mind the enormities of the 19th century, but nobody can complain of the way in which the present restoration is being carried out. A sum of almost £300 was raised this year at stalls and sideshows, but much more is required, if anyone is feeling generous.

The fete at Comberbach was a more elaborate affair. The village was decorated. There was a queen, a baby show, a fancy-dress competition, sideshows of great variety and even a skiffle group, whose singer had a voice of extraordinary penetration. The famous morris dancers from Manley gave exhibitions of their art: they had come from another village, it is true, but the precision of their delightful capers was to me the feature of the afternoon.

A. W. B.

COLD COMFORT FOR THE TARN-BAGGERS
November 14 1959

The end of a long, cold story for two Grasmere men came the other day when, shivering in a shower of hail, they scrambled out of a tarn high on a shoulder of Esk Pike and shook hands. There are, they estimate, 463 tarns in the Lake District – some large enough to sail a yacht on, others little more than rock pools – and they had just bathed in the last one.

The younger of the two is Mr Collin Dodgson, who keeps the tea gardens at Grasmere and serves mint cake to the tourists; the elder is Mr Timothy Tyson, the village shoemaker. Mr Dodgson is 49. Mr Tyson will be 76 in February.

'Doing the tarns' – a feat never tackled before and perhaps not to be repeated for many years – is only one of their remarkable achievements. A few years ago Mr Dodgson became one of the first men to reach the summit of each of the 543 peaks and tops in Scotland more than 3,000 feet in height. He has also climbed each of the 2,000-footers in England, all the Welsh '2,500s' and every mountain in Ireland more than 3,000 feet high – and on the great majority of these expeditions Mr Tyson, who did not start peak-bagging until he was approaching 50, has been with him.

Mr Tyson is unknown in the mountaineering world, but he completed the ascent of all the 276 'Munros' in Scotland – the lifetime ambition of hundreds of younger men – several years ago (nearly always in winter) and kept his mouth shut about it. He was almost as reticent about the story of the tarns.

'It certainly wasn't done as a stunt,' Mr Tyson told me in his tiny cabin, surrounded by photographs of snow-covered Scottish peaks, as he sat hand-sewing an old pair of climbing boots. 'It was simply because we like wandering about on the fells. We tried to keep the whole thing as quiet as we could and we feel we have discovered the Lake District afresh, for you often find tarns in the most unlikely places.'

Wintertime

They had to do most of their bathing in winter, because Mr Dodgson is too busy catering for the tourists in summer; and it had to be done on Sundays, for Mr Dodgson has to work on other days. They were always back in Grasmere by midday, having normally set out at six or seven o'clock. Nobody ever saw them bathing and they never used bathing costumes, as there seemed no need. One morning they 'did' 14 or 15 tarns.

The decision to bathe in all the tarns was taken on July 30 1951. But long before that, during petrol rationing, they had gone to Tarn Hows every Sunday morning to bathe, and later they extended these trips to other tarns. First they did the bigger and best-known tarns and later, by studying the six-inch maps and surveying the land from the mountain tops, they found more and more tarns and began to arrange them in groups. Some of the tarns are not marked, even on six-inch maps, but provided they were permanent, not too small and deep enough to get into they were counted, and doubtful small pools have been excluded from the final list.

Often they have had to break the ice to get in – once on a group of tarns on Glaramara, which they think has more tarns than any other Lake District mountain. Once they could not find their chosen tarn – a little pool in the Martindale Deer Forest – until they had scraped away the snow and found the ice. But these were not the coldest bathes, but rather their dips in Hard Tarn on Helvellyn and in a tarn on Red Crag on High Street. The coldest summer bathe – they managed an occasional evening bathe out of the main holiday season – was on Scales Tarn on Blencathra. The highest Lakeland tarns, they agree, are that on Broad Crag, which lies exactly at 2,750 feet, and Foxes Tarn on the Cam Spout side of Scafell at about the same height. The deepest tarn is probably Blea Water in Mardale, while Devoke Water is the largest and Foxes Tarn, a tiny gem in a cluster of rocks, probably the smallest.

Favourites

They have been screamed at by geese, quacked at by ducks, barked at by dogs and trumpeted at by wild swans when they invaded their territory. On one occasion a farmer moved a bull so that they could bathe undisturbed, and once they had to cut short a late-night dip just before Christmas when ducks rose noisily and windows opened at a nearby farm. They expected any minute to be taken for poultry thieves and shot out of hand.

Inevitably they have their favourites. Mr Dodgson's are Blind Tarn, near Coniston and Small Water, and Mr Tyson speaks particularly of Hard Tarn, Lambfoot Dub, Broad Crag Tarn, Innominate Tarn on Haystacks, and Low Water.

The old man also speaks of little tarns whose names he has forgotten. 'I remember passing one this summer,' he told me, 'just a pool on the fell. But with the light on the water, the grey rocks, a little island with heather moss and a patch of yellow asphodel in flower, it was a lovely sight I can never forget.'

My Tyson finished sewing his climbing boot and took off his leather apron. 'It is always a bit sad,' he said, 'when the tasks are finished – the mountains and now all the tarns. But I believe it is a good thing in life to have something to strive for, even if it's bathing in tarns.'

A. H. GRIFFIN

A COUNTRY DIARY: MACHYNLLETH

November 28 1959

It is just two years since I recorded in this diary that grey squirrels had really begun to entrench themselves in this westernmost strip of mid-Wales. Now, besides becoming ever more plentiful, they are getting less timid, a sure sign that they are settling down and beginning to feel confident in their hold on the place. I have read that there are parts of the world where even herring gulls are retiring, wary and rather silent, because they are there on the fringe of their range and therefore scarce; a dominated instead of a domineering species.

And so until recently were our grey squirrels. We knew they were here, but they kept extremely aloof. But now quite suddenly they are beginning to show very faintly the other side of their nature: that boldness and familiarity which if encouraged would make them more like the favourite pets they used to be in the London parks.

So, early one morning recently a grey squirrel scuttled along our bedroom windowsill; a few days later one raced across the garden; another coolly showered me with half-chewed pine cones as I stood and looked up at him. And I doubt if it is the slightest use killing them. Tens of thousands have been killed, but that has not stopped their advance, probably not even slowed it. Think of the millions of rabbits that used to be trapped. Did that affect their numbers at all?

W. M. C.

A COUNTRY DIARY: LOWER NIDDERDALE

December 24 1959

The farmer next to us has just bought a load of black Irish bullocks for fattening and turned them into the Home Field next to us. They arrived in a large cattle wagon and seemed bewildered, but relieved to be out of it. The farmer, his dog and the driver had no difficulty in herding them into the field; the bullocks were no doubt thankful to be on a firm footing in a green field once again.

Before the days of the cattle wagon they would have had a leisurely journey by quiet, devious routes, from Scotland more probably than Ireland. The wide, green tracks – the old drove-roads – are still to be found, especially high up in the moors, still green after the manuring of centuries, and kept so now by the moorland sheep who graze these appetising parts closely.

Now even the short trip from auction mart to the slaughter house is done by wagon. It certainly relieves the congestion in the streets of our market town. But we have lost the excitement of chasing a sheep that had made a dash for it into the nearest house – ours once, round and round the kitchen table. Then there was the expression of utter disbelief on my mother's face the time she came up the cellar steps to find herself confronted by an enormous woolly sheep, blocking the cellar door and all ready to make the descent.

M. A. M.

☙ CHAPTER FOUR ❧

Making hay
1960–1979

After seven years of war and a further nine of rationing – bananas were not available until 1955 – Britain was ready to escape from centralised government and an unusually long period of good behaviour and respect for those in charge. The flowering of satire and protest in the 1960s was a relief, an overdue letting-off of steam. It was also an awakening of sensible, serious public opinion to some of the havoc which had been done in its name.

Typical of the period were articles in the normally staid establishment newspaper *The Times* by one of the first of a new generation of what today we might call 'eco-journalists', although the phrase then was 'environmental campaigner'. Tony Aldous eventually collected his opinions in a book called bluntly *Goodbye Britain?* (1975), whose chapters included one headed 'The Destruction of the Countryside'.

His readers had been prepared for polemics by books such as Rachel Carson's *Silent Spring*, a devastating indictment of pesticides published in 1962. It appeared soon after the English countryside had been fouled by the appearance of thousands of dead or dying rabbits, victims of deliberately induced myxomatosis. Hedgerows were being grubbed up by 'factory farms' and the march of the pylon (which matched the TV aerial as a cartoonists' icon in the late 1950s) had been followed by the spread of ugly silage silos, unimpeded by any need for planning permission.

In these circumstances, a newspaper such as the *Guardian* with a radical, campaigning tradition, could not allow itself to be beaten to the tape by *The Times*. Aldous's persistent but sometimes generalised pieces were soon matched by specific attempts to change trends in the countryside or government policy towards it. The *Guardian* analysed a particular example of woeful behaviour and then went for it. One of the first successful and very colourful battles was over the nectar of the British countryman and woman: beer.

It was led by Richard Boston, a large, boisterous freelance contributor to the

Guardian, who had suffered what he called 'a severe cash-flow crisis' in the late 1960s and resolved it by hackwork for an American firm which was publishing a guide to pubs. Boston's discovery of the dismal spread of bland keg beer in country pubs, which had once served a marvellous kaleidoscope of local draught bitters, coincided with a reader's letter to the *Guardian*. This noted the fact that every paper had a wine correspondent, but none did a similar job for beer. 'May I write you one?' Boston asked the features editor Harold Jackson and his deputy Mike McNay. The reply, recalled by McNay in his obituary when Boston died in 2006 aged 67, was 'Good idea. Your round.'

It was a good idea, for Boston's lively and knowledgeable columns caught a mood and then ran with it brilliantly. The Campaign for Real Ale was one rapid result, and the return of local draughts in all the glory which we enjoy today, a longer-term one. Ever a man for interesting experiences – he served as a film stand-in for the French comedian Jacques Tati and was notable as someone who could wake himself up by laughing in his sleep – Boston moved on to further work on behalf of the countryside. His book *Beer and Skittles* (1976) helped to revitalise village pubs, with guidance on everything including the best pets for landlords (cats, budgies and chickens – yes; mynah birds and hedgehogs, as tried at the Mendip Inn, Gurney Slade, Somerset – no).

Boston's genius lay in correctly identifying a rural wrong and setting about righting it relentlessly. But he was not a new phenomenon. He could mull back through the pages of the *Guardian* to find others who had trod similar paths years earlier. One of the three great threats to the countryside identified by Aldous was unimaginative forestry (along with misguided farming and under-regulated quarries). And it was dim-witted forestry which had incensed the newspaper's readers in 1911.

The match was lit by Canon H. D. Rawnsley (the co-founder 16 years earlier of the National Trust), who had been outraged by the Manchester Corporation's treatment of the beautiful Lake District valley newly flooded to make Thirlmere reservoir. Manchester had to drink and wash, and the battle over the flooding had been reluctantly conceded. But now the city seemed intent on turning the wild valley of the Lake poets into one of its shrubbery-dominated parks. The *Guardian* had just reported the Lord Mayor of Manchester claiming complacently: 'Ruskin in the past had talked about the spoiling of scenery; but if Ruskin could come to life again, he would admit that the City Council had improved the scenery instead of damaging it.' Oh yes? replied Canon Rawnsley in a letter to the paper of some 2,000 words. Improved the Lakes by replacing oaks and bracken with laurels and 'monotonous

A Cumbrian sheep farmer herds his flock. DENNIS THORPE

Ramblers walk a footpath at Lyme Handley, Cheshire in 1962. TOM STUTTARD

Men and machinery at work in the fields, 1952.

A snow-covered hedgerow in Diseworth, Leicestershire. DAVID SILLITOE

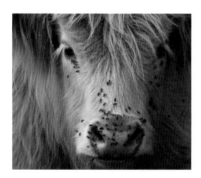

Highland cattle are brought to graze on Sudbury Common Lands every summer. The ancient riverside pastures have been maintained through traditional grazing for over 800 years. GRAHAM TURNER

A chicken perches on a wire fence by allotments in Oswaldtwistle, East Lancashire. DON MCPHEE

A cow in the river Waveney, Suffolk on a misty morning. GRAHAM TURNER

A fisherman catches a 19lb pike in Cambridgeshire. GRAHAM TURNER

Three sows piggyback in Yorkshire.
DON MCPHEE

In the heat of a summer's day, cattle keep cool in The Mill Pool, the Stour, Sudbury, Suffolk. GRAHAM TURNER

Crab fishing in Cromer, Norfolk.
GRAHAM TURNER

Walking in the Lake District National Park.
DON MCPHEE

belts of conifers', and importing Isle of Arran red stone and blue Welsh slates into a landscape with its own very different and beautiful geology?

Rawnsley's condemnation, taken up by the *Manchester Guardian* (and no doubt privately urged by its senior journalists on city councillors – they all knew one another), prevented further excesses on quite such a scale. When Haweswater reservoir was created in the 1920s greater sensitivity went into the landscaping, even though the project remained controversial. These were very big targets for a newspaper to take on and not ones in which complete victory was ever likely. But patient, well-argued articles changed minds and policies on the countryside, as Boston was later to do.

Another example, less vivid than the beer and pubs but just as significant, was the *Guardian*'s help in protecting the Soil Survey of England and Wales from abolition in Margaret Thatcher's civil service cuts. The specialised department of the Ministry of Agriculture seemed an easy target to those charged with making savings. The public would hardy rise up on its behalf. But the government reckoned without an alliance of *Guardian* journalists – from the economics expert Harford Thomas to the Country Diary writer Bill Condry – who understood how important it was that an index of soil type, fertility and changes should be available to farmers, foresters and those such as National Park authorities who needed data to fend off the threat of housing and forestry. Another diarist, Virginia Spiers, actually worked for the survey, sorting farming land into five grades in a way which still has her crumbling different soils in her palm and telling the value by look and feel. The clash was given some spice by assertions that the survey was covertly in the sights of 'prairie farming' interests who resented its findings about the soil erosion caused by hedge removal. At all events, the regular articles had their effect and were invaluable to the director of the survey Professor Peter Bullock, who fought his own tenacious corner at the famous Rothamsted Experimental Station which was his HQ.

Funding was reduced but the survey survived and was eventually taken under the wing of Cranfield University where it continues as the National Soil Research Institute. Bullock continued too, adding the online resource Soil-Net.com and the World Soil Survey Archive and Collection to his many achievements before his death in April 2008. He also lived to receive perhaps the ultimate accolade in his profession: a share in the 2007 Nobel Peace Prize as a member of the intergovernmental panel on climate change.

RECLAMATION OF SPOIL-HEAPS

April 28 1960

For years Lancashire and the north have been blemished by spoil-heaps, which spread across the countryside like a rash of gigantic molehills. Once, the spoil-heaps were regarded as permanent features of the landscape, dreary and immovable. Now, however, there is hope that Lancashire's progressive planning department has found a solution to the problem of improving the landscape.

The experiment began about eight years ago on a 10-acre heap at Bickerstaffe, near Ormskirk, where 20,000 young trees were planted in nothing but the shale. Some are now about 10ft high and the losses have not been much higher than the average rate of loss on more fertile ground. Fifteen acres of ugly red shale next to a housing estate at Skelmersdale have likewise been transformed, and children are now playing football and cricket on a mound that was once little more than an eyesore obstructing a fine view.

It is part of the planning committee's policy to encourage other local authorities and individuals to follow its example. One such adherent is Mr Michael Graham, the former Director of Fishery Research at the Ministry of Agriculture, Fisheries and Food. Mr Graham had heard of the efforts being made to reclaim the county's spoil-heaps and was determined to spend his retirement doing what he could to help. His offer was readily accepted and since August 1958 he has been hard at work growing blades of grass where virtually none grew before. Although he keeps very closely in touch with the planning department and is working with the support of the Community Council of Lancashire (with a grant of £100 a year for two years from the Development Commission), he is left largely to his own devices. Clearly, he would not have it otherwise and is happiest when he is working with only his Arab bay mare and a few children for company.

'Stop the Wash'

He now lives at Eccles, within daily riding distance of any spoil-heaps to the east of Tyldesley, but he often travels farther afield to places such as St Helens and Billinge, four miles to the north, and, instead of returning home each day, camps out in his green and yellow caravan – a real gipsy affair with his full name and decorations (C.M.G., O.B.E. (Mil.), M.A.) emblazoned on its side. In his breeches and black bowler hat he would not look out of place in the jumping ring at an agricultural show, and with his extensive knowledge of the soil he is in a position to approach his task of rejuvenating spoil-heaps from a highly scientific angle. Having decided that his expenses must be kept to a minimum, he began to experiment in the belief that the bareness of spoil-heaps is due to erosion. Acting, therefore, on his slogan of 'Stop the Wash', he adopted the classic anti-erosion technique of contour-ridging – simply by riding up and down the gentler slopes on his beloved bay mare.

And it is the mare that has attracted Mr Graham's other source of labour. When a slope is too steep for her the children who flock round her are easily induced to take over and dig contour ridges, using entrenching tools where the mare's hooves have failed to gain a hold. Mr Graham then sows the shale with grass seed or wild white clover, following this up with a layer of barn sweepings or anything fibrous which may seed itself, and finally a dressing of lime. In all, the department has planted three quarters of a million trees and reclaimed nearly 150 acres of land.

GENTLE PERSUADERS

August 31 1960

A face peered through the window. The small black eyes above the flattened nose followed us about the room. Another face soon joined it, then another, until the window seemed to be dotted with eyes peering inwards.

Only our guide was unconcerned. 'You get used to them,' said Miss Eileen Keating with the aplomb of someone accustomed to living in the public eye. If your home is National Trust property open to the public, you probably have to get used to strange faces.

The garden that day was crowded with holiday visitors come to inspect Plas-yn-Rhiw, as the old manor house near Pwllheli is called. It was not visiting time, but they had all been allowed in to walk around the grounds overlooking the bay. Once in they seemed to spend their time at the windows and returned our looks with cold stares as if it were we who were the intruders.

A Waugh-like mood might have descended on us had we been the Misses Keating, but the three sisters – Miss Eileen, Miss Honora and Miss Lorna – welcome visitors with the enthusiasm of an artist showing his pictures. They derive obvious satisfaction – and perhaps encouragement in their efforts to keep the area as it is – from strangers' appreciation of Plas-yn-Rhiw, for they have transformed what was a wilderness into a Welsh estate worthy of the National Trust.

When they bought it in 1938 both house and garden looked their age. The sisters had to enter by a side door until the overgrown garden was cut down to size. The inside of the house was in comparable condition. Planks were needed to cover some of the holes until the dry-rotted floors could be replaced. As the signs of neglect were gradually cleared away, the true character of the old manor house emerged again. The Second World War delayed some of the repair work, but house, garden and views of Hell's Mouth and beyond were soon back on the local beauty list. 'A vivid experience,' Sir Compton Mackenzie was able to call Plas-yn-Rhiw after a visit in 1950.

But the Misses Keating's work was not finished – at least by their standards – when their home was ready to be given to the National Trust in memory of their parents. Having restored Plas-yn-Rhiw, they also set about helping to preserve the area of Wales of which it is a part. Let even a prominent acre go to industry and all eventually might be lost, as in so many other formerly green areas of Britain. That roughly is their argument. Thus they have protested or supported petitions against a nuclear power station, a radar base and a telecommunications aerial mast to mention but three local proposals they have found threatening in the last few years.

'We're not rebels. Don't think that,' said Miss Eileen, who is 74, while pouring out another cup of tea. Nobody could have thought her in the least rebellious – or the other sisters, Miss Honora, who is 68, and Miss Lorna, who is 70. The afternoon tea scene – we were in an upstairs room safe from peering visitors – looked serene enough for Jane Austen.

'We're very law-abiding,' said Miss Lorna.

'People talk about what we are fighting for,' said Miss Honora. 'We don't fight. We are merely trying to preserve beauty after seeing it lost in so many other areas.'

'We have always had very considerate letters from all the Ministries,' added Miss Eileen. 'We have corresponded with them all and put our point of view. We're not rebels at all. We just feel very strongly that there's now very little of Britain that's unspoilt.'

Some of their opponents – who tend to simplify the controversy into scenery or jobs – call them foreigners, depicting them as inconsiderate outsiders from England not concerned in the local struggle for existence. Miss Honora, who is the author of a book about Plas-yn-Rhiw, has a firm answer to that: 'We have been ratepayers in Rhiw for 41 years since 1919, and my mother and sister permanent residents since 1934.' Mrs Keating lived at the house, now a memorial to her, until she died.

'People must have jobs. We realise that as well as anyone else,' said Miss Eileen, 'but it does not profit industry to come where the scenery is most beautiful.'

'There are usually other sites equally suitable where much less harm would be done to the beauty of the area,' said Miss Lorna.

'But you have to keep watch. It is possible that a proposal might be made by someone for whom the area is just somewhere on a map,' said Miss Honora.

'It was proposed to build a nuclear power station where the National Parks Commission had declared an area of outstanding natural beauty,' said Miss Eileen.

'We're very glad to say that has been postponed indefinitely,' said Miss Honora.

'We're not fighting alone –' began Miss Eileen.

'Preserving, not fighting,' corrected Miss Honora.

'There is really so much support,' said Miss Eileen. 'We are on the side of various organisations like the Council for the Preservation of Rural Wales. For one petition there were well over 2,000 signatures.'

A visitor from industrial regions knowing well the opposite extreme to the Lleyn Peninsula, may have his moment of fantasy amongst the roses – which flower from April to near Christmas – and wonder that everyone does not support every campaign to keep the area just as it is. The visitors' book shows how many people take advantage of the Misses Keating's gift to the National Trust and they are all welcomed. They even get help in parking their cars.

'We're really quite old,' said Miss Eileen that day, while helping her sisters to direct some of the visitors' traffic with the efficiency of policemen half their age. With them were their dogs, including the stray they have adopted who responds only to calls in Welsh.

They looked as independent then as the woman in Elia Kazan's film *Wild River*, who refused to make way for the Tennessee Valley Authority and obstinately waited to be evicted. The difference is this. If a TVA threatened Plas-yn-Rhiw and the Misses Keating disapproved of it, there would not be any passive resistance. They would go straight to the ministry involved. There would probably be a petition. And in any such battle between Whitehall and the Misses Keating it would be a rash man who bet on the government department. In a little matter about which they are concerned at present, if justice isn't done, they may write directly to Mr Butler, the home secretary.

W. J. WEATHERBY

A COUNTRY DIARY: WESTMORLAND

September 5 1960

The agricultural show just up the valley takes place on a steeply tilted field at the foot of the fells, for there's no level ground in the neighbourhood. When you drive in you take your car to the top of the slope, for you know that if it rains – as it generally does – you'll never get out on the level, except at the end of a tractor rope. But by sliding downhill through the mire you might just manage it. This is essentially a farmers' show – no stands or fancy marquees or side shows or youngsters jumping ponies. Just the cows and the sheep and, almost apologetically, the sheepdogs. Oh, and a bit of wrestling this year, in case there might be some strangers uninterested in shorthorns and roughs. There's not even a notice on the main road to tell passers-by about all the excitement going on behind the wall, and unless you happened to hear the man with the loudspeaker calling, say, Class 22 into the judging ring, you'd drive right past the place. And only one tent on the field for president, secretary, judges, the press or anybody else who wants to get out of the rain – that is, if you don't count the beer tent. But to compensate there's a pleasant absence of restrictions – nobody to tell you where not to park your car and nobody even to keep you out of the judging ring, if you want to go there. Not to speak of the best show lunch in Westmorland. Nobody is getting excited about it, but this is the centenary show. That's why the prize-winning cows and sheep are wearing coloured rosettes this year instead of bits of cardboard. But perhaps you didn't notice.

A. H. G.

SOBER COLOURS FOR CARAVANS: NATIONAL TRUST'S CALL TO MAKERS
October 15 1960
A call for caravan manufacturers to concentrate on 'sober and suitable colours to the exclusion of shades of orange, pistachio and cream which are now so much in evidence' is made in the annual report of the National Trust. The report welcomes the recognition of the need to control the siting of caravans and adds that, in some situations, a caravan or a tent can be harmless if it is an inconspicuous colour.

REFUGE AT ROSTHERNE
February 11 1961
The establishment by the Nature JL Conservancy of Rostherne Mere as a National Nature Reserve will insure that a principal refuge for wildfowl in England will be safeguarded. Thousands of ducks, which have learned to rely on the mere as a

sanctuary when other waters are disturbed, will continue to enjoy the strict protection which was given them by the late Lord Egerton. The mere and some surrounding woodland is a gift to the conservancy from his executors, and an additional area will be included in the reserve by agreement with the present owner and the farmers of land overlooking the mere. The neighbouring Tatton Park with its meres, having already been handed over to the National Trust and the Cheshire County Council, will provide for public recreation, and the Nature Conservancy will maintain strict control over access and disturbance to the Rostherne Mere Nature Reserve.

Among ornithologists Rostherne has long been famous, for both T. V. Coward and A. W. Boyd ('A. W. B.' of the 'Country Diary') did much of their birdwatching here. Boyd, in particular, devoted much time and effort in his later years to insure that the mere should remain a bird sanctuary, and through the appeal for the establishment of an observation post at the mere as a memorial to his work, it is hoped to recognise this permanently.

It is as a wildfowl sanctuary for wintering duck that the mere has mainly gained its reputation among ornithologists. There is little doubt that the numbers of wintering duck there have steadily increased since Coward recorded the birds here in the first quarter of this century. In mid-winter there are often 4,000 mallard on the water, with over a thousand teal and many shovellers, widgeon, tufted duck and pochard. In general, the surface-feeding ducks greatly outnumber the diving ducks at Rostherne because, for much of its area, the mere is deep – 101 feet in its centre. This makes it less attractive to the diving duck than certain other, shallower, meres in the same district. But no other inland water in north-western England shelters such great flocks of duck.

Another feature of the winter bird population of the mere is the huge roost of gulls that assembles there each evening. This may consist of as many as 10,000 birds, mostly black-headed and herring gulls, with a few common and lesser black-backed gulls with them. Black terns, on passage migration to and from the Continent, are often to be seen in spring or autumn fishing the shallower parts of the mere.

Rostherne has always been a stronghold of the great crested grebe, which breeds in the reed beds surrounding the mere. Last autumn there were nearly 60 of these birds on the mere, both adults and young birds. The rare black-neck grebe has also bred here, and the little grebe does so regularly. The reed beds around the mere also shelter colonies of reed warblers and Rostherne is the most northerly place in western Britain where this bird breeds in any significant numbers. The sedge warbler is also fairly common as a breeding bird.

In the coverts surrounding the mere, many of the more common passerine birds occur and breed. The green, greater spotted and lesser spotted woodpeckers have all been recorded, though only the greater spotted woodpecker is known to nest regularly. The nuthatch, a bird that has greatly increased in North Cheshire lately, can be seen regularly in the Rostherne coverts. Blackcap and garden warbler are both present in summer, together with reed and sedge warblers. The willow tit and hawfinch are rarities that also occur regularly.

There is no heronry at Rostherne; though herons may be seen at the mere throughout the year. These birds probably come from the large heronry at nearby Tabley Mere. Occasionally, a bittern is disturbed from the reed beds: it would be a notable addition to Cheshire birds if a pair stayed to breed. There are no extensive mudspits or sandy verges that could attract wading birds and consequently Rostherne is not noted for its records of waders. However, the common sandpiper nests each year on the slopes beside the mere and the snipe breeds regularly in the adjacent meadows.

Although the mere is principally noted as a refuge for birds, it is also of great interest to the freshwater biologist. Much is known about the biological and chemical composition of waters in the Lake District, but lowland lakes, such as those scattered over Cheshire and Shropshire, have been less intensively examined. Some work at Rostherne Mere and other places in Cheshire has revealed that these lakes are generally much richer in mineral salts than the Lake District waters, and this seems to be associated with a greater abundance of phytoplankton. In this respect Rostherne Mere has much in common with Lough Neagh and resembles many of the shallow lakes in Denmark. It undoubtedly calls for further research.

The mere is also remarkable for its content of the smelt or sparling. This fish is normally an inhabitant of salt water, but frequents estuaries and ascends rivers into fresh water in the breeding season. It is a permanent freshwater resident in some Swedish lakes, but in Britain it is known only from Rostherne.

TOM PRITCHARD AND STUART SMITH

EMANCIPATION ON RIVER BANK FOR COMPLEAT WOMEN ANGLERS
July 1 1963
There was no lack of male sympathy, advice and encouragement from sons, fathers and husbands for the 100 women who competed in the first all-England ladies'

angling championships on the banks of the Avon at Pershore, Worcestershire yesterday. After all, was it not the Pershore Working Men's Club – no less – which agreed to let the ladies use their stretch of water for the contest? 'We were,' said the secretary Mr Ray Summers, 'unanimous in our decision.' In the words of a rain-drenched but loyal husband, crouched on the bank inside a plastic mackintosh, while his wife fished from the shelter of his umbrella: 'It's a damned poor sport who doesn't let his wife do a bit of fishing.'

Another similarly loyal husband – whose wife, Mrs Helen Wright of Swadlincote, Burton-on-Trent, thought up the idea of the championships – made it perfectly plain that journalists were not to treat the event flippantly. Mrs Wright, however, after speculating briefly on an empty net, recalled that her idea for the championships was born as a domestic joke: 'My husband was late for lunch one day. He had been out with the Swadlincote anglers. I chided him for being late and said, "Right, we ladies are going to have a match of our own now and you can stay at home and cook the lunch instead." It was only a joke of course.' Mrs Wright sent a letter to the *Angling Times* suggesting the all-England ladies' championships, with the result that 200 women said they would like to compete. She was, to put it mildly, 'surprised'. The contest was won by Mrs A Harrison of Manchester, with a catch weighing 3lb 9oz 8 drams.

Mrs Anne Wilson, the organising secretary, did not welcome any suggestion that she and the other 99 women contending for the championships were intruding upon a realm of male dominance; but she was clearly grateful for all that the men had done, including the diplomatic erection of ladies' toilets in the meadow.

NORTHERN ACCENT: RURAL DEPRESSION

July 15 1963

All last week a company of rather special soldiers toiled on top of Warden Law in County Durham. They were taking apart a beam engine put together by George Stephenson and his lads, a long shift of 140 years or so ago. All is not over for the grand old engine. After a lyke wake journey of 20 miles or so she will be put together again in an open-air museum of folk ways, buildings, tools and machines, just over the hill from Durham Cathedral.

There will also be, I hope, a reconstructed farmhouse with red pantiles and a cow byre with a witchstone hanging: scythes, hayforks, ploughshares (where are all those shire horses now?) , and maybe a haywain – I know where there is a nest of no less than three all in mint condition. I hope there is a waterwheel as well as Geordie's engine: they may do more than create a wonderment of our children's children: after Armageddon men may use them as models.

The pang I feel for forgotten tools, abandoned engines and crumbling buildings is eased a little by the noble work of preservation. But what of the run-down rural districts? The current annual report of the Northumberland Rural Community Council makes melancholy reading, not for want of interest or energy on the part of countryfolk, but for the lack of means which could make them truly fruitful. Who was it talked of a country's 'haemorrhage' of people a few days ago? In the last 10 years, Northumberland's rural labour force has declined by around 3,000 or 30 per cent. The percentage puts the matter in perspective, especially when you remember that families are involved as well. Then think of the other rural areas that spread out from the Pennines. The report remarks that most of the villages were established a century ago when the rural population was bigger than it is now, and continues: 'Despite increased mobility, people demand more and better local services than they had then, but there are fewer people to pay for them. Selection of a reduced number of villages and hamlets for development is inevitable.' We must build arks among the meadows.

The conclusion is sound, but there is no noise to be heard of hammers or concrete mixers, so far as I know, and I am thinking of 'truly rural'. Voices cry in the wilderness for better housing, amenities, communications, and the trend moves inexorably in the reverse direction. The other evening I took part in a preliminary discussion about a forthcoming issue of the *Northern Architect*, one of the brightest and most useful of all our specialist publications.

It will be devoted to the theme of 'Folk, Place, Work', and it is hoped that it will help to project the new environment which is in the making in the north-east. I was struck by the ferment of creation and re-creation in the area stretching from Middlesbrough to Blyth, and extending roughly from the coast to the Great North Road. New city centres, new towns, new roads, bridges, tunnels and a variety of amenities are in the making – and not before time. I was also struck by the absence of activity, or proposed activity, in the rural west.

Is it that we unconsciously – and jealously – wish to leave the country alone? Or do we class it as a land where 'our' kind of problems simply cannot exist? If so, it needs stressing again that the country is a sight more than a 'lung' for the urban-dweller. It is a land with people, problems and values. All are in danger. We read about the Irish Famine; we talk about the Irish Famine; we talk blithely about enclosures for sheep and dispossession for deer, and forget a contemporary, creeping decay.

Thinking of the 3,000 (first shire horses, then man, woman and child), I find a list of industries a shade pathetic – catamarans, coin cabinets, aqualungs, fishing rods, souvenirs, mead and plastic mouldings, it is believed, may offer extra jobs. What is obvious is that as farming becomes increasingly mechanised, and as mineral resources decline, the need for larger 'planned settlements' and a massive diversification of rural industry become really urgent. Otherwise our haemorrhage of people, skills, and traditions will continue unchecked.

The waste in terms of space and potential is not so dramatic as it is, say, in Sicily. But in our terms it is just as significant. To murder by neglect, to kill by apathy or by a kind of urban arrogance, to drain away a noble heritage of folk is a crime for which the nation must pay. Better to pay now and prevent the desolation of the more remote fells and dales from spreading out to the open, gentle countryside.

One can think of a whole string – or necklace – of rural towns which could become strongpoints for a rejuvenated rural economy: Richmond, Reeth, Barnard Castle, Staindrop, Stanhope, Alston, Haltwhistle, Rothbury and Wooler could provide an opportunity for thousands to return and root themselves in good, rich soil.

Hamlets and villages within easy reach, nourished by new industry and amenities, could lend themselves to bold and imaginative planning; socially as well as architecturally we could set about building a rural society in contemporary terms. In terms of history, the countryside is to us what the virgin lands are to the Russians. The smiling fields and hedgerows hide a challenge. After all, the Jerusalem of William Blake was not in heaven. It was a re-created, rural England.

SID CHAPLIN

A COUNTRY DIARY: LONDON
December 18 1963
The 25 years during which I have been contributing to 'A Country Diary', which pressure of work compels me reluctantly to give up doing, have seen many changes in the face of the English countryside. In the South Midlands, the part of England that I know best, intensified farming and new techniques have not only altered the look of the land, they have banished the corncrake from the river valleys and the nightjar, virtually, from the commons; reduced the number of stone-curlews

and wheatears on the downs and of sparrowhawks everywhere to a handful; and made those once commonplace delights of a country walk, butterflies and flowers, comparative rarities. Yet, if one looks farther afield, all is not lost. Wrynecks and red-backed shrikes, in addition to the birds I have mentioned, may have become scarce, and there may be grave fears for the future of several sorts of bird of prey; but black redstarts and little ringed plovers have colonised London and the Home Counties, avocets and black-tailed godwits are breeding again respectively in Suffolk and Lincolnshire, and golden eagles are trying to nest in the Lake District. The avocets and the godwits, like the ospreys in Scotland, owe their success to the voluntary Royal Society for the Protection of Birds. Hope for wildlife in general and for the countryside as a whole also lies not only in statutory bodies like the Nature Conservancy and the National Parks Commission but in voluntary ones, such as the recently created Council for Nature and the growing number of Naturalists' Trusts, which reflect and harness the great interest in nature and its preservation that has arisen since the war.

J. F. A

HOW MANY EGGS FROM ONE BASKET?

May 9 1964

If M. J. B. Eastwood, who already produces 12 million broiler chickens a year, carries through his enterprise to house another 12 million laying birds, turning out between two and two and a half thousand million eggs, he will not exactly have cornered the market. But at least one sixth of the eggs which reach our breakfast table will then be coming out of a single basket. The egg market is near saturation: it is no wonder that the Egg Marketing Board and the smaller producers feel uncomfortable.

Mr Eastwood is only a symbol of the revolution in food production methods. Factory farming, which started with broiler fowls, has already spread to eggs and is rapidly spreading to beef and pig meat. It raises all sorts of problems, financial, social and emotional, not only for farmers but for everybody. Mr Charles Jarvis, chairman of the British Farm Produce Council, gave good advice when he told the Association of Agriculture this week that new methods of food production should be treated with the seriousness they merit and not be dismissed in an atmosphere of emotion and hysteria.

The vast farming enterprises have one object in common – to cut production costs by streamlined methods. This is desirable as long as a fair proportion of the reduction is handed on to the consumer. But while it is easy to say that there is no reason why Mr Eastwood or anybody else should be discouraged from producing eggs at 1s 4d a dozen when the present government-guaranteed price is 3s 8d, the problem is not as simple as that. Vertical integration on this scale affects more than a few poultry farmers. Feeding stuffs compounders, faced with the threat of rations mixed on the factory farm, are wondering whether they ought not to go into the business themselves. Is the grain producer and the livestock breeder going to be forced into the position of selling under contract to the factory farm, which will process his output into the final egg or meat product, tailored to the needs of the supermarket? Will he then be reduced to the factory farm?

These are questions vital to the future of farmers and to the social and aesthetic pattern of the countryside. But there are others. Experience does not suggest that the setting up of monopolies in any industry will, in the long run, benefit the community at large. Favourable prices prevail only as long as there is competition. Living creatures, however they are treated, are not factory products and are subject to hazards beyond those of normal factory breakdown. If unexpected disaster hits the Eastwoods of the farming world there would be a serious dislocation of food supplies. Finally, there are all the unanswered questions about the wholesomeness of food produced under conditions which many people believe to be unnatural, and the feelings aroused among those who sincerely hold that it is cruel to deprive living creatures of their natural environment. These are the considerations which are least susceptible to proof and most susceptible to emotional imbalance. But they cannot be disregarded.

Factory farming is likely to remain with us. Those who approach the problems it poses with the sobriety that Mr Jarvis advocates will have to determine, in the end, how far it should be allowed to go, and how the more traditional farming pattern can be fitted into it. It must be hoped that those who like their eggs from free-range hens and their beef off the grass, in spite of what the analysts say, will always be able to find their genuine 'country fare'. But they may have to be prepared to pay more for it.

WOMEN FARMING

February 24 1965

An attractive woman in her 30s has just taken over the entire management of her deceased father's Yorkshire Wold farm of 500 acres. I wish her joy, just as if she were newly married; for if she carries on with it she will have little time or opportunity for marriage. Many men will respect and admire her ability, but they will, unfortunately, be rather scared of her for the same reasons. Most farms, of course, are managed by a husband. His wife gives him food and sympathy at the right times, and puts his slippers out after a tiring day in the market.

In this wide area of Yorkshire, which includes the Wolds, there are wives looking after their husbands' herd of milk cows, and daughters helping their fathers to keep the farm records, but I know of only two single women managing all the departments of a farm – the one I have already mentioned, and myself.

When my mother and I bought our 450 acres 'problem' farm of poor land 12 years ago, we decided to be partners. I was to take on the more active part of the management and we would discuss all matters of policy together. I was 30 and full of energy and enthusiasm. Looking back over the past 12 years, I wonder how it has been possible to carry on, faced with the difficult problems that farming and our peculiar land have presented.

However, there has always been the challenge: what a man can do, so also can a woman. Superior physical strength does not enter into it nowadays on a farm of this size. At first we were given much advice. Locals shook their heads knowingly and were slightly suspicious of us. Women might not understand the land, they said, and probably could not keep good labour. But we thought that no man had ever understood this curious land anyway, and that sensible agricultural workers might not object to sensible women bosses. We engaged a foreman whose experience was extensive, and also his son, an ex-army mechanic, as our head tractor man. They are still with us after 12 years.

Two hundred acres of our land is peat with water about two feet below it. This land, known locally as Seamer Carrs, was once a lake, and is peculiar only to the sea end of the vale of Pickering. The flat, dreary waste throws up ancient bog oaks buried by the Ice Age, flint arrows left by Neolithic man and, worst of all, a godforsaken atmosphere of hopelessness. When we first moved in, National Agricultural Advisory Service men with first-class degrees came to test this land. They agreed with local opinion in advising us not to risk spending money ploughing this part of the farm.

If by a lucky chance we could grow a crop of grain on this land, it would be almost impossible to harvest it, they said, as a binder or combine harvester would sink in and bog. With the willing cooperation of our key men, we went against their advice. We ploughed the peat land, racing against oncoming winter, because when it rains heavily some of this land reverts to lake-like conditions. When spring came we sowed oats. The seed drill sometimes bogged and often had to be pulled along with two tractors. But the oats germinated. Each spear-like blade showed along the drill rows, a brilliant healthy green – so did the weeds.

Locals had said that you 'couldn't' spray with selective weedkiller in Seamer Carrs, because it 'didn't work'. I found they had always engaged a contractor to do it for them and he had applied the wrong quantities, so naturally it had not worked. Although our capital was rather low, we bought our own spraying outfit and our head tractor man applied the right quantities. It worked all right. With no weeds choking it, the oats grew well and in July the heads shot out and swayed and rustled in the wind. One day, just before harvest, one of the Agricultural Advisory Service men who had been to test the land came to see us again. I took him to the oats. He stared at it and his only comment was, 'I always said this land would grow good crops if someone tried it.' That night there was heavy rain. Next morning the oats were flat to the ground – it looked as if a steamroller had been over them. The thought of local farmers saying – or even thinking – 'we told you so' gave us all strength. We attached a pick-up reel to the combine and it lifted the laid crop satisfactorily as it harvested. But the combine harvester bogged repeatedly. The foreman and his ex-army son lined our four tractors up, and time and again all our men pulled the dangerously tilting monster on to drier ground. It was a slow process but worth it, because from each acre on which we had sown 12 stones of oat seed in the spring, we combined a ton and a half of oats at harvest. The satisfaction of producing tons of grain where only weeds and rushes have grown before is reward enough, but we needed the money too.

We have served a tough apprenticeship for 12 years, and though the Seamer Carrs land can still play some queer tricks on us, we have tamed it. During this 12 years, British agriculture has seen quicker, bigger changes than have ever taken place in its history. We like to feel we have, in a small way, taken part in this revolution.

Now local farmers sometimes consult us for advice, and occasionally they ask at what 'college' I spent my student days. I suppose they refer to 'learning farming'. I hedge, and say that I was brought up in the country and have farming ancestors, which is true. I do not tell them, in case they think it is some kind of joke, that my only official qualification – which at least taught the keen observation of land, people and objects that is essential to farming – is a London University Diploma in Fine Art.

ANN WILLATT

PLODDER'S PROGRESS
April 17 1965

Next Saturday the minister of lands, Mr Willey, will formally open the Pennine Way and a 30 years' war will have come to an end. It has taken us that long to acquire this precious strip of land so that any one of us may walk there without being told to get the hell out of it. The Americans have their Appalachian Trail, the New Zealanders their Milford Track; next weekend we shall have our Pennine Way, which is neither as grand nor as formidable as the other two, but which is good enough for this claustrophobic country.

There is nothing else like it in England. Dartmoor is a featureless hump by comparison, the South Downs a genteel stroll. It starts at a log bridge across a Derbyshire stream and it ends at a valley just inside Scotland. In between it rambles for 250 miles over eight counties and 10 sheets of the one-inch Ordnance Survey maps. In doing so it is traversing – if you discount that last brief Celtic lap – the only English landscape which is magnificent rather than just charming or pretty. From its beginning across the boggy plateau of the Peak, then up the hard spine of the Pennine divide, until it swoops across the windy solitude of Northumbria, it is all of a piece in this sense. But it has its own variety.

A man walking the Way will find himself at some of the weirdest spots in England, like High Cup Nick and Malham Cove, and one of its most torrential, like High Force. He will stand on one of our highest hills at Cross Fell and if it is a clear day there he will be able to see Ireland. As he plugs his way up Teesdale he will be moving through the most exotic collection of botanic specimens in the land. And as he strides over Hadrian's Wall he will be upon our most colossal ancient monument and, with Stonehenge, our most haunting. Provided he is well shod, well protected from the wind and rain and self contained, anyone with tolerably good lungs and legs can try all this now; though he would be a fool to cross some parts of the Way – the disconcertingly similar hills of the Cheviot, say – without a map and compass. If he is in his prime and accustomed to rough walking he can cover the whole route comfortably within a fortnight.

We have had a long struggle in getting the Pennine Way open from start to finish. It was conceived in 1935 in a *Daily Herald* article by Tom Stephenson, and if ever a man deserved to take the victory salute on his battlefield, as he will on Saturday, it is the 72-year-old Stephenson, secretary of the Ramblers' Association. It was fought for doggedly, sometimes literally when walkers and gamekeepers coincided on the same grouse moor; in the 1930s five men went to prison after a demonstration against restricted access to Kinder Scout. It was argued over in a succession of committees established to bring – in the ramblers' war cry – 'freedom of the hills' to all of us. It was tramped over in 1948 by a party of sympathetic MPs, one of whom was Mr Willey, another Hugh Dalton. And when Dalton, then a power in the Labour government, said that we had waited long enough for completion of the Way it looked as if we might be enjoying that particular slice of freedom pretty soon.

But Dalton, Stephenson and the rest had underrated the tenacity of the landed interests involved. Although the Labour government designated the Pennine Way in 1951 and urged local authorities to establish rights of way along it, the battle went on. The corporations of Manchester and Huddersfield took some shifting because they were anxious about their water resources being polluted. A few individuals were concerned lest the number of game birds available for their private slaughterings should be diminished.

The last obstruction, a Northumbrian gentleman, was not reduced until a couple of months ago. But now the Pennine Way is open. It was seen by the Hobhouse Committee in 1947 as one of several long-distance walking tracks in England and Wales – the Pennine Way, the Pilgrims' Way, the Chilterns to the Devon coast, the South Downs to Salisbury Plain, Offa's Dyke, and the Thames Towpath. Having taken more than a quarter of a century to get the first of these open it is probably going to exercise us for several generations to come before we get the rest. We must comfort ourselves with the thought, meanwhile, that at last we are getting somewhere.

GEOFFREY MOORHOUSE

A COUNTRY DIARY: CUMBERLAND

March 14 1966

The most famous bit of rock in England is Napes Needle, perched high up among the ridge on the side of Great Gable and looking down on the patchwork fields of Wasdale Head nearly 2,000 feet below. It was first climbed just 80 years ago by W. P. Haskett Smith, a young Oxford graduate who was later to be revered as the 'father' of climbers, and its ascent was the first significant landmark in the development of the new sport of rock climbing. Haskett Smith climbed it alone, leaving his fell-pole at the foot, and left his handkerchief jammed in a crevice on the top block to prove it. Fifty years later, at the age of 74, but roped this time between two other distinguished climbers, he went up again and seated on the top block, made the extempore remark that has since passed into history. 'Tell us a story,' shouted somebody from the admiring crowds below, and the old man, never at a loss for words, replied on the instant: 'There is no story. This is the top storey.'

Since the first ascent, all sorts of indignities have been heaped upon the old Needle. It has been climbed thousands of times by at least eight different routes; small boys and girls have been hauled up, stunt climbs and speed record attempts have been perpetrated on its smooth walls, and it has been photographed, sketched, filmed and televised. People have lit fires on top, stood on their heads, eaten meals, shaved and danced jigs and, if there are three of you on the edge of the top block, you can gently rock it. I know, I've done it. But the other day the Needle looked none the worse for its harsh treatment, except a little polished here and there.

A. H. G.

A COUNTRY DIARY: MACHYNLLETH

July 30 1966

We were becoming afraid of the giant hogweeds we had planted in our garden. They looked so huge and fecund we feared we were in for everlasting trouble. But after last Saturday's 'Country Diary' we got a letter from a kind-hearted reader. 'Don't worry about the giant hogweed,' he wrote. 'I never see them but in ones or twos.' We took courage. Besides, we said, this is a plant esteemed by the best authors. Gertrude Jeckyll, for instance. Still, we had to admit, maybe Gertrude never thought in terms of gardens as small as ours. Indeed, looking up her actual words we found that she thought it would look excellent 'about old water-mills'.

So gloom again. On top of which came Wednesday's post bringing a letter from another reader with very definite views about giant hogweed. 'I am writing to warn you that this plant can be very dangerous. Earlier this year we cut back a lot of it and our children played with the huge leaves. It happened to be very hot and the children were wearing few clothes. Two days later they were covered with a rash and huge blisters formed, up to four inches long and half an inch high. Which leaves me not only panicky but puzzled, for I have never heard of hogweed being poisonous. I wonder if any other reader has had a similar experience or can shed any light on the mystery?'

W. M. CONDRY

COUNTRY STOMACHS TURN

January 22 1970

Countrymen who have grown up in the lee of a manure heap without even noticing the smell are finding that they cannot stomach the smell from the new large-scale broiler houses. Complaints from distressed villagers were leading to battles between public health officers and the broiler firms, the Hertfordshire county health inspector, Mr J. L. Stringer, told a conference of the Association of Public Health Inspectors in London yesterday.

'Intensive farming methods meant the broiler houses could produce vast quantities of highly septic manure,' Mr Stringer said. He added: 'One high farmer, to my knowledge, takes his wife and family abroad when the seasonal emptying of the catch-pits from the poultry houses takes place. Unfortunately, the local villagers are not able to take the same step.' He argued that the law needed to be strengthened to cope with the problem of animal smells from intensive farming. There should also be some means of ensuring that old and unsuitably placed buildings could not be converted piecemeal into intensive farming units and jeopardise the well-being of country dwellers.

Various Uses

Poultry manure has its uses, he pointed out. Mixed with barley, it could be used as cattle food. A cow was able to use the nitrogen in the manure, so reducing its need for protein. Would it be possible, he asked, for cows and poultry to learn to thrive by a mutual exchange of droppings?

Intensive farming was also attacked as a possible health hazard to the consumer. In a letter yesterday to the National Farmers' Union, Miss Anne Coghill, chairman of the Farm and Food Society, said: 'There is now a mounting pile of evidence to show that factory farming methods, which over the last decade have made rapid advance with the full support of successive governments and of the NFU, hold health hazards for the consumer.'

Disease among intensively housed stock had reached frightening proportions, Miss Coghill claimed, quoting an estimate that its cost to the country was £150m a year. Many people would like to hear that farmers were fighting for better farming, and not merely their own betterment.

PUBLIC FOOTPATH THROUGH THE LAUNDRY WINDOW
May 13 1970

To say the least, life can be bewildering at Bilbrough, a village near York. Mr Robert Wybrants, who lives in Cat Lane, has just learned that his house, which cost £12,000, was built across a public footpath and that anybody is entitled to walk right through it.

Yesterday the *Guardian* reported that Bilbrough had a dispute over the ownership of what must be the smallest village green in the country, 40ft by 9ft. And 10 days ago it reported that the village had failed to get an ugly water tower demolished, because water from Bilbrough would be needed in any nuclear holocaust.

Bilbrough may be short on knowledge of the nuclear holocaust, but it is long on experience of the peculiar hullabaloo. Mr Wybrants said yesterday that he was a keen golfer and was prepared to tee-up in his garden, yell 'Fore!' and bang golf balls at anybody trying to exercise a right of way. There are, it seems, three ways of following the public footpath through the house of Mr Wybrants. The easiest (which Mr Wybrants would not allow, anyway) would be to go in through the front door and out of the kitchen door that would leave the walker facing the way he came in. The second way, more difficult, would be to climb up the walls and walk over the roof. And the third, following the right of way exactly, would be through the laundry window, over the washing machine, through a brick wall, through a broom cupboard into a food cupboard, through another brick wall, into a dining recess and out through a window.

Mr Wybrants bought his land freehold and was told of no restriction on it. He learned about the right of way when he was shown an old map by a councillor, and he is to ask the West Riding County Council for it to be diverted. The passage of the footpath through the house in Cat Lane was discovered at the height of National Footpaths Week, a campaign by ramblers to clear obstructions and generally tidy up rights of way. Mr Wybrants need not fear that his house will be tidied out of the way. A local member of the Ramblers' Association, Mr R. B. Brewster, said he knew of no plans to walk that particular footpath.

MICHAEL PARKIN

VIGILANCE URGED TO HALT THE SPREAD OF SUBURBIA
August 28 1970

Never before has the need for careful planning been more urgent, says a report published yesterday. Wrong decisions now could ruin the face of England for ever. Constant vigilance is urged in the annual report of the Lancashire branch of the Council for the Protection of Rural England to prevent rural areas from being turned into straggling suburbia, and more water being provided at the cost of irreplaceable land and wildlife. It says no county in England stands to gain more than Lancashire from the careful husbandry of countryside. Few counties, however, present greater problems.

On the one hand, there was the grim inheritance of bad housing, derelict areas and the need for new industries to replace those in decline. On the other, there was the ever-increasing population demanding more and more expendable commodities and expecting, and needing, the refreshment of the countryside.

Dense Population

In an already overcrowded county, the Irwell Valley was more densely populated than the valley of the Ganges. By the year 2000 the country's 54 million would have increased to around 70 million. The report makes these points:

- *Education.* 'If we fail now in focusing public opinion on the problems of the Lancashire countryside, we will be too late and unable to leave a decent environment for our children. Time is not on our side.'
- *Sites.* Wherever possible, the siting of public works and motorways must be exercised with good taste and judgment.
- *Water.* 'We are especially concerned with water supply, there are few problems more threatening to the landscape. Because of this we are carefully watching the investigations into the Morecambe Bay barrage and other schemes.'
- *Rubbish.* Expanding rubbish dumps were products of 'this throwaway world'. At present, it was cheaper and easier to dump rather than dispose of, or recover, waste.
- *Houses.* Private housing development was a continual headache, the report says. Ill-coordinated individual developments could transform pleasant rural areas into a straggling suburbia. Tighter control was called for.

A COUNTRY DIARY: KENT

October 9 1970

Egg Pie Lane leads out of Seaharbour Lane and winds its narrow way through coppiced woods and unkempt hedgerows on steep clay banks. It is one of those lanes that conceals more than it reveals. The occasional wayside cottages stand half-hidden behind pond and orchard and the reddening chestnuts. In one of them, W. H. Davies lived for a short time in 1905. I try to imagine the conversations he had with Edward Thomas, the poet, who lived at nearby Elses Farm and encouraged Davies in his writing. Thomas spent two of the happiest years of his short life at the farm, though he is not remembered in the district now. The place has hardly changed since he lived there. The small farmhouse built in Flemish bond, red and grey brick alternating, is set well back from the road, standing behind big black-timbered barns and two round oasts. Over the meadows to the north is seen the tall tower of St George's church, high on the hill above Sevenoaks Weald. Here are many of the images that the poet stored in his imagination and used later to celebrate his devotion to the rural scene. Some of Thomas's poems are almost incantations of country names. I wonder what he made of Egg Pie Lane and Seaharbour?

J. T. WHITE

TERRIERS KILL 80 RATS AN HOUR

November 16 1970

Dogs bred by a Breconshire woman are killing rats infesting many parts of mid-Wales at the rate of 80 an hour. Mrs Margaret Williamson of Blaenantllwyd Farm, Llandeilo, Breconshire, who has been breeding Bedlington terriers for 50 years, says she is unable to supply all the farmers who want to buy them. The 'super-rat' menace became apparent in 1966 when it was discovered that this strain was immune to many poisons. The National Farmers' Union (NFU) said the rats had been advancing towards urban areas at a mile a year.

The Bedlington seemed the answer to what had been becoming a national problem. Mr David Lloyd of the NFU in Welshpool said farmers in Wales had been trying dozens of different methods of rodent control. 'But this seems to be the best method we have had so far.' The Ministry of Agriculture's recent announcement that the rats were advancing had worried many people. Now there was some hope that the problem would be contained.

According to Mrs Williamson, Bedlington terriers were first bred by Gypsies in Northumberland about the middle of the last century and were used to clear country estates of rats. She charges £10–£15 for dogs and £20–£25 for bitches.

RAMBLERS TO PROTEST AT 'SPOILING' OF SNOWDONIA
September 27 1971

The simmering controversy about the sanctity of national parks in general, and Snowdonia in particular, will come to the boil at the end of next week with an open-air rally to protest about industrial exploitation of Snowdonia.

The rally at Capel Curig is being organised by the Ramblers' Association, which has 22,000 members. It is being supported by the Council for the Protection of Rural Wales, and members of the North Wales (Hydro Electric) Protection Committee will doubtless be there in force.

There are three targets for the protest: Rio Tinto-Zinc (RTZ)'s plan for opencast copper mining on a large scale around Dolgellau; the Central Electricity Generating Board (CEGB)'s examination of three sites, all within the national park, for another pumped-storage power station; and the growth of conifer forest around hill farms. The organisers could well add a fourth: the chance that the government could still order the CEGB to site its proposed nuclear power station on the Lleyn Peninsula instead of on the Dee estuary in Flintshire.

RTZ is not without support in Merioneth, however. Only this week the Welsh nationalist party, Plaid Cymru, has approached Rio Tinto with a view to setting up a commitment to recruit local labour for mining in Merioneth. The Deudraeth rural council, also in Merioneth, would 'in principle' welcome a 1,000 MW power station in the locality. The attitude is similar among local people at the other two possible sites, Llanberis and Dolwyddelan.

Sad tales of drowned villages abound in Welsh literature, but the prospect is now viewed with equanimity if it provides work. 'I have no objection to drowning the weekend retreats of affluent Midlanders to provide jobs for some of the 30 per cent of young people who leave Merioneth every year,' said Plaid Cymru's policy director Mr Dafydd Thomas. His view is not an uncommon one. Until someone comes up with a policy for providing employment, and stemming depopulation, within the national park, the voice of conservation will largely be an English one. And while this situation continues, planning applications for development in the park will be examined with interest, if not actually welcomed.

The conservationists are perhaps beginning to see this. The secretary of the Ramblers' Association, Mr Chris Hall, agreed yesterday that economic problems in the national parks would have to be examined by someone. It was perfectly possible, he said, for suitable light industries to be established near existing built-up areas – industries that would provide more permanent jobs than many of the developments now threatened. Sir Jack Longland sympathised with Welsh local authorities over the financial burden placed upon them by having to administer the national park. 'We have always said that the cost of maintaining national playgrounds should be borne directly by the Exchequer.' The development of tourism offered the best prospect of solving unemployment.

JAMES LEWIS

OIL TEST CASE CENTRES ON HIGHLAND HAMLET
November 12 1973
The tiny crofting hamlet of Drumbuie in Wester Ross has emerged from peaceful obscurity to become the centre of a test case which could determine the future course of oil-related development in the West Highlands. The issues at stake are the social and environmental effects of heavy industry on remote rural communities, and the need for Britain to establish a home-based construction industry to serve the North Sea oilfield.

These conflicting interests and the specific case of Drumbuie will be examined over the next six weeks at a public inquiry which opens today at Balmacara in Wester Ross. Two construction groups – John Mowlem Ltd and Taylor Woodrow Ltd – have applied for planning permission to build concrete oil-production platforms on land at Drumbuie which is owned by the National Trust of Scotland.

Those proposals have produced a remarkable surge of public opposition and an embarrassing clash of government policies. Ross and Cromarty County Council decided last month by a majority vote to appear as objectors at the inquiry. The National Trust says it is prepared to take the case to Parliament and has raised £17,000 in a few weeks to cover the cost of its campaign. It is supported by more than 380 formal objectors who include local people and national conservation bodies.

The intending developers are being backed by the Department of Trade and Industry, which sees Drumbuie as the first step towards establishing a new industry with international prospects in Britain.

The National Trust for Scotland says that heavy industry is unacceptable anywhere on the West Highland coast. It is in a strong position to resist, as it holds the Drumbuie land 'inalienably' in trust for the nation. The Trust can only be compelled to sell by an Act of Parliament and that would mean a further public outcry.

Disputes over land and tenure are an integral part of Highland life and the record shows that many an apparent lost cause has been won. There was the classic case 90 years ago of the lamb of Kintail, near Drumbuie, when the wealthy American owner of Kintail estate claimed that the pet lamb of a crofter's small son was trespassing on his deer forest. He took court action to compel the crofter to fence in the lamb. The crofter's response was a counterclaim that the landlord should enclose his deer forest.

The case became a national controversy and funds were raised to support the crofter's cause. After a prolonged legal battle he finally won his point in the Court of Appeal. The landlord was heard after the decision to say that it would have been cheaper for him to give the child a model of the pet lamb in pure gold.

JOHN KERR

REAPING HARVEST OF A FARMING REVOLUTION
January 26 1974
One of the first dairy farmers in the country to recognise the potential of delivering crates of milk to schools was a shrewd Yorkshireman called Tom Foster. He had the bright idea of supplying isolated school in the Yorkshire Dales with their daily milk and although some of his farming friends are said to have pulled funny faces at him, he became known as something of a pioneer. His efforts meant that long before schoolchildren were either loathing or loving their official milk breaks in Britain, he had built up a private and highly profitable milk market on his home ground.

When he died, his son, Rob, now 52, took over his 600-acre farm at Airton, just outside Malham. Now it is a vast new market – the Common Market – which is challenging the Fosters, and Rob Foster says he has a barnful of reservations about Britain's entry. He will tell you there is a point on his land where, given a clear day and good imagination, he can turn around and see 'most of England'. However hard he peers to the south, he can never see Europe.

He runs New Field Grange with his son Simon, two labourers, Michael Riley and Rodney Wainman, and a 70-year-old stockman, Wilf Kipling. Simon, aged 19, has one regret about farming – that he did not start sooner. After passing nine O levels he went to a farm training college, left after three weeks, and came home with a youthful impatience to run his father's farm. As it is he could not have picked a more exciting or exacting time to begin farming. The Fosters and thousands like them are in the middle of a farming revolution. The industry is seeing more changes than it has for probably 20 or 30 years.

Exactly what are the changes? How are British farmers being affected by the Common Market and the rise in world prices? What effect is the gradual introduction of the common agricultural policy having on them? How are the farmers shaping up to the problems? The major changes facing farmers include a new system of support for cereals, sugar, milk and beef; much better support prices for beef, but gradual abandonment of the indirect subsidies which have been so important to the British producer in the past; prices for milk products well above traditional British or world markets; a reduction in the protection given to the pig producers; and much tougher competition on the British market from other Community farmers.

It is clear that to benefit from Europe, British farmers are having to look closely at their own farming systems. As far as marketing is concerned within the enlarged European Economic Community (EEC), British farmers are in a different world. They are competing directly against farmers from other member countries. This, together with the need to get the full return from the open market and not from guarantees, is already forcing a reappraisal of British agricultural marketing.

Farm systems that have traditionally been highly profitable are becoming, almost overnight in farming terms, only marginally so. World price rises are playing a part here, although the clear pattern of profitability within the different systems that has existed for around 20 or 30 years is changing.

Mr Laurence Gould, chairman of Lugg & Gould of Warwick, one of the country's largest agricultural consultants, says: 'Tremendous changes are taking place in farming because of the EEC and because of the rise in world prices. The pattern over the years has, more or less, been the same. Pig production has been one of the most profitable concerns, followed by potatoes, vegetables, dairy farming, cereals and sheep farming, with beef a long, long way behind. But it does look as if this order is being turned on its head.'

Beef: Europe is still extremely hungry for beef. As incomes improve, beef consumption rises and there is a demand for quality cattle. One side-effect of this demand is of great significance for British agriculture. Now that Continental markets are more accessible to the Irish, they have begun diverting supplies of beef away from the British market. Beef prices on the Continent have traditionally been higher than in Britain. The gap between the British and the EEC levels was to have been closed gradually over five years, but the world price rises have virtually wiped out much of this difference in the past year. Prices for best British cattle were going around £13 a live hundredweight in 1972. Now they are about £17 or £18.

Cereals: The cereal farmer is having a boom. He has never had a year like last year. If he was making £12 or £15 an acre a couple of years ago, he would have doubled that figure in 1973. But the high cereal prices hit directly at the country's livestock producers. They are now expecting even higher increases as British support levels go up, and because of this they are beginning to use substitutes in animal feed where they can.

Milk: The most striking difference between dairying in the EEC and the United Kingdom is the consumption per head of liquid milk. In the United Kingdom the figure is about 31 gallons a year compared with only 18 gallons in Europe. The introduction of support buying for butter and skimmed-milk powder will have important consequences for the dairy industry in Britain. Until recently these sectors have been unprofitable for producers who concentrate their efforts on milk for drinking. The introduction of support for the products will step up production on the manufacturing side, and the country's import needs, in particular for butter and cheese, are likely to fall rapidly.

Under the EEC's new regulations there is a real incentive to switch from dairying to beef, another example of the changing farming patterns. Grants are being introduced to encourage farmers to make the switch, although it is not yet known how many farmers are taking up the offer. A dairy farmer who kept 11 or more dairy cows on June 4 1973, a reference date, is eligible for a grant, providing he gives up selling and supplying milk and milk products for a period of four years and changes to keeping beef cattle or sheep, or both, and to maintain his livestock numbers throughout the four-year period.

Pig producers: Those who stand to lose most in the switch to the common agricultural policy are the producers of pork and bacon and other pig products. They are finding themselves without the complex support system that has operated in the United Kingdom and they will have to get their returns from a free and open market where the competition is extremely tough.

Horticulture: The British industry is facing many problems and as far as the Common Market is concerned is exposed to two dangers. One is well-organised competition, particularly from the Dutch. The other is competition based on natural climatic advantages – from the Italians, for example. The industry did not feel any great pressure in 1973, but there is every chance this picture will change this year, and many say that the 'marginal producers' could find themselves in deep trouble and might even be forced out of business.

Many farmers are also facing major problems in financing their farm operations. Credit from the agricultural merchants who deal mainly with the banks is going to cost farmers more in future because of the high interest rates. Merchants are paying at least 30 per cent more for their goods now than a year ago and according to the BASAM, the merchants' trade association, rising prices and the need for more working capital at high rates of interest have caught the merchants in a trap. A lot have to pass on the extra costs. Laurence Gould comments: 'I believe that the problems of United Kingdom farming are not going to be problems of profitability in the future but of liquidity. With costs rising, farmers are going to need something like 30 per cent more to finance their business concerns. There will be a great need for capital to be made available, certainly over the next two years. The farming industry has swung round from being very afraid of the EEC to feeling very optimistic. Farmers went through a period of utter despondency to a state of euphoria, and are now reasonably optimistic. They have reservations in certain directions and liquidity is going to be a big problem.'

In practice, British farming has operated under a capital grants system whereby farmers have been given grants of about 40 per cent for building expansion, farm improvement, land draining, etc. Through the transitional period of entry the grants are falling away. On January 1 the new EEC scheme came into operation and means that drainage grants are cut, pig producers can receive grants only after stringent limitations and poultry producers do not receive any kind of assistance. Sir Henry Plumb, president of the National Farmers' Union, says that the problems the farmers are facing over finance will undoubtedly have its effect on farm expansion and modernisation. 'It will also remove the opportunity for a number of young farmers to come into the industry.'

A breakdown of farming finance shows clearly that the bulk of money for reinvestment needs to come from outside the industry. If the net income from farming, now £800m, is divided between the country's 200,000 farmers, it works out at £4,000 per farm. With half this figure needed for living expenses and a further amount for tax, it is easy to see, even in this crude example, that there is little left for reinvestment. Added to the financial problem is the fact that land prices have soared over the past year. According to the Ministry of Agriculture, prices went up by £126 per acre during the six months up to the end of September. The average price for the 228,608 acres sold during that period was £506 an acre, compared with £380 an acre for 227,800 acres sold six months previously.

The biggest increase in land prices has been in farms of fewer than 50 acres and in large sporting estates. This means that Britain is now rapidly catching up with the highest prices for land within the EEC. The National Farmers' Union firmly believes that the combination of high land prices and higher interest rates could well lead to a slowing down in the farm expansion rate. The dramatic rise in world prices coincided with Britain's entry into the Common Market and affected farmers greatly during 1973. The world grain situation has swung from surplus to deficit and made prices soar. This makes it extremely difficult to assess the direct effect of entry on Britain's farmers.

In egg and poultry meat production feeding stuffs can be as high as 80 per cent of the total costs, in pig production as high as 75 per cent, and in intensive beef, 65 per cent. In dairying it is between 50 and 60 per cent. So any rise in feed prices strikes straight at the heart of livestock profitability.

Another problem is that because of the long production cycle in livestock farming there is always a time lag between buying the feed and being paid for the product, straining the cash flow even further. There is little escape from this situation for the intensive livestock producers, but the cattle and sheep farmers are able to make more use of grass to cut their costs.

To try to discover the exact effects of the EEC agricultural policy on British farming the agricultural adjustment unit at Newcastle University is building a 'computer farm' based on some 50 average farms. The unit hopes eventually to be able to find the best farming system under EEC conditions – something most British farmers, including Rob Foster, would like to know.

MALCOLM PITHERS

BLAZING THE OLD TRAILS
April 22 1974
There is a strange irony in the fact that more than 300 men and women are riding about quiet country places on noisy, smelly motorcycles claiming as they go that they are preserving our British environment. They are members of the Trail Riders' Fellowship, whose object is to seek out and keep open off-road trails which might otherwise fall into disuse or be ploughed up or barred off to suit the convenience of farmers or landowners.

The trail riders are very serious about their mission, although of course they enjoy themselves into the bargain as they blast over grass, mud and stones on purpose-built machines. Their trail-bikes, mostly Japanese, are catalogue models made for on or off-highway use with knobbly tyres, good ground clearance, upswept exhaust pipes and high footrests. They are a cross between what used to be called trials machines – used for mud-plugging over rugged courses and up impossible hills – and normal road machines. Trials have largely given way to motocross, which is like grass-racing with all the grass worn away and allied to great leaps into the air.

Trails are more gentlemanly than trials. The riders go out in groups for a potter round their special routes, which they look up on the definitive maps in local council offices to establish that there is a right of way. However, farmers do not always agree and they have been met with shotguns, just as rally-drivers have met burning straw bales on their routes. Sometimes the ground rides are sponsored in aid of charities and these can raise hundreds of pounds.

All this sprang from the Countryside Act of 1968, under which local councils are required to survey what the riders call Green Lanes and decide their category. A Green Lane may be either a Rupp (Road used as a Public Path), a CRF (Cart Road Used as Footpath) or a Boat (Byway Open to All Traffic). Equally, it might be a footpath (for walkers) or a bridle path (for horses). Eventually, if everybody lives long enough, they will all be categorised. The trail riders want to keep as many as possible open to wheeled traffic.

They have succeeded in preserving Pisspot Lane near Luton, which might have been lost when the new Offley bypass was opened; averting closure of the old London Road near Henley; and successfully pressing for an underpass on the M40 near Stokenchurch. When the survey is complete they may ride on Rupps which will become byways, but CRFs will still be open to argument.

Mr E. A. Wrigley, director of the Trail Riders' Fellowship, lives right on the dual Hendon Way into London, fortunately behind double glazing as befits a country lover. He is a wild enthusiast, house decorated with one-inch maps, correspondence files with the British Horse Society, the Countryside Commission, the Ministry of This and That. He recalled with glee the time when a police car came to deal with a shotgun farmer. The crew disappeared into the farmhouse. An hour later a second police car came to rescue the first. The riders won the day.

Unsurprisingly, the motorcyclists are not always popular with fellow country lovers. Trail riders say: 'Horses create hell. One place we had three hunts in a week galloping through and they made the lane impassable.' But John Blackmore of the British Horse Society said: 'We are agreed with them over keeping green roads open, but the motorcycle and the horse are not good bedfellows, because motorcycles are so noisy. We prefer that Rupps should be downgraded to bridle paths.'

For the walkers, Christopher Hall, national secretary of the Ramblers' Association, said: 'We don't always see eye to eye with the Trail Riders. As far as keeping open tracks is concerned we are in agreement. Our disagreement is over whether Rupps are generally suitable for use by motor vehicles of any kind. Our line is that there is need for tracks in the countryside where you don't have the internal combustion engine.' Back to Mr Wrigley: 'A big group of ramblers makes for more noise than a motorcycle, and we have opened up for others many lanes not used for years.'

So if you are out walking on a Rupp or a Boat or a CRF and a motorcyclist showers you with mud and smoke give him a cheery wave and try to remember he claims to be preserving the environment for your family.

GEORGE BISHOP

ENGLISHMEN'S CASTLES: 'THE DESTRUCTION OF THE ENGLISH COUNTRY HOUSE' AT THE VICTORIA AND ALBERT MUSEUM
October 9 1974

European Conservation Year has opened with a massive plea for the preservation of the English country house, and it could scarcely have come at a worse time. In a climate of economic crisis we can hardly be expected to have much sympathy for the lord who is forced through economic straits to 'transfer his flag to a smaller house'. Who can raise a tear for the withering of the great estates at a time of land and housing shortage?

For the kind of country house in question is the real thing: the massive pile complete with estate, farm land, landscaped gardens, art collection: the lot. The reason for such alarm on the part of the conservationists – and as expressed in Roy Strong's exhibition – is the fact that such entities continue to disappear or be broken up. Since the war 250 major examples have gone, and that was after the post-war Gower Report recommended government help and relief to the owners in maintaining their seats. Such help immediately raises a host of political questions and principles, the most obvious of which is inevitably why should public money be used to prop up the possessions of a privileged few?

The visitor to the V&A exhibition is given a disagreeable choice: either he is identified with the pitiless vandalism of the demolition man's ball or he is asked to sympathise with the 'luckless owners', with those 'who actually struggle to live in a great house'. Strong admits that there are moral problems involved in it all, but his rhetoric has the same arm-twisting effect. He finds an analogy in the smashing of the monasteries at the Dissolution. He appeals to the British sense of history and pomp: 'The great houses of England and their occupants represent a continuity within our society.'

Another contributor to the exhibition, John Harris, refers to the great estate system as ruled by the landed gentry around 1875 as 'a way of life that at its enlightened best was perhaps one of the happiest social structures that western man has ever achieved'. But this is nothing compared to the cloud cuckoo land inhabited by another contributor to the Thames & Hudson book/catalogue. James Lee-Milne sings sad stories of the woes of privilege and property. He traces the cause of the downfall of the English country house: 'The few left fulfilling the purpose for which they were built are inexorably doomed. The causes are only too well known: penal taxation and the dearth of domestic helpers. Furthermore, the spirit of the age is against what is termed "privilege". God knows, the privilege of slaving in a palace without help and with responsibility for valuable contents is less than that of living carefree in a cosy cottage with every mod con. But how often is this factor appreciated by the increasing millions who visit the country houses which they – as the electorate – are busy destroying?'

Such garrulous hysteria is not only loony (to use one of Dr Strong's favourite words), it is also counterproductive. These houses were built through the dynamism and the greed of the families who held power in a certain form of society. Few people are so unobjective that they would deny that the visual traces that remain of this power have taste and flair and beauty, and that it would be a good thing to keep them as well as possible for the pleasure of everyone. But to suggest that because continuity is involved (cf. Jane Austen, Henry James, Virginia Woolf, Evelyn Waugh, etc.) the position of privilege that produced them should be maintained or reproduced through public money is patently nonsense.

There are ample examples illustrated in the exhibition of former stately homes that have been turned over for uses more in keeping with a less feudal society. It would have been wiser to concentrate on these than moan on about the poor rich, again with the suggestion that the alternative is the bogey of nationalisation. The National Trust and the Historic Building Councils alone cannot cope financially for the whole responsibility and neither is there any point in turning all of them into dead museums.

The encouragement of local authority involvement is a positive alternative to Harry Hyams of Ramsbury, whether for division into flats, expensive though it is, or for public use. There is no reason why – if the problem were placed on a more public basis and organised properly – the gardens that are probably the greatest visual contribution the English ever made, should be allowed to wither away. And neither is there any excuse for the restriction of access to miles of the finest land in the country.

CAROLINE TISDALL

PEOPLE'S HISTORY*

May 1 1975

All is not safely gathered in, even by diligent historians who can liken themselves to those stooped figures coming long after the swish of the scythe to glean the stubble left upon the vast acres which stretch back to the dense thicket at the edge of the mist. But the old cry of 'Harvest home!', a shout of triumph at the door of the barn, can justly greet the first sheaves from the history workshops held at Ruskin College for the past eight years. *Village Life and Labour* is indeed a fruitful start to what will be a dozen volumes designed 'to offer some examples of what "people's history" is or might be about'. It is a marvellous book, unexpectedly moving, zestful and yet plangent in its sweep and feeling, as clear to the mind as the rasp of the stone that once sharpened the fagging hook.

The four essays begin with a short piece from Raphael Samuel which indicate the extent of our ignorance about the life of the village labourer of the 19th century. The birds wheeling and screaming behind the plough have had their diet and their nesting places described with more loving care than the men, women and children bent at work upon the fields. Yet the very act of asking the right questions about what has been ignored compels the reader to shift his imagination into the cramped cottages and the gaps between the hedges or ditches. The ploughmen, stockmen, shepherds, harvesters and travelling gangs who toiled from dawn to dusk, adapting to the seasons, clearing the smallest shelter for themselves against the bleak imperatives of poverty, begin to emerge out of the anonymities of orthodox history.

The English countryside was more densely peopled and extensively cultivated by the middle of the last century than ever before or since. At harvest time a great throng of workers swarmed over the land, cutting, shocking and tying the crop. David

* Raphael Samuel (ed.), *Village Life and Labour* (London: Routledge & Kegan Paul, 1975)

Morgan's alert description of how the harvest altered the rhythm of rural life and, for the only time of the year, gave work and a little bargaining power to all the family, pulls one closer still to the life of the farmhand. 'It was because the fields were so crowded and so much extra labour of all ages was employed that harvest time was an occasion of drama, of distress and even of tragedy.' The voices can now be more distinctly heard, though still as from a great distance, out there where the horse-rake has passed and before winter presses down in hungry and frozen silence.

Women and children found it a bit 'easier' to earn a pittance when the ripe corn stood ready for the blade. In the third segment Jennie Kiteringham details the many domestic handicrafts, the uncelebrated resilience and the endurance of labouring women out in all winds and weather, skirts tucked up in an 'immoral' bundle, mud sometimes halfway up to the knees; the endless striving of village women to keep some food on the plate and some hope in the cupboard. Perhaps in inevitable reaction to the male-orientated obtuseness of much history this is the only part of the book which tries to underline what it reveals.

But if ever justification should be sought for the methods of the History Workshop, the final contribution – which takes up half the book – is sufficient answer. Described as 'an essay in oral history', Raphael Samuel's 'quarry roughs' brings us nearer to the present and closer to the town with an outstandingly remarkable account of life in the village of Headington Quarry, near Oxford, between 1860 and 1920. 'All 'oles and alleys and 'ills, that's what Quarry is, all up and down,' this plebeian settlement has no postcard ivy or village green, and none of 'Akenfield's' mellowed charm. A struggling community opens out before us, alive at first bounce in the speech and memory of its oldest survivors.

'I can remember as if it was yesterday,' comes a voice, one of many. The chopping block at the back door, the jug for boot money on the shelf, the dog and the rabbit, the sweat and scrimping and modest hope, a people's history to the marrow of the bone. A distillation so tangible and human, so full of the means by which working men and women faced up to their narrowing horizons with all the skill and wit and tenacity of their own resource of spirit that it is surely impossible to read it without quickening emotion and gratitude. I urge you to get hold of this achingly lucid book, if only to temper the cynicism and weary cant which is the late harvest of our own thermoplastic capitalism. Today's publication date is not fortuitous.

DENNIS POTTER

COUNTRY MATTERS

June 28 1975

When Gordon Beningfield cuts the grass in his back garden he mows round a cluster of buttercups and daisies. They are too pretty to destroy. The rhubarb has keeled over because there's knee-high coltsfoot thrusting through the clump. It would be a shame to disturb it.

Land that runs down to the trout stream is a rampant wilderness of cow parsley and dandelions, nettles and thistles, grasses and so on down the index of the wildflower guide. The drone of a thousand insects rises into the glaring June afternoon. Large whites and small whites dither over the flower heads; young sparrows, L-fliers, crashland on telegraph wires; bullfinches hunt the caterpillars; a mouse-grey flycatcher darts from a branch and it's the end of the afternoon for someone.

Beningfield, naturalist and artist, is afraid that unless more gardens are treated as nature reserves it will be the end for most wildlife, too. For its Environment Year effort – an Endangered Species exhibition at the Tryon Gallery, London – the Flora and Fauna Preservation Society sent him to paint the large blue and tortoiseshell butterfly, the dormouse and the monkey orchid. But there are any number of creatures doomed because their food supply and habitat are being snatched away.

'Our agricultural methods of tearing and smashing everything apart are entirely to blame,' he says. 'Butterflies, for example, are all endangered now because their habitat is wiped out with the hedgerows. All naturalists can do is ask people to leave nettles and patches of rough ground around in their gardens for the butterflies' food. Instead gardeners and farmers are spraying insecticide and weedkiller like mad, killing off food plants and, eventually, whole species. Sometimes I think spraying is the disease of the 20th century.'

His 1630 cottage was derelict on the corner of one of Hertfordshire's big country estates when he began to haggle for it. He fought a building society who said it didn't comply with building regulations and he transformed it into a much admired home for his wife, daughter and their pets – a deerhound that mumbles in his sleep, a terrier and a tortoise. The land was derelict, too, but the neighbours who looked forward to lawns sweeping down to the trout will stay disappointed.

He's sure that the Victorian craze for collecting specimens and eggs did far less harm than modern chemicals in the countryside. 'We have banned insecticides in the past few years and the manufacturers have made others safer. They tell us they have stopped killing the ladybird, but they did it for 20 years without a qualm. And they are proud they have invented a selective weedkiller. Well, they should have thought of one in the first place. I don't understand how they could make so many mistakes.'

Born a Londoner, Beningfield moved to Hertfordshire when he was three, has lived in the county ever since and can't remember a time when he wasn't passionately interested in the countryside. After St Albans School of Art he worked 13 years for an Anglican firm producing stained- and engraved-glass windows, heraldry and sculpture. But all the while he was studying natural history and selling his paintings. Then, with six months work ordered by the Tryon and pressure to take on more, he realised he had to give all his time to his painting.

That was 10 years ago, 10 years which saw him become one of the most successful wildlife artists in Britain. His vast knowledge of natural history gives him a scope unequalled by competitors restricted to one or two fields. Benington's work moves on in phrases. There was a time when he was 'the dormouse man'. Another time he was into badgers. Now it's butterflies.

So what would happen if he took a fancy to something with less eye-appeal? Suppose he felt an urge for beetles or spiders or anything else with a high shudder ratio? It wouldn't matter, he says. He was warned off butterflies because they wouldn't sell like birds or furry little animals. They did.

He sees his roles as artist and naturalist inseparably entwined. 'The most important thing about natural history paintings is that they should excite people to go and look at and think about the real thing. If something has great beauty and subtlety people will appreciate it, but I feel an artist should add a little bit of his own quality, use a little licence. If I'm painting thistledown I feel I must make it appear even softer than it is, even more delicate. For an exact reproduction I could take a photograph, but that is not what painting is about, it is about stressing the beauty of the subject.'

He sketches as much as possible from real life, only resorting to specimens when the subject is very scarce. It is a life that finds him all over the country. The Endangered Species exhibition took him to several regions, including the Thames Valley for a secret rendezvous with the elusive monkey orchid. A series on bird life and mammals in Scotland sees him crossing the border frequently. Butterflies and wild flowers often mean Dorset, where they were reluctant to hack down their thick hedges.

'When I sketch an animal I am trying to capture the character and attitude of it. Details like the fur or the colouring I can check later. I don't need to catch butterflies to keep any more – if I need a specimen I can buy it from a farm – but I go and watch them as much as possible. It's very exciting catching them, more exciting than any sport. Fifty or 60 years ago you could rush around like a maniac with a net gathering them up, they were everywhere. Now you've got to find one before you can start.'

There was a television film of him once doing just that, running up and down a ride through the forest with a butterfly net in his hand. It was a programme which fed the growing public interest in the countryside and so he was glad to take part. It taught him something, too. 'There was a dandelion clock so I sat down to draw it. They filmed the clock, then me drawing it and then superimposed my finished painting. The response was fantastic. The number of people who rang the television people to ask about buying it was amazing. They had all suddenly realised that a dandelion clock is a beautiful thing. They had been made to realise; I had shown them.

'People will not make these value judgments on their own. They are afraid to. It's partly that we are growing away from the countryside, forgetting how to look at it. When you drive through it you can't see the hedgerows and have no idea what is growing or living there. Wildlife programmes on the television or radio are popular, but so many people who enjoy them cannot even look at a dandelion clock without help and say "This is beautiful."'

Although he's keen to educate and bolster an interest in wildlife, he has not moved into the expanding book market. Every approach for illustrations has been rejected. 'Illustrations are not works of art, they are just a job and need a different approach. But I so much want to bring the fate of our butterflies to the public eye that I would like to publish a book of paintings on them. When I paint I like to give an idea of the whole countryside, its colour and its warmth. The butterflies I want in my book would have a great quality of the beauty we are throwing away.'

LESLEY GRANT ADAMSON

VILLAGE CHAMPION

July 1 1976

The driver of the Coldharbour post bus is also the postman, and as the scarlet and yellow mini-bus climbs the lanes from Dorking he stops to check the post boxes planted in overgrown hedgerows. At Coldharbour, the highest village in the southeast of England, the bus pauses briefly at the Plough and the post office before plunging through the narrow green lanes down the side of Leith Hill towards Ockley, leaving the Coldharbour passengers to walk home past one of the finest views in Surrey. In summertime the Coldharbour post bus carries a number of sightseers who ride just to look at the scenery, but for the villagers it is the only regular public transport they have.

The successful fight for a post-bus service when the regular service was chopped was one of Mrs Irene Jackson's proudest achievements. She was president of the local Women's Institute at the time and because of the bus and because of her long experience in the WI – she's now vice-president of the Surrey Federation – the Council for the Protection of Rural England (CPRE) invited Mrs Jackson to join their working party on the Future of the Village. 'They wanted someone at grass roots level. In fact,' said Mrs Jackson, with a giggle, 'they said they wanted me because of my experience on the ground.'

The working party was set up when the council decided that its approach to rural life had concentrated too much on the visual aspect, the roses round the door. So it asked a panel of experts on rural life to look into the realities of the village, into housing, social services, job opportunities, and to come up with a serious national policy on the future of village life in Britain. The working party has just completed its findings and they hope that the report will be published later this year. One thing they all agreed on was what a village was, the essence of what they called 'villageness' being community spirit rather than stone and thatch.

'You can have a country village which is not really a village,' explained Irene Jackson, 'and on the other hand you can have villages in a place like London. People who've lived in towns often appreciate village life very much more than the people who've lived there all their life. In Coldharbour the people who've lived here all their lives don't mind change. It's the incoming people who want to preserve the place exactly as it is. I came first from Woodford in Essex, which was absolutely suburbia. You didn't know anybody around. Then we moved to North Holmwood near Dorking, and 13 years ago we moved to Coldharbour. There was a bus service every hour 13 years ago and when we first moved here there was a village school – I think when the school goes that's the beginning of the end of a village. Now, oddly enough, we've got enough children to support a school, but it's gone and that's that.'

It is Mrs Jackson's experience as a fulltime member of a village community that has made her of value to the CPRE, coupled with her natural common sense and practicality. In addition she has had the experience in the WI of travelling all over Surrey to other villages. Despite its proximity to London, Surrey still has large pockets of rural England and its villages are as vulnerable to decline as anywhere else – as likely to be affected by the cutting of transport, the neglect by councils, the unemployment that means death to a living village.

'When you're in the WI you do get to know so much about village life. I see an amazing difference between populations of villages that are the same size. In some villages they still have the proper balance of age, social standing, occupation, but once you get an overwhelming preponderance of commuters then it does throw the balance out. In a WI meeting you can see whether there's a good cross section or whether there's a more coffee-morning sort of feeling. In Coldharbour at the moment I'd say we're fairly well balanced. We've lost something from the wealthy end and from the other end too. There are about 200 people and we still have a lot of people who've lived here all their lives, but as houses fall vacant they're being bought up by people with more money. I should think there are three weekend cottages in the village, though lots of people commute to London and quite a few people work locally.'

One of the tasks of the committee was to draw up a list of the facilities they considered essential to a living village. First on Mrs Jackson's list was some sort of meeting place, a village hall. Then a church, although she admits that the church as a centre of village life is dying. Third came a proper village pub, not the kind which serves expense-account dinners; and fourth was a general store and post office. Coldharbour has all of these, and it runs a lively sports and social club which takes part in cricket and football tournaments in the summer. Both Mrs Jackson and her husband, a lecturer at Guildford County College of Technology, take an active part in most village activities.

'I think that since I've lived here Coldharbour has gained villageness, but then when we moved it was possibly at a very low ebb. In previous years it had been so go-ahead, they'd had a brass band and a flourishing WI with around 50 members. There are 27 members now. Then it fell off, people grew older, the school closed, the buses stopped. No village is static. They have ups and downs and there's no real rhyme or reason in it.'

Although Coldharbour has retained its villageness, its original function as an estate village for a large house has entirely gone, and with it the social structure that used to be at the heart of village life. The house now belongs to Oliver Reed, the actor, and the village looks outwards for services and social care. Coldharbour has kept a spirit of concern for its inhabitants – not noseyness, says Mrs Jackson – but with the arrival of commuters and weekenders the English village has become inhabited by part-timers and in many villages the problem of loneliness has arisen.

'Old people do get lonely. In Coldharbour we look out for people and we call, but where you get a change in the village is when people come and don't want to take part. In the days of the big house the social services were provided by the lady of the manor, but that's all over. Nowadays you get loneliness and this is where social services are required. Things like Meals on Wheels bring not only a meal but they bring company.'

The future of the village, according to Mrs Jackson's personal experience and her findings on the working party, is not too bright. Through the findings of the committee she has become aware of the problems of villages which are suffocated by the building of large new estates which fail to integrate. And on the other hand there are many villages suffering from sheer starvation and lack of facilities. Lack of work is at the root of the village's decline and she feels strongly that small industries must be brought back to villages if they are to grow naturally and without any loss of villageness. She is also realistic enough to realise that some villages are inevitably doomed.

'I would be sorry to see villages disappear, but I feel it's inevitable. I can't help feeling a little bit dismal about the future of little villages. You can't expect councils to pour money into transport and services so they will become retreats for people who really want to get away from it all – and that's not what a village is.'

LESLEY GARNER

A COUNTRY DIARY: KESWICK

June 13 1977

I had a note recently from someone connected with the 'Country Diary' who said, with perhaps a touch of nostalgia: 'When I was a kid, dogs used to run after cars and woodlice rolled up like armadillos when poked with a finger; neither seem now to behave in their ancient ways, is there a thought here for geneticists?' Dogs elsewhere may not run after cars but some sheep dogs here still crouch in the grass and run at them – very unnerving. The second remark set me turning over old wood in the garden, but there was never a curl in any common woodlouse. Were his armadillos, perhaps, pill beetles, which curled to look like small peppermint humbugs – or have I missed something? Some things have taken on new ways, like the crows who drop on to motorways to snatch tit-bits under the very wheels of the traffic – and how many do you see killed? Almost none.

Some places, some creatures, however, stay happily much the same. I spent part of a hot day lately on a peat moss in south Cumbria; butterflies drifted over it; there was a froth of May blossom and cow parsley; birds sang and the man who was working there had time to talk in a leisurely way. Rows of chocolate-brown peat lay to dry in the sun. Adders, he said, are very plentiful this year, all over the moss and even looped on the road – 'Give you a nasty nip, they will,' and with that he hurriedly picked up his jacket from the turf, shook it vigorously, and draped it on a thorn. Adders like other people's clothes and I was reminded of another man who used to dig peat from a 'flow' beside the Solway Firth. He said that if he left his gold watch in his waistcoat pocket there he might expect to find an adder curled close about it. What attracted them, I wonder, the sound or the feel? It needs a herpetologist, not a geneticist, to answer that one.

ENID J. WILSON

COUNTRY MEETS FOLK
August 29 1977

South, scree plummets sheer into chill blue lake. East, the great giants of the Lake District, the barrier between Wasdale and the rest of the world – Great Gable, Scafell, The Pillar: barren, bleached, the colour baked out of them by the 80 degree severity of a summer sun they are unused to. North, across the lake, some green land struggling to force the darker green of the rough fell to retreat up the lower slopes – not much, but enough for Jos Naylor to scrape a living from Bowderdale Farm.

Scrape is Jos Naylor's word. Given the option of describing the living he makes as 'good', 'comfortable' or 'scraped', that is his word. He says it softly, but the meaning rings through the stone-cool kitchen; walls built thick not to keep out this summer sun but to parry the fury of biting winter winds carrying sleet and snow and misery to the farm from the ice-peaked mountains. 'Scrape.' Yet Jos Naylor is the iron man of the Lake District, the marathon man of the fells – 108 miles taking in 72 peaks at over 2,000ft – run by him in the 24-hour race with time to spare. He allows himself to be pleased with that record made two years ago. But it takes a feat of that stature to impress him. So when he says life as a Lake District fell farmer is hard, you believe him.

Wet, cold, wretched; 15 miles a day, thigh-deep in snow searching the fell bottoms for sheep – a way of life in winter on the big farms. And on the small ones – something like a thousand sheep to shear single-handed in summer. In spring, crops to sow, then haytime, and five times a year the hundreds of acres of cruel, steepsided fell and gully to climb and cover, one man and six dogs, raking in the sheep – lambing, clipping, dipping, tubbing and in the winter just keeping them alive.

And in between – feeding, ditching, walling, you name it, it needs doing and not enough hands to do it. 'Stone walls, whitewashed farmhouses, slow-voiced farmers, sheep dogs, sheep' – the visitor's image of Lakeland described by the National Trust regional information officer, Christopher Hanson-Smith. The same scene represents a hard slog to Jos Naylor, with no money to pay for labour on small farms these days and no skilled labour if you could pay for it. 'A farmer isn't going to work himself to death to pay somebody a better wage than he pays himself.

'I was up at 10 past three this morning to fetch some sheep in before it got too hot for the dogs. Cruel to dogs this weather. We were back here by half-past eight.' Then his day began. It didn't finish until gone midnight. 'Some nights in summer I don't get to bed at all.'

But this is how it always was: the physical privations, the financial hardships taken for granted. Like their Herdwick sheep, they became a special breed. 'Put a hill farmer on a lowland farm and he'd be lost,' said one farmer. 'But put a lowland farmer on the fells and he wouldn't survive. These men know every wretched inch of land and every wretched sheep.'

Jos Naylor's time-off is tougher than his work. He regularly tops off his day in the early hours with a punishing jog-trot 800 feet up The Pillar. 'It is the freedom of being up there at night alone.' The farm demands the same kind of mental commitment and physical endurance as his fell running. 'It is the price you pay,' he says, 'for living surrounded by such beauty.' And here is the real hardship that has hit the fell farmer.

For now the real asset he once had has been taken from him. The remoteness, the splendid harsh, satisfying grandeur, the close-knit dalehead communities are saturated with sightseers, backpackers, hikers, climbers, the quiet, the curious, the crag rats in every conceivable nook and cranny.

'You should see them in a morning leaving the National Trust camp site at my brother's farm. It's like flies off a dead sheep's back – they just scatter in every direction over his land to get on to the fells. He's virtually had to go into hiding to shear his sheep. He couldn't get on with the job for the number of people wanting to watch him.

'If it carries on it will be impossible to farm this valley in another 10 years. You can't move sheep on the road for the number of cars. A lot of them won't give way if they see stock on the road or a dog working with the sheep. And gone are the days when you could leave stock in a field and expect to find them in the same place the next day. People seem to think that because this is a National Park the public own the land, but that isn't so. And some of the worst offenders are those who have paid their subscriptions to the National Trust and feel they have a right to go anywhere.'

The Trust owns 85,000 acres in Cumbria, including 71 hill farms. Its latest acquisitions are seven farms – including one down the road from Jos Naylor at Nether

Wasdale – a gift from the Lake District Farm Estates. But while its prime object is to preserve the character of the area, its initial function has been to support the farmers. 'We are in business to keep the farmers in business, because they are the ones who preserve the land in the traditional pattern,' said Mr Hanson-Smith. But some farmers resent the presence of the Trust, feeling it has access to financial resources, unavailable to them, which allows it to buy farms from under them. Private farmers could no longer hope to pay the staggering price of farms in the face of competition from organisations or wealthy individuals looking for holiday homes. 'We could if we could buy the place first, then advertise on television for the money through public subscription,' accused one farmer.

Even the Lake District Farm Estates, a society with parallel aims to the Trust, which set out to buy farms within a 20-mile radius of the Langdale Pikes to preserve the most isolated and therefore commercially vulnerable daleheads, has gone to the wall. Unlike the Trust, which is a charity, it did not benefit from tax concessions, and the gift of its last seven farms to the Trust because of 'the rising cost of farms and the high interest rates on borrowed money' is the epitaph on its work.

Not that hill farming has become less profitable than it always was. 'But it is difficult to keep farms going if you intend to keep them looking like Lake District farms – the cost of renewing a slate roof with slate is a different matter to putting on asbestos,' said the society's chairman, Mr Cuthbert Acland. The cost of prettying up a farm in Lakeland tradition – planners can control farm building, but grants are discretionary – has no direct commercial return. Indirectly, it attracts the visitors with a subsequent rake-off for whoever fills a need. Yet the visitors are killing off the very valleys the National Trust is trying to preserve for them.

It is a problem which has been occupying the Lake District Planning Board for some time. And in its recent draft plan for the National Park it acknowledges that it is the small farms like Jos Naylor's which epitomise the character of the Lake District and which must be preserved – it doesn't quite say 'at all costs', because perhaps then somebody might ask where the money is coming from. But perhaps the emphasis is in the right place.

The plan spotlights the dangers of losing more small farms – between 1963 and 1973 the number fell by 20 per cent, with a 23 per cent decrease on the labour force. At one time farmhands, needed during haytime and shearing, were put to work repairing walls and maintaining the farm in the slacker periods. Now they are an unobtainable luxury. 'This landscape, which reflects a labour-intensive form of farming, continues to show many signs of neglect, such as collapsed walls and the invasion of bracken,' reports the draft plan. 'A further loss of farmers and farm labour due either to farm amalgamation or further decline in the viability of hill farming will not only result in the continued deterioration of the landscape but will also add to the problems of rural depopulation' – another essential ingredient of the area's character.

'The hill-farming areas are naturally disadvantaged – the combination of poor and variable soil quality, a short growing season, difficult accessibility and frequently severe winter weather conditions made it the least viable of all farm enterprises.' But not the least important. The hill farmer is the keystone in the national pattern of agriculture, supplying breeding stock and livestock for fattening on lowland farms. 'The Lake District hill farmer is by no means an anachronism,' said Mr Hanson-Smith, and this year the National Trust has initiated a cooperative scheme with a lowland estate to try to increase the hill farmer's slice of the profits. The value of total output from livestock production in the Lake District was estimated at £16m.

'If you wanted to run the Lake District on strict agricultural profits, it could be ranched on 100 or 200 farms,' said Mr Ken McKean, county secretary of the Cumbria branch of the National Farmers' Union. 'But we believe that would be a dreadful thing to happen here, and indeed it can't happen because the National Trust owns so much of the park. But if you are going to maintain your smaller units, you have to allow additional income – quarrying, tourism – and this is the next problem we have to tackle. Already some farmers have broken the planner's county code by erecting bed-and-breakfast directional signs where they shouldn't and have been threatened with prosecution. Conversely many National Trust farm tenants agree to take in visitors.

'The answer is that in the end if you want the scenic pattern and variety provided by the smaller farm, you have to pay for it,' said Mr McKean. 'If the British consumer insists on paying rock-bottom prices for farm products, then the public will have to decide how it wants to pay for the small farm, whether it is a tourist tax, payment for entry to the park or subvention through the government. The small farm can't just be held as a museum piece.

'The Planning Board has appreciated the fact that it cannot have a worthwhile Lake District without an economically viable agriculture. We have the words, now we want the deeds.' At the same time, Mr McKean acknowledges the success of the board's Upland Management Scheme, which involves 'the lads on the ground' and uses local labour rebuilding dry-stone walls, repairing footbridges and stiles, signposting footpaths; improving the quality of life for both farmers and visitors.

In the future, 'the board will consider acquiring a suitable hill farm for use as a demonstration farm, managed to combine the interests of efficient farm production with the need for conservation of the landscape and wildlife, and the promotion of recreation.' It has already organised farm tours and farm trails and places some faith in education as the answer to the problems between farmers and tourists. But realistically, if, pessimistically, it confesses: 'There is no obvious solution.'

Indeed, there is only one certainty. It is that for the likes of Jos Naylor the isolation and the solitude and the deeper satisfaction of surviving harsh environments is gone for ever. 'Imagine the entire population of Birmingham or Manchester walking into your office and watching you work,' said Mr McKean. 'That's just what it's like for the hill farmer in a National Park. The Lake District will be killed by over-visiting.'

And no matter where they park the cars, draw the footpaths or channel the visitors: with planners, conservationists and crag rats all breathing down his neck, the farmer is suffocating. And while they might preserve the shell, if the present trend in tourism continues, there is no way they can save his soul.

CYNTHIA BATEMAN

SOFTER AIR PERVADES VALLEY WHERE IRON USED TO RULE

August 16 1978

Rescue operations are being attempted for two of Britain's few remaining industrial villages built when iron was master. One of them is a crumbling community in the Pennine foothills at Ashton-under-Lyne, which may become the focus of an unusual partnership between a private builder and a local authority. The other is Golden Valley, a mid-Derbyshire hamlet where restoration work starts this month at a cost of £220,000, the most ambitious rescue project yet by the county's Historic Buildings Trust.

Park Bridge, the works and village near Ashton, is today strangely silent and pollution-free after the deafening hammers and sulphurous smoke of nearly two centuries. Until the iron-works closed 15 years ago the village was tenanted by 150 workers and their families out of a labour force which reached 800 at the height of the Industrial Revolution. In 1783 it had an iron mistress as well as an iron master when Hannah Buckloy married Samuel Lees, the first of a Lees dynasty which lasted until 1963.

They took over the forge of a whitesmith (dealing with metal in a different way from a blacksmith) and gradually Park Bridge developed into a dynamic industry.

Mainly, it made rollers for the cotton industry, but as cotton declined so did the works. Yet the big forge with its long slate roofs, undulating now with age, the huge building and chimneys of brick, the church, the cottages and the stables for 30 horses (before the railway came) still testify to a second Iron Age.

A former ironworker, Mr Norman Harvey, spoke about the boom time in one of the brick-built cottages where he has lived all his life. The works made quite a noise, the hammers going and smoke billowing out, blackening the houses and the sulphur scorching the grass. Today the tenants find it pleasanter to recall the Park Bridge garden fetes, harvest queens, billiards in the institute and tennis – provided by the philanthropic Lees. Mr Harvey now explains how green is his valley, with grass growing where the ground was bald.

The danger now is that the works – and still to some extent, the village – will be bulldozed to make the landscape for the Greater Manchester Council's continuing Medlock Valley countryside park. But Mrs Peggy Quinlan of Dingle Terrace says they will have to dynamite her out.

The Tameside Borough Council has been considering buying the village compulsorily for demolition, but is making one last effort to save it by proposing a deal with any private builder willing to buy the property at a nominal price and restore it, an idea put forward by the deputy leader, Councillor Alan Fearn. One basic condition: providing sewerage.

In Golden Valley 36 canalside cottages, originally homes for iron and coal-workers in the early Industrial Revolution, are virtually all that is left of the settlement near Ripley. Local craftsmen, however, will use original materials to turn the derelict cottages into comfortable and moderately priced homes. Financial aid is being given by the Civic Trust and the district council is making available historic buildings and general improvement area grants. Built around 1793, the stone cottages were for workers in small coal pits and iron stone mines.

MICHAEL MORRIS

ANGLING IS AS MUCH A COMPULSION AS INDECENT EXPOSURE
June 13 1979
If you have got a box of pinkies in your fridge and can mix a bucket of cloud so that it clings together in mid-air; if you can tell a brandling from a lob and prefer a fixed-spool to a centre-pin, you are probably too preoccupied right now to pay attention.

If, on the other hand, you haven't a clue what I'm talking about, then you are fortunate enough not to be a coarse angler. Luckier still, you are not married to one.

For next Saturday is the opening day of the coarse fishing season and some three million men, women and boys will converge on Britain's lakes and rivers. Each will be carrying anything up to half a hundredweight of gear, the value of which is probably a secret between the angler and the tackle dealer, but is certainly astronomical. Some will fall in the water; some will break something, a thermos flask, a rod or a leg. One or two may die and some will have to be rescued. All will be cold, damp, mosquito bitten and will return home smelling of a curious blend of mud, water weeds and fish slime.

Correction: only those who have caught fish will smell of the slime, and that smell, coupled with a mood or euphoria as opposed to bitter rancour or black despair, will be the only proof that they have actually caught anything, for almost without exception all the fish they have gone to so much time, trouble and expense to catch have been carefully returned alive to the water, to be caught again.

In fact trying to explain to a non-angler why a grown man should spend his leisure hours up to his scuppers in mud, blood and duckweed trying to catch a fish he can't eat, and probably wouldn't want to if he could, is like trying to explain to a Pakistani immigrant that while it is perfectly decent and honourable to hunt foxes with horses and hounds, setting two drunken quails to fight is not only despicable and cruel but illegal to boot. He may get the message, but he'll never understand.

I doubt if the anglers themselves understand why they angle. Many acres of print (to which, I confess, I have added my share) have been devoted to the rationalisation, or the poetic justification, of an act of sheer lunacy. Certainly anglers themselves, however articulate, cannot account for their addiction, and there is perhaps a PhD awaiting the guy who can shed some light on the mystery. He'd need to be a brave man, however, for anglers tend to get on the defensive when questioned about their motives. Perhaps an attractive woman would fare better.

True, angling satisfies the basic demands of the libido, providing a soothing sequence of desire, frustration and satisfaction, but one would have thought that other forms of human activity could cater for such needs better. I don't know, though. Frustration in one field has often led man to explore others, and if you think there's no post coitum triste in angling, try chatting up a tench fisherman after he's spent a night by the lake.

Some might argue that the fishing match or angling competition provides an excuse for mass insanity, and to be sure the thought of material gain, which at times can be considerable, is a point of contact between the angler and the non-angler.

Unfortunately, it is an historical fact that the fishing match evolved in those areas where water was so polluted and the fish so small that they weren't worth catching unless there was an additional motive. If they were honest, most anglers would admit that they would rather catch big fish than win a big match.

It's safest, perhaps, to dismiss the whole of angling by saying that it is as much a compulsion, in its way, as indecent exposure, although fortunately not carrying the same social stigma or penalties. Yet there are those who would like to see the sport so stigmatised and incur similar penalties. This is illogical, in a way, because while they might pity the flasher they feel no sorrow for the angler bowing under his burden of compulsion, and it is short sighted. So, like most myopic individuals, they are in danger of throwing the baby out with the bath water.

Coarse fishing is considered by many to be both cruel and unnecessary. Cruel it may or may not be, but all forms of human activity with animals involve cruelty from the keeping of domestic pets to factory farming, all of which are also mostly unnecessary. Angling is unnecessary, but so are all other forms of leisure activity, and at least angling is low on energy consumption.

Anglers at least serve one useful role in society, and though they should not for one moment be suspected of altruism, they nevertheless confer a greater benefit to mankind and his environment than many other sportsmen. The specimen fish that comes to the angler's net is the end product of a healthy, varied and incredibly complex way of life, and for this to occur, the water in which it all takes place must be free from pollution.

In theory we could have unpolluted waterways without anglers. In practice we could not. It is, I believe, as simple as that, for anglers have ever been the watchdogs of society in this respect, and always they have been the ones who have fought hardest to prevent and remedy water pollution. I suspect it will ever be so. Certainly it will until those who wish to abolish angling are prepared also to devote the same time, energy and finance as the anglers have done. I doubt if they are so willing.

All that the banning of angling will achieve will be to throw three million more neurotics on to the National Health list, and there they will stay, for angling is a form of hunting, and hunting is an old madness. It drove Neanderthal man from the warmth and comfort of his cave into the post-glacial wastes of Europe. It will drive the coarse fisherman out of his bed on Saturday and future morns. It is a madness too deeply engraved on the psyche to be erased by a few purple pills.

EWAN CLARKSON

FUEL FEARS OVER AGRICULTURAL SHOW

July 2 1979

The threat of a fuel shortage hangs over the Royal Agricultural Show, which opens in Stoneleigh, Warwickshire, today. As if to make the point, more than 100 heavy horses will be displayed, but the show will be dominated by new machinery and equipment, and more sophisticated breeding methods, seeds and chemicals, to enable farmers to produce crops and fatten animals quickly and profitably.

Demonstrations will show how keeping cows indoors throughout the summer leads to much steadier milk yields. Farmers will be shown how intensively stocked deer can be as economical to produce as lowland sheep. Mr Richard Butler, president of the National Farmers' Union, has said that farmers can make a strong claim on available fuel supplies and that farming was 'already a very efficient user of fuel'.

He has also urged farmers to conserve fuel, though at least one event – a pulling contest for tractors – encourages them to waste it. Carefully manicured pigs and cattle will belie the reality of the big business that agriculture has become. And exhibitors will pay special attention to visitors from abroad, who this year include delegations from China and Syria as well as at least three oil-producing countries – Venezuela, Nigeria and Qatar. But some research into energy-saving will also be apparent – a windmill and the potential of solar energy for drying grain.

RICHARD NORTON-TAYLOR

THREAT TO LAST SAXON FIELD SYSTEM

November 26 1979

Tenant farmers at Laxton, Nottinghamshire, are urging Mr Peter Walker – who, as minister of agriculture, is their lord of the manor – to think again before selling off the only village in England where the open field system of farming has been practised continuously since before the Norman Conquest.

The feudal fields of Laxton are part of the national heritage. Thousands of people visit them every year to see how today's farmers cultivate three fields in strips, with rotated crops, in much the same way as the serfs of Geoffrey Alselin, lord of the manor in 1086.

The Ministry of Agriculture bought the Laxton estate from the Earl of Manvers, 35th lord of the manor, in 1952. It is now to be sold as part of the government's rush to dispose of its assets for cash. No firm value has been put on the Laxton estate, but 1,860 acres, the farms, cottages and other properties should fetch well over £2m. One tenant farmer, Mr Edmund Rose, said: 'That kind of money is not going to put the country back on its feet; it's a drop in the ocean.'

The three Laxton open fields, covering about 500 acres of the estate, are not some kind of ancient monument, with a preservation order stuck on them. Only the goodwill of the tenants and the sensitive and sensible management of the Ministry have kept the open field system as a living part of history, an example of social and economic life that probably goes back to the time of the Saxon lord Tochi, son of Outi, before 1066. What worries Mr Rose, the other 13 tenant farmers and the four smallholders, is that the land will be sold off to some investor who, tiring of archaic farming, would scrap the open field system to get a better return for his money.

Though nobody at the Ministry was prepared to say as much, it is clear that some of its officers are unhappy about the proposed sale. The Ministry is hoping that 'some organisation such as the National Trust will be interested in preserving Laxton'. But the National Trust, anxious though it is to see the open fields preserved, does not have the kind of money needed to buy the estate. A spokesman said that since the government was intent on selling off assets, it was most unlikely that the National Trust would get Laxton as a gift.

If the Trust cannot afford Laxton, who else would buy it? The Ministry is busy making soundings of 'sympathetic people'. If it cannot find anyone willing to preserve the open fields, it would then have to reconsider the proposal to sell it. Mr Rose said: 'I don't think any of the tenants could afford to buy with the present high rate of interest. It would finish the open fields if they were sold off in the open market. Business interests would come in to sell a bit off here, a bit off there.'

The three open fields contain 150 strips, all without hedges or other boundaries, ranging in size from about half an acre to eight acres. The Ministry has pursued a policy of deliberate fragmentation so that a tenant does not have adjoining strips to farm. This may involve him in having to move half a mile from one strip to another. Such piecemeal farming is uneconomic, and this is reflected in the rents the farmers pay. Mr John Hoare, the Ministry's regional surveyor, said that if the farmers once started amalgamating strips, this ancient system could disappear within 30 years.

Until 1968 one field was sown with winter wheat, one with spring corn, and a third allowed to lie fallow. A special meeting of Laxton's baronial court leet then decided to change the system. Instead of leaving one field fallow, the spring corn was undersown with grass to be harvested as a hay crop in the following year. The court leet, of which Mr Rose is bailiff, sees that the old system is maintained by imposing fines of from 20p to £5 on farmers who encroach on other strips, leave the ends of their strips untidy or dump manure heaps on the sykes – permanent grass strips which play no part in the rotation of crops. Half the money raised in fines goes towards the meal at the village inn for the court leet jury. The other half goes to the coffers of the lord of the manor.

MICHAEL PARKIN

MILLIGAN EGGS ON BATTERY FARMING PROTEST
December 12 1979

A former Goon came to the defence of the hen yesterday when Spike Milligan presented a petition to 10 Downing Street calling for the phasing out of battery farming. Mr Milligan, who has eaten only free-range eggs since being shown round a battery farm seven years ago, said that it was a symptom of declining morality in Britain that our laws should permit such cruelty to animals.

'If it goes on like this, we could end up with battery cows in concrete farm jungles where the animal lives and is killed and packed up in tin foil at the end. I should hate to be alive when that happens.' He called on people to give up eating battery chickens or their eggs, even if it meant paying more. 'If you are going to support cruelty because it's cheaper, then we're no longer living in a Christian society,' he said.

Mr Milligan was speaking at a press conference, flanked on one side by a 16in by 19in cage containing five battery chickens, and on the other by a scaled-up cage containing two humans aimed at showing the conditions in which 95 per cent of our hens are kept. He then headed a deputation to Downing Street, where, with the playwright Brigid Brophy, he handed in a 190,000-signature petition calling for the outlawing of battery farming by 1989. He had high hopes that Mrs Thatcher would take up the cause.

The protest was organised by two groups, Compassion in World Farming and Animals' Vigilantes, who claim the battery system leads to deformities in hens and means they can never fulfil maternal instincts or build up 'meaningful relationships'. In their cages, they say, birds have only four inches in which to spread their 32in wing span. The system leads to feather-pecking and cannibalism, as well as variations in protein and vitamin content of eggs. Miss Brophy said that to allow such a system was similar to the fascism which led to concentration camps being built in Nazi Germany.

Mr Peter Roberts, general secretary of Compassion in World Farming, said that other European countries, notably West Germany and Switzerland, were planning legislation to ban battery farming. Poultry had been excluded from our Protection of Birds Act because of vested interests, he said. Mr Roberts said the National Union of Farmers had been resistant to supporting the ban and added: 'They are not acting in the interests of the chicken farmers but to protect the interests of big business.' He said that a straw-yard system poineered over the past 10 years in Cambridge provided a viable and humane alternative to battery farming. It needed more space and used more labour, but was less costly to set up and could make vast savings in energy. Under the straw-yard system each bird is allowed three square feet – six times that given to battery birds – in a covered yard with straw at least a foot deep.

ALAN RUSBRIDGER

❧ CHAPTER FIVE ❧

Chop and change
1980–1989

In 1974 the implementation of Lord Redcliffe-Maud's suggestions for new county boundaries changed the face of the countryside. Abruptly the long familiar pattern of urban county boroughs and rural shires was shattered. Strange new names appeared for counties – Cleveland, Avon, Humberside – and for district councils – Wansdyke, Tameside, Kirklees. Bradford burst its urban boundaries to take in Ilkley and its famous moor. The Saddleworth villages of West Yorkshire were disgusted to wake up in Oldham, Greater Manchester.

There were plenty of angry petitions for a reversion to the old state of things and much vandalism of new border signs. The red rose which Lancashire county council placed on its new library in Barnoldswick, part of historic Yorkshire, has never stayed in place for long. Some of the most crass decisions were reversed in due course and Humberside vanished in 1996 as swiftly as it had originally appeared. But a sense of impermanence replaced the old order of things which had seemed, for so many years, as immutable as the countryside's seasonal pattern of ploughing, sowing and reaping. It was compounded by successive governments' restlessness about the agencies designed to help the rural population and economy. The Countryside Commission gave way to the Countryside Agency and powers moved to and fro between changing national regional bodies.

Alterations even threatened to create two RDAs working in the same field – the Regional and the Rural Development Agencies – until the latter was changed to the Rural Development Service. To journalists, this version of perpetual motion deterred inquiry into what was really going on. When English Nature decided to call itself Natural England in 2006 much of the media absent-mindedly carried on using the old name for well over a year. There was perhaps, too, an irritated, deliberate element, as in the case of the *Guardian*'s former northern editor Harry Whewell, who was rung up one day to be told: 'In future, the Midland Hotel will be known as the

Golden Clover Traveljoy Midland Hotel' (or some such). 'Not by me it won't,' he said, and put the phone down.

The complications which so muddled rural opinion and initiatives have been brilliantly set out in chart form by the Plunkett Foundation, an excellent trust which promotes agricultural cooperatives with a legacy from an Anglo-Irish aristocrat, Horace Plunkett. He began a transformation of the Irish economy in the dying days of the old, often absentee landlord system before independence. When he died in 1932 he was buried beneath a telling and well-deserved headstone with the simple inscription: 'The sower went forth to sow.'

The Plunkett chart covers an entire A3 sheet of paper with squares, circles, stars and hexagons, more than 120 of them and each representing one of the agencies which a farmer or rural entrepreneur may expect to encounter. The European Union is there, of course, but so is the Federation of Small Operators, the Wetland Grants Scheme and an organisation called Eat the View. Linked to them by pathways which represent the likely journey of an applicant for funding or advice is a fantastic array of initials and acronyms: ADAS, FBASplus, BiTC, LANTRA, ViRSA and TENTO.

If journalists, even persistent and well-educated *Guardian* ones, find this a dispiriting maze, the effect on country people is so much the worse, because they are not just inquiring about the galaxy of bodies but depending on them. The House of Commons committee for the environment, food and rural affairs found this out in June 2008, when it held a meeting away from its usual room beside the Thames at Westminster. They convened instead in the creamery at Hawes in North Yorkshire, which makes the celebrated Wallace & Gromit Wensleydale cheese.

The MPs got a right earful from people whose nearest democratic authorities, other than parish councils, were 27 miles away in the case of the district and 37 miles in the case of the county council. Ruth Annison, who heads Outhwaite's the ropemakers in Hawes, told them despairingly: 'When we came here, we had an organisation called the Council for Small Industries in Rural Areas, and that was followed by the Rural Development Commission. That was subsumed into the Countryside Agency, and all of that work is now with the regional development agency, Yorkshire Forward.' The gradual creep of decision-making away from the doorstep to a distant county hall – or Yorkshire Forward's HQ in Leeds – had also encouraged policy-making based on data, rather than experience, in the view of the dales people. Rima Berry, chairwoman of the Upper Wensleydale Business Association, produced a startling example. The valley had lost out on extra aid for its many elderly, she suggested, after it was lumped in with Catterick, Europe's largest garrison town, which naturally swarms with young men.

Statistically, that made the area look as though there were, relatively, hardly any old people at all.

Such treatment suggests that an originally enlightened process has gone wrong: the planning system which began in 1949 with the National Parks and Countryside Act. It was only with this measure that a place known as the 'countryside' was first designated in law, and the now-familiar system of foot and bridlepath rights of way, national parks and other protected areas and similar zoning came into effect. The measure was just in time, for the later 1950s and 1960s saw national prosperity on a previously unmatched scale, with suburban housing developments, motorways and large-scale infrastructure such as power stations demanding their share of empty space. The profound scare of food shortages in the Second World War at the height of the Nazi submarine blockade led at the same time to the farming subsidy system, which guaranteed low prices for consumers but enmeshed agriculture in paperwork (in return, it should be added, for handsome payments). Land values soared as a result, if only because, as Mark Twain observed with his usual combination of astuteness and wit: 'Buy land; they're not making it any more.'

The way to turn this maze of legislation and supervision of the countryside into something more coherent remains uncertain. But there is hope in the increasing use – from Whitehall to village hall – of the word 'sustainability'. A sense of the urgency of making sense of the often conflicting or duplicating authorities in the countryside runs through the English Rural Development Programme 2007–2013, produced by the Department for the Environment, Food and Rural Affairs. Sustainability is its second watchword, and perhaps most significantly, its budget of £3.9bn is double the funding of its predecessor, which covered the previous seven years from 2000.

A COUNTRY DIARY: THE LAKE DISTRICT
February 11 1980
There is a particularly soothing rhythm in the ascent of snowbound fells on skis fitted with climbing skins. You gain height steadily in easy, ascending traverses, choosing the most comfortable angle, and the motion is so measured and relaxing that all your attention can be directed to the enjoyment of the gradually widening views. If you feel like it you could compose a poem or even a 'Country Diary'; at a pinch you could close your eyes for a time. In ideal conditions it can be the easiest way to get up a mountain – provided you're not in a hurry. Recently, on a perfect day of sunlit snows,

just before the 'high' slid away to the east, I enjoyed a lone traverse of the Troutbeck fells on skis, exulting in the contrast between the leisured ascents and the exhilarating, and sometimes rather undignified, downhill swoops and turns. Two walkers, doing the ridge in the opposite direction, found the crusted snow rather tiring: But, using skins, the uphill sections were almost effortless, taken slowly, and the descents, on varied snow surfaces, proved ideal or awkward, but always interesting. As on previous visits to the high fells during this spell of winter perfection, the clarity of the views and the complete absence of wind were quite exceptional. You could sunbathe in comfort by the icicle-hung cairns on Ill Bell and look across half of winter Lakeland to the bold dome of Great Gable, 15 miles away. Much closer, to the north, High Street surfaced like a great white whale and, to the south-west, the long length of Windermere reached out to the sparkling, sunlit waters of Morecambe Bay. Only two or three times each winter can you capture days like this.

A. HARRY GRIFFIN

KNOWING YOUR PLACE IN THE FIELD FULL OF FOLK*

May 15 1980

It has become the custom for institutions to have their origins, achievements and aims all put in some reassessed and readable order after they have lost some of their crusading spirit and novelty, and when the future in which they are to be particularly involved begins to cry out 'Which way?' and 'What next?'

Richard Mabey's summary of the work of the Nature Conservancy Council, which includes a mass of comment upon the score or more adjacent protective bodies with which it has become intertwined during the last quarter century, might be called a landmark in such briefs. It lucidly sets out, it records, it warns. It avoids prophecy, both hopeful or dire. What it concludes is this, that nature itself being in a state of perpetual evolvement, and our attitude towards it still being one of rationalised exploitation and economics, the battle between its protectors and its destroyers is certainly going to be something far more continuous than a 30 years' war – which is about the length of time it has taken to formulate our current notions of how it can be both used and saved.

* Richard Mabey, *The Common Ground: A Place for Nature in Britain's Future?* (London: Hutchinson/The Nature Conservancy Council, 1980)

So what next? Mabey rightly sees plenty of further fight and enlightenment spreading in the Nature Conservancy Council itself and in all like-minded groups with their special interests, but as one comes to the end of his book there comes the feeling that, with all the eyes they have opened, the time has surely arrived to draw up all the best and irrefutable discoveries which these watchful societies have made on Britain's behalf into a policy on how we should use the land.

The chief land-users, the farmers, the sportsmen, the foresters, the developers, even the armed forces, no doubt, will all say (and with much justification) that it is they who made the landscape and that time will green their mistakes, and so why attempt to alter what to them is a natural interference anyway? But as Mabey's book proves plain enough, God knows what would have happened if the Council for the Protection of Rural England (1926), the Countryside Commission (1968), the National Trust (1895), the World Wildlife Fund (1961), the Royal Society for the Protection of Birds (1889), the doughty Greenpeace (1971) and a host of similar agencies had not stepped in to check and educate.

Britain remains an enchantingly beautiful place despite so much ravaging of its surfaces in late years, but the losses incurred are far greater than is popularly understood. Now that international operators are licensed to change the scenery and international parliaments allowed to decide what crops and transport should prevail, and now that home interest in bird, beast and flower could easily be deflected into becoming a charmingly suitable hobby for our dangerously cosy, country-loving selves, can our soil and plants and creatures in future have anything like the protection they are going to need from the admirable protectionist societies by themselves?

In other words, is the Department of the Environment enough? Or do we dare to examine once more that ancient and most revolutionary concept of all, the land and ourselves, its true ownership and its usage as a trust? For countless commercial and political reasons, much of what the naturalists advocate is quietly ignored in both government and farmhouse, and an idea that so long as we can protect 'sites' and thus save species and at the same time recreate ourselves by visiting them, we are progressing, so to speak. But Richard Mabey rightly asks, are nature 'museums' the answer? The word 'reserve' gives the go-ahead in many quarters fully to exploit the unreserved. We should not have to drive for miles – as one does in some areas of East Anglian monoculture or indeed on some Scottish grouse moor – to find a certain common flower or creature. They must co-exist and we must co-exist.

Mabey describes in a fresh and exciting language our national losses and gains, chiefly since the last war. Highest among the latter must be an educated eye, in the generally informed sense. We have come a long way from 'nature study', pressing flowers, and birds' eggs and shell collecting, and the sentiment which used to accompany the subject. As with music, there has been a swift and remarkable development in a properly informed appreciation of the countryside. It is an influential advance, which owes almost everything to the various protective societies, and those who have gained by it, and who might be lulled into some feeling of a battle won because Minsmere or Loch Garden are secure, need now to address themselves to far more important issues, and not think that groups such as the NCC, the RSPB or the SPNC, etc., which converted them, will convert our legislators, for they will not.

Only the realisation by society as a whole that its own habitat – so fascinating and infinitely pleasurable, and so essentially a part of itself, its art, literature and worship – is being subjected to unprecedented violations and dangers will bring the all-over change in land law. The farmer spraying everything but his oats out of existence will take his family at the weekend to see the oxlips in the officially protected patch, and will not think it odd. But maybe the rest of us should.

'At its roots,' says Mabey, 'nature conservation seems to me to be a human celebration of the diversity of life,' adding later on, that at the moment we 'are thinking about creating entirely new "natural" landscapes in the corners left over by intensive agriculture. We have invented the notion of the "living museum", which, while it would not literally contain plastic trees, nevertheless suggests the depressing idea that our remaining wildlife might become a collection of living fossils. We have become aware that the survival of the network of wildlife on the planet may be inextricably connected with our own survival and we argue this very persuasively, though we know it is an intellectual defence, a kind of "nature in the head". And none of these alternatives come anywhere near to making up for what we are losing. The dispiriting procession of transient, unfamiliar, distant experiences they offer makes us realise that what we want from conservation is not a museum of nature, a remote collection of undifferentiated wild "things", but the community of distinct, familiar forms that is part of our cultural history.'

Mabey gives heartfelt thanks for all that has been saved and taught by the preservationists, but says that now is the time for us to take stock of their vocabulary. Let us begin talking of 'place' rather than 'site' or 'habitat', for example, 'as this seems to catch the element of human significance better than specialised or abstract words'. Let us not be preoccupied with the exotic and rare, for this would be the ideal activity for us in the eyes of those who don't want our inconvenient meddling with their plans to 'develop' the ordinary scene. Let us do challengingly large-scale, confident things, such as planting woods as well as trees. Let us be central and not peripheral. 'Nothing but good can come of the planting of woods amongst, say, intensive arable fields, new housing estates and industrial spoil-tips.'

Quoting Langland's famous Malvern hilltop dream, Mabey asks us to trespass into the curious countryside which has emerged since the new farming and the new preservationists fixed their boundaries. Both abuse the land ethic, the land being community, not commodity. What burrows, what flies, what shoots from the ground, whether marketable or not, is inextricably bound up with our own life on earth. We cannot simply just sell it or visit it as something quite other than us.

Langland thought that the whole countryside, whether it was the bits which fed the body or the soul, its harvests and its wilds, needed walking in, seeing, touching and somehow 'joining' by men and women if both needed to retain a total naturalness. Mabey agrees: 'A countryside full of people "worchyng and wandryng" is, I think, a happier prospect for the future than the empty monocultural desert dotted with barricaded nature reserves that seem to be the dream of many planners. John Fowles said that it was impossible to write of nature in the 70s "except in terms of lamentation and sermon" and that we would never make any real progress until we got back to the pleasure principle. This is the strongest argument for trying to change ordinary attitudes from pseudo-scientific to the poetic, from the general to the personal.'

The subtitle of this very good and sensible book is *A Place for Nature in Britain's Future?* and this is the key question for the present. Are we to make pilgrimages to Nature at her little cult centres and venerate avocets, fritillaries, purple orchids, wildfowl, or are we to take steps to see that our economic greed should no longer relegate her to an existence and concept so unnatural?

Mabey opens up the prospect before us persuasively and knowledgeably. As always, he writes excitingly about his great loves, woodlands, neglected corners, lichens and rare spirits such as the Reverend John Henslow, who, after instructing Darwin, revealed the marvels of botany to village children. But the uncomfortable and prevailing issue of *The Common Ground* is that of the special area versus the rest of Britain. The special areas – even where they allow some members of the same species to breed and others to be exterminated – are the government's sop to the concerned. The entire land of Britain being our special area, should we not, having learned so much about it from those who have managed to safeguard its more remarkable features, insist on having our say on how it should be used as a whole? And should not each of us who have supported our own favourite special area leave the 'temple', as Mabey calls it, and teach ourselves the shore-to-shore doctrine of a land-use policy, nothing less? If we do not, we shall be kept in our place, along with some creatures or plant, whilst commercial interests far more overwhelming than anything which this country has known before manages our natural acres for us.

RONALD BLYTHE

JEWEL OF ENGLAND THREATENED
October 20 1980

One of the last great unspoilt jewels of England was under nuclear threat, an MP told an outdoor rally of 600 people in Northumberland yesterday. 'If permission is given to dump nuclear waste in Northumbria it will mean not only that a highly dangerous substance is stored under the soil,' said Dr David Clark, Labour MP for South Shields, 'but there is no provision for the inspection of the waste, which will remain dangerous for 500 to 600 years'. It would be better to store the waste above ground, where it could be inspected, until safer disposal techniques have been found. Dr Clark was speaking at a protest rally at Wooler, organised by the Ramblers' Association. A public inquiry is to be held in Newcastle-upon-Tyne tomorrow week into a plan by the Atomic Energy Authority to carry out test drilling in the Cheviots for possible sites to store nuclear waste. Northumberland County Council has refused planning permission.

NO ROOM FOR SENTIMENT
March 23 1981

Let me declare my interest. I am a farmer. An intensive farmer (as all farmers are, of course, in varying degrees). I rear chickens in large, enclosed, environmentally controlled buildings. I fatten pigs in large, enclosed yards. I grow corn with the aid of herbicides, pesticides, artificial fertilizer, seed dressings and many other scientific boosts to higher yields. I am unrepentant.

Now let me try and explain to you worthy *Guardian* readers, whose idea of farming is sadly naïve, and who – as you baste your cheap broiler chicken or munch your meaty hamburger or crunch your expensive potato chips or select the 'duck with orange sauce' as a restaurant treat – also mouth your disgust at 'modern' farming methods, let me tell you that you do not know, or understand, what you are talking about. You have lived so long divorced from primary contact with the soil that it has lost its real significance to you.

For that fickle jade, Mother Nature, has to be rigorously controlled, her fertile potential for growing crops both vegetable and animal carefully exploited, for us to survive at all. The great breakthrough in civilisation – so my history teacher told me, and I believe him – came when primitive man learned how to grow his food. He stopped chasing it, became settled, not nomadic. He began to dominate nature.

That dominance is the crucial point. The whole process of producing food for our continuing and increasing needs is forced, unreal, un-natural. All farming is un-natural in the sense that it is imposed. All our farm animals bear as little relation to their primeval ancestors as a domestic cat to a tiger. They have all been skilfully bred to provide us, their masters, with easy meat. Present-day cereal or root crops are so developed to provide us with their bounty that they would not last a season without our protection.

So those critics who demand a 'return to nature', in that we grow crops or rear animals the 'natural way', are asking for the impossible unless we wish to starve. They are akin to the pastoral idealists who hanker for the horse and plough crossing the skyline and bemoan the noisy tractor. They have never had to tramp for hours and days on end with one foot in a muddy furrow, behind an obstinate team of horses and an arm-wrenching plough, nor have they experienced the comparative luxury of a weather-tight cab and fingertip controls, nor have they to feed the five thousand.

In our gardens, if we are lucky enough to have one, we till the soil, hoe the weeds (poor things), spray the blackfly, cross-fertilise, create order from riot, that our fruit and vegetables may win prizes in the show and may feed us through a long winter. Farming is just the same. But it is when we apply basic farming principles to animals that criticism is provoked. Suddenly it becomes inhuman to cage an animal we have created in the warm and dry, with plenty of food and water, and protection from its worst enemy – its fellows, and from other predators, in order that its full potential may be realised.

It is, for some extraordinary reason, preferable to leave the poor brute in the open, prey to the elements and its wild brethren (have you ever seen what a fox can do in a jolly murderous mood?), to hunger and to thirst, to be tantalised by flies or buried by snow (until rescued by helicopter). Survey the hunched misery of out-wintered stock and reflect how much better off they would be in even the most basic shelter, let alone in a snug, insulated one.

Those who advocate wishy-washy ideas of 'extensive' as opposed to 'intensive' methods, or any feeble compromise in between, have never had to farm animals for a profit in a hard, cruel, rapacious economic climate. They might then learn and come to understand, over a period of time, that a farmer has perforce a completely different, and not necessarily worse, attitude to animals than has his critic. Animals to us are not just cuddly toys or household pets, they are living creatures who provide us and the rest of humanity with food, and they will stubbornly refuse to provide eggs or meat or milk if they do not thrive. And animals will not thrive if they are abused. It is no good having a factory farm if the products die halfway along the line, and that explains why that industrial term can never be accurately applied to farming.

If I felt anguish as each lorry left my farm en route to the slaughterhouse I could not survive or do my job. Those animals have served my purpose by growing successfully and profitably into saleable meat: they will serve your purpose by providing a succulent, nourishing and cheap meal. We have all manipulated them from cradle to grave (or rather, from incubator to plastic bag), but with adequate care and compassion and attention for them to have lived a contented, non-stressful existence. Any comparison with human life is meaningless.

I do not consider I am particularly hard-hearted, unsympathetic or cynical. Just realistic. I reject the cruelty and callousness from which far too many animals suffer unnecessarily. But what can appear to a decent, liberally minded urban proselytiser to be cruelty is usually but long-established farming practice, developed over the years to get the best results. If you think today's methods are new, look back to how for instance, Henry VIII got those nice fat capons. Or to how milk was produced in Islington. Or prime Scotch beef for the rich man's table. Only the scale has changed. But then, so has the size of the population and our capacity to cope with numbers.

As you choke into your milk over these words, consider that to give you that milk a calf had to be taken from its mother at a few days of age, bleating piteously, so that its dam could plod profitably through the milking parlour. Could anything be more unnatural than that? Yet more inevitable? Every branch of farming can similarly be described in such emotive words, yet they are all part of the process of growing food. In contradiction to this inspired popular belief, the vast majority of farmers care sincerely for the animals in their charge. We live with them, we feed them, we doctor them, act as their lavatory attendants, watch carefully and help as they give birth, encourage their progeny to healthy growth. (Regard, O you of little faith, the gentleness of a shepherd as he acts as a midwife.) But we are also only too aware of the practicalities and the realities of our jobs. Our animals must keep us, not us them. Their end, untimely death excepted, is pre-ordained. If we do not do our job well, you quite literally starve. Our consciences are quite as admirable as yours, and I suggest you leave us to wrestle with them unhindered, while we also try to cope with your demands for cheap and plentiful food.

PETER ASHLEY

THE NATIONAL TRUST HAS ACQUIRED A SITE IN NEATH
May 25 1981

The National Trust has acquired a site in Neath, Glamorgan, which is not only a beauty spot but also a birthplace of industrial Wales. It is Aberdulais Falls, where the smelting of copper began in 1584. Metalworking has since transformed the district and much of south Wales. The site was given to the National Trust by Neath Borough Council. A grant of £55,000 has come from the fund, which was set up by the government last year. But more money is still needed to consolidate the ruins, partly restore the site and present the history to the public. Copper ore was first brought there from Cornwall in 1584, because coal was available for the smelting. By 1667 an iron forge had been set up and tinplate was rolled. Power came from water which drove a wheel: the weir has survived. The beauty of the four-acre spot – with the river, ruins, a magnificent waterfall, the remains of a three-arched bridge – attracted artists including Turner, who were in search of the picturesque. Copper ore was brought from north Cornwall across the Bristol Channel in small boats. Charcoal for the process of smelting was scarce in Cornwall because woods and forests had been chopped down. Wood was plentiful around Neath and so was coal. Water power was used to work bellows for the furnaces. The process involved several meltings of the ore. The ore was repeatedly drenched in water – again plentiful – so that the impurities, mainly sulphur and arsenic, were released in clouds of steam and smoke. Skilled workmen, mostly Germans, came to Aberdulais from Keswick; the secrets of the smelting were closely guarded. But the enterprise ran into difficulties. Capital was short at Aberdulais and in Cornwall, so that wages could not be paid. The Cornish mines were troubled by water in the workings. Boat owners were reluctant to cross the Bristol Channel in winter.

The National Trust hopes to have an audio-visual presentation at the spot. This project is different from its usual ones of preserving fine buildings and places of scenic beauty.

A-HUNTING I WILL GO, WITHOUT SHAME
December 28 1981

I live deep in the country where the horse, hunting, and the pony club has a strong hold. I work hard and keeping a horse is my one dear indulgence. It has taken me nearly 50 years to get to own my dream-horse, nearly too long to acclimatise to the riding of it – not quite, but breaking my back in a fall nine months ago and coming back again after the lay-off has emphasised afresh how much riding means to me, what spiritual resources are to be drawn from riding off the roads, through the bridleways, over the stubble. Walking does it too, but being on a horse adds an extra dimension, and cements through long hours of each other's company the relationship between horse and rider which brings such satisfaction.

However, I do sometimes go hunting too. I adore hunting and am not ashamed to admit it. One Saturday a few weeks ago I sat on my mare in a small wood on the top of a hill overlooking a river estuary. It was a morning of very high tide, of bright sunshine, but bitterly cold. Ahead the green grass stretched to meet the sky and on either side, both inland and to seaward, it sloped away down to the seawalls and sheets of wave-flecked water which seemed to fill the landscape as far as the eye could see. Good enough just to sit there drinking it in – from a viewpoint one normally has no access to – but then to see hounds stream down over the grass followed breakneck by the bright coats of the huntsman and whippers-in, feel the mare's excitement, wanting to go but having to hold her back until it was the field's turn, cantering slowly at first and then being overtaken and, striding out faster and faster down the hill in a great melee of horses like the Charge of the Light Brigade, knowing there was a hedge at the bottom and one had to stay in control somehow ... after five days of desk work to feel the adrenalin running like that is indescribable ... see the bars in the hedge loom and feel the mare's wild effort, see your friend alongside and find yourself laughing because it is so marvellous ... how can you not love it, if you do it? But, of course, if you don't do it you only see the hunting people when they are on the roads and holding up the traffic (a very small part of the day), enjoying themselves when other people are working.

If hunting people did not so obviously enjoy hunting, but did it as a duty, would they attract such a bad press? I am always deeply suspicious that the cruelty-to-the-fox angle of those against hunting is only part of the argument. I think they partly resent foxhunters enjoying the sport so much and looking as if they are superior and rich and privileged. Anyone on a horse is forced to look down on anyone not on a horse, so is willy-nilly superior. Quite a lot of hunting people are rich – all sports have their rich and poor – but contrary to common opinion not all fields are made up entirely of Prince Charles and his friends. The hunt I belong to is small and unfashionable and most of the followers are farmers who hunt to have a day off with their friends at the season of the year when they can afford the time. Hunting takes place from November to March in the worst of the weather when the mud is deep, the rain cold. Sunny days are a bonus.

Yes, it is cruel to kill a fox with a pack of hounds, but is it more cruel than to kill it with a gun or strangle it in a snare? Hounds kill a fox quickly if they catch it, but guns and snares often do terrible damage without killing. Foxes breed too readily to go unculled. A farmer in our village has shot over 20 this winter.

In our local paper last week there was a letter exhorting protestors to demonstrate at the Boxing Day meet. In the same paper is an advertisement offering good prices for winter fox pelts. A wood near my home is full of fox snares to try to satisfy this same advertiser. (My daughter, home for the weekend, walking the dog, was told to keep the dog out of the wood in case it got in a snare.) Do the foxes caught in these snares lie down and die peacefully? Nobody is holding demonstrations concerning their much more lingering and agonising deaths. Why not? Presumably because nobody is having a good time in the killing, merely making money, which is a much more understandable motive and therefore not worth making a fuss about.

KATHLEEN PEYTON

SIZEWELL INQUIRY

June 18 1983

The Sizewell B public inquiry has been engaged in trench warfare most of this week, with the Council for the Protection of Rural England (CPRE) chipping away at the economic case surrounding the Central Electricity Generating Board (CEGB)'s proposal for the UK's first pressurised water reactor (PWR). Mr John Taylor, QC, for the CPRE, has forced witnesses from the board to concede that the CEGB has been overoptimistic in its assumptions over future exchange rates and fossil-fuel prices, factors which are crucial to the economic justification for the £1,200m nuclear power station planned for the Suffolk coast.

The CPRE, like other objectors, should have a chance to test the sensitivity of the board's case to differing assumptions over economic growth and fuel costs now that the inquiry has been offered the use of a computer model developed by the Energy Research Group at the Cavendish Laboratory of Cambridge University. The group, a leading independent research body, receives funds from the energy industry – including the CEGB – and earlier this year carried out its own analysis of the PWR, which concluded that there was a 60 per cent chance that Sizewell B would be justified on economic grounds.

Although detailed economic matters have dominated the 20th week of the inquiry, now sitting at Church House, Westminster, safety issues have also had an airing. Friends of the Earth failed in their attempt to have the safety part of the hearing postponed for 18 months. The Greater London Council, another principal objector, announced that its case would rely in part on a report which suggests that a catastrophic accident at Sizewell B could in certain weather conditions cause up to 24,000 cancer deaths among Londoners and make it necessary to evacuate up to half the capital's population. That is the prediction of the National Radiological Protection Board in a 'worst case' analysis of the effects of a core meltdown at Sizewell leading to a plume of radioactive gas blowing over London carried by north-easterly winds.

The CEGB said this week that the possibility of such an accident was so remote that it could be discounted. A spokesman put the risk at no more than once in 100 million years. There has been a significant development over the question of the safety of the pressure vessel, which critics believe is not yet proven. Sir Alan Cottrell, who as a former government chief scientist voiced doubts about the safety of the PWR, has agreed to chair an advisory committee which will monitor the design, fabrication and in-service testing of the pressure vessel. Sir Alan, a distinguished metallurgist and now master of Jesus College, Cambridge, will act as the watchdog over the work of the Inspection Validation Centre, which the United Kingdom Atomic Energy Authority will build for the board in Cheshire to test the pressure-vessel components and massive steel forgings.

Next week the inquiry reaches a significant stage when the CPRE, as the first objector to present its case, calls its first witness.

THE INTIMIDATED ANGLER

January 5 1984

The director of the Salmon and Trout Association which, as its name fails to imply, speaks not for the fish in its title but for those who try to catch them with meretricious flies, is quoted as saying on one of the great unresolved questions of our age, recently revived: 'My own feeling is that fish do not feel pain, but I think they can feel panic.' A distinguished neuroscientist reportedly takes a neutral stance: 'This question borders on semantics, philosophy, even religion ... You cannot ask a fish if it feels pain. I think it is impossible to answer.' But the Hunt Saboteurs' Association (HSA), in keeping with the moderate, live-and-let-live image it sedulously omits to cultivate, has no doubts on the matter, brands angling as cruel and has just announced a campaign of obstruction. Well, almost no doubts. Two senior HSA officials have resigned on the politically correct but inherently illogical ground that a campaign against angling, the pastime of up to four million people, could cost the HSA support for its main cause against blood sports. Another quintessentially British orgy of logic-chopping on cruelty to animals is at hand.

As only an estimated 200,000 Britons go fly-fishing, we can conclude without fear of contradiction that most anglers are coarse. This impression is confirmed for some by observation of the behaviour of certain members of the species *Piscator piscator* in their native habitat, the crumbling banks of the typical public angling facility with its haphazard sprinkling of nameless (or unspeakable) rubbish. The pre-dawn air fills with strange oaths as ill-fitting and treacherous boots sink into the potholes on the towpath in the dark. It is almost always raining, especially in the early hours of June 16, when the coarse-fishing season opens in most of England. The delicate plop of the sounding fish soon makes way for the erratic gurgle of the slowly submerging beer can. Ritual cries greet the passage of boats as they innocently stir up the groundbait and the mud, break the odd line and drive away the quarry. Swans die quietly from the lead in abandoned fishing weights. Now to all these delights are to be added interference by the HSA, which may very soon find that it has bitten off more than it can chew.

No better evidence for the French observation that 'the English take their pleasures sadly' exists than this kind of coarse angling. If Izaak Walton was right in saying, 'Angling is somewhat like poetry,' he must have meant a dirge. This does not mean that those who indulge in it are going to surrender it lightly. Until we manage to plug into the nervous system of a fish we shall not know for sure whether it feels pain. We do know it lacks the vocal cords to express it, and we can see from its behaviour when caught that it would prefer to be free. We already have an RSPCA, hopelessly riven over foxhunting; we have the HSA; we even have the Animal Liberation Front (ALF), which has its priorities so confused that it seeks to maim and kill people to protect animals. The real question is: do we need, courtesy of the HSA, an Organisation Against Fishing (OAF)? The answer seems to be, probably not.

HELP FOR WILDLIFE DOWN ON THE FARM
December 29 1984
Bill Ackworth was explaining the advantages of not ploughing up an old pond on his Berkshire farm when a large hare leapt up to prove the point. It bolted from a clump of grass and tore away across a field until it reached the safety of a hedge.

'Right on cue,' said Joy Greenall, who had been listening with approval as Mr Ackworth described how the tangled dip in his field was a wildlife refuge. The hedge was another and so was a nearby spinney with its newly planted saplings and nesting boxes.

Mr Ackworth is chairman of the Berkshire and Oxfordshire farming and wildlife advisory group, one of more than 50 county associations which are bringing two bristly countryside camps together. Farmers and conservationists sit in equal numbers on the groups, and discuss such things as the best way to encourage barn owls to nest or the effect of hedge shadow on crop yield.

Ms Greenall is the latest of 12 full-time wildlife advisers appointed by the advisory groups. Farmers and land owners in Berkshire and Oxfordshire have provided £6,000 as a down payment for her salary on a contract lasting three years. There were 125 applicants for the job she took up in October, and she already has a waiting list of farmers who want a wildlife survey of their property.

Bad publicity over practices like rooting out hedges and a growing awareness that wildlife and farming can be complementary have prompted a friendlier approach to conservation. 'There should be room on any farm for wildlife havens even if they are not always where the farmer thinks they ought to be,' she said.

One farmer went to some lengths to remove an unsightly fallen tree from an old pond, but in the process destroyed a purpose-built refuge for insects and birds. Unsightliness, Sir Ackworth agrees, is a familiar obstacle to conservation, especially in lush, tidily farmed areas like most of Berkshire and Oxfordshire. He and Ms Greenall, who previously worked for an East Anglian naturalists trust looking after 35 nature reserves and 1,100 acres of land, hope to persuade the 2,200 farmers in Oxfordshire and Berkshire to adopt a policy towards 'wildlife land'.

Modern, highly intensive farming has brought the realisation that the wildlife may not always be there and that its survival may be important for pest control, suppression of weeds and the safeguarding of the landscape. 'We want to see farmers drawing up an annual management plan for wildlife areas on their farm in just the way they do for their farming land,' said Mr Ackworth. On his 143 acres at Little Hidden Farm, near Hungerford, some five or six acres are given over to wildlife – about the appropriate ratio, he thinks.

There is a price to pay. Mr Ackworth's spinney casts a long shadow on an oilseed rape field, stunting the crop for several yards out from the hedge. He would also gain a bit of extra cash if he ploughed up the pond where the hare was hiding. 'But there are plenty of advantages,' he said. 'A grass barrier round a field can eliminate weeds more effectively than spraying right up to the hedge. And a farm increases its capital value if you have a stock of wildlife for shooting and pleasant natural landscape rather than a prairie.'

The progress of the advisory groups, which are coordinated nationally by the Countryside Commission, the Ministry of Agriculture and farming and conservation groups, is being encouraged by a gradual shift in government grants in favour of conservation-minded farming.

MARTIN WAINWRIGHT

WHEN LAMB PROVIDES THE BEEF
June 23 1986

In the Lake District, where sheep unsafely graze, lamb was off the menu at many restaurants and hotels in tourist spots yesterday. And today there will be empty sheep pens at the weekly livestock auction in the town of Cockermouth, where Wordsworth was born – the first market to be affected by the ban.

There are 1,000 flocks on farms in West Cumbria covered by the restriction of the movement and slaughter of sheep; and throughout the weekend 10 Ministry of Agriculture field staff continued to collect lambs as samples for analysis by food scientists. In Carlisle, both the Ministry of Agriculture and the National Farmers' Union (NFU) dealt with scores of calls from members of the public asking if it is safe to eat lamb, and from farmers with more serious queries about whether the emergency meant a setback or ruin.

The very worst scenario, which sends a shudder through the sparse population in its lakeland of sombre greens, is that high levels of caesium might be so prevalent among lambs tested that whole flocks would have to be eliminated. That is the unthinkable. Sheep farmers, taking their patience from the seasons, do not panic easily.

It is easy, and alarming, to see why. For though the contaminated rain cloud, which drenched sheep and shepherds, ballooned in from Chernobyl, this is the county which has lived with the nuclear reprocessing plant at Sellafield smack in the middle of its coastline.

How Cumbria copes with the crisis will be illuminating, for it has kept its rural structure better than another part of Britain. It has managed a balance between farming, the nuclear industry and tourism – even though two of the components are troublesome.

Cumbria grins and bears Sellafield. It was unwished for, as are the local Herdwick sheep. The county NFU chairman calls them Alice in Wonderland sheep; they exist on next to nothing; have one rib more – and therefore one chop more – than other breeds. And many farmers are saddled with these lambs because Beatrix Potter, lakeland resident, persuaded the National Trust 80 years ago to make keeping Herdwicks a condition of the lease on its many farms in the district.

However, it is farmers on the coastal strip who will be the first to feel the financial effects of the ban. Their lambs are born earlier and, therefore, fatten quicker than those on the high fells. This week, for instance, Patrick Gordon-Duff-Pennington was preparing to send the first of 1,000 lowland lambs to market. Every week they remain unsold, the guide price drops. He will lose about £15 per head. Even for Mr Gordon-Duff-Pennington £15,000 would be a thumping big loss. He is county chairman of the NFU, but hardly a typical Cumbrian farmer. His family supplements his income by taking in guests; their home is their castle – Muncaster Castle, actually – and the family have so skilfully combined tourism and farming that he is one of the few landowners in the area who admits to not being in debt.

However, for the majority of NFU members who farm on the fells, the worrying time will come in the autumn when their Herdwick lambs, born a couple of months ago, will be disposed of at the autumn store markets; that is, sold to be fattened in other parts of the country, rather than for immediate consumption.

'What worries me is that the people in the high fells cannot afford to take any more of a knock,' says the county chairman. Lou Howson, at the opposite end of the economic and political spectrum, couldn't agree more. He farms just 60 acres at Wasdale. The Howsons will have 150 lambs for sale in September. Mr Howson is worried that, at worst, the scare will last until then and that the public will turn against buying lamb. He is afraid also that, with fell lambs hard to sell – because they will be too fat – unscrupulous dealers might try to pass them off as coming from other parts of the country when they resell them.

However, Howson's biggest underlying fear is about the collective blind eye which the farming community turns to the nuclear business, wherever the risk comes from. His son Jim says: 'Sellafield is the only source of money in the area. So many people depend on it, directly or indirectly, that they are just as worried about it closing down as melting down.'

There is, indeed, a quiet connivance by many in agriculture at the existence of the nuclear plant. For lakeland sheep farming is the very opposite of agri-business. It is still mostly a matter of one man and his sheep dog. Mr Bob Rawlin, whose family have farmed in Ennerdale for 400 years, says with patient modesty:

'Hill farming isn't the Rolls-Royce of agriculture. The economy of West Cumbria depends on Sellafield.'

His family concern, Hollins Farm, was featured a week ago on a Channel Four documentary which placed sheep farming in a romantic frame; so it is perceived increasingly by the public. It deserves stone walls rather than uprooting hedges, there is no scandal of over-production or massive subsidy (though about half farmers' income comes from the government and the EEC). And it offers an acceptable degree of diversification. Tourists enjoy farmhouse hospitality, then wander over the hills kept trim by the chewing of innumerable sheep. And derelict cottages are saved for occupation by the Sellafield folk.

Mr Rawlin says: 'We'll have Greenpeace telling people "Don't eat this bloody Cumberland lamb or it'll kill you", as sure as eggs are eggs.' Other farmers are at least aware of the need for vigilance, and even Mr Gordon-Duff-Pennington, though a friend of Sellafield, reckons the campaigners did well to warn of safety defects at British Nuclear Fuels. He is all in favour of more openness about any possible dangers to the local population. However, it is easy to meet hoteliers who are almost paranoid about what they see as excessive coverage by the media of all scares – including this latest one.

Nearer to the mark is the laird of Muncaster Castle when he says: 'The battle now is not so much about agriculture, as keeping a population in a rural area.' Throughout the next few weeks, West Cumbria will be hoping that it can preserve the delicate balance of interests which just about sees it through.

JOHN CUNNINGHAM

THE ARCHERS
December 24 1986
Brookfield Farm. Cue: Dum, de-dum, de-dum, de-dum. Christmas Eve. Jill and Phil (no more Lill or Dill or Bill, alas) hold open house. Enter WALTER: (*Bows, scratches long-johned groin and takes cheese-straw from mouth*) 'Ello me ol' pal, me ol' beauty!'

> TOM: (*Doffs cap, pats brilliantined hair, wipes hand on lovatey-tweed lapel and then on Walter's smock*) Now, look 'ere, Walter, I allus say, I've been around, I keeps my ear to the ground, and I've 'eard stories that'd freeze the blood.

JILL: *(Breezily)* Have a nice mince pie, Uncle Tom.
PHIL: *(Sighs in exasperation, clears throat, shuffles bank statements and snuffles adenoids)* ...

Drippy Phil. Dear Jill. Prattling Tom and kindly Walter, me old pal, me old beauty. They never close. We've been together now for 36 years and it ain't twice-a-day too long-27,000-odd episodes, including Christmas Day. And tomorrow morning, just after the 8a.m. news, Radio 4 doles out the presents and mince pies down Ambridge way for a special-day Special of country folk.

Producer Liz Rigbey has opened up the archives and a whole life (yours and theirs) will swim before you. Old ones, new ones, loved ones, neglected ones. And lo, even Dan, late and great, appeared among them on the hillside on Christmas morning and said to Shula, 'Why should we consider ourselves different just because we're the Archer family? We're not any different to anyone else, y'know.' Stay tuned.

On Whit Monday 1950, a couple of weeks after 'Wor Jackie's two humdingers had hissed the Wembley rigging behind Blackpool's Farm to take ty' Cup to Tyneside, the regulation Oxbridge voice on BBC Midland Region cleared its throat to announce: 'We present *The Archers of Wimberton Farm*, on the fringe of the village of Ambridge.'

FADE IN ODD FARM NOISES, COW MOOING OFF-MIKE.
DAN: Well, Simon, what d'you think?
SIMON: Ah well – 'er might and 'er mightn't.

In fact, there was no doubt. She was off and long-running. Since when we devoted legions have stood by their loved ones through thick and thin, sick and sin, hatches, dispatches, matches, madness, manslaughter (acquitted at Gloucester Assizes), prison, pillage, primness, plague and pestilence in the form of liver fluke, foot-and-mouth and warble fly. Not to mention skeletons in Nelson's closet.

By the evening of September 22 1955 Ambridge was already so much part of the fabric that the BBC chose the villagers as its taskforce to scupper the very first night of transmission by ITV – and hoity-toity, lace-knickered Grace Archer (née Fairbrother) was incinerated at Grey Gables while trying to rescue her horse, Midnight. The body was cold before the ambulance reached Borchester General – and a nation, stunned, could think of nothing else all evening but to sit sobbing over cups of tea (sorry, nice cups of tea). Certainly the martyrdom and grief put a stop to any thoughts of watching the new-fangled ITV. It was probably the BBC's best and last throw, as the *Manchester Guardian* leader writer hummed in verse next day:

> *"She was well-loved and millions know*
> *That Grace has ceased to be.*
> *Now she is in her grave, but Oh*
> *She's scooped the ITV."*

Since when, for over 30 years, and in spite of more martyrdom, more fires, a heck of a lot more fluke, flather, hobgoblins, Horobins and Grundys, this newspaper had not been stirred to rumble again. Till 1986. For this year Ambridge was traumatised by what seemed to be its most diabolic visitation yet. A new boss was brought in and the feathers flew at Cosy Comfort Farm. Not only that, but this new supremo of the squad was a woman, and not only that but a woman of infinite determination and oomph, and not only that but a mere slip of a gel of 29 who wasn't even born when Phil met Jill, let alone when Grace got charred. And now she's got Betty charring. The nerve of it.

The hoo-ha began just because Liz Rigbey got the job. She hadn't been on anyone's shortlist and Broadcasting House seethed with jealousies like the back bar of The Bull wouldn't credit. The *Guardian* letters editor winced as the shires shook fists. Liz Rigbey was accused of being 'a pestilential nuisance to proper village life', 'a "weekender" full of o'erweening ambition' who had introduced 'an infiltration of spoiled brats, disreputable liaisons and people to whom pragmatism is more important than principles'. And our leader column warned her that, unless she laid off, 'the future disposition of Brookfield Farm may well take on dimensions which will ultimately place it somewhere between the Electra of Sophocles and the steamier works of Tennessee Williams'.

Ms Rigbey, 5ft-nothing, stood four-square. It was heroic. She endured, and Ambridge stopped kicking and screaming, and grew up, and now, for my money, the villagers are strutting and fretting and farming in a reality as never before.

The *Guardian* leader hurt her most of all. 'It was longer than the accompanying one on South Africa. Of anyone, I thought you lot would have understood what I was trying to do – get to grips with real farming in a dramatic way. OK, I admit I might have set off too dramatically. But I was new, and I was learning, OK?'

She is not what I thought when the flak was flying. She is bright as a blazer button, bubbly as a soap opera, pretty as a picture, with china-blue, saucery eyes, a wavy hayrick of Sunsilk-ad brown hair, a ready smile and a whippy wit. The notion put about in the summer that Ambridge had been saddled with a harridan-battleaxe even more stubborn than Antrobus, the dog-woman, can here and now be discounted. In fact, Ms Liz reminds me of one of my all-time pin-ups – Miss Elizabeth, the beguilingly breezy space-seller on the *Borsetshire Echo*.

After English at Exeter University, she was a junior sub-editor on the *Chartered Quantity Surveyor*, then a reporter on *Farmers' Weekly*. With sights still firmly set on big-time TV current affairs, she set her alarm for a 4a.m. to be dogsbody on Radio 4's live dawnwatch, *Farming Today* – milk yields and fat-stock prices – after which a lie-in on Saturday mornings with the more featurey, pre-recorded *On Your Farm*. Being proclaimed May Queen of Ambridge surprised her most of all.

'I freely admit that when I started I made quite a few botches by going at it too fast. I was in such a spin those first months that I was totally unaware of any personal opposition to me, till it began to filter back through gossip columnists and the like. All the resentment came from London, none from Birmingham. And let's face it, no one actually stuck a real dagger in my back.'

As well as her own admission of starting off 'much too dramatic, much too plotty-plotty', she was accused of four other heinous decisions that were, in fact, her predecessor's final flings – killing off Dan; introducing Nelson's illegitimate daughter; giving tedious Nigel the boot; and betrothing the simpering Sophie to honest-to-goodness David. Each split the nation – but not half as much as the one Miss Rigbey dreamed up to explode Brookfield's cosiness for ever. The taxman cometh, and the world went potty.

'After Dan's death, Phil became patriarch. (I think I've done a lot with Phil as a character, don't you?) So who takes over from Phil? Such is the very stuff of British farming families. It dominates all of them – the dreaded handover of the generations – when and how the eldest son takes charge. Honestly, there are thousands of 70-year-old farmers in Britain with sons of 45 or more who do all the work but are not allowed even to sign a cheque. They are just waiting for their fathers to die.

'On *Farmers' Weekly* I did a survey and about 90 per cent of the old farmers said they would never retire, they would die "in the saddle" no matter what age they reached. That's unique in all working Britain, isn't it? So I thought we should address the problem at Brookfield, plus all its ensuing death-duty ramifications. It's a unique worry, also fascinating, sometimes upsetting to the whole family. It affects fathers and sons, and also mothers and daughters too.'

Especially, I say, if a daughter had married a scheming solicitor like the earnest grasper, Mark Hebden? 'Well, yes, that was a very nice aside for us, just sitting there.' So does David take over? 'You wait and see. Jill and Phil say "Not till marriage with

Sophie works out." That's another classic situation happening all over the country this minute. Farming families are scared stiff of divorce – it can destroy a whole farm.'

Well, clever clogs, it hasn't yet destroyed South Fork, Dallas, has it? More's the pity. 'OK, but fair's fair, the producers of *Dallas* are pretty clever in realising the highly dramatic potency in the handover of the generations in a family business. Like them in oil, what we are doing at Ambridge is exploring the potential of the drama that happens on almost every farm in Britain.'

In this same vein, did I perceive, too, that the Grundy family has changed in these last few months? 'Well spotted. Because, you know, there are a heck of a lot of real farmers like the Grundys. So I refuse any more to use them just as comic relief; they are poor, struggling farmers, down at heel but doing their best; that fact is not intrinsically humorous. OK, Eddie's a lovable rogue, and at present Joe's lovelorn, but that's nothing to do with their farming, is it? (Darling Clarrie's real-life impersonator, by the way, is off having a baby: so at present there are lots of shouts to her in the kitchen, but no actual dialogue.)

All right, I say, you've convinced me that Ambridge is growing up. But I'm a big boy now, as well, and I want the full facts, girl. Like, is the YTS laddo, Art, going to get his mitts on juicy Lucy Perks? Or come to that, is Sid going to have it off with the schoolmarm, marm? Or even with Betty Tucker? The lovely eyes narrow. 'You have fallen for some classic Ambridge gossip if you think Sid and Betty are...'

The only time sheets have ever been ruffled at Ambridge is when Jill or Phil turn to get their cocoa mug off the bedside table. There was also, just once, I shudder at the memory, the rustle of a breast-stroke when the squirming, soppy Sophie tried out the back seat of David's new car. So, what I want to know is have they progressed from there? The eyes frost over like the parkiest of December mornings.

'We did pick up a storyline about their sexual problems when I first took over. Certainly the engagement was a bit shaky. Don't you remember she wouldn't share a room with him in France on holiday? So Sophie wanted an engagement first – ergo, after the engagement should we have David at once wandering around with a stupid grin on his face? No, we simply haven't pursued the subject for some time.

'You see, one thing I'm trying to do is make Ambridge more like real life, not so predictably tailored – something flares up, goes on for a few months, then dies down, then it might come back in a big way. In other words, instead of three or four intriguing storylines popping up regularly, we might have 30 or so waiting to be brought to the boil at any given time every three or four months.'

Like Freddie Danby's libido? 'Precisely.' She laughs, then throws her eyes to heaven when I persist with inquiries about Freddie making it with Martha. Or perhaps even the Dog Woman? No? OK, what about dear ageing Caroline? Will she finally get goosed by the quack? Or does she still love the smarmy Brian? The question is, to all intents, ignored.

'We've got some really nice storylines for Caroline coming up. We still get hundreds of letters saying Brian's such a bastard, can't Caroline get her own back? She will, don't worry, but in the nicest possible way. Now Brian's a really interesting character, don't you think? A lot of people these days don't like farmers generically, for all the reasons that any *Guardian* reader must know – you know, featherbedding, butter mountains, ecology and all that. I didn't want them to feel that about Phil, I wanted to isolate it on one character and say, OK if you're going to hate farmers, hate Brian. So let's give him a helicopter, when Phil's got a tax bill; or get him tearing out a hedge when Tony's getting all organic.'

I still want to know about Lizzie, my honey bun. With the terrible Pargetter out of it, big-banging in London, who might (oh, horrors) give Elizabeth her first big bang?

Oh, grow up, man, says the look. 'You must realise the very essence of Ambridge is that you can't go there. Only I can, I suppose. I'm the only one who has to live and breathe the romantic idyll every day, 24 hours a day. And it's true, the real me wakes every morning and I'm really in Ambridge. Honestly, I dream about Ambridge every single night. I wake up saying "What a great storyline!" And then promptly forget it, of course.'

The baby's come a long way – and even longer under the splendid Ms Rigbey. Listen tomorrow morning and you will see. As Dan and Doris sit around the fire listening to the 1951 budget: 'Petrol up, oil up, eh? I'm glad we got the heavy ploughin' done up Lakey Hill, dear.' At which Philip bounds in to say, 'What's for tea, old girl? Partridge! Whackho!' Happy days. Little did he know that a slip of a girl who wasn't even born would have the For Sale signs up in a Brookfield some 35 years on, me old pals, me old beauties. Dum, de-dum, de-dum, de-dum …

FRANK KEATING

A COUNTRY DIARY: MACHYNLLETH
October 24 1987
Today I can't help looking backwards, because it was in October, 30 years ago, that I wrote my first *Guardian* 'Country Diary'. I have it before me now, brown with age and getting hard to read. The three decades that have passed since then have seen two major

changes for the worst. The first is the loss, which is still continuing, of ancient pastures, ploughed and reseeded to increase the production of meat we do not really need. The second change is the never-ending encroachment of spruce plantations, which get ever more huge now that the wealthy are putting more and more of their money into forestry. Too much of our countryside is now stifling under the conifer blanket. Certainly we need more woodlands, but not more exotic conifers. There has been a third major change. When I first began to write about nature conservation it was quite hard to find any kindred spirits hereabouts, whereas today there are plenty of them, many of them very active and enthusiastic. But though we have moved into an age of nature reserves and nature trails I sometimes wonder if this trend is as wonderful as it may seem. Is there a danger that we are gradually accepting a world where there won't be any wildlife worth talking about except what is protected in reserves? That would truly be a depressing sort of countryside to live in. But it need not happen and it is up to the conservation movement to make sure that it doesn't. A good start has certainly been made with the provision of incentive schemes to encourage wildlife conservation on farms and in woodlands, but the momentum will need to be maintained.

WILLIAM CONDRY

A COUNTRY DIARY: KESWICK

April 18 1988

If you want to get a wide view of the Cumbrian mountains, then the only thing to do is to get to the top of one of the higher ones – or go right outside their ring of fells and look back. That way you can get, too, a wonderful feeling of freedom and of elbow room, which many people need from time to time. One sunny noonday lately, I went east and took the steep and twisting road up to Hartside in the Pennines. I was last up there in late January with snow on the road and a threat of more to come, but now there was time to stop and look back to Hellvellyn and Saddleback and their attendant outliers. They still had old snow on their tops beyond the fertile valley of the Eden, which lay open to the warm sun. There were a lot of sheep and their growing lambs on the patchwork of small vari-coloured fields. Curlews rose and fell, calling, above the rougher land where the light gave a strange gold to the leafless ash trees and a shine of silver to the lichened thorns close at hand.

Primroses were fully opened in the lee of a conifer wood. The Eden had been in flood in January and disconsolate gulls waited on the muddy fields, but now a tractor was ploughing those same fields and an excited cloud of gulls circled overhead to drop and feed along the newly turned furrows. The top of Hartside was almost a different country. The east-facing block of Crossfell was thickly plastered with winter's snow and one lonely curlew flew, silent, over the heather. Was it, like me, distrustful of the weather? It might well have been – there was new snow on most of the fells a few days later.

ENID J. WILSON

DEVASTATION IN THE EYE OF THE STORM
October 15 1988

On the morning after, gardeners across the south of England couldn't believe their eyes. Here four of the guardians of great Wealden estates remember the October night that scarred their landscape and changed their lives.

Sheffield Park, Fletching, Sussex

Archie Skinner, head gardener for 17 years: 'When I woke in the night, I kept saying to my wife, "I've never heard a wind like this before." At 5 a.m. I couldn't stay in bed any longer. I knew it would be bad. I went out at six o'clock and it really shattered me. Two eucalyptus, both over 100ft, and a blue cedar were lying on the ground on top of one another. My heart was in my mouth. You couldn't walk on the footpaths. You had to clamber around.

'When you've devoted yourself to a garden – and most head gardeners look upon a garden as theirs – it's a part of your life. This was just the same as bereavement. It really hurt. And it still does. It's a loss that can't be repaired in my lifetime. It'll be 50 years before those trees we're planting will be up.

'We were a three-tier garden. We have lost the top storey: the dark green summer backdrop, it's a beauty in the autumn, and with it the intimacy. A garden is like a beautiful woman: you should never see everything in one glance. Thank goodness for the rhododendrons. They survived and will make a good show.

'We'll have a hundred new specimen trees in by autumn: scarlet oaks, beech, more conifers, rarer trees like the Syrian juniper. The emphasis will be, as it's always been: autumn colour.'

This 200-acre National Trust estate first entered history as the manor of Simon de Montfort and was landscaped by Lancelot 'Capability' Brown. Gibbon wrote part of his famous history in the library; and the third Earl of Sheffield, after whose family it is named, entertained the first Australian touring cricket team there in 1876, donating a trophy for Australia's premier domestic competition. Arthur Soames, father of Christopher, bought the garden in 1909 and planted it with exotica: 300 different conifers and 300 rhododendrons. It attracts 150,000 visitors annually.

Leonardslee, Lower Beeding, Horsham

Robin Loder, owner of the estate: 'It started to blow around one o'clock, but I thought at half-past one, "Well, half-an-hour of gale must have blown itself out by now." I just put my trousers and jersey over my pyjamas, slung a pair of shoes on, and wandered out. I drove my car down the driveway as far as I could go – fallen trees and whatnot – and then thought, "This is a bit hairy."

'I hopped over the fence into a field. I was suddenly conscious of things going zoom past me. "Can't be ponies," I thought. "And we haven't any bullocks or sheep." I caught the next one in the torchlight: big pine branches, about four feet long, going across the field rather like sage brush in a western movie. So I hopped back over the fence and stood under a couple of rhododendrons. I waited for the next lull before coming back to the house.

'I spent the rest of the night looking out of the bedroom window with powerful torches, literally counting all the trees disappearing, and realising what a better view we were going to get of the great out of doors. We've normally 80 trees in our view, so when we could see only two we knew we'd lost a bit. There were 1,000 trees down, as it turned out, and 6,000 to 8,000 in the surrounding shelter belt. The pinetum lost 98 per cent. Twenty trees are in the lakes. Quite attractive. Good for kingfishers.

'I look on the bright side – what else can you do? The majority of the trees were fully mature or very over-mature and would have come down in the next decade or two in one of the many winter gales. It's a blessing in disguise. We had too many big old trees; not enough planting space. When you've a fine tree with lovely shrubs under it, you tend to postpone the evil day. The local council isn't keen on felling trees; probably lumber you with a preservation order.

'We are planning to increase the area open to the public by 50 per cent. If that isn't positive thinking, I don't know what is. We've got quite a number of champion trees still. It'll be a different garden, but in many ways better.'

Robin Loder's great grandfather, Sir Edmund, bought the estate in 1889.

Nymans, Handcross, Sussex

David Masters, head gardener, another Sheffield Park apprentice: 'When it became light I looked east out of my bedroom window, and instead of a solid bank of conifers there were two trees standing. It was a lot worse than I had expected. There was a wide-open sky we had never known. I couldn't get anywhere. It was an obstacle course the whole way round the main garden.

'We are 500ft up. The country slopes away in every direction. We had a 400-yard pinetum shelter to the east. That was virtually obliterated. We lost 80 per cent of our trees, 90 per cent of the conifers. More than 500, I would say.

'The bit that survived best was the car park, the highest point of the garden. Woodlands in the valley you thought would have been protected were devastated. It took us three days to open up the access roads. I thought it was a dream, initially, and I would eventually wake up. It was the equivalent of a horticultural hell. We're battered, but there's still plenty to see.

'We shall replant a section of the shelter belt before spring. The western hemlock rather than Norway spruce – we lost every last one of them. You do learn, even from a nightmare.'

Nymans is the home of Anne, Countess of Ross, who supervises the gardens for the National Trust and Royal Horticultural Society. It has the intimacy of a family home. Three generations of the Messel family have created one of Britain's finest collections of South American and Far Eastern plants and 28 of the trees were among the country's biggest and best. Of the record-breaking trees, eight remained. Some others were winched back from 45 degrees and staked. The plants, camellia and rhododendron, one of the great glories, largely survived.

Emmetts Garden, Sevenoaks, Kent

George Fillis, the head gardener, who was taught his craft by Archie Skinner, looked out of his cottage at 3a.m.: 'I could see all the way up to the mansion. I couldn't do that before. I counted 60 trees blocking the drive. You just felt shock and horror. Time I met my assistant up at the house we were both almost in tears.

'The first effort was to get the roads clear up to the village. The people from the mansion came out to drag the stuff away and it was a marvellous effort by everybody.

'Gardens are always an ongoing thing. In a way, the storm gives us a marvellous opportunity to put our own stamp on a place which never really had a theme, except as a nice park collection. We shall go for Japanese maples and a few exotics from the Victorian period, such as the monkey puzzle and redwoods.'

A pro-hunting protest at a Countryside Alliance event held at Melton Airfield, near Melton Mowbray, Leicstershire in 2004. DAVID SILLITOE

A lamb waits for its bottle feed at Mark Graham's Hunt House Farm in the North York Moors National Park. DON MCPHEE

Sheep graze in a field opposite the Watchtree site near Carlisle, where half a million animals were buried during the foot and mouth outbreak of 2001. DON MCPHEE

Above and below: Cattle at Netherplace Farm in the town of Lockerbie are culled and burned on the farm – a response to the outbreak of foot and mouth disease in 2001. MURDO MACLEOD

Checking for symptoms of foot and mouth disease on a farm near Longtown, Cumbria. MURDO MACLEOD

Above: Strawberry pickers work in fields near King's Lynn, Norfolk. GRAHAM TURNER

Below: Sizewell nuclear power station, seen from across the sea at Southwold, Suffolk. GRAHAM TURNER

Above: A crop of rapeseed in a field near Hoxne, Suffolk. The distinctive yellow flowering crop now covers 3.5 per cent of England's farmland. The oil is harvested for use in processed foods, cooking oil and margarine. GRAHAM TURNER

Around 80,000 rooks and jackdaws gather for their evening roost on Buckenham Marshes, Norfolk. It is one of the largest known roosts in Europe. MARTIN ARGLES

A poppy field in Hoxne, Suffolk.
GRAHAM TURNER

Winter pike fishing on the Forty Foot river
near Ely, Cambridgeshire.
GRAHAM TURNER

This 100-acre estate – acquired by the National Trust in 1965 – bore the brunt of the storm. It stands behind Toys Hill, 300 acres of woodland where a 140ft tree, a Wellingtonia or Sequoiadendron giganteum, the tallest in Kent, still stood like a petrified monument amid the wrath of the storm. Every major specimen tree on the estate had been slain.

JOHN SAMUEL

LIFE BEYOND THE M40
April 27 1989
Do you feel tired, jaded, depressed by the fumes and congestion of city life? What you need is a weekend in the country. Driven by the desire to hear birdsong, to see green fields, real trees and – who knows? – the occasional ferret, thousands of us regularly set off on a journey of expectation down the motorway in pursuit of a vivid, rustic dream.

Country life, we believe, is somehow nearer our true nature than life in the city. Some of us may have a weekend cottage in Wiltshire, Oxfordshire or Norfolk, to which we grimly ferry the children, providing a wide range of in-car entertainment – tapes of *Winnie the Pooh*, *Alice in Wonderland* and *Children's Favourites* – to keep them going. Some of us favour weekend breaks in country hotels, where a ramble round the grounds and cocktails in the bar get us into the country spirit. Some of us fervently believe that, one day, we will finally move out of the town for good and spend the rest of our lives eating home-grown carrots and fresh-picked parsley. None of us actually lives in the country yet. But we all believe that rural life is 'out there' at the end of the motorway, waiting to welcome us. What a pity it only lasts from Friday until Sunday, when we all have to head back to town again.

Each of us likes to think of ourself as a country person at heart. Few of us feel like Mr Salter, the demoralised foreign editor of Waugh's *Daily Beast*, who regards the country as highly dangerous: 'There was something unEnglish and not quite right about "the country" with its solitude and self-sufficiency, its bloody recreations, its darkness and silence and sudden, inexplicable noises.' You hear few people insisting that they prefer, say, Birmingham or Birkenhead to the Yorkshire Moors or the Cotswolds. Everyone is at pains to claim an affinity with nature, even if the nearest they get to the countryside is a trip to the garden centre in a pair of green wellies.

We still think that 'country children' have a better time than town ones, picturing them running wild over hills and dales, although in a recent *Harpers & Queen* survey, country-loving mothers confided that they no longer felt happy about letting children roam unsupervised. 'When I was eight or nine,' wrote one, 'I used to roam free for hours on end. When Alexander and Nicola want to do the same today, I have to say no. There are too many strange people about. It's a very great tragedy.'

Of course, it is not strictly necessary to live in the country to be a 'country person'. You need not spend weekends training your pointer to 'flush' or 'peg', or practising with your Coggswell & Harrison gun on basic targets (going away, incoming, crossing) to see yourself as a person whose heart lies in country matters. Merely putting on a Barbour to go to work indicates that you are someone to whom an office is a foreign land, a place where you go merely to earn money.

Driving a Range Rover (Nissan Patrol or Daihatsu Sportrak are acceptable alternatives) through choked city traffic demonstrates to those crawling Fiestas and Escorts that you are really more at home bumping over a muddy grass track. Even if you live in a high-rise, hi-tech apartment, the Laura Ashley catalogue can furnish you with a country house-style interior, complete with dried flowers and coordinating chintzes.

If you are still not quite sure how to achieve the authentic country lifestyle, there are plenty of magazines to help you to do it. Indeed, it seems that when they are not shuttling up and down the M40 (the direct route from Chelsea to Gloucestershire), country people do little except read about country life. Best of all for an instant insight into country living, is the glossy *Country Homes and Interiors*, a magazine which combines the pleasures of stately homes and shopping. Here are Grania and Hugh Cavendish taking us on a tour of the family seat, Holker Hall in Cumbria, which is open to the public. The house is magnificent, the family is fun, affectionate and relaxed, but, we learn, old, almost outdated formalities still persist: 'At lunch, the children and their friends stood up as we, the grown ups, entered the dining room.' A helpful feature at the back tells us how to create and where to acquire what we have admired. Candlestick lamps, like those at Holker Hall, are available for £48.50; the manners of the Cavendish children are presumably more expensive.

Next come interviews with the famous, who also turn out to be 'country people'. All-purpose 'country lovers', like Tim Rice and Jilly Cooper, are a real threat here, but this month we discover that the famous spy sleuth, Chapman Pincher, is a countryman too, bringing up his children in a sprawling Elizabethan farmhouse in unspoilt Surrey countryside, which he vigorously defended from ramblers and herds of cows (not very rural of him, surely?).

Country Life is indispensable reading matter for all those who fantasise about acquiring a little 'country property'. Inside its stiff, colourful pages, crammed with property advertisements, you can find the charming April Cottage, a 300-year-old thatched cottage at Minstead for around £100,000; or the lovely Grade II listed Berkshire cottage with its own woodland and views across to Inkpen Hill and Combe Gibbet for £260,000. Property advertisements take up two-thirds of the magazine, but if you plough through them you get, at last, to 'Warbling Among the Oaks' by Philip Radford.

The Field describes itself as the 'magazine for the country' and is altogether more pugnacious in its approach to country matters. Here is Lord Denning doing battle with county councils over their classification of green lanes as Byeways Open to All Traffic and consequently being ruined by young vandals on motorbikes. There is a fascinating essay on silage. And a very angry piece on behalf of Devon landowners complaining about the midsummmer migration of 'hippies' to the south-west and the reluctance of the police to tackle the problem. 'One wonders what the police's attitude would be if a few of the hippies could be persuaded to decamp to the inviting lawns which surround the Devon & Cornwall Constabulary headquarters?'

Members of the Animal Liberation Front or those squeamish about Mr Salter's 'bloody recreations' should steer clear of *The Shooting Life* or *Countrysport*, magazines devoted almost entirely (with the exception of property advertisements) to killing things. A matter of raging controversy here is the 'commercial' shoot, an unsporting arrangement where tame, hand-fed pheasants are kept on short rations until the Range Rovers roll up. Seduced by the whistling of their feeders, these unfortunate, but gullible, birds rush out from the woods to be fed, only to be shot by aspiring sportsmen. One keeper describes his astonishment on a commercial shoot to see a couple of hundred pheasants running out of the wood to meet him. 'Soon they were all around my feet almost pecking at my bootlace eyelet holes. They thought I was there to feed them.'

All these magazines are on sale, of course, in the city and its suburbs where nearly all of us live. The rural newsagent doesn't exist. But then, it is only town dwellers who need to read about country life. Real country people – the handful who are left – are too busy shooting foxes, digging up hedgerows and spraying pesticides over the fields to bother with *Country Homes and Interiors*. The countryside, I suspect, is an altogether nastier place than 'country people' ever imagine from their rapid weekend visits. Surely Mr Salter was wise to prefer his 'cosy horizon' of slates and chimneys.

JANE ELLISON

TO THE GREEN AND PLEASANT?
THE PROSPECTS AND OPTIONS FOR FARMERS NEXT YEAR
December 22 1989

The British farmer is about to wander into fresh woods and pastures new. In the course of doing so he could change the face of Britain. He could grow 'biomass' for biotechnology. He could – in theory – farm for the pharmaceutical companies. He could diversify into new crops like meadowfoam, lupins, borage, linseed and flax. In some areas he could plant his land with windmills. If the climate changes a bit more, he could grow sweetcorn in the south and wheat in the north. He could farm alpaca, deer and wild boar. He could take up organic farming and selling nurture as nature intended to a consumer market now seriously worried about E numbers and Alar. He could take up agroforestry; he could convert to timber; he could take up government agency schemes and grow winter grass mixtures for geese to graze upon, or engineer his fields to be a home for the stone curlew. He could grow hedges and wildflowers instead of sugar beet; he could turn his fields into areas of 'quiet countryside enjoyment'; he could restore ancient coppices and chalk grassland.

He could also go broke – last year, farm incomes fell by 25 per cent. His land could tumble down to scrub and nettles and eventually untidy woodland. Or he could sell most of his land to Mr Big and his house and a few acres could fall into the hands of a merchant banker who wants somewhere quiet with a paddock for the daughter's ponies.

Then Mr Big could try diversifying. But he, too, would run into the same problems. Britain is over-producing: there will have to be some way of reducing output. There is a ministry proposal called 'extensification'. It means that the whole farm has to produce 20 per cent less. One scheme is already in place. It is called 'set aside'. A proportion of the farm – or for that matter all of it – is set aside, left fallow, mown once a year, while the farmer draws a set fee per acre and manages on the rest or gets another job.

Either way, the countryside changes. There are various calculations about how much land is potentially redundant: it could be as many as three million acres. For the first time in decades, the nation has a chance to decide what to do with it. Conservationists, farmers and government agencies all agree that there is an opportunity right now for debate and then decision. But there is no debate, and any decisions are likely to be taken piecemeal and by default. On the horizon is a field of view overgrown with nettles, which no one seems to want to grasp.

One of them is the geography of decline. Miss Melinda Appleby is environmental policy adviser to the National Farmers' Union (NFU). She says one fear is that land in the hills will become redundant. 'These are areas where you could say farming was marginal. As profitability declines, they would go out of farming. There is a big fear in the hills that in order to maintain businesses in the lowlands, people will diversify into sheep and the profitability of sheep in the lowlands will be greater.'

In fact, the Countryside Commission has just announced an imaginative scheme for 12 'community forests' on marginal, urban-fringe farmland. But the community forests – plus the Commission's other plan for 100,000 acres of new forest in the Midlands, which will also soak up redundant land – together with new land released for development, will barely scratch the surface of the problem. The NFU doesn't like the idea of set aside. In the first place, the scheme only operates for five years, with no guarantee of continuation. There are also emotional objections. 'We wish to see as many farmers as possible occupying the countryside,' says Melinda Appleby. 'We want to see a working countryside and we don't want to see it fossilised so it's almost like a theme park.' Farmers have higher hopes of the 'extensification' programme in the wings. Under this, farms would have to reduce output by 20 per cent. Some farmers are likely to achieve this by converting to organic farming.

Unfortunately, even this won't be enough: the output figures from well-run organic farms are only between 6 and 12 per cent below those from intensive estates. So 'extended' farms will have to leave a wide strip of unsown soil in each field, and let the hedges grow. But only a few will make the change. Most will still be farming what they always farmed. And they still won't feel enthusiastic about extensification. 'To a farmer it's anathema not to produce on his land and therefore it's not that he is not being responsible in meeting the challenges.'

Many farmers, it turns out, wouldn't in the least object to making the countryside – their countryside – more attractive. It depends on what is defined as attractive. It would also depend on some serious stimulus from the conservation lobby. 'People were extremely disappointed that conservationists could not come up with exciting, positive solutions for potential land that might come out of agriculture,' says Miss Appleby. Another problem is that the wildlife lobby is divided even over simple things like the future of old farm woodlands. Most of these were 'coppiced' – cut to the ground every 20 years or so and then allowed to regenerate. Should these go back to coppice? Or be allowed to go on growing? She goes on: 'The problem with taking a management decision out of a farmer's hands as an economic decision and putting it into conservationists' hands is that the conservationists don't always agree. In the future, it seems, we are going to be taking arbitrary decisions about what we want from the countryside: the large blue here, a certain bird there, and we are going to manage for those species, which will mean that everything else will go.' The countryside may be changing. It will go on changing. The Agriculture and Food Research Council (AFRC) reckon cereal yields could be increased by another 25 per cent this century, freeing even more land.

In a bid to meet the problem halfway, the AFRC has also invested £730,000 in a five-year study of the relationship between wildlife and farming – and what will happen as land use goes on changing. The point is that for the first time in decades the environmentalists have a powerful voice – and a government which claims to listen. Three million acres or more of Britain's countryside can't be left to tumble down to nettles, bracken, Oxford ragwort and rosebay willow herb, punctuated by leisure centres and car parks. Or if it can – there is a case for that, too – it might as well be thought about first. Both the farmers and the conservationists agree that there ought to be a debate. They also agree that a debate doesn't seem to be taking place. There is a nettle for a somebody – it might as well be the new environment secretary – to grasp.

TIM RADFORD

෨෨ CHAPTER SIX ෨෨

Right to roam
1990–1999

Guardian editors have an enviable record of long service, with the sad exception of C. P. Scott's promising son Ted, who drowned in 1932 in Lake Windermere, where his friend Arthur Ransome had introduced him to the pleasures of sailing. He had been in charge of the paper for only three years, a span dwarfed by one of his most significant successors, Alistair Hetherington, who edited the newspaper between 1956 and 1975. Hetherington saved the *Guardian* by staying up all night to write a memorandum on its unique virtues, which rallied enough support on the newspaper's governing Scott Trust to reject a planned merger with *The Times* in 1966. Had he gone to bed instead and turned out the light, there would be no *Guardian* today. He was also an intimate of leading politicians, conferring regularly with the Labour prime minister Harold Wilson just as Scott had done with Herbert Asquith and David Lloyd George. But in spite of these distinctions, he is remembered best by his friends as a countryman, a cragsman and a tireless, long-distance walker.

At the editorial conferences over which he presided, where (most unusually for Fleet Street) alcohol was never served, the rosy-cheeked Hetherington regularly picked out rural stories, complimented the day's 'Country Diary' or enquired about possible coverage of farming or, particularly, environmental issues. His passion for walking extended to London, where he marched about between the *Guardian* office, Whitehall and other important places, scorning taxis and on one occasion, when it was snowing as strongly as in his beloved Scottish Highlands, rejecting a lift from a Rolls-Royce, which was conveying his very different colleague Peter Jenkins, a comfortable socialite and townsman who ran the labour desk, from a long lunch with a wealthy business contact.

Hetherington tramped the Cuillins of Skye with his Scottish correspondents, the Lake District with the country diarist Harry Griffin, and Blackheath or Greenwich Park with his children Lucy and Tom. He kept Ordnance Survey maps of the whole of Britain in a cabinet at home, and after moving from the *Guardian* to become the BBC's controller in Scotland, he sent nature notes to the *Listener*, the corporation's excellent but now sadly defunct magazine. In August 1983 he described how the water supply to his neighbour on the Isle of Arran had been blocked by an eel, which had squirmed through the filter on the intake from the nearby burn and got wedged in a pipe. On another occasion he took issue with Scottish churchmen on the island of Lewis who were demanding Sunday observance in its strictest sense, condemning even rural strolls. Hetherington asked in the *Listener*: 'Must young people incur the censure of the elders if, having been to the long morning service, they go walking in the country on a Sunday afternoon? Why not encourage them to enjoy the beauties of nature, with which Lewis is so richly endowed? Modest enjoyment of the countryside on a Sunday afternoon does nobody any harm. It is at least as spiritual as doing what I know some Lewisians do, which is go to bed or doze in an armchair until it is time for evening service.'

Hetherington was a man of his time, and also of demure Scottish Presbyterian stock. His own eyebrows went up when he came across visiting geologists 'of both sexes' swimming in the icy water off Coire Lochan beach on Arran. But his countryside interests made him a man of his time in another sense, especially in the great debates about access to wild land which absorbed rural Britain in the second half of the 20th century. Appropriately, these had their roots in Manchester. On the day after St George's Day in 1932, April 24, two large groups of determined ramblers were organised by the British Workers' Sport Federation to carry out a pincer movement on the Peak District summit of Kinder Scout, which had been declared off-limits by the landowner, the Duke of Devonshire, and the gamekeepers who protected his grouse. The Manchester and Lancashire contingent, 400-strong, marched up from Bowden Bridge and brushed aside a picket of keepers strung across William Clough, slightly injuring one in a scuffle. Surging triumphantly on, they reached the plateau and the dramatic rock formation of the Kinder Downfall, where they linked up with the second front, whose members had tramped from Sheffield.

The Kinder Scout Mass Trespass was accompanied by a special correspondent from the *Guardian* who was given the then enormous allocation of 954 words (in a paper of only 16 pages) to describe the scene in detail. He recounted the curious mixture of sudden violence – 'There will be plenty of bruises carefully nursed in Gorton and other parts of Manchester tonight' – and cosy moments, such as regular stops for cups of tea and the decision of the local police inspector to allow the returning procession to march, singing, into Hayfield, led by himself in one of the Derbyshire force's 'Baby' Austins. The newspaper also covered the subsequent imprisonment of five of the ramblers after a trial in which prosecution evidence included the possession by one of the trespassers of a book by Lenin. The judge at Derby Assizes observed, in the classic manner of all judges, 'Isn't that the Russian gentleman?'

The grand jury at Derby consisted of two brigadier generals, three colonels, two majors, three captains, two aldermen and 11 country gentlemen, and this had a lasting significance in the long debate about access which ensued. The British countryside has been divided for most of its history between masters and men, to an extent seldom matched even in the harshest Industrial Revolution towns. The access issue reopened this ancient division, albeit with much assistance from urban ramblers like the members of the British Workers' Sports Federation and its bicycling counterpart, the Clarion Club. Prime among these was one of the Kinder Trespass leaders Benny Rothman, a lifelong Communist but a genial and practical man, who was a good friend and contact for three generations of *Guardian* reporters. He lived to take part in the 60th anniversary celebrations of the trespass, which the paper liberally reported, helped in the creation of the Pennine Way, which crosses the Kinder plateau, and even in his late 80s, confined by a stroke to a wheelchair, fought successfully with his wife Lily against his local council's plan to close a short but vital local footpath, which gave mothers with pushchairs a safe route to the primary school. After his death aged 90 in 2002, a high-speed locomotive was given the name 'Benny Rothman – Manchester Rambler' by the then environment secretary David Miliband at Manchester Piccadilly railway station. By then, Benny's dream of a national 'right to roam' had been law for two years and was agreed, even by the majority of previously restrictive landlords, to be working sympathetically and without damaging change to Britain's wild places and those who work in them. Fittingly, too, among the other locomotives which the 'Manchester Rambler' passes on its journeys between London, the north west and Scotland is another called the 'Manchester Guardian'.

FARMERS FEEL INSULTED BY ENVIRONMENTALISTS
December 14 1990
From where I farm, high up on the edge of the Brendon Hills in Somerset, there is an eagle's-eye view across an ethereal landscape moulded by centuries of occupation by small family farms. But this year I have watched three of my four neighbours having to throw in the sponge. And as the new owners have moved in, I have wondered what

fate would befall the beech copses, the steep-sided coombes cloaked in oaks, the old *linhays*, the badgers' sets and bluebell woods.

One neighbour has just sold out to a big 'efficient' farm business operating from an HQ in the Taunton Vale. After the first day under this new ownership, the philistines moved in with chainsaws and bulldozers and proceeded to fillet out the backbone of one of the finest beech and oak hedgerows in the vicinity. Despite the fact that this hedgerow had taken years of natural evolution and diligent human tending (with the help of grant aid) under the previous owners' occupation, it was impossible to find any existing legislation or powers under the Tree Preservation Orders to help safeguard the unique patchworking of this land.

Another neighbour, the last of a long family line, has been shut away in a geriatric mental home. For centuries, this traditional farm has hosted timeless summer evenings fanned by the wings of horseshoe bats, cockchafers and chiffchaffs. Buzzards have presided over the groves of alders and orchids. Last month his farm was sold to an agrochemical director; men arrived with chainsaws, teams were hired to gas the rabbit warrens, new plans for developments were submitted to the council's planning department. Another neighbour is simply fallowing the livestock from his fields, and hopes to weather the storm in an armchair.

Symptoms of the financial squeeze are becoming increasingly evident as the agri-grapevine reports sightings of the bailiff in nearly every farmyard. Across the pages of the local papers there is an ever-growing frequency of farmers reportedly convicted at police roadblocks by the weekly cattle market for crimes of untaxed, uninsured vehicles. And yet, even after the most financially crippling season, farmers have found themselves stereotyped as factory-farming fiends. Even bodies like the Council for the Protection of Rural England (CPRE) have been proposing a 100 per cent subsidy slash in the Gatt talks. They propose payments geared towards 'developing environmentally beneficial features'.

To do this would simply mean that small farmers would hit the dirt first and green objectives would fail still further. A small farmer's financial status is precarious: if you remove our subsidies we just would not be able to produce food any longer. The environmental grants would go nowhere near making up the difference. The only likely survivors would be the Big Farmers with the financial clout to buy their way into the freehold of the bankrupted areas flooding the market. And those characters would be the least likely to take up the environmental grants on offer.

People must learn to differentiate between the small family farmer as landscape and ecological benefactor and the big company farms as the real culprits of rustic ransack. It is no good if the environment lobby persists in remaining so divorced from the realities of those that work the soil. The diabolical misunderstandings cross-flowing between the two groups will never establish common ground for fertile developments. Farmers and the greens are like two sociological satellites on different orbits, frequently in collision; yet both are part of the same universe and could be potentially well-cemented allies. Farmers feel insulted by environmentalists. They sense they are the misappropriated targets of the green vendetta and that they are not respected for their insight and wisdom into the workings of the natural world.

The CPRE's latest publication, *Future Harvests*, demonstrates this well. Being all about the future of agriculture, the research for this pamphlet failed to consult a single working farmer. The resulting text serves little more than to alienate the farming community from the start, suggesting the need to resurrect yet another consortium of officials to police farmers. My mailbox already receives up to three bureaucratic letter bombs each day, whilst my farmyard hosts a whole Piccadilly Circus of nit-picking officials; do I need any more environmental Adolfs telling me what to do?

Despite the media's hypothetical generalisations about farmers, many of the smaller family farmers are on the 'all-go' for environmental objectives. They have been for years, long before the concept became fashionable. But farmers are mistrustful of the sincerity and practical abilities of the conservationists. They believe that the endless assortment of trusts, societies and associations magnetise a riff-raff of urban-refined, holier-than-thou do-gooders. These self-important souls appear to struggle desperately for any outlet through which to exercise 'eco-clout' over others, particularly us. Meeting houses are full of pretentious cliques, back-scratching their way up a fiercely competitive and acidic hierarchy. Projects rarely seem to venture out from the world of word-processed, recycled paperwork into practical fruition.

Farmers keen on conservation are put off still further. They are confused when so many of the conservation king-pins spearheading the movement appear to be suffering from eco-schizophrenia. One day we read about David Bellamy ranting on about the dangers of agrochemicals applied to the soil, the next day we see him fronting an ICI schools video promoting the wisdom and eco-compatibility of these same chemicals.

One farmer I know on the Brendon Hills accidentally ploughed out a footpath. Surprisingly, the Ramblers' Association ordered this farmer to spray off the growing crop with herbicide to demarcate the line of the footpath again. After a BBC Open Space film about my own anti-pesticide campaign was broadcast, the Ramblers' Association were one of the first to be in touch with me, expressing their concerns about their members' exposure to farm chemicals!

The macho man can be a green man, and I remember some years back when, after milking my cows in the evening, I used to descend the hills on to the west Somerset coastline and play saxophone at a night club. The bouncer was typical of the 20-stone, close-cropped, tattooed bovver brigade; yet I remember being curiously captivated by his talk of his voluntary, self-appointed daily task as 'minder' to a Peregrine falcon's nest on a local cliff ... 'The lads here think I'm namby-pamby, but I tell you, I'll smash any ... er that has it in for those hawks. They're wicked magic, those birds.'

Quite frankly, if the environment movement integrated a bit of the macho instinct into their campaigning, some real action might be achieved. Whenever I've tried to get a local trust involved with the protection of some species in my vicinity, they have generally been most untrustworthy in their response. In the last year I have tried to call out several full-time field staff to trace and stake out a stone curlew's nest for a 'no-go' spray zone on a neighbour's farm. Similarly, a roosting haunt of the greater horseshoe bat needed a protection order slapped on it before a change of land ownership threatened the bats' survival. Sadly, not one of the trusts I contacted could be coerced into any kind of positive reaction.

The inept impracticality of conservationists has led to a high degree of eco-stupidity at trust level. A classic example of this was when the Woodland Trust sold 32,000 deciduous trees to another trust. The purchasing trust returned all 32,000 specimens, claiming they were dead; after re-examination, the Woodland Trust got back to the purchasers stating that the trees were not dead, they were leafless because it was winter. What a waste of transportation resources! Where is the greenery of the greens?

The environment lobby and small farmers alike must identify their common ground before it is too late. The small farmer's demise is the ecosystem's demise, and would be the biggest crisis to conservation this century.

I'm a family farmer, but I hardly have time left for my family once the 16 hours a day, seven days a week drudgery of hard labour is over. My personal scheme for survival has been to write a letter to the National Trust, asking if they could finance a preservation project by signing and sealing my farm and family up for life (and after life in cryonics and taxidermy) as a sort of national monument to the traditional small farmer. The public could view us at work forking farmyard manure, talking in West Country jargon, being macho, rising early in the morning and dressing in rustic rags.

MARK PURDEY

A COUNTRY DIARY: WHARNCLIFFE
January 12 1991
It's exactly a century ago that those two gritstone pioneers, Puttrell and Watson, put up the first rock climbs on Kinder Scout. The promontory on Upper Tor and Primitive on neighbouring Nether Tor may seem tame these days but were a real pioneering effort in 'forbidden' territory on the Peak District's best-known upland, overlooking Grindsbrook. Kinder Scout is not, though, where outcrop climbing began: that honour seems to belong to the long-overlooked but once mightily popular Wharncliffe Crags high above the Don Valley. Puttrell, Watson and Co came here in the early 1880s and put up several interesting routes on what is actually coal measure sandstone, not gritstone. It has a good supply of positive, incut holds so the techniques required are more akin to those of our volcanically derived mountains than the friction methods of most gritstone crags of the area. Wharncliffe became notorious as Britain's dirtiest climbing ground on account of the copious deposits of soot – the edge lies immediately down-wind of the former Samuel Fox's steelworks at Stocksbridge and high above the Sheffield–Manchester 'Woodhead' railway. Though the elements have cleaned the rocks in the years since the steel works and railway went electric, few climbers come here now. Looking north along the crest of Wharncliffe the other day as the soft, winter sunlight slanted through the silver birches, no living soul came into view. What a contrast to the early postwar days, when cragsmen came by bus to Deepcar, or by train to Wortley station, and climbed through those birch woods to the foot of the rocks, Others came 'via devious leafy glades' from Grenoside and Chapeltown in the east. As I went along the sunlit crest, jackdaws shouted to one another in the trees below, a Swaledale ewe watched me from a rock pillar. The stage was set for Puttrell's ghost to come swinging up from Deepcar, a hemp cart rope slung across his shoulders.

ROGER A REDFERN

THESE BOOTS WERE MADE FOR BAGGING
August 3 1991
Rain sweeps in curtains across the bleak expanse of Rannoch Moor, the largest and most inhospitable tract of saturated peat in Britain. The grey day dawns to show ragged clouds clinging to the black cliffs of Glen Coe and the burns are ribbons of foam. Motorists swishing by on the A82 turn up the heater and switch the wipers

to double speed. Warm and cosy, they can afford to spare a thought for the bedraggled walker plodding through the heather on her way to the hills of the Black Mount. But our lonely soul needs no sympathy. She is bound for a 3,000ft mountain and a bright fire burns within, sustaining her over the miles of bog and boulder slopes. It's a fire first kindled by Sir Hugh Munro 100 years ago.

Munro was a founder member of the Scottish Mountaineering Club at a time when the Highlands were being explored for the first time. He spent years poring over maps and walking the hills, in all weather and usually alone, clasping an expensive altimeter. Munro's research findings, his Tables, were published in the September 1891 edition of the *Scottish Mountaineering Club Journal*. The Tables listed 283 separate mountains in Scotland over 3,000ft high (a total which has since been reduced to 277 following recalculations by the Ordnance Survey). At once the Munros provided a cast-iron framework for hillwalkers in Scotland and only 10 years passed before the first Munroist claimed his prize.

Imagine the scene: a late summer's day in September 1901 and a small party of walkers, dressed in tweeds, is approaching the summit of Meall Dearg, a 3,118ft peak at the east end of the Aonach Eagach ridge in Argyll. With great emotion one of the party, the Rev A. E. Robertson, rushes to the cairn, kisses it and then turns to embrace his wife and shake hands firmly with his friend, Lord Moncrieff. History was being made, for Robertson, aged 31, had become the first Munroist, the first climber to have ascended all the 283 mountains in Munro's Tables.

Since that date the sport of Munro-bagging has gathered pace and today there are nearly 800 Munroists, including Chris Smith, Labour MP for Islington South. Munroitis is increasingly addictive and the annual total of completions is accelerating: 24 in 1980, 62 in 1985 and 76 in 1989. Final Munro parties are wonderful celebrations and many become legendary in their extravagance. After all, they have been planned and debated hundreds of times by half-frozen wretches as they plodded over remote Highlands.

Last year, one Munroist was accompanied to the summit of her final peak by a kilted piper, while another chartered a train to take his support party of 80, plus supplies, to the base of Beinn na Lap. Recently, we struggled in a snowstorm to uncork the champagne and malt whisky on the bleak summit of Slioch to celebrate a Munro completion.

Munro's Tables provide one priceless asset for the hillwalker: motivation. The thought of another tick in the Tables is usually enough to get you out of your sleeping bag, however vile the weather. During 10 years of Munro bagging, I suffered an inordinate amount of bad weather; you don't drive 800 miles just to doze in the tent.

Apart from the joy of 'bagging', the Munros have their own rewards. Days when the rain stops at lunchtime, the clouds roll away and you enjoy clear air and intoxicating views; stormy days when the wind tears holes in the mist to expose savage and dripping crags; days when you crunch up frozen snow with the ridge, snaking ahead, set against an azure sky, and autumn days when you stride back down the corrie with a delicious ache in your legs and some new Munros under your belt, marvelling at the rowan berries and the moor grass burnished by the evening sun.

The disease of Munroitis can lead to one-upmanship. I remember the raw Easter day when I reached the summit cairn of Spidean Mialach, having traversed the ridge from Gleouraich, at the same moment as another walker who had approached from Quoich dam to the south. We nodded to each other. 'One ninety-eight,' he said. 'Two thirty-five,' I replied. His shoulders drooped slightly, while I headed towards the valley with a spring in my step.

Hugh Thomas Munro was born in London in 1856. At 17 he was sent to Stuttgart to learn German and he started climbing in the Alps. He was ADC to General Fielding and went to South Africa as private secretary to the Governor of Natal. On the London scene he had a reputation as a magnificent dancer. After the Basuto War he returned to Scotland and managed the family estates at Lindertis in Fife for his father, Sir Campbell Munro. He stood as unsuccessful Conservative candidate for Kircaldy.

The Highlands in Munro's time differed greatly from today. The estates and deer forests were thriving then and Sir Hugh knew personally many of the lairds. It was always possible to find accommodation in the abundance of lodges and bothies. He was often transported by his man in a 'dogcart' to the base of the mountains; later he bought one of the first motor cars.

From his writings, we can see that Munro was a tough and single-minded hillwalker. He hated to lose time by a late start and was known to leave for the hills after dinner and walk through the night. Winter blizzards were faced stoically and he describes powder snow filling his pockets and drifting between his shirt and waistcoat where it froze. Back home they had to chip the frozen snow off with a knife. Sadly Munro died of pneumonia in 1918 while running a troops' canteen at Tarascon in France. He left two mountains unclimbed: the Inaccessible Pinnacle on the Cuillins of Skye and the Carn Cloich-mhuilinn in the Cairngorms, which he was keeping for his final party.

The Munro round lends itself to all manner of records. Hamish Brown has climbed them all six times. Martin Moran has completed a winter round in 83 days. Fred Wiley took 57 years from first to last peak and Hugh Symonds recently ran the

Munros without using wheeled transport in 67 days. Hugh continued his run and completed all the 3,000ft mountains in Britain and Ireland in under 100 days.

When all the Munros have been climbed, can we hang up our boots? No, is the answer. We simply start on the Corbetts!

J. Rooke Corbett was born in 1877 and, although living in Bristol, he passionately loved the Highlands. In 1930 he was the second Munroist and went on to climb every 2,000ft eminence in Scotland. Corbett's list of Scottish mountains between 2,500 and 3,000ft was published in 1952. It contains 221 splendid peaks and only the Corbett-bagger will visit spectacular regions such as Rhum, Ardgour, Arran, Flowerdale, Applecross, Coigach and the Reay Forest.

When we have seen off the Corbetts are we to start on Docharty's list of 2,000–2,500ft hills? Surely we can't go on making lists of objectives based on height alone or our last years might be spent sweating up Cambridgeshire's Gog and Magog, or every molehill on the garden lawn. Yet if we disregard Docharty's list we can never enjoy the Ochils, Ben Stack, Criffel, Suilven, Stac Pollaidh, Heaval and Ben Mor Coigach.

However, the Munros set the pulse racing and for this we must thank the great man himself, whose ghost stalks every cairn.

HAMISH BROWN

PILLAGE CHURCH OF ST LOOT

August 16 1991

Car boot sales have overtaken Sunday morning religious services in popularity, but the new religion may be nearer to the local church than is imagined. The Revd David Atkins, Rural Dean for Chelmsford, believes that the increase in thefts from his four parish churches has much to do with 'the new joys of car boot sales': 'The nearest church to my house has nothing at all of any real value, but it's been done twice in the past month. They took the mowing equipment, and exactly the same happened in a neighbouring parish last Saturday night. We think they get sold the next morning. The turnover's pretty rapid.'

From lawnmowers to stained-glass windows, nothing since Henry VIII's dissolution of the monasteries 450 years ago compares with the current pillage of the churches, according to the Ecclesiastical Insurance Group (EIG). One of Britain's 16,000 Anglican churches suffers theft, vandalism or arson every four hours. Places of worship of other denominations are at similar risk, with one in four a victim in 1989.

The crimewave is of particular concern for the Church of England, which lost property worth £4.5m last year. Incidents of claims have risen from 5,000 two years ago to 6,500 last year and a projected 8,500 this year. 'We try to keep premiums down to the minimum, but if these thefts continue we will have to consider making increases,' says Jim Scott of EIG, which insures 95 per cent of Anglican churches.

This has worrying implications for the rural parishes, struggling to pay an average £600 a year for comprehensive insurance, which are a soft touch to the amateur opportunist burglar or the professional gang stealing to order. 'Increasingly, we are having to keep our churches locked,' says the Venerable Neil Robinson, Archdeacon of Suffolk. 'Parishioners are anxious to keep them open, so in some cases we encourage the whole village to keep an eye open for strangers.'

But low-tech answers to theft have not stemmed the tide of burglaries. A parish chest was taken from St Peter's at Cretingham, the name of the village carved below the date 1660. On the other side of the country, thieves with crowbars smashed an ambry, containing the sacrament, from the wall of St Michael's in Newquay, Cornwall. A 17th-century chair worth £2,700 disappeared from St Mary's at Shipton Solers, Gloucestershire. In Pleshey, Essex, a Jacobean altar and a medieval vestment chest were removed from the village church in broad daylight. Felsham, near Bury St Edmunds, suffered the loss of two Jacobean chairs after thieves cased the church and returned at night, forcing the heavy doors open. All along the Kentish Weald villages have tales to tell of stolen goods. Hawkhurst and Sandhurst, within miles of one another, each had unwelcome visitors who made off with altars, tables and chairs.

'St Peter and St Paul at Alpheton is a little gem hidden in the countryside next to a farm up a lonely lane and it was stripped of everything,' says the Venerable Donald Smith, Archdeacon of Sudbury. Luckily the silver was in a safe, but six medieval chairs went, as did a credence table (on which are placed the communion vessels) and a coffin stool. Its pair had been stolen during an earlier visitation. 'That took place on June 9 and three days later they came back to see if there was anything else.'

In nearby Great Barton another church was stripped of everything movable. The archdeacon is convinced that organised antiques gangs are behind the robberies: 'We're very near the coastal ports here, and I think they're people who've got a container and they get it straight over to the Continent.'

This month's edition of *Trace*, which specialises in retrieving stolen works of art and antiques, is going to press with an appeal for readers to keep a lookout for a wooden carving of St George and the Dragon, removed from a Staffordshire church. Editor Philip Saunders says the theft of church silver and furniture is booming. 'During a four-month period last year we had 28 Bishop's Chairs stolen, worth between

£1,500 and £2,500 each. The problem is that churches can't afford to insure their things properly, so they go for new for old. When an Elizabethan chalice gets stolen it's replaced by a £300 silver one. If a dealer is offered something, the thieves are so plausible no one ever suspects it's stolen. The thieves are helped by the churches, who don't catalogue their valuables or take photographs of them.'

Mr Saunders paints an appalling picture of the churches slowly but surely disappearing before our eyes. 'Stained-glass windows are going as well. There were two taken down in Kent and another in Hampstead, north London. And literally hundreds of brass plates from church floors and walls have gone.' While the Revd Atkins warily eyes the crowds drifting off to neighbourhood car boot sales, he has taken drastic action to preserve the sanctity of his church. 'We've installed what I call Colditz lights. They come on automatically whenever anybody comes within 50 yards. It's one of the few churchyards where you can tend your graves by floodlight. Cut down on courting no end, too.'

A colleague describes the looting as the spirit of the age, but the Venerable Terry Gibson, Archdeacon of Ipswich, believes there is nothing new under the sun. 'It's far less here than I was accustomed to on Merseyside in the 1960s. We had 38 people employed full time repairing damage. We used to buy £300 worth of second-hand window panes per week. It was a daily routine checking if the guttering was still there.'

DAVID SHARROCK

THE LIE OF THE LAND: THE FARMER'S WIFE
February 12 1992
The phone rings in the farmhouse kitchen in Kent. 'Yes,' says Leslie Manington patiently, 'yes, they can bottle-feed the lambs. Pardon?' She looks upward in a perfect Beattie Telecom impression. 'Piglets? Well, yes, we can do piglets if the pigs get the timings right. When exactly were you thinking of coming?' Moments on and the latest bed-and-breakfast booking is in the bag. The farmer's wife, in her role as bookings secretary, jots it down in the diary. 'I can see the day when the guests are our bread and butter,' she says, 'and the farm will be no more than one big tourist attraction. Farmers may hate the change, but you've got to move with the times or starve.' With ham sandwiches in abundance, we won't go hungry today, though Manington apologises that as it isn't Friday, they have only sliced bread. Friday is farmhouse loaf day, because Friday is the day she buys it from the local baker.

Not only does she not bake her own bread, Leslie Manington also does not have rosy cheeks or an apron with ducklings embroidered across the hem. She's a youthful 46-year-old farmer's wife who smokes rather more than is wise and who readily admits to being on hormone-replacement treatment. It's this, she says, that gives her the energy she needs to cope with looking after not just her farm home, but also the farmhouse cottages, the bed-and-breakfast business, the caravan park, the designer, machine-knit farm jumpers, the tea shop, the shire horses, the seven- and five-year-old children and the farmer husband.

She is a modern-day farmer's wife and we all know the nursery rhyme about how much the farmer wanted one. But for the farmer's wife, the farmer's den is a rather stressful place to be these days. Latest statistics show that, on average, one farmer commits suicide every day, making farmers currently second top of the league table, after the medical profession, of those taking their own lives.

Debt, poverty and isolation have conspired to make killing fields of the green and pleasant land, with farmers turning to their work tools – guns, poison, ropes – to escape harsh economic realities. The average income for a medium-sized Lake District farm has fallen from £9,000 to around £3,000 in the past three years. In the same time, the Samaritans have started running special teams to fight rural depression. Says Leslie Manington, 'I had no idea what I was taking on when I got married. I was happy to marry a farmer. I'd been working for the National Farmers' Union for years, I knew what the life was like, I sympathised over lost crops. But I was totally unprepared for the reality of it. You would need to have been brought up on a farm to understand what you were going into.'

Manington's family had come from Durham, with some roots in farming, but she lived an urban life in Brentford where her parents ran a cycle shop. She went to the local grammar, on to business studies, then, inspired by farm holidays in Durham, took a secretarial job at the National Farmers' Union (NFU) in Knightsbridge. She did so well that she was soon running committee meetings, editing newsletters and writing articles for *The Grower*. She met John Manington on a trip she organised to France to look at fruit and while they went out for two years, she never expected to be a farmer's wife, because she never thought he would ask. 'It was a stormy relationship and eventually we decided to part. I was amazed when a fortnight later he came back to pop the question and to say, "I'm sorry, it's farming that makes me the way I am."' He was talking about the uncertainties of farming life, but it was the first hint that farming itself is part of the relationship. It's more than a job – it's a culture, an upbringing, a way of thinking as well as living. 'I was 31, independent and because children didn't come along immediately, I continued to commute to the office in London and didn't get too involved. But there are things you don't properly anticipate – even down to it being a family business and where will the family go? Will the parents move out of the farmhouse or will you live on their farm? In some marriages, even just the generations living so close can be an issue.'

Manington says she knows homes where the closest analogy would be the royal family. The son is set to inherit – but when? The older family set the tone and everything must be done as it was before. 'Some women I know sympathise with Princess Diana, because it's not easy being the wife when your husband feels he has no real role and time is passing. I didn't mind becoming a farmer's wife full-time, but there are strange pressures. It seemed important that I should have a boy to be the heir. It's weird to be forward-thinking, yet find yourself caught up in a medieval system.'

Manington says firmly that all farmers are chauvinists. Their lives are physically tough and they are used to thinking they deal with the outdoors and women should deal with the indoors. 'There is no doubt it's a hard life. Farmers tend to be very solitary and bottle things up. They are too tired to have hobbies, they can't go away easily, they fear letting down their forebears and once the economic climate turned against them, they hit real emotional difficulties. Around here you see it all the time; farmers hanging or shooting themselves, or taking mistresses.'

A spokesman for Acre, the charity that aims to improve rural life, put it like this: 'Roses around a thatched cottage are not everything. Rural poverty exists; it mirrors the problem in the city in different surroundings. And you can't eat scenery.'

A few years ago, the Maningtons got to the point at which the farm wasn't making any money at all. The recession meant garden centres were not buying the conifers they were growing. They had a Tudor farmhouse with a cluster of five pretty oast houses and more tourist spots nearby than you could expect to visit in a week: Sissinghurst, Chartwell, Leeds Castle, Hever Castle. Diversification was the answer: 'We set up our caravan park, took on bed and breakfast, holiday lets, a tea shop. It's exhausting, but there is a little white light at the end of the tunnel and I feel that in two years we could turn things round and have a lot less money worries.'

She also feels it is good for farmers' wives, because they have to be treated more equally now. It's a thesis supported by Dr Ruth Gasson of the University of London's Wye College. As a senior research fellow in agricultural sociology she has seen the problems created by the financial squeeze. 'It's very hard for the farmer's wife, because she is always on the premises having to absorb a lot of stress. But there are grounds for saying the position is improving as more farmers are marrying outside the community. Research suggests the patriarchal system will have to break down and allow women to have a more formal say or they will be generating income from running their own businesses. They see the status young women have elsewhere and will want it too.' Dr Gasson believes, however, that tradition will always play a large part in forming attitudes and change may be slow. When she set a questionnaire recently, asking women how they liked to be described, she found 'farmer's wife' was still the most popular term, as opposed to farmer, woman farmer, farming partner or housewife.

The theme of weight of farming history is echoed by Jenny Cornelius, a tutor in stress management with the Agriculture Training Board. She started her courses after being surprised, as a nurse, by the ill health of farmers and recognising the stress relation. 'Some young farmers who come to my courses tell me they want their wives to lead more modern lives, but fear that once they have families, they will slip into the old ways and start coming in from the fields expecting their dinner on the table. It's hard to break the habits of generations.'

Anne Dillon Roberts of the NFU is certain that change will come. The government has set the agenda by changing its directives to farmers. No longer are they encouraged to produce as much as possible and the government will buy; now farmers must also find their own markets. And women are the ones in the household who know about consumers.

'There is a sense coming from the branches,' says Ann Dillon Roberts, 'of increasing sympathy to the idea of women being more actively involved. A desire to see them actually involved in NFU policy processes, not just making the tea. My intention is for us to move away from talking about farmers' wives and have more women farmers,' she says. 'But farmers do need guidance and time to do it. Many men don't realise how Neanderthal they have been and some would probably have a breakdown at the thought of more women in farming. I'm looking forward to the day when we can have a creche at Agriculture Hall, but it may take a while.'

CARMEL FITZSIMONS

May 6 1992
Halfway between clifftop and boiling sea, the Grease Gang comes off a shift, swathed in sweat and Swarfega. Along 105 miles of Cornish coastline the National Trust is battling open mineshafts, eroding beaches, Hottentot Fig and vandals. But at the Levant tin mine near St Just, it leaves the volunteers of the Grease Gang to get on with it – restoring an 1840 beam engine, 62 years after it last ran and 57 years after

it was bought back from a scrap merchant for £25. The volunteers are members of the Trevithick Society, named after the 18th-century Cornish engineer, and include former miners, a local farmer, a retired engineer and a policeman who cycles from Croydon every summer for two weeks' filthy holiday.

In 1985, after two years' work, the National Trust had repaired the stone buildings, and inside the rusted metal had been scraped clean, missing parts had been replaced, and the geraniums – a Cornish engine driver's tradition – were on the windowsill. Then Milton Thomas, the chief engineer, spoke the dreadful words: 'Let's get the engine to go.' They hope to finish the job this year: steam trials (fuelled by oil) are due in autumn, and next year tourists should be able to watch the machine that lifted millions of tons of ore from 350 fathoms below the sea.

Reg Goodman, the retired engineer, has documented the process. Two years ago, after filming alone with a camcorder, he found the microphone had picked up a Cornish voice which could clearly be heard, 'in an urgent whisper', giving the order: 'Take it down to 10.' The team is convinced it is the engineer ordering the engine driver, in October 1919, to take the skip down to level 10 to recover the bodies of 31 men killed in the mine's worst disaster.

Mr Thomas, aged 70, drives his team as remorselessly as any mine boss. But what will he do when Levant is chugging again? Pipe and slippers? He snorts. 'By God, I've got another one, for the King Edward mine!' he says joyfully. 'That is in bits and pieces in a yard in London – it's going to be a bugger!'

MAEV KENNEDY

QUEEN REQUESTS £300,000 GRANT
July 13 1992

An application by the Queen for a £300,000 public grant to help protect one of Britain's most important remnants of ancient Caledonian pine forest ran into fierce criticism yesterday. Opposition politicians attacked the royal family for sponging off the state while paying no taxes, and conservationists dismissed the Balmoral estate plans as environmentally misguided.

The row follows the *Guardian*'s revelation on Friday that public scrutiny of the £10m paid each year to the Queen and her family out of the public purse has been barred until the year 2000. The Balmoral estate has applied to the Forestry Commission for help under the native pinewood grant scheme to encourage the regeneration of Ballochbuie forest on Deeside. The forest is dying out through red deer eating young trees. The estate plans to fence the 1,000-acre site to keep out the deer. The application for £300,000, the largest known to have been made by the estate, is likely to be granted in the next few months.

Balmoral's application to the Forestry Commission – revealed in the *Scotland on Sunday* newspaper yesterday – follows the breakdown of prolonged negotiations with the government's Scottish Natural Heritage agency, which wanted the estate to cull more deer. Negotiations were not helped by the fact that royal land cannot be designated as a site of special scientific interest. 'Many people will find it remarkable that the royal family is so assiduous in claiming grants for absolutely everything that they do – much of it with no public benefit,' said Brian Wilson, Labour's Scottish rural affairs spokesman. 'If you don't pay taxes you should not be able to claim grants.'

His criticisms were backed by Alex Salmond, the Scottish National Party leader. George Kynoch, Conservative MP for Kincardine and Deeside, said the Queen was entitled to apply for the same grants as other landowners and her application should be treated on its merits. Dave Morris, the Ramblers' Association's Scottish officer, said: 'If massive sums of public money are going to be spent on Balmoral to help the Caledonian forest they should be directed towards increased culling of red deer, not on ineffective, intrusive fences.' Balmoral, which is run by the Duke of Edinburgh, prefers fencing to culling, because it leaves more stags for sport. Conservationists say that although fencing can lead to pine regeneration it creates an unnatural forest. It damages the landscape and endangers rare birds.

Buckingham Palace confirmed that a grant had been applied for, but regards the details as confidential. The Forestry Commission said the application was within the terms of the woodland grant scheme and was under consideration.

ROB EDWARDS

ROADS PLAN THREATENS THE CAIRNGORMS
December 7 1992
Deep in the heart of Britain's most valued and vulnerable wild mountain area, John Dibben, a Wiltshire businessman, is planning 18 miles of roads which will change the face of his 42,000-acre estate at Glenfeshie in the Cairngorms. His plans have been condemned by environmentalists.

Mr Dibben, who made his fortune from luxury kitchens, wants to extract 1,800 acres of maturing commercial conifers planted by his predecessor, the late Lord Dulverton. To do this he plans to bulldoze an extensive network of roads across the heather: seven miles for heavy goods vehicles and 11 miles for large tracked diggers. He has applied to the Forestry Commission for about £90,000 to assist in a 66-year woodland management programme, which also involves fencing off 1,200 acres of native pines to prevent them being eaten by deer. But because of the proposed access roads, the commission has requested an independent environmental assessment, due this month. Mr Dibben recognises that a high density of roads in a national nature reserve is undesirable, but he insists the network is required for forestry management. 'I don't want to see the landscape scarred in any way that is not necessary, but how else can we get out the commercial crop?' he asks.

The Ramblers' Association is so appalled by Mr Dibben's intentions that it is calling for Scottish Natural Heritage to use its compulsory purchase powers to buy the estate. 'Mile upon mile of roads and deer fencing would be a grotesque intrusion into the wildness and splendour of Glenfeshie,' the association's Scottish officer, Dave Morris, says.

It emerged at the weekend that the advisory committee set up by the Scottish Office to recommend a management strategy for the Cairngorms is split on the issue of national parks. A minority of the Cairngorms working party, chaired by the presenter of *Mastermind*, Magnus Magnusson, believes that only a park authority with planning powers will be able to prevent landowners from damaging the environment. The majority, including landowners, councillors and businessmen, favour a 'partnership board' which would bring together local authorities, land managers and conservationists in an essentially advisory role.

When he receives the working party's report in the next few weeks, Ian Lang, the Scottish secretary, is almost certain to back the majority view. This will disappoint – but perhaps not surprise – the two dissenting members of the 16-strong working party: Eric Langmuir, a mountaineer and member of the north-east board of Scottish Natural Heritage, and John Hunt, reserves manager for the Royal Society for the Protection of Birds. Mr Magnusson, who also chairs Scottish Natural Heritage, said the working party had reached a clear decision on its recommendations.

ROB EDWARDS

FOREVER ENGLAND: FIRST RAPE AND THEN JUST THE MILDEST WHIFF OF
EXHAUST FUMES
March 30 1993

It's been a funny old year for Mr and Mrs Robert Andrews of Sudbury in Suffolk. On the first Sunday in January they woke to find that their magnificent estate had been entirely turned over to yellow oilseed rape; and on the first day of February, a dark-suited stranger with a brand-new executive car started to snoop on them.

These incidents would be of no more than local interest were it not for the fact that the Andrewses are one of the most famous couples in English history. They stare out at us from Thomas Gainsborough's exquisite 'conversation piece' from 1756. Since being bought by the National Gallery from the Andrewses' descendants for £130,000 in 1960, it has become one of the most famous and haggled-over English paintings. The left have seen it as an apologia for privilege and property, while the right have seen it as an apotheosis of unadulterated country life.

Mrs Andrews is a dainty nymph in a blue satin dress perched on a park bench. She is overlooked by a sturdy oak, and by Mr Andrews, a dapper fellow who leans insouciantly against the back of her bench. He comes with waistcoat unbuttoned, legs crossed, hunting rifle under arm, dog in attendance. On the left is their dreamscape estate. It is populated by stooks of grain, feathery trees, fluffy clouds, and by sheep in a faraway fold.

What happened in January is that a picture editor from the *Sunday Times* Culture section replaced the Andrewses' estate with a photograph of a field full of rape and functional farm buildings. This montage illustrated an article by Robert Hewison in which the heritage industry was warned about 'over-idealising' the countryside. If we do not accept the landscape as dynamic and changing, he argued, there is a danger that our view of it 'becomes that of Mr and Mrs Andrews, as though we, too, were 18th-century landowners, while someone else gets on with the work'.

What then happened to the Andrewses in February seems to confirm Hewison's worse fears. The painting was featured in a pair of striking posters that appeared on 2,606 billboards around the country. Here it hung in splendid isolation in a white-walled, pine-floored art gallery, scrutinised from close range by a thirtysomething male in a dark suit. In one poster the man stood with his hands in his pockets, and in the other, with his jacket slung over his shoulder. To his left, stretching out luxuriously, was a curvaceous blue car. A caption read: 'The New Safrane by Renault. Take a Private View.'

The Renault campaign was orchestrated by Tago Byers, Douglas Thursby-Pelham and Mel Williams at the London office of Publicis, a French advertising agency. For

Williams, the Andrewses are a middle-class couple supremely at ease with themselves: 'About a year ago we were looking for a different reason at some art and the Gainsborough picture of Mr and Mrs Robert Andrews struck us instantly. It came into our minds that these people were our target market. It's the 18th century, and here are our people! It's not Lord or Duke so-and-so, it's Mr and Mrs. They're not aristos and they're not *Sun* readers. The husband is leaning against the tree with his hunting gun, and his wife looks perfect sitting on the chair. They're totally relaxed. They're completely at home with themselves. Had they been selling cars in the 18th century, these people would have been the target market.'

The point was developed in press and television campaigns that began on February 5. The press campaign used similar mises-en-scène, but the Gainsborough was supplemented by three other paintings: *The Cradle* by Berthe Morisot, *Tropical Storm With A Tiger* by Henri Rousseau, and *The Return* by a contemporary British artist Peter Szumowski. Texts explained the link between each artwork and the car. The Gainsborough stood for 'refinement' and 'elegant poise'; the Morisot for 'comfort, security and perfect tranquillity'; the Rousseau for 'stealthful pursuit with the inevitable ability to overpower'; the Szumowski (a Magrittean dreamscape used because rights to a real Magritte, at £50,000 to £100,000, were prohibitively expensive) was about 'resisting the obvious'. In the TV commercial, shots of a man looking at the pictures in a gallery, purpose-built at Shepperton studios, were combined with footage of the car in the Arizona Desert.

When I point out that the paintings are pastoral rather than metropolitan, Williams remarks: 'In the 80s everybody was doing ads with thrusting Mr Businessman in a pin-striped suit shouting "Sell! Buy! Sell! Buy!" down a mobile phone. We're a barometer of popular culture and that really is distasteful now. We're saying there are other sides to people. This car is part of that. It's relaxed. It's not saying, "Let's drive down the M1, then take the M40, then we'll go to a meeting in Birmingham and come straight back." This is saying, "OK, we know you're going to do that sort of thing. But look, the difference we can offer you is that you can take a breather. Why not take some time to look round a gallery, for example – it's a fantastic experience." It's no accident that there's a nun with buck teeth out there on TV explaining art to people.'

Though the Gainsborough is the centrepiece and catalyst of the campaign, it does stick out in this company. The other paintings fall broadly into the category of modern French art. Morisot and Rousseau are, respectively, French Impressionist and Post-Impressionist, while the Szumowski comes into the orbit of French Surrealism. All this makes sense for a modern French car. Yet the Gainsborough, intriguingly, is 18th century and an icon of Englishness. Is there not a soupçon of cultural imperialism here – when a French car confronts a classic English landscape and looks set to take possession of it?

Thursby-Pelham denies this. They could just as well have used a French 18th-century picture to make the point about refinement. As for cultural imperialism: 'People in this country are very interested in buying into a Latin quality of life, and that's fine. But the idea that there is some sort of French cultural invasion is very unattractive and certainly not one we want to propagate.'

And what would Gainsborough make of Mr and Mrs Andrews' latest fate? The chances are that he would see it as another instance of Gallic sleight-of-hand. He regarded Watteau, no less, who invented the genre of the conversation piece, as a 'very fine painter taking away the French conceit'. After much deliberation, he would undoubtedly advise the Andrewses to stick to the Land Rover Discovery, with the Conran interior.

JAMES HALL

A COUNTRY DIARY: OXFORDSHIRE

April 9 1993

I remember I was five and our destination was a cottage in the deer-park adjoining Wychwood Forest, and the wagon carrying the family – this was 1910 – passed in the dark November night through a scaring display of red and green lights. I eventually learnt these were the eyes of the deer reflected in the two candle lights of the wagon.

The estate where my father went to work must have been the major employer next to agriculture. Apart from butler, footmen, hallboy, housemaids, scullery maids, cooks, housekeeper and chauffeur, there was a groom and nightwatchman. In the four acres of walled garden, the glasshouses produced tomatoes, bananas, peaches, pawpaws, figs and melons. Of the 14 men under my father three were 'bothy-men', apprentice professional gardeners who lived in the bothy on the edge of the garden. In addition there were foresters, carters, masons, stone-wallers, hedgers and ditchers, sawyers, carpenters, gamekeepers, painters and decorators, and even a full-time molecatcher. The estate must have provided work for over 100 local craftsmen and labourers. Here I lived for 21 years until my father died, but I continued to have access to the vast acreage of woodland and farmland as long as the estate was still in the same family ownership. Then I left for an appointment in Berkshire.

After 21 years away I returned to the area to live. In my beloved forest the greatest change had been due to the cessation of copsing, when sections of the forest, planted with hazels, used to be cut down every 10 years or so, leaving open areas for a rich flora such as primroses, orchids and bluebells and habitats for warblers and nightingales. The copses were now overgrown and the shaded conditions no longer favoured the former flora and fauna. The other sad change was the disappearance of the red squirrel (one used to enter our scullery to clean up the cat's plate) on the sudden colonisation by the alien grey squirrel.

The other big change, still in progress, has been the predominance of commuters in the population and the scanty remains of the old population depending on agriculture or private estates for employment. The large local estate, my childhood home, on the advice of computers and accountants, has realised it is cheaper to purchase flowers, fruits and vegetables than to employ a gardening staff, and to hell with the aesthetic aspects. We no longer have craftsmen such as blacksmiths, shoe-makers, saddlers and tailors, and our nearest banks, of which we once had two, are now seven or eight miles away.

What I miss most is the old Oxfordshire dialect. I no longer hear such expressions, with Germanic overtones, as 'Wurr bist thee a-gooing, you?', answered by 'I bent a-gooing nowurr – I be a-coming back.'

W. D. CAMPBELL

THE QUIET WAR FOR OUR EMBATTLED ANCIENT CHURCHES
April 24 1993
'The church is the people, not the building.' Those words are uttered in despair, or defiance, by many rural clergy when faced with five or even 10 ancient buildings in their charge, each requiring thousands of pounds to maintain, while their days are absorbed by an unending round of jumble sales and fetes. The people themselves see things differently. To them the church is the building. Over 90 per cent have no interest in Sunday worship, but they will raise money to repair the roof, they will mow the churchyard, polish the brasses and decorate the altar with flowers.

Though a rural parson myself, I know the people are right: they recognise that the church building is the heart of their community. Each generation has made its mark, putting in a new window, constructing an aisle or installing a pulpit, so the history of the community is embodied in wood and stone. And over the centuries that building has witnessed the greatest joys and sorrows of the community at christenings, weddings and funerals, and when people come in at times of hardship to pray.

Even today, when the institutions of the church have lost their influence, the buildings continue to serve their traditional purpose. Belief in God remains stubbornly strong, and the church represents His presence in our midst.

Visitors from the cities also make use of our hundreds and thousands of country churches. Taken together the parish churches of Britain form the greatest single tourist attraction. But, more importantly, they are the heart of our nation. Though most British people live in cities, their imagination remains firmly rural: and the village church, surrounded by thatched cottages, is our national vision of heaven on earth. Yet currently a war is being fought for the preservation of our ancient churches. It is largely hidden and voices are rarely raised; indeed the antagonists themselves are often only dimly aware of the conflict.

On one side are the ordinary people in the villages struggling to keep rain out. On the other side are their enemies: first, the clergy themselves – or rather the ecclesiastical hierarchy charged with deploying them. Owing to a combination of bad luck and bad management the amount of money the Church Commissioners can give to rural dioceses will dwindle to nothing by the end of this decade.

Thus the stipends and housing of the clergy must be borne by the parishes themselves. With the present number of clergy this can mean that a small village of, say, 300 people – of which only 20 attend church regularly – will have to pay £4,000 or £5,000 each year. Outside the stockbroker belt, no village can afford this sum and still maintain its building. And if the church is indeed the building, the answer must be fewer paid clergy – a fact which bishops and clergy are understandably reluctant to face.

The second enemy are the experts in conservation. Parliament requires quite rightly that the Church of England should operate a system of planning controls to ensure that work on churches is of high quality. Unfortunately, the men and women who act as planners, while often replete with academic knowledge, are largely ignorant of both finance and modern building methods. For some reason these experts believe that techniques and materials used in the 19th century represent perfection. So often ludicrously expensive standards are imposed, which may be beyond the pockets of the parishioners, and vital work is left undone.

The third enemy are the architects and builders specialising in church work. By law every church is required to employ an architect, approved by the diocese; and he in turn employs the builders to repair the churches. In most areas there is a handful of builders doing church work who often charge monstrously high prices. And since the market is effectively closed, and since the architects' fees are a proportion of costs, the normal competition forces do not apply. The result is that parishioners cannot afford all the necessary repairs.

The people in our village have until now been too willing to submit to these forces against them. They have grumbled at the amount required for clergy stipends, but paid up. They have railed against the experts, the architects and the builders, but have played by the rules.

Yet if the battle is to be won, we need a resurgence of that sturdy independent spirit for which the British yeoman was once famous, and which at their best still activates our middle classes. If the people in the villages stopped paying so much for the clergy, ignored the dotty ideas of the conservationists, and refused to employ the approved architects, the authorities would be helpless.

Faced with the great social and ecological problems which confront the human race, it may be felt that the preservation of rural churches seems trivial. Yet these buildings embody a vision, an ideal, which is as relevant to the future as to the past. If our species is to survive and flourish we must rediscover the virtues of stable, sustainable communities. Our village churches are beautiful symbols of such communities, and so can inspire and strengthen us as we confront the next millennium.

ROBERT VAN DE WEYER

BIRDWATCH: FLIGHT OF THE SKUAS – HEBRIDEAN HERALD
May 17 1993
Aird an Runair is, as Private Frazer of *Dad's Army* might have called it, 'a wild and lonely place'. On the north-western edge of the island of North Uist, in the Outer Hebrides, nothing but the Atlantic Ocean separates it from North America. This makes it the perfect spot to watch the British weather approaching from the west, the clouds moving in from the sea like time-lapse film.

One May during the mid-1970s, a Kentish birdwatcher, David Davenport, made the long journey to North Uist to see some of the island's breeding birds. Spring is a fine time to visit the Western Isles; tiny flowers carpet the meadows, breeding lapwings perform tumbling flights over the machair and, if you're lucky, a splendid Golden Eagle may soar into view. Most prized of all, the exclusive and mysterious Corncrake, returned from its African winter quarters, keeps islanders and visitors awake all night with its repetitive call. With such delights on offer, it's perhaps surprising that he found time to look out to sea. But he did, and in doing so discovered one of the most extraordinary avian spectacles in the British Isles – the Hebridean Skua passage.

Skuas are the hawks of the sea, scourge of weaker seabirds such as terns and auks. They prowl around a seabird colony until they spot a bird which has just caught a fish. Then they pounce, swooping down on the unsuspecting victim and harassing it until it drops or regurgitates its catch. Two species of Skua breed in Britain, the Great Skua or Bonxie, and the more falcon-like Arctic Skua. Both nest on the moors of northern Scotland and the Atlantic islands. But two other species of Skua also visit our shores from time to time. The bulky Pomarine and the slender, tern-like Long-tailed Skua, are rare passage migrants, usually seen only briefly as they pass by our coasts in spring or autumn. These two species breed in the high Arctic, sharing their nesting-grounds with polar foxes and Arctic hares.

As David Davenport looked west from Aird an Runair that windy spring day, he was astonished by the spectacle he saw. Tight flocks of Pomarine Skuas flew over the waves in close formation, like a squadron of fighter planes. These birds with their extraordinary twisted tail-feathers were joined from time to time by delicate Long-tailed Skuas, many sporting the magnificent elongated tail-feathers worn by breeding adults. What brought the Skuas so close to land was the weather conditions that day. A deep low-pressure area moving north past the islands brought strong westerly winds, veering north-westerly. These had blown the Skuas close inshore – so close that some passed directly over the beach.

Given suitable weather conditions, the Hebridean Skua passage has been noted most years since. The record was set in mid-May 1991, when 622 Pomarines and an astonishing 1,346 Long-tailed Skuas flew north in a fortnight, shattering the previous record of 388 birds in May 1983. The greatest spectacle was on May 19, when lucky observers logged 540 Long-tails and over 100 Pomarines. Two days later the numbers were down to 180 Long-tails, passing in a single, dramatic flock.

But Skua-watchers already packing their bags for the Hebrides may be disappointed. When the winds fail to blow from the west or north-west, a whole season can pass by with hardly any Skua sightings. 1990 was the worst year ever, with only eight Pomarines and just a single Long-tailed recorded. Observers had plenty of time to enjoy the many other delights of the islands, while contemplating the unpredictability of birds, and of the British weather.

STEPHEN MOSS

BUTTERFLY TO MAKE FENLAND RETURN

June 4 1993

Britain's largest butterfly, the Swallowtail, is being reintroduced into Cambridgeshire where it became extinct in 1951, the National Trust announced yesterday. The Swallowtail is three inches across and lives on the rare milk parsley plant which – after nearly disappearing itself – is thriving in Wicken Fen, Cambridgeshire. The fen is one of the oldest National Trust properties, having been acquired in 1899, but yesterday it was declared a national nature reserve by English Nature, the government watchdog. Although it had been protected, Wicken was in danger of drying out through the draining of surrounding farmland. The fen was once in a hollow, but now stands 9ft above the surrounding countryside. Consequently its water was leaking away, endangering many rare plants. It was because the milk parsley became scarce that the Swallowtail disappeared. In 1989 a waterproof membrane nearly two miles long stopped the leakage and restored the fen's ecology, with the milk parsley making a comeback.

The National Trust is taking the gamble of reintroducing Swallowtail caterpillars this month, in the hope that next year visitors will see the butterfly on the wing. The caterpillars are from eggs from a colony in Norfolk. Dr Jack Dempster, formerly of the Institute of Terrestrial Ecology, said previous attempts to bring back the Swallowtail had failed because there was insufficient plant food. 'We now hope there is enough water on the fen for both plants and butterflies to thrive.'

The Swallowtail was at one time common in England, being collected on the Thames at Battersea, but the draining of river margins and fens confined the survivors to tiny colonies on the Norfolk Broads.

National nature reserve status will give special protection to Wicken Fen, one of four fenland sites remaining. Where once there were 3,000 square kilometres of fens, less than two kilometres in all are left. As a result of draining, ground levels have dropped between 9 and 13ft in the last 150 years.

Songbirds should also increase in numbers this summer, the British Trust for Ornithology said yesterday. Its annual study shows that last year saw significant increases in young wrens, dunnocks, robins, sedge warblers, reed warblers, lesser whitethroats, common whitethroats, blackcaps, great tits and treecreepers. If winter survival has been good, the increase 'bodes well for the 1993 breeding season'.

PAUL BROWN

RURAL ENGLAND LOST IN CONCRETE
July 29 1993

Urban sprawl has swallowed up close to two million acres of the English countryside since the Second World War and more than a million acres of farmland has been lost, the Council for the Protection of Rural England (CPRE) said yesterday. Unveiling what he called the most reliable survey of land use available, the council's chief planner, Tony Burton, said the rural face of England was changing much faster than the government was willing or able to admit. Trends were 'extremely worrying'.

'None of the government's past or present systems of monitoring land use provide an accurate or comprehensive record,' he said. A tightening of national and regional planning policies was needed to protect the countryside, and especially existing green belts.

An area equivalent in size to Berkshire, Hertfordshire, Oxfordshire and Greater London combined had been lost to urbanisation, which included new motorways and roads. The government's transport programme, Mr Burton said, was causing more environmental damage than any other policy. 'We want the government to revise its planning policies and transport plans,' Mr Burton said. 'We need to get our environmental priorities right and we need to value land much more effectively.'

The CPRE favoured more local control over land use. Planning permission was necessary today for a second satellite dish, but not to plough up an entire hillside. Decisions were made in Whitehall and Brussels without consideration of local implications and priorities. According to CPRE estimates, the current rate of 'countryside loss' to all urban uses was now about 25,000 acres a year – more than twice the figure given in official returns by the Department of the Environment. By the middle of the next century, one fifth of England would be urbanised, against the present 15 per cent.

Regional highlights from the report include:

- South-east: Urban area up by nearly 470,000 acres (44 per cent) since 1945, more than equivalent in area to Greater London and almost twice as much as any other region. Buckinghamshire, Bedfordshire and Essex were gravest offenders. Twice as much farmland lost as any other region.
- West Midlands: Urban area up by more than two-thirds with loss of 200,000 acres of rural land, more than twice the size of Birmingham.
- North-west: Now the most built-up region in England, having lost more farming land relative to size than any other region. The spread of Greater Manchester and Merseyside needed careful control.

- East Anglia: Farmland covering area eight times the size of Norwich lost; new housing accounted for urban spread of 30 per cent since 1945.
- Yorkshire and Humberside: Urban area up by 'staggering' 88 per cent, the largest increase in the country.
- The North: Urban area up by more than 50 per cent, equal to Tyne and Wear.
- East Midlands: Urban area up by almost 75 per cent, with spread of Derby, Leicester, Northampton and Nottingham causing most concern. Farmland down by 190,000 acres.
- South-west: Well over 300,000 acres of moorland and rough grazing lost, including large tracts of Dartmoor and Exmoor. Urban area up by over 70 per cent, mostly new housing.

MICHAEL SIMMONS

DOWN ON THE FARM

August 14 1993

I seem to remember we had a memo saying 'ironically' was out. (That's enough 'ironicallys', Ed.) But if ever a programme made a good case for 'ironically' it is *Highgrove – Nature's Kingdom*, a *Survival* special from Anglia.

Here we have this downright idyllic do. On Prince Charles's Gloucestershire estate the nuthatches are hatching, the poppies are popping and every creature that can noodle is canoodling. The whole place seems to fluff up and heave with happy activity like a flowered eiderdown. Except the house itself where, clearly enough, hell is breaking loose in large lumps.

Maurice and Carroll Tibbles, a husband and wife team, (ironically) filmed Highgrove over '91 and '92. And that, as my father used to say, accounts for the milk in the coconut and the hair on the exterior. Plenty of Prince Charles, but no Princess Diana and only one sighting of William and Harry, lubricating the stockman's glove before he hauled out a lamb. An unsentimental introduction to birth.

Highgrove goes with the flow of nature. It is charming farming. Prince Charles has refreshed ponds, planted hedgerows, left tussocky grass where owls can hunt and newborn calves rest. Did you know cows preferred to hide their calves? Nor me. No pesticides are used and wildlife and wild flowers flourish together. It looks the way Eden would if God had had a bit more money.

Still, the honestly fascinating thing is the royal sewage system. No organic farm is short of manure and Highgrove has an embarrassment of riches. The third time the septic tank overflowed, the Prince looked into other solutions. So to speak. Now the effluent is filtered through bark beds ('What's left behind can be used as compost') and reed beds ('The roots of the reeds draw up the soluble nutrients') and no newt turns its nose up at the result. This, Monica, is simply gripping stuff.

There was photography, which I will call loving because that is what it felt like. I have never seen a better shot of a badger than the determined chap, like a baseball bat with bristles, who came trotting at the camera, brushing past blindly. Bees in their own thatched home. PC Tudor Davies policing 83 nesting boxes. Koi carp by Sir Yehudi Menuhin, old roses by Lady Salisbury and wild flowers by Dr Miriam Rothschild.

I bought a pair of Lady Salisbury's shoes at a Hatfield House fair. They seemed quite new. 'She never wears anything but Wellingtons,' said the seller. Miriam Rothschild wears white plastic boots. It is an endearingly eccentric crew. And I still haven't got around to Jemima Parry-Jones, 'a well known expert on owls'. You feel that the whole bunch could go to sea in a beautiful pea-green boat. It is as if the place itself were a beautiful pea-green boat. Almost an ark.

I wonder, your Royal Highness, if you've met Professor Bellamy? You two would get on like Chas and Dave. *Blooming Bellamy* (BBC1) reminded us of the medicinal power of plants. This is clearly serious science. When the big drug companies move in, you'd better believe it. You, sir, might like to try borage, which maketh man merry and driveth away sadness. I am trying ginkgo, which improveth the memory. Or it would if I didn't keep forgetting to take it.

NANCY BANKS-SMITH

TWIGGING THE TRUST
March 7 1994

At this time of year, with every crocus that shows its nose, I start to test the air. I am waiting to catch the scent of wax polish, which says that the National Trust is open for business, ready to receive visitors.

The pot-pourri industry must by now be working overtime. The satanic mills where they seeth and skim great vats of English rosebud soap are surely bubbling away, three shifts a day. The strange world of the National Trust shop, where honeysuckle clings to every letter-card and kitchen apron, has to be stocked with the symbols of life in whatever nation it is the Trust represents. You know, pottery cottages, fudge and lavender bags.

The National Trust seems to me a country in its own right. I am drawn to it, as a tourist from everyday, real Britain. We shall cross the border and visit National Trustsylvania again this year. We'll probably go to the garden centre where, last time, a Jack Russell wandered up and cocked his leg over our newly bought delphiniums. This may be a local custom.

If we stroll around the gardens, my hands will remain firmly in my pockets. I wouldn't dream of helping myself to the merest cutting after hearing a first-hand account of the case of a woman horribly denounced for theft in a National Trust garden. A Trust member, bursting with righteous indignation, came bustling up to report this crime to the authorities. 'A woman,' she said, 'is stealing your plants! I've left my husband to keep an eye on her. Follow me!' An embarrassed member of staff trailed off behind this flying vigilante to make the arrest. He must have expected to step around the lupins and find an organised gang at work with a mechanical digger, excavating the entire herbaceous border. Instead he was pointed towards a rather timid lady. She was being followed down the gravel paths by a gent, flitting from shrub to shrub and bristling like a sniffer dog.

'That's her,' said the informant, loudly, gesturing with an accusing brolly. Husband and wife, plus various onlookers, closed in for the unmasking of the garden criminal. The staff member sprang into action with all the natural authority that the natives display on these occasions. 'Err. Excuse me. So sorry. Would you mind ... I mean, could you? Have you been? That is to say ... Have you, well, taken any – uhhm – plants?' The woman, shamed to the core by the violent force of this outburst, clicked open her handbag and revealed a tiny twig. Yes, she confessed, tearfully, she had indeed snipped one cutting.

She asked for 17 other offences to be taken into account and was immediately strung up from a pergola by a lynch mob of National Trust members. I'm sorry, that last bit is ever such a slight exaggeration. I expect, though, that the guilty party went straight home without stopping for her National Trust tea or pausing to buy a Gertrude Jekyll-style oven glove from the National Trust shop.

The public humiliation of this woman has made me terribly cautious. Never again will I pluck so much as a lavender head or a sprig of catnip. This is tough news for our cat, who flings himself into a frenzy of a vaguely erotic nature given a tiny fix of the stuff – but there you are. I have the feeling that a certain section of the British public would sooner see offences committed against the state, or even against the person, than against the National Trust. You might with impunity flog arms to a deranged dictator or beat up a bus shelter or run off with an old lady's wheelie basket. But don't mess with the NT. Don't even dare touch anything within its hallowed walls.

The sense of reverence and obedience is palpable. I have to admit that once – a long time ago and after a very good lunch – I amused myself in the garden of one of our stately homes by approaching visitors and saying: 'Excuse me. Do you mind not walking on the gravel?' Without exception, they nodded politely, stepped off the paths and walked on the grass.

This sort of thing can go to your head. It's only one pace removed from strolling up to visitors and lecturing them: 'That portrait – there, to the left of the fireplace – is of my great-grandfather, the 11th Earl. He had a raging affair with Mrs Pankhurst. My great-grandmother collapsed in a heap after finding them, stark naked, in the conservatory ... Please feel free to step over the ropes and handle the Sèvres porcelain.'

I rather like the volunteers, particularly National Trust ladies, who provide a more restrained commentary. It is especially pleasing when they have come to identify themselves entirely with the house and the great, dead family that once occupied it – and which wouldn't have dreamed of allowing the ghastly public on the premises. Certainly not by the front door. It was hard enough to get landed families to pay their butcher's bills.

'We have to take enormous care with the curtains in Lady Sybil's bedroom,' says the volunteer. 'We had them hand-sewn by local girls, at a cost of one shilling and fourpence, when Queen Victoria visited us – and Prince Albert swung from them in his nightshirt.'

The National Trust garden does, of course, provide a welcome break from real gardening – from actually doing it. Kipling may have said (in fact, he did say): 'Our England is a garden, and such gardens are not made / By singing "Oh, how beautiful", and sitting in the shade ...' But that's exactly what the pilgrims do, with almost religious respect. Then they retire to the old stables or servants' hall to be served English scones by women in English mob caps and aprons. Yes, there is honey still for tea.

It all gives visitors from overseas such a picture to take away. A glimpse of a very charming, deferential sort of never-never land, smelling of beeswax, distilled rose petals and sanctity.

ANDREW MONCUR

RAMBLERS JOIN OUTCRY AGAINST WIND FARM FALLOUT
March 26 1994

One of the biggest countryside groups will throw its weight today behind the growing campaign against wind farms in remote upland areas. The national conference of the Ramblers' Association, which has 173,000 members, is expected to vote to reverse its policy of favouring the turbines as a pollution-free source of energy. Buffeted by gusts across the moors above Bradford, the association's executive set out their case yesterday in a pre-conference hike along the Pennine Way. 'It's getting to be known as the Wind Farm Way,' said Alan Mattingly, the national director, against the susurration of 23 windmills at the joint Yorkshire Water/Yorkshire Electricity farm on Ovenden Moor. 'We originally saw wind power as a benign and environmentally friendly resource, but that has not proved the case in practice. Our members are telling us very loudly that they do not like wind farms at all.'

Association delegates will be told that turbines are proving visually intrusive at almost all the 30 sites approved by the Department of Trade and Industry under its promotion of non-fossil fuels. 'Noise has also proved much worse than expected,' said Mr Mattingly, 'and there are growing concerns about danger. Apart from the possibility of blades shearing off, you can see for yourself the warning notices here at Ovenden about ice being flung from the turbines.'

The association will call for a comprehensive review of the effect of existing farms, with the government's non-fossil fuel subsidies frozen pending the outcome. A further 230 projects are being considered in the third phase of wind-farm development, although Tim Eggar, the energy minister, has said that only about 20 are likely to win approval.

MARTIN WAINWRIGHT

A BIRD IN THE BUSH
September 16 1994

Beyond the trees broods Sizewell nuclear power station. From the west come the first chill autumn winds and over the sea must be Holland. All around, you just know, is bird food. Billions of squiggly things deep in the mud and the sand and all those reeds. Nature's little helpers toiling away selflessly in one of Britain's few remaining quiet corners.

This is Minsmere on the Suffolk coast, one of the Royal Society for the

Protection of Birds' senior nature reserves. Somehow you expect Hitchcockiana under this mackerel sky; the air should be flapping with all that space. Where are the noisome, tumultuous, joyous coos and caws of the birds?

The reeds hiss, some sand blows off the wide beach. A solitary gull rises westward and a few pheasant chicks near the cafeteria do a stiff walk behind Mum. Big deal. I've seen more birds in SE1. But there are lots of people. Not the obsessive twitchers ticking off their rarities, but craggy couples teetering by, strung with binoculars and tripods. Weathered, booted folk dressed in anoraks who stop you on their tracks.

NO 1 BOOT: 'Good news about the marsh harrier, eh?'

(What news? What marsh harrier?)

NO 2 BOOT: 'Had a sparrowhawk, too.'

(Where, dammit?)

NO 3 BOOT: 'Seen that bustard over there? Look ...' (We spin round, binoculars ready. Great view of a tree. No bird.) 'There, on the fence. Against the sky ... no, no ... it's gone behind the spinney.'

'Bastard.'

'No, bustard'

NO 1 BOOT: 'You're new to birdwatching?' He turns away, kind eyes lost on some far horizon. 'You'll get the hang of it.'

And so to a bird hide. The reserve has eight immense chicken coops where Those in the Know (there are almost two million RSPB members) sit for hours at a time on chaste benches, scanning Minsmere's shallow lagoons through long slits in the wooden front. They're a mix between chapel and commentary box.

A jovial ex-pig farmer and his wife ('The business is ruined; we've been on holiday for the last six months') are slavering over a little grebe just 30 feet away. 'Lovely,' he says. 'Mmmmm,' she murmurs. And in 10x50 Zeiss vision (you can hire binoculars on-site) it is beautiful. The colours sting. Its head twitches twice. It stares ahead. It's motionless in the mud for three, no, five minutes. The tension is unbearable. Then BING. Supper. How the ...? Who cares? The heart soars.

Out on a little man-made island (all Minsmere is man-made, fed and watered by sluices and ducts, a giant playground for hydrologists to fine-tune the habitat to the tastes of individual birds) some ducks are being rude. A cormorant circles twice, lands on a mallard and pisses off the coots. There's mayhem. It hangs out its wide black wings to dry; the water drips off and peace drops too.

'Is that a gadwell?'

You get the idea. Relax. Birds do it as and when they want. A kingfisher dives into some reeds, all thrilling blues and greens. There it is again, hopping past the redstarts. Some avocets swing left. Stints, sandhoppers, wagtails fly in and leave smartish. For the next month or more finches, pipits, wagtails and warblers will be gathering before the long journey to wintering grounds in southern Europe and Africa.

Minsmere will hum and flutter; the whole of the north Norfolk coast, too, will be alive to flights of geese and duck. The butterflies and the dragonflies will be long gone, but the red stags will be fighting in the reserve's woodland and heath and, if you're lucky, the otters will show and you'll return with the boom of the bittern in your ears.

And No 2 Boot may still be there, too. 'There's nothing like birds,' he says later. 'Here, let me show you that marsh harrier. That's it. Just below the horizon, low and left. You've got it.'

JOHN VIDAL

THE REAL EARTH MOVERS
December 7 1994

> *A powdery layer of lime dust lay 5cm deep on the road in the Piave valley. George and I raced along it at full throttle. A vast plume swelled out behind us. We terrorised the pedestrians; it was like making a gas attack; their faces contorted and we left behind us a world without shape.*
>
> ALFRED DIESEL, INVENTOR OF THE DIESEL ENGINE, 1902

Last week in London, a few hundred 'pedestrians' bit back at the terrorist mentality of Herr Diesel and the latterday British government modernists. The massive display of force, money and technology needed to evict 350 peaceful protesters, breach their rickety, festooned 100ft tower and snuff out the M11 road protest was as outrageous to the government as it was to most of the local community. As the colourful hordes leave Claremont Road, though, it may be forgotten that this broad social protest led directly from one of the first serious direct actions taken against the government's £23bn road programme.

Two years ago this week on a muddy chalk down above Winchester, with Celtic field systems and ancient paths leading down to some of the richest fields in Britain, 40 rather naïve people with little more than cooking pots, blankets, axes and canvas had gathered to 'protect' a threatened hill. Just by living on it.

And just as last week's people on the Leyton roofs were not the usual hard-left political agitators of the 80s, the young Twyford Downers had little in common with traditional British countryside defenders: they were not members of any establishment environment group, describing themselves in global terms as 'indigenous Englanders', or as descendants of rural Levellers; they had no jobs, but did not see themselves as dropouts.

They talked of the environment in a language common in the Third World but rare for Britain – in terms of marginalised people, human rights, civil liberties, justice and spirituality; most were urbanites and though they were 'defending nature', some barely knew the names of the plants and birds around them. What united them was learning survival skills, the down and their broad anger at the likes of Mr Diesel's engine – a symbol for many of societal suicide.

The extension of the M3 London–Southampton motorway through Twyford Down had been fought through the courts and inquiries for 20-odd years. A few people had given the better part of their lives to stopping it, yet their best arguments had consistently been overruled. There was nothing to do, it seemed, but look on in horror and get back into their cars.

The £45m cutting, designed to shave a few minutes off the London to Southampton car journey, was to be an engineering triumph, but no one had reckoned on the 'Dongas'. By early December 1992, the first frosts had come and gone and the contractors were exchanging jokes with the mud-daubed bunch on the hillside. There had been skirmishes as the first trees had been grubbed up, but on 'Yellow Wednesday', December 9, everything changed.

As they had many times before, the Dongas broke on to the site, threw themselves in front of the machines and stopped work. But this was the first day that private security guards had been employed on a road site, and the Dongas were bewildered at the new tactics. The guards, drawn from the dole queues like the Dongas, went for the protesters.

There followed brazen sexual and physical assaults, broken heads and arms, torn ligaments and punches. Women, kids just out of school, were battered. There were screams, tears and chants. At one point four people lay waiting for ambulances. David Bellamy and others tried vainly to attract the police. In 20 years' protesting around the world he said that he had never seen anything like it.

The 'Battle of Twyford Down' raged all day. That night the Dongas – bloodied, exhausted, triumphant – danced wildly around their camp fire in the woods. The next day the police turned up in force and proceeded to duff them up, too. The powerful modern image of private money hand in hand with the machinery of state together rolling over the economically weakest to appropriate common resources was given perfect expression. The subtext for environmentally aware youth was obvious: to the list of oppressed people in Latin America, Indonesia and elsewhere, add the English.

The aftermath was perhaps worse. The intelligence services then spied on the Dongas, the Department of Transport (DoT) spent £250,000 hiring private detectives to investigate, film and, in scenes reminiscent of the Keystone Cops, chase them across the country to haul them through the courts. Thirteen of them broke the court injunctions and returned to Twyford with 700 others; 12 people were jailed and the DoT, claiming it was not punitive, last week demanded that 76 people who dared question the destruction of one of Britain's loveliest places, should pay £1.2m for delaying work.

The cutting is now complete; 20,000 or more businessmen now get to their offices a minute or two quicker each morning and all there is to show for the protest is a small stone memorial on the hillside above. But the kickstart the Dongas gave to others to stand up to the government was sharp. Indirectly, too, the changes they helped trigger in the environment movement, in government departments, in new laws and in wider social change organisations, were considerable.

It started with roads: within a year of Twyford some 200 ad hoc anti-road groups had been set up and dozens of Earth First and other direct-action groups were raising hell. Umbrella alliances and information networks formed, coherent alternatives to the whole philosophy of road-building were refined, many middle-aged, middle-class protesters learnt to use the courts and the media to their advantage – and a lot of young people learnt how peaceful protest can provoke violent responses.

The Dongas themselves dispersed, some to work the land, some to invigorate other road protests round the country. The last two years have seen hundreds of arrests as non-violent direct actions were broken up in Newcastle, Bath, Skye, London, Oxford, Cornwall, Lancashire and north Wales.

People are now living rough to stop the M77 outside Glasgow: a camp has been set up in Newbury where a new road will plough through several old battlefields; there have been people living in woods in Lincolnshire, hanging off cranes in Liverpool, occupying Oxford towers to object to pollution, 'damming' the doors of the ODA and raising hell in Manchester, Leeds, Leicester and elsewhere.

Concurrently, the protests moved into other areas. Just as the Dongas dispersed after the battle, so the angle of fire for direct environmental action has spread into the occupation of supermarkets, timber firms, chain stores, Oxford towers, annual meetings of banks and Bretton Woods organisations, all of which are seen as promoting or encouraging destructive development.

In the two years since Twyford, the environmental mood in Britain has changed out of recognition. The remote government-packaged global nihilism of the 1992 Earth Summit, reflected in the head office missives of elite eco-groups, had left a policy vacuum in many organisations and a feeling in the public and in political parties that real environmental change was not achievable. Into this green hole – and picking up on the general political dis-ease, unemployment, and the evident disintegration of many British communities in the last decade – came the angry direct-action protesters with their social agenda. They talked not just about their own patches, as the house-price-watching Nimbys did in the mid-1980s, but about the whole culture of progress, economics, development, communities and corporate ethics.

The sluggish, only semi-accountable establishment groups, long used to slipping in and out of bed with politicians, reacted curiously. Paranoia about their patches being hijacked turned to fears that their financial support would falter if they were seen to side with controversial protesters. But while they are now happy to applaud and feed off the resistance they see on TV, they do not feel obliged to help. None have even commented on the Claremont Road evictions.

Greenpeace quietly contributed a few hundred pounds to the M11 protest, but the 14-months resistance was otherwise funded entirely by individual donations – running at about £1,000 a month. But the debate about direct action has been intense within the groups. Many would like to help the protesters more and argue that they should help 'empower' their membership.

Now they are in danger of being left out of what is quickly developing into significant social expression. There is a quietly growing public appreciation that the environment is only partly to do with cuddly animals, pretty countryside and Third World forests, and that the eco-agenda so single-mindedly pursued throughout the 1980s is now changing into one of values, culture and societal responsibility in Britain. There is also a new sense that real change is possible: 'Viva los Zapatistas, viva los Scaffoldalistas!' cried the M11 protesters, echoing this year's Mexican revolt, as they were led away by the police.

People, in short, are coming back to the centre of the British debate. It is being fuelled by radical new economics, local initiatives like LETS schemes, credit unions, new indicators, consumer alternatives like fair trade and using new technologies, new media-grabbing ideas. From feeling powerless, communities are linking in common local protest at everything from toxic waste to asthma, electromagnetic fields, airports, supermarkets and waste tips and are coming up with solutions.

But where are the established environment groups? They may tub-thump less about global issues, focus more on Britain and are looking more at cities now than they ever used to and, as in the Far East and Latin America, there has been a significant merging of intellectual agendas with human rights, social justice and libertarian groups. Even so, few groups are willing to question, let alone condemn even the Criminal Justice Bill, parts of which were designed to stop the sort of protests that gave them legitimacy in their own salad days.

Yet when they act together and stand up to government the results can be powerful. Faced with 5,000 people from eight major groups declaring they were ready to take direct action, a twitchy government last year pulled out of destroying London's last remaining old forest at Oxleas Wood. Correctly reading the new mood, the government has been forced to cut, and cut again the road programme. The intellectual battle between the Department of the Environment and Department of Transport has been all but won by John Gummer.

Academics and others have leapt in, too. New research has moved the environment debate firmly into health and housing, shed new light on the broader effects of the car, and real fiscal, intellectual and developmental urban alternatives are increasingly discussed and tried out. The recent Royal Commission study on transport was damning; the Labour Party has finally embraced some of the tenets, if not the full spirit, of 'sustainable' development.

Faced with all this, the prospects for the megaliths of commerce, industry and government are not so good. Many people living near massive developments like roads, airports, incinerators, factories or even supermarkets have now been radicalised and are linking cars and social conditions, access and culture, pollution and consumerism, quality of life and urban decline.

The protesters seen on the roofs of Michael Howard's and John MacGregor's houses, at Parliament and Wanstead, are the modern equivalent of the Greenpeace boats bobbing in front of whalers 20 years ago. Today's protestors are just as likely to move on to the roofs of Messrs Harrod, Toyota or Sainsbury, as into the boardrooms of oil companies, think-tank meetings or to dance on Herr Diesel's grave, to make their points.

Two years ago the Dongas lit the undergrowth of an environmental and societal bonfire. The oxygen of the established groups, with their millions of semi-detached or completely frustrated but generally willing supporters, may now be vital if it is to spread.

JOHN VIDAL

COUNTRYSIDE MARCH: HUNTERS CARRY TORCH TO LONDON
February 28 1998

They are a mixed bag. Aristocrats, nouveaux gentry, townies who hunt on their days off, shooting enthusiasts, butchers, farmhands and Conservative politicians nostalgic for their red boxes. Shortly after 10a.m. tomorrow this strange, amorphous procession will set off from Victoria Embankment and move in an orderly fashion towards Hyde Park. At the front, a clay-pigeon shooter will carry an Olympic torch. There will be a brass band and some Highland bagpipers in pinstripes.

The Savoy is providing breakfast before departure, and has abolished its jacket and tie rule. No dogs are allowed, but there will be singing ('probably "Jerusalem"', one organiser said), together with a lot of twiddling of radio sets as marchers tune in to their own special radio station set up for the day, March FM.

But what, exactly, are the 200,000 people expected to turn up to the Countryside March in central London actually saying? The Countryside Alliance, which organised it, makes little secret of the fact that it is motivated by a single issue: the desire to carry on hunting.

There are other concerns which cause rumblings of discontent: the beef crisis, rural housing, lack of public transport and the right to roam, but broadly the march is about the right to preserve a minority sport which the majority finds barbarous.

The demonstration has been timed to coincide with the third reading next Friday of Michael Foster's private member's bill banning fox hunting. It has been refused government time, despite the vote of 411–151 in favour at its second reading. Clever tactics by its supporters may ensure that it stays on the agenda by going to the Lords. The well-funded pro-hunting lobby remains anxious. 'The Countryside Alliance is first and foremost a defence of field sports organisation,' said a spokesman for the alliance, which is a subsidiary of the British Field Sports Society.

Critics of the march accuse organisers of disguising what is essentially a pro-hunting rally with a 'pro-countryside' agenda so vague as to be almost meaningless. (The enveloping aura of romantic shire nationalism was typified yesterday by a free Save Our Countryside poster in the *Daily Mail*, showing a field with cows in it.) The alliance insists it is not anti-government, and the early signs suggest that Tony Blair is listening carefully. Inside the Department of Agriculture itself confusion reigns on how to deal with this rural uprising, and whether it carries an electoral portent.

Lord Donoughue, the junior agricultural minister, is taking part in the march on behalf of the government. His colleague Elliot Morley, meanwhile, spent yesterday complaining that the rally had been hijacked by the blood-sports lobby and the Conservative Party, and ignored the real issues which beset the countryside, such as housing, health and jobs.

Many of the march's financial supporters do not even live in this country. It emerged this week that a Chicago-based shooting enthusiast, Eric Bettelheim, had helped mastermind the funding campaign. Britain's wealthiest man, the Duke of Westminster, has lent more than £1m to the march, and Michael Heseltine, the former deputy prime minster, has offered a tour of his arboretum as a prize in a fundraiser organised by his local hunt.

David Beskine, of the Ramblers' Association, accuses the alliance of having a hidden agenda. 'People's emotions are being manipulated. The message is: "If you are against beautiful fields being destroyed, come to London." The alliance is really made up of field-sports enthusiasts and a small band of rich landowners and shotgun manufacturers with vested interests,' Mr Beskine said. 'Something stinks about the whole bunch of them, but they are very good at PR.'

The National Trust is not taking part in tomorrow's rally ('We regard it as politically motivated'); nor are the Council for the Protection of Rural England or Friends of the Earth ('dangerously simplistic'). The Transport and General Workers' Union points out that casual rural workers earn just £3.06 an hour. 'Many of the landowners and farmers funding and taking part are doing so to defend their right to exploit the modern farm subsidies system, together with their right to maintain feudal systems of employment, land ownership and control,' said spokesman Barry Leathwood.

The alliance counters by saying its concerns, over the green belt, for example, are genuine, and the pro-march National Farmers' Union (NFU) points out that British farming is in dismal shape. 'Thousands of livestock farmers are still facing enormous problems caused by the beef ban, which still exists,' an NFU spokeswoman said. The union claims farmers' incomes fell by 47 per cent last year, hit by the BSE fiasco and a resurgent pound. 'The farming industry is in a period of crisis,' she added.

The alliance reserves its greatest ire for the ramblers, who are pressing for statutory legislation to open up the four million acres of Britain closed to the public. 'They can piss off,' a spokesman said. The landowners' argument against 'right to roam' is that ramblers might fall down slurry pits or be charged by cows, so farmers would need to be expensively insured. Ramblers dismiss this as 'absolute rubbish'. The government is reluctant to legislate, and has given landowners three months to come up with a voluntary code.

LUKE HARDING

A COUNTRY DIARY: THE LAKE DISTRICT
September 28 1998

The other day, warm with a pleasant breeze on the tops, I went back to Dow Crag, where I had started my climbing almost 70 years ago. But we weren't climbing this time, just walking over the top from Walna Scar to try to catch something of the flavour of those more adventurous days in the late 1920s. On the way we visited a secret place where, last month, we had sadly scattered the ashes of my only son, a fine mountaineer.

The modest ascent seemed more demanding than it used to be, but the splendour of the view kept me going. For there are few ridges in Lakeland more rewarding than this one, with the long length of Dunnerdale, perhaps the least-spoiled valley in the area, stretched out far below and, straight ahead, the Scafells, the highest land in England with every tiny detail etched sharp against the sky.

From the top of one of the gullies on Dow Crag I looked down and watched two climbers on Trident Route, a well-remembered climb – the only two climbers we saw all day. Years ago there would have been dozens; perhaps climbers prefer quarries and climbing walls nowadays.

But, scrambling about the summit and walking along the ridge were scores of people – from grannies (and at least one great-grandmother) to small children (including two babies in rucksacks) and several dogs. Other noticed changes were the grossly-eroded, stony tracks, where there used to be grass, the growing profusion of unnecessary cairns and, above the fell-gate, more parked cars than I have ever seen there before.

Mountain bikers on Walna Scar pass, and pony riders on the lower slopes, added to the variety while, in the air, there were silent parascenders and buzzing microlights and, away to the south, a couple of balloons inching northwards, no doubt from Holker Hall. Big changes indeed, for, years ago, this used to be largely climbers' territory, but, happily, the beauty of these hills remains unchanged.

A. HARRY GRIFFIN

ENGLAND'S GREEN AND PLEASANT BAND
December 3 1998

The Women's Institute seems to signify the soul of Middle England: untroubled and untroubling, complacent and conservative, but good-hearted. WI members –

there are 250,000 of them – have a reputation as a movement of wives rather than women, accessories to men, with time on their hands and coffee mornings to organise. But if the WI confirms some stereotypes of compliant jam-makers armed with doilies, it is also more than that. Radicalism nestles in its respectability.

The WI was formed in 1915 as a progressive countrywomen's movement, inspired by the cooperative movement in Canada. And while cooperatives did not take hold in the British countryside, the WI did. In North Yorkshire, a region of flat farming land and wooded valleys, there are 3,500 members and they have just decided to support a campaign of direct action against the construction of 229 pylons along the Vale of York. Some members will quietly lobby politicians, others will take to the streets, or rather the lanes, to obstruct the construction of the new electric transmission line, planned as part of the National Grid's privatised competitive culture.

'They'll have a hell of a job,' says retired farmer Margaret Hill, a member both of the WI and Revolt, the countryside campaign against the pylons. Like many members of her rural community, she is on a telephone tree – a fast communication system whereby each person calls the next on the list. When the contractors arrive next year, the tree telegraph will be activated and the resisters will turn out in their Range Rovers – from National Grid to gridlock in the blink of an eye.

'It will be totally legal,' says Margaret Hill, proudly. Her farm, now run by her son, already has one pylon and seems doomed to acquire another three. 'We have got slow tractors and slow cars,' she adds, conjuring an image of mechanical immovable objects confronting irresistible force. 'We've got slurry-spreaders as well.' She laughs.

'This power isn't for us in North Yorkshire, it will go to the south of England,' says WI campaigner Janet Wright. She started going to meetings in her village near Sowerby after a life revolving around her children. She says: 'I suddenly got tired of just being a mummy. You end up feeling very cut off.'

Her neighbour suggested going to a WI meeting and she loved it. Her local WI, which has acquired new members through its stand against the pylons, has just been going through its political priorities for the annual conference, ranging from rape victims' sexual histories being revealed in court to genetically modified food and the treatment of ovarian cancer.

Pat Shotton is a middle-aged woman who moved to her village near York when her husband retired from the RAF. The WI is the one organisation she has joined and though she expects to stick to lobbying rather than engaging in direct action, she seems secure in being part of a movement that allows its members to choose.

'The WI is a platform. Unless people speak up, the government won't know, will they?' She wears a WI sweatshirt proclaiming 'Extraordinary women.' Retired geography teacher Ann Johnson lives in the Vale of York. She is ready for everything, including gridlock. 'We are not Swampies,' she says. 'We haven't experience of politics; we're on a steep learning curve.'

The WI's endorsement of the campaign and the alliance between women, farmers and environmentalists disrupts predictable portraits of political activists. Like the surprising coalition that blocked the traffic in live calves, this movement consults its own experience of the countryside, rather than relying on party affiliations to sponsor its mutiny. The WI was anti-nuclear power before the TUC and when the Conservative government deregulated Britain's buses, the WI was one of its most formidable opponents.

At a time when debate and disagreement are being purged from politics, the WI holds fast to its own democratic culture. Each institute formulates resolutions for its national conference; they then go to the federation HQ, which distributes them throughout the movement. Local institutes choose their own priorities, which are then sent back to HQ. By the time the annual conference meets – and famously sings 'Jerusalem', William Blake's hymn to England – the agenda is the product of a long, inclusive process.

WI members are, of course, women interested in influence rather than political power. Its founders, faced with two power blocs – landowners and men – 'hoped to inspire courage in those who feared to express an opinion lest it prove unpopular at the big house', writes WI historian Inez Jenkins. The WI flourished during the First World War, faded when the men returned from the trenches, revived and faded again in the 'hooray for motherhood and apple pie' 50s. Jenkins points out that its revivals have often coincided with waves of feminism. 'It was their aim,' she says, 'to give a voice to wives, sisters, daughters who had come to think it the only proper behaviour to leave the men to do the talking.'

BEA CAMPBELL

LESS BARK, MORE BITE: THE COUNTRYSIDE ON TELEVISION
February 20 1999

A great barking and yapping has broken out over the BBC's plans to put down the long-running BBC2 series *One Man and His Dog*. One of the *Daily Telegraph*'s columnists, Robin Page, attacked this decision last Saturday with a venom only partly attributable to the fact that he is the programme's presenter; since when, the paper has been 'inundated' with complaints, mostly from people who see this as confirmation that the BBC is nowadays run by incurable townies, hatching their plans in north London wine bars. Some correspondents see clear links here with a broader BBC agenda, which extends to the persecution of hunting folk by Labour MPs. How, it is asked, will the time that is saved be used? A *Telegraph* leader fears it may simply follow the pattern it sees in *The Archers*, 'which now chiefly concerns itself with matters such as illegitimacy, adultery and the homosexual landlord of the Cat and Fiddle'. The stakes, we are asked to believe, could scarcely be higher. To sweep *One Man and His Dog* from our screens, wrote Lord Buxton, Miriam Rothschild and others in a letter to yesterday's paper, seems all the more incredible when the countryside and rural communities are facing their gravest crisis for 70 years.

Some may doubt that televising *One Man and His Dog* can in practice do much to counter the countryside's gravest problems, its areas of grievous poverty, the collapse of its transport services, the loss of the shops and schools which sustain village life. Even so, the coverage of rural life on TV is hardly so lavish that any relevant programme can be easily spared.

If the BBC intends to stick by its decision, and let *One Man and His Dog* find a new home with Sky, it needs at the very least to produce some substitute which demonstrably serves countryside interests better; and preferably at a more convenient time than Saturday afternoon. Let us add, for the avoidance of doubt, that replacing Robin Page with a Vorderman or a Smillie, or even a Zoë Ball, is not what we have in mind.

VISIONS OF ALBION: THE CHOCOLATE-BOX VILLAGE
March 27 1999

Potpourri. Polished dark-brown, antique tables with barley-twist legs. An equally well-polished and regularly serviced four-door Nissan, with National Trust or RSPB stickers neatly aligned on the inside of the rear window. Rayburn or Aga. Copies of *Country Life*, *The Field*, and magazines with names such as *Kentish Life* stacked limply in a bright, copper-lipped coal scuttle. Coiffured thatch. These are some of the essential ingredients of the thousands of picturesque English cottages that adorn the most beautiful English villages. Or, they are in the imagination of those of us who do not live in such rural bliss but know it only as a passing temptation when we drive through on high days and holidays and say, with a wistful sigh, wouldn't it be wonderful to live in such a perfect place?

In larger English villages, between the estate agent and Spar mini-mart, you are very likely to find a second-hand bookshop run by a nice buffer in cardigan, corduroys and half-moon glasses hanging on a string from around his neck. He is bound to stock, among slightly foxed tomes on fishing, military history and obscure railway branch lines closed by Dr Beeching, at least a dozen devoted to the celebration of rural England, its thatched villages with names that appear to have been bestowed on them by poets. Or should I say bards? Ryme Intrinsica, Fontwell Magna, Huish Episcopi ... The best of these books are from the turn of the century and not much later than the First World War. Some are written by Edward Thomas, who was desperate for cash at the time and had yet to make his name as a poet. Nearly all these books boast softer-than-Andrex watercolours of charming village scenes, painted by local artists in a style somewhere between Constable on a bad day and Beatrix Potter without the wit. Like an exotic dancer in seven veils, each coloured plate is half-hidden from the browser's view by a gossamer tissue of cloudy paper, as if to half-protect and half-highlight its soft and downy charms.

For a while, I liked to collect such books. They presented a view of England that was as illusory as a Victorian vicar's magic-lantern show. They were the stuff of gentle fantasy, for whenever I cycled out to find the watercolour villages, they were never there. They were marked on the *AA Book of the Road* all right, but where were the ducklings waddling across the ford in the middle of the ancient high street laced with willow herb and forget-me-not? Where was the straw-sucking shepherd ushering his flock at sunset between rose-bedecked cottages?

Instead, there were yellow lines, 'No Entry' signs, speed-bumps, crew-cut hedgerows, vast litter bins on the green, huge notices braying BUMPINGTON TWINNED WITH ÜBERHUNDWASSER-AM-RHEIN, strings of Range-Rover and Subaru estates pushed up to the car-battered walls of the local pub. Neighbourhood Watch signs in beetle-browed windows. Signs barking PRIVATE PROPERTY. KEEP OUT. And ostentatious notices declaring THE MOST BEAUTIFUL VILLAGE IN ENGLAND, 1978.

On the edge of the village, what were meadows had long given way to the sort of 'vernacular'-style housing specified from a junk-mail catalogue, or perhaps designed by a local architect who in his youth admired Le Corbusier, but has since donned patched-sleeved tweed jackets with which he rubs shoulders over a pint of local brew with local planners and small-time developers in the Fox and Hounds.

He has come to see the errors of his mildly radical youth and now rather admires the Prince of Wales.

Of course, there are many beautiful villages in England, but most have stayed that way because they are truly remote or else pampered and pickled in heritage aspic by wealthy types who 'discovered' their village in the mid-60s on a 'wonderful' holiday to Bumpshire – with the aid of a *Shell Guide* written by John Betjeman and illustrated by John Piper. Many of these marvellously decent types own a house in west London, too. The perfect cottage in the most beautiful village in England is accessed not by a sweet roam across clear streams and dewy fields, but by Mercedes estate down the M3 or M4, turning off at the A59765 intersection (A DEPARTMENT OF TRANSPORT INITIATIVE IN PARTNERSHIP WITH THE EUROPEAN REGIONAL DEVELOPMENT FUND. HELPING TO CREATE BETTER ROADS. APOLOGIES FOR ANY DELAY). From there, the newly widened B44332 bypasses Cidercombe, the one semi-industrial town on the way ('frightful place'), and then it's a full-bore spin down the long straight above the valley, so much faster now that the bends have been ironed out. Left down the hill, and here's Sloane-on-the-Wold (MOST BEAUTIFUL VILLAGE IN ENGLAND, 1982, and again in 1997).

The weekend motorway set and most of the rest of us, too, remain, at the tail end of the 20th century, either in love or bemused by a rural idyll that, if it never really existed – save in the plates of those floury-papered Edwardian books – certainly doesn't today. No great insights are needed to understand why we are so enchanted with the idea of the perfect village with its doll's-house homes. A return to childhood, a retreat into innocence. A chance for townies to dress up, learn to ride and take up hunting, as if to the manor born. The desire to grow old conservatively, to grow pears, plant a kitchen garden, make fires, keep dogs and to wear a sexless uniform chosen from a rack of thick woollen tights, fisherman's hats and muddy boots.

The last time I walked through one of the 'most beautiful villages in England', it was jammed with a fleet of day-tripping coaches with loudly hissing air-brakes. Cars – no, not vintage Bentleys – surrounded the pond. The pub (heavily restored) was crowded. Only the church was empty (KEY FROM MRS CHARMINGBUTT-BOSSY, MANOR COTTAGE, FIRST ON THE LEFT IN BACKSIDE LANE).

No. The best way to experience such rural fantasies is in the pages of books devoted to preserving the myth. Now, if only a publisher was to offer a scratch-and-sniff book of the most beautiful villages in England – the scent of thatch-eave roses on page 26, potpourri on page 94 – we could happily sit in our towns and cities, secure in the knowledge that rural perfection existed somewhere without us having to drive along motorways and new bypasses, past distribution depots, to find them. Or just open a tin of lavender-scented polish or a bag of potpourri from a frou-frou shop in Notting Hill and dream of England.

JONATHAN GLANCEY

HOW TO SURVIVE A SUMMER FETE
July 17 1999

In the summer months, the villages of Britain are studded with fetes designed to show that merciless commercial exploitation is not only the preserve of the Square Mile. If you're going to organise a fete, the first thing you need to do is to catch your village idiot. You then attach the idiot to a public-address system and get him to do a running commentary on the sale of every raffle ticket, as well as announcing every time the rat is batted – Bat the Rat is the financial bedrock of any village fete, and involves dropping a sand-filled sock down a short pipe and then whacking it with a stick before it hits the ground. The stall usually raises about £19 on a good day, and provokes unimaginable brutality when combined with local cider.

If you're at a village fete that has stands such as Guess the Age of the Cow Pat, then the village is actually in the commuter belt of a major metropolis. If there are stalls such as Touch the Computer or Watch the Traffic Light, then you are in a rural heartland. The best feature of any fete is the cake stall, where you can pick up for 25p a freshly baked cake that cost well over a pound to make. Unfortunately, this is such good value that it attracts the professional fete scavengers. When you arrive at the fete 10 minutes after opening time, they will already be leaving with their estate cars loaded down with bedding plants and fairy cakes. There should be a rule stipulating that you can go to the fairy cakes stall only after you have been around the Count the Flies and Bat the Rat stalls.

At any fete, always remember to set aside at least half an hour to watch the Cubs and Brownies do their carefully choreographed displays of unarmed combat, or whatever it is they do these days. And also take a moment to visit the second-hand-books stall, packed with old textbooks on caravan maintenance and property law. These are exactly the same books that turn up at every village fete – the act of buying any of them is, in fact, the secret way to join the masons. At most fetes, the place you'll end up in is the St John Ambulance stand, where you get your two aspirin for the horrific ploughing injury you sustained in the Blind Man's Tractor Game.

The climax of the day is the raffle, when someone wins the lovely picnic set and deck-chairs that you thought you'd laid out under a tree an hour before.

GUY BROWNING

SPY WRITER FIGHTS FOR CLIFFTOP PARADISE
July 24 1999

On a hot summer's day, the view from the study of David Cornwell's clifftop home could not be more tranquil. Small fishing boats rest quietly on the sparkling water far below, butterflies flit from bush to bush and only the quiet hum of a mower disturbs the peace of an extensive and lovingly tended garden. But for the man better known to millions of readers as the bestselling author John le Carré, these are anything but peaceful times at Tregiffian, the Cornish coastal hamlet he has called home for the past 30 years.

Though his latest novel *Single Single* is selling well in hardback, the main focus of the writer's attention in recent weeks has been a planning row that has seen him condemned in some quarters – unjustly he insists – as an egotist and intolerant resident. His most recent appearance in print was a stinging letter to the local paper in which he criticised a neighbour's plans to build a house on land overlooking the Cornwall coastal footpath as a calculated assault on a precious piece of British coastline. By ironic coincidence the chief protagonist in this unneighbourly dispute is the farmer who first sold the millionaire author the cottages and barn that have been so painstakingly converted into the magnificent home that remains his continuing obsession.

Bought with the proceeds of *The Spy Who Came in From the Cold*, when the author was seeking sanctuary during the break-up of his first marriage, it has witnessed the birth of 11 more novels, *Smiley's People* and *Tinker, Tailor, Soldier, Spy* among them, in the three decades since he moved there.

At the heart of the planning row that has deflected Mr Cornwell from his latest project – a novel set partly in Africa – was an application by a local farmer, Jimmy Thomas, to build a 4,000 sq ft house and a shed to house 160 head of cattle on land some 200 yards behind the writer's property near St Buryan. The site, which cannot be seen from Mr Cornwell's house, lies within a designated area of outstanding natural beauty in a river valley that leads down to the rocky coastline.

Earlier this week a full meeting of Penwith district council rejected Mr Thomas's plans to build an agricultural dwelling. But Mr Cornwell fears a decision by the council at the same meeting to allow further negotiations on the cattle shed could prove to be the Trojan horse that enables the dwelling to be built. A pressing agricultural need has to be shown to build a house in an area of outstanding natural beauty, and Mr Cornwell believes that Mr Thomas, with the help of a new livestock building, may eventually be able to convince planners he needs a house.

Mr Cornwell has vowed to continue the fight and is considering using funds from a charitable trust to help fight other intrusions of property along Britain's heritage coast. Standing on the footpath below the proposed new dwelling yesterday, the author warned that if the building was allowed it would be the only new building you could see between Lamorna and Porthcurno along the coastal footpath. The agricultural buildings that would attach to it and be the justification for it would be 'a blot on the landscape'. The whole of the hillside would be polluted.

'It makes me very cross when people say this is another bit of celebrity Nimbyism, that this is my backyard. This is everybody's backyard – not just every Cornishman's backyard, but every tourist's backyard who comes down here. It is of concern to everyone who walks this coastal path.'

Mr Cornwell, whose 27-acre property includes a one-mile stretch of the cliffs along the path, was backed in his opposition to the building by the National Trust, the Council for the Protection of Rural England, Friends of the Earth and the Ramblers' Association, but was critical of the lack of teeth shown by such organisations in planning disputes. He believed he was put in the position of having to act as a 'spearhead'.

The battle, in which he enlisted the help of lawyers and agricultural consultants, has given him an appetite for a wider war to protect Britain's heritage coastline. 'What I would like to do is establish – and if necessary share in the funding of – a ginger group of some sort which would watch the coastline nationwide. It would attack vocally and vigorously any abuse of the planning system, particularly through this agricultural loophole. There is a new force abroad of people who say we have built enough.'

Funding for the proposed ginger group would come from the £1.25m charitable trust set up by Mr Cornwell and his wife, Jane, to support west of England causes.

Celebrities with Trouble Next Door
- John Major: The former prime minister wrote to the government in February 1998, objecting to plans for a 24-hour air-freight terminal development yards from his home. Protesters said the development would be used for 15,000 aircraft movements a year, mainly at night.

- Laurie Lee: In 1995 the 80-year-old author led the successful campaign to prevent a housing development in Slad valley in the Cotswolds, where he based *Cider with Rosie*.
- Gary Barlow: The former Take That singer and owner of a 60-acre country estate, Delamere Manor in Cheshire, outraged his neighbours in 1998 by refusing to allow the Delamere Manor Fly Fishers' Club to use its trout lake. The club had fished there for more than half a century and even stocked the lake, but Barlow said his privacy was more important.
- Bernard Ingham: Margaret Thatcher's former press secretary had been feuding with his neighbours in Purley, south London, over their home improvements. In December 1998 he was accused of denting their car in a row over their use of a track to both homes' garages. He was bound over to keep the peace and the charges were eventually dropped.

GEOFFREY GIBBS

✹ ✹ ✹

BRITONS ALL OF A TWITTER OVER BIRDWATCHING
August 20 1999

Birdwatchers, like trainspotters, have long suffered from an image of compilers of lists and wearers of unfashionable clothes, but birds are fast becoming one of the nation's favourite hobbies. Although still behind the £3bn-a-year gardening and angling industries, watching, counting, recording and photographing birds is booming.

The Royal Society for the Protection of Birds (RSPB), the largest conservation charity in Europe, has seen its membership double in 10 years to well over 1m. Its reserves have turned into busy tourist attractions, and the British are now spending £80m each winter feeding garden birds.

The interest has been fuelled by television series like Sir David Attenborough's *Life of Birds*, which attracted up to 9m viewers a week, and made his book of the same name into a £1.5m, 100,000-copy best-seller. Sales of birdwatching equipment like binoculars and cameras have reached £25m a year, according to specialist shops, and twitchers – the keen fringe who drive hundreds of miles to see a rarity – are paying up to £800 for Swiss binoculars.

Sir David yesterday explained Britons' fondness for birds. 'I think it is because birds are the one wild creature that almost everyone sees every day, unless they are unlucky enough to be locked up in prison. It is the link of ordinary people to the wider wild world. I am delighted the television series captured the interest.'

The RSPB estimates the annual spending of British birdwatchers is now about £200m, and 17,000 visitors are expected at the British Birdwatching Fair starting today at Rutland Water, which runs until Sunday. The specialist bird holiday trade has boomed and Titchwell Marsh in Norfolk, the RSPB's most popular reserve, had 127,600 visitors last year. Part of the attraction at Titchwell is the only resident black-winged stilt – a Mediterranean wading bird which has long pink legs – in Britain. For the past seven years it has remained at Titchwell, while others of its species, rare summer visitors, always head south for winter.

Tapes and CDs of bird sounds, books about them and where to watch them are proliferating and there are 5,000 birds books available compared with only 1,000 in 1985. Perhaps the most astonishing finding is that two thirds of British households now claim to feed birds two or three times a week in winter. It is estimated that 30,000 tons of wild bird seed and 15,000 tons of peanuts are fed to birds in British gardens every year and a vast range of bird feeders and bird tables are sold.

Despite their newfound love of birds, many people are still pretty ignorant of the subject. Robins – the most popular bird and aggressively territorial – start singing in January to warn off competitors and claim a breeding site. Because street lights are so bright they can be heard singing at night and are frequently mistaken for nightingales. The robin was officially chosen as the British national bird in December 1960 and has long been a favourite.

For the enthusiast, hundreds of specialist overseas tours are available, many costing thousands of pounds, and about £10m is spent on foreign 'bird' holidays. These go as far as the Aleutian Islands in the north to Antarctica and from the Himalayas to the Dead Sea in search of rare species. There are also live images on the internet with cameras trained on seabird colonies or the osprey nest at Loch Garten in the Highlands.

Britain's choice for 'the most beautiful bird':
> Robin (20 per cent)
> Kingfisher (11 per cent)
> Golden Eagle (7 per cent)
> Blue Tit (6 per cent)
> Kestrel (6 per cent)
> Barn Owl (5 per cent)
> Magpie (5 per cent)

Mute Swan (4 per cent)
Blackbird (3 per cent)
Jay (3 per cent)
Song Thrush (3 per cent)
Chaffinch (3 per cent)
Source: Mori

PAUL BROWN

❧❧ CHAPTER SEVEN ❧❧

Harvest home
2000–2008

Reynard and John Peel are so deeply embedded in the British national consciousness that it seemed unbelievable to many when, four days after Valentine's Day in 2005, a ban on fox-hunting finally came into force. Since then, the situation has been a vintage British muddle, with most of the famous names in hunting continuing to flourish, albeit sometimes under humiliatingly untraditional titles such as 'pest control operators'. Simon Hart of the Countryside Alliance, which has done much to force a rural agenda on to national newslists in the last decade, gave a fair summary during the round of interviews which marked the debut of the new law. 'You can hunt a rat, but not a mouse, a rabbit, but not a hare, an artificial scent, but not a real one,' he said. 'The definitions of legal and illegal hunting are so blurred that the police are being asked to make impossible judgments.' But although the rights and wrongs, legalities, conflicts and perceptions and realities still require careful scrutiny from the *Guardian* and other media, the principle that killing a fox for sport is no longer acceptable has been established.

The Hunting Act 2004, which followed a similar measure in Scotland two years earlier, was the culmination of a debate which the *Manchester Guardian* was covering almost as soon as it was founded in 1821. It looked sceptically, for example, at a business prospectus which envisaged the Church of England breeding horses on a large scale to pay for the restoration of dilapidated rural rectories. 'This is only to be explained on the supposition that the scheme was projected by a knot of the fox-hunting parsons, once so common in England,' the newspaper surmised. The absoluteness of the way that hunting was part of English life at the time was also shown in the unexpected form of a schedule for a Manchester carnation show, held at the Swan Inn and recorded in the *Manchester Guardian* only two months after its first edition had appeared. Among prizewinners in the 'scarlet bizards' class of the flowers was a bloom called Fox-hunter, which was as red as a huntsman's coat.

The idea of banning the sport was inconceivable throughout the 19th century, when far more devastating assaults on the nation's wildlife were also treated as a matter of course. When the current Conservative spokesman on justice, Edward Garnier QC, was a night lawyer at the *Guardian* in the 1990s, he would recall his ancestor Thomas de Grey, the 6th Baron Walsingham, who shot a record 1,070 grouse in a single day on Blubberhouses Moor near Harrogate. The moor is hourglass-shaped and Lord Walsingham stood in the neck in the middle, banging away as the beaters pushed the birds to and fro over his vantage point. By the end of the day, staff said afterwards, some of the grouse were walking or hopping, too weary to fly.

This extraordinary tradition continued with little social disapproval for decades, with two singular examples in 1923. The Duchess of Bedford won her unofficial crown as the best woman in the butts in January by downing 273 pheasants with 366 cartridges from one 16-bore shotgun. Eight months later, the Marquess of Ripon dropped dead at the age of 71 on one of his favourite moors, Dallowgill near Ripon, after shooting 165 grouse and a snipe. His obituaries recorded that his many possessions included a lifetime tally of 556,813 game birds and animals. He was outdone for neatness, if not mass, by Captain Horatio Ross of Rossie castle near Montrose who bagged 82 grouse with 82 shots on his 82nd birthday.

It is easy to mock these people now, but the *Manchester Guardian* always – and the *Guardian* usually – recognised that many of them were extremely knowledgeable about their prey and the countryside habitat which birds, deer and fish require to flourish or sometimes even survive. Walsingham was a formidable authority on insects who made one of the world's most important collections of microlepidoptera, the very small species of moth and butterfly which are too much for most entomologists' patience. He was a valued trustee of the British Museum, partly because of his natural history expertise, but also because, as a Tory whip in the Lords during Benjamin Disraeli's second government between 1874 and 1880, he had political and fund-raising clout. He gave his specialist library and 260,000 preserved insects to the Natural History Museum where they remain a major scientific asset, unlike his grouse which ended up on dinner tables over 100 years ago.

In the same way, Captain Ross was one of Britain's leading authorities on deer in the 19th century, and in this he prefigured an interesting member of the *Guardian*'s staff. Harry Tegner was a founding member of the British Deer Society and a prolific writer on the subject. His daughter Veronica Heath, who took over his 'Country Diary' duties in 1977 when he felt too confined by ill-health to his home near Morpeth, remembers being spellbound by his stories of the animals' secret ways, including his discovery of 'deer playgrounds' deep in the forests of the Scottish highlands where the animals had trampled grassy glades in figures of eight.

Tegner's stalking and support for fox-hunting, which was an unremarked way of life in rural Northumberland, did not ruffle *Guardian* readers. Things were different for another sportsman contributor, George Muller. He patrolled the Cumbrian beat for the newspaper for 40 years until his death in 1950, also writing 'Country Diary's, but contributing many longer articles besides. In the 1920s, these included a series on fox-hunting which was approved by C. P. Scott, but led to outrage among one influential group of *Manchester Guardian* faithfuls, the Quakers, who were strong in northern Lancashire and the Lake District. Muller was reined in and for a while confined to his weekly diary. He wrote to Scott's successor A. P. Wadsworth many years later saying that he still mourned the loss of the weekly guinea. And many of his fellow countrymen mourned the loss of the countryside expertise shown in the articles, which did not dwell on the excitement and terror of the chase, or the blood.

Muller was also one of the country's leading authorities on otters, which were also hunted by packs of hounds at the time, and he was a superb fly-fisherman. His family were of German origin, but he spent his teenage years in the United States where he acquired a mixture of Hawkeye's frontiersman skills and the love of nature shown by Thoreau in *Walden*. Muller's obituary in the *Manchester Guardian* included a tribute by his friend and fellow angling devotee Arthur Ransome, who recalled being stoned by poachers with Muller when they were guarding salmon and trout in the deep pools of the river Marron. 'No man in England knew more about otters than Muller,' wrote Ransome. 'Long after he had all but given up fishing he used, evening after evening, to go down to look at the river to renew his acquaintance with the otters and to watch the salmon leaping. It is sad that he will watch them no more.'

A final member of this band of what we might call journalists-turned-gamekeepers was John Masefield, the Poet Laureate from 1930 to 1967 who was an influential member of the *Manchester Guardian*'s staff before the First World War. He invented the 'Miscellany' column, which was to become one of the newspaper's most famous and long-lasting features, and his writing glowed with a love of the countryside, bred in a briefly idyllic childhood in Herefordshire before his parents died. He was influenced, too, by another experience he had in common with Muller, teenage years in the United States where he was a vagrant and carpet-factory worker after deserting from a clipper ship whose crew he had joined in London. The eventual result was poetry such as 'Sea Fever', 'Cargoes' and, in 1919, *Reynard the Fox*. This last, which the *New York Times* compared at the time to Chaucer, perhaps sums up the uncertain mind with which so many British people, including countrymen and women, view the hunt. Reynard is the hero of Masefield's 166-page epic, but so is the hunt. Reynard escapes, but another fox whose scent is taken up in error by the hounds dies.

COUNTRYSIDE ALERT
March 29 2000
Tomorrow Tony Blair turns his attention to another creaking area of public policy when he hosts a farm summit at Downing Street with ministers and leaders from the farming and food industries. The issue? How to take British agriculture out of its current doldrums.

It's an odds-on bet that short-term problems will dominate the agenda: an unusual alliance of organisations, including the Royal Society for the Protection of Birds (RSPB), the small farmers' alliance and the young farmers, feels sufficiently confident of this that they have organised an 'alternative' summit. Why do these bodies feel that their interests are in danger of being left out in the cold?

There is an extensive history of governments talking a long-term game on farming and the environment, but adopting short-term tactics. If this government falls into the trap of concentrating on the immediate economic crisis, it risks losing the opportunity to reflect the developing consensus about the long-term future of farming.

There is no doubt that, across most sectors, the farming industry is in crisis. The role of agriculture in the rural economy has been declining for decades. Stuck with a 'dig for victory' emphasis on food production, farming policies are badly out of kilter with modern needs. This has had a knock-on effect on rural communities. The total number of UK farmers and farm workers has declined from over 1m in the 1960s to 605,000 in 1996, and many farming families survive on annual incomes of less than £5,000.

But it would be a mistake to think that, apart from agriculture, the countryside is in good health. The rural environment is in crisis too. Only recently, the government published quality-of-life indicators showing that countryside bird populations continue their massive declines: millions of wild birds have vanished from the skies in a quarter of a century. In just one three-year period in the early 1990s, 54,000km of hedgerows were lost across England and Wales. This week, BirdLife International published figures showing that 42 per cent of the most important bird areas in Europe are threatened by intensive agriculture. These statistics are indicative of what is happening to the farmed landscape and wildlife countrywide.

No one can blame the farmers; they have simply responded to market demand and the outdated priorities of the Common Agricultural Policy. However, opinion polls show the public increasingly wants agriculture that is about more than just mass food production at lowest cost. Food safety scares, BSE, genetically modified crops and the impact of modern farming on the landscape have intensified consumer anxiety about the way we produce our food. There is a growing recognition that farmers should be rewarded for their wider roles in the countryside – contributing to a diverse rural economy and providing an environmentally rich landscape. In convening his summit, Blair has a prime opportunity to find solutions for redirecting public money to provide what the average taxpayer really wants from British agriculture. But the omens for this are not good.

The RSPB has long been an advocate of the need to reduce the environmental impact of pesticides and the £100m annual costs to the taxpayer of removing them from drinking water. Introducing fiscal incentives through a pesticides tax is one option. But this has been shelved by the government in favour of an as yet unseen package of voluntary measures from the agrochemicals industry. Until it is demonstrated that the latter has real substance, this can only be construed as gesture politics taking precedence over long-term policy solutions.

The switch from paying sheep farmers on a headage to an area basis made environmental and economic sense, as it would have reduced sheep numbers on the hills and produced fewer, higher quality – and therefore higher-value – lambs. With sheep prices at an all-time low and overgrazing continuing to blight the uplands, both hill farmers and the environment will lose out as a result of the Ministry of Agriculture, Fisheries and Food's decision to keep payments closely linked to sheep numbers. An opportunity has therefore been wasted to move towards a more environmentally sustainable and economically viable agriculture in a struggling sector.

Ministers have repeatedly stated that they want to see an agriculture industry that is competitive on the world market and rewarded for its increasingly important roles in providing rural development and environmental stewardship. The government has made positive first steps towards this vision. But if ministers fall back on short-term expediency rather than grapple with the long-term solutions then everyone will be a loser: farmers, taxpayers and the environment.

The primary justification for continued state intervention in agriculture should be to safeguard the future of the countryside as a resource for the whole of society.

If the government accepts this vision, it has to face up to the challenge of modernising agriculture policy so that it delivers value for money to the taxpayer. As Blair himself said last month: 'There is a healthy future for farming, but it means change.'

GRAHAM WYNNE

A COUNTRY DIARY: RETURNING TO THE PURPLE – THE STIPERSTONES
April 4 2000

Swooping low over the Devil's Chair, the buzzard covered a half-mile of rock and heather in seconds until it reached us, then wheeled overhead, slowly spinning the scene in its scrutinising gaze. We watched the buzzard, saw the morning sunlight flash on bronze underwings, felt the piercing surveillance, as if the mountain itself had sent a spy.

What did the buzzard see? A group of people milling about, an odd collection of vehicles, a horse. The buzzard snapped the scene in its head and soared off back behind the craggy ridge.

A Landrover returned from the hill with a dead sheep in a trailer. The previous day this corpse had not only attracted a large gang of ravens but also a red kite. No kite around today, but groups of ravens, in twos and threes, tumbled through the warm, spring morning air and barked across the still expanse of The Stiperstones. All eyes swung east towards the Longmynd as a characteristic noise became a black dot making its way towards us. A small red helicopter arrived and the ravens, skylarks and stonechats fled or kept low in the heather. Heather and helicopter was what this peculiar gathering was all about.

As part of the Back to Purple project, which aims to restore lost areas of heathland to The Stiperstones, English Nature (EN) had arranged for an aerial seeding over a cleared conifer plantation. The Gatton plantation covered 16 hectares of hillside and is now largely bare. Some natural heather regeneration has occurred, but EN wanted to get heathland cover as soon as possible.

Heather seed was collected and processed and now, like some bizarre cookery demonstration, the seed was being mixed with water so it could be sprayed from the helicopter. Apparently, 112m near-microscopic heather seeds were needed. The heather-seed soup was loaded on to the helicopter to be sprayed from nozzles in plastic tubes. The chopper worked back and forth across the hillside, sometimes only 15ft above the ground, spraying, then banking deftly, hawking across the hill like a huge red dragonfly from another age.

PAUL EVANS

WILDLIFE ACRES TO BE TREASURED
June 21 2000

Sixty wildflower acres and a Nissen hut were ranked with Turner landscapes and Wren churches yesterday as among Britain's most valuable treasures. The heads of the National Trust and English Nature trekked from London to a Yorkshire smallholding to honour the work of Walter Umpleby and his scythe.

Tucked beyond the reach of slurry wagons and fertiliser sales agents, the patch of Malham Moor was declared the newest national nature reserve at a farmyard ceremony. Scientists have been astonished by the wealth of plants preserved by Mr Umpleby's 'outstanding' management of one of the last true hay meadows in the northern uplands. Martin Drury, director general of the National Trust, said: 'We call this an agri-environmental benefit. But in truth it is a great national treasure, as fragile, rare and important to this country as an ancient building or work of art.'

The survival of the meadows at New House Farm, almost 2,000ft above sea level, is due to Mr Umpleby's dogged use of traditional meadow management for 40 years. The regime, maintained since Mr Umbleby, now 72, retired and sold the smallholding to the National Trust, involves a single mowing in July, prompt removal of the hay, and no soil nutrients.

MARTIN WAINWRIGHT

COASTLINE RESCUED FROM MAN-MADE HORROR: NATURE RETURNS TO CO DURHAM'S *GET CARTER* LUNAR LANDSCAPE
July 29 2000

On the limestone cliffs high above the rocky shoreline a rare butterfly flutters in the July sunshine. Skylarks swoop overhead while a variety of seabirds – purple sandpipers, little terns, oystercatchers – wheel above a reclaimed beach or waddle on the sand. Walking along a newly created clifftop footpath, weaving between high grasses and a profusion of harebells, speedwell, sea sandwort and other wild flowers, John Goodfellow swore that the landscape could easily match Dorset, Cornwall or nearby North Yorkshire. 'Would you believe that, until very recently, everyone turned their back on this area?' he said. 'It just wasn't a nice place to be.'

Five years ago, only the brave and foolhardy ventured on to the badly scarred cliffs and the blackened beaches of County Durham. After 100 years of mining it had the most heavily polluted coastline in Britain, and probably western Europe. A series of huge overhead mechanical conveyors had dumped at least 100m tonnes of colliery waste on to the cliffs and into the sea. Scores of pipelines pumped black liquid across once-sandy beaches. Parents warned children to keep away. The lunar coastline was the backdrop to the final grim scene in the 1960s film *Get Carter*, as Michael Caine struggled with a mobster on the conveyors preparing to tip waste high above the North Sea.

The film graphically illustrated the man-made horror below: years of indiscriminate tipping meant that the Durham coastline had the distinction of being the only part of Britain that had extended into the sea – by about 100 yards in 50 years, according to Ordnance Survey maps. When the last of the six big coastal collieries at Easington closed in 1993 local councils faced a choice: write off the coastline or attempt to bring it back to life.

As the collieries were demolished the councils opted for a massive reclamation scheme in the hope of restoring the area to its former glory. A partnership with national agencies and conservation groups was launched, boldly titled Turning the Tide. With funding from the Millennium Commission and other sources running to £10m, the four-year scheme is due to be completed next spring, and has exceeded the wildest expectations of a small project team. John Goodfellow, one of its senior officers, lists a string of achievements, not least the return of the Durham Argus butterfly (brown, with orange-spotted wings), which has been attracted by rock roses on the reclaimed magnesian limestone cliffs, along with many varieties of wild flowers. Partly as a result, the coast has become a national nature reserve.

It has been a monumental task. For a start, 1.3m tonnes of waste, sometimes 30-feet deep, has been removed, although some slag has been retained, because it is considered necessary to stabilise the cliffs. Footpaths, including a spectacular 12-mile coastal route, and cycle ways have been created, and a string of sculptures erected. More public art is planned. To improve access and encourage flora and wildlife, around 500 acres of farmland has been bought from local farmers and converted to limestone grassland.

'On a summer weekend, you can't move for people on the beach,' said David Smith, a former miner, as he walked his dog towards Easington sea front. 'It's now clean and lovely – but you've got to watch, because the tide now comes in further with all the muck gone.'

Ambling along the coastal path with her daughter Amy, Tracy Kirkup, whose father was a miner, vividly recalled the 'horrible beaches' of her childhood. 'You'd go on to them and come back all black. I grew up with it, and it was awful. I remember that at school our old head teacher once showed us some photographs of sandy beaches and we couldn't believe it. Now it's getting to be lovely once again.'

At Seaham, the northern point of the path, Alan Willis licked an ice cream on his mountain bike and recalled how most people boycotted the beaches during his youth. 'You turned your back on them and went somewhere else. Now they've been cleaned up, you can clearly see rocks through the water. Before it was all black.'

Now that millions are being spent improving hotels in the area, some brave souls are even predicting the emergence of a holiday trade. 'Maybe that's going a bit far,' said Tracy Kirkup. 'It's still nice to go abroad. It can be cold and wet here.'

PETER HETHERINGTON

GROWING PAINS: TWO THOUSAND YEARS OF FARMING ONE FIELD
August 9 2000

The wheat growing in the field known as the Horse Ground is now tall, golden and ready to be harvested. With Cotswold cream houses as a backdrop, it is a scene any visitor would relish. But the farming practices that govern the field are not so picture-postcard. In a 10-month growing season, it has been sprayed with herbicides, pesticides and growth regulators a minimum of seven times, as well as having two applications of liquid nitrogen.

Frequency of spraying is not everything, since chemical concentration also counts. But by any standards, this farming is intensive. And it is potentially toxic – at least to those directly involved. The seed grain planted last September was itself coated with fungicide. The hazard data printed on the sack ran to seven paragraphs, including the warning that PVC gloves and a respirator should be worn when filling the seed drill.

'This is not what someone with a weekend cottage wants to hear,' says the farm manager responsible for the Horse Ground's 14 acres, plus another 2,000 acres. 'But we are producing a commodity, just as on a factory floor.' He was prepared to speak about the field and the way it was farmed provided he was not named. 'We have to maximise return,' he says. 'In the present financial climate, even the big farms are suffering.'

The grain the Horse Ground grows this year will fatten pigs and poultry. Feed wheat that fetched £120 a tonne in the mid-1990s now sells for less than £60. 'Highly efficient farms are probably still an acceptable investment, but they are certainly not highly profitable,' says Dr Dick Morris, senior lecturer in environmental systems at the Open University. 'Intensive agriculture is like a treadmill. The more you put in, the more you have to put in. If you sow treated grain, you've paid for the treatment as well as the grain, and you've probably chosen an expensive variety. Faced with that investment, you would have to put in other treatments necessary to protect it.'

Take out the herbicides, fungicides and insecticide and the yield would fall by a third from its current four tonnes an acre, the farm manager estimates. Take out the liquid nitrogen as well, and the yield would be down two-thirds. For the Horse Ground that would mean a reduction in income from the anticipated £3,250 to little more than £1,000. The chemicals used on the field cost around £700 (£50 an acre), and little labour is involved since the entire field can be sprayed in half an hour. So leaving out the chemicals saves little, while slashing returns. The best organic farmers in the UK harvest 70 per cent of average non-organic grain yields. But it takes years of altered management to reach this level, and it is almost impossible to succeed with organic arable farming unless animals are part of the system. And that would require prohibitive capital expenditure.

Ironically, the Horse Ground was once part of a flourishing dairy unit, abandoned under the economic imperatives of the late 1970s. 'We moved from dairying into arable, taking the subsidy available from the Common Market to cull the cows,' recalls Archie Piper, then land agent responsible for the field. Cynics might suggest that as a result the field switched from contributing to a milk lake to contributing to a grain mountain. But Morris contends: 'There were intermittent surpluses at the time, but in global terms they were molehills.'

Whatever the economics at play, the 1970s switch out of dairying ended at least 500 years of pastoral use. But the Horse Ground's long history as pasture began with an equally hard-headed financial decision. In the late 15th century the future was not cereals but sheep. Wool destined for the continent was England's dominant export.

'At the time, part of the Horse Ground was cultivated, but about a third of it was lived on,' says Tim Copeland, an archaeologist who knows the area well. 'It might have been home to 50 people. But it was more profitable for the lord of the manor to have a herd of sheep than a dozen tenants, and they would simply have been forced out.' The abandoned village left its mark on the landscape for five centuries, until it was obliterated by the ploughing in the 1970s that prepared the ground for grain. That was a loss to archaeology. But the environmental costs of farming the Horse Ground so intensively are probably more pressing.

Aside from the potential accumulation of chemical residues in food, pesticides and herbicides contaminate water supplies. Since privatisation, the water companies have spent an additional £970m in removing pollutants from drinking water. But they regard farmers as less to blame than local authorities and railway companies who spray herbicides on to hard surfaces with rapid run-off. A reduced range of flora and fauna is the undisputed price we pay for intensive farming.

What we gain from it is ample home-produced food. For Neil, who ploughs, plants, sprays and harvests the Horse Ground, that is a significant achievement. 'I sometimes wish people in this country would go hungry for a while,' he says. 'Then they'd appreciate farming more.'

Even on a small scale, commercial and environmental considerations do not always pull in different directions. Today's tight profit margins mean that, for example, agrochemicals that increase yield by 10 per cent, but cost more than farmers recoup on the extra grain, will no longer be used. And there is an appreciation that integrated crop management can maintain yields while lessening input of costly chemicals. One year in five, peas are grown to fix nitrogen in the soil, reducing the need for fertiliser.

The wheat the Horse Ground grows does not go to the mill at nearby Shipton-under-Wychwood, but prices there indicate the extra cost of not using chemicals. Organic Cotswold flour is 20 per cent more expensive than the non-organic equivalent. If more consumers are prepared to pay that premium, history suggests that agriculture will respond.

The two big changes in the last millennium – when the Horse Ground shifted from arable land to pasture and back again – were both driven by economics. Pottery shards Copeland dug from the field show the Romans used the land, which lies close to the site of a large villa. 'The Romans practised what we would recognise as commercial agriculture,' he says. 'And it is likely that even then someone was counting the sestertia it generated.'

ROB STEPNEY

A COUNTRY DIARY: SOMERSET

August 22 2000

We found the little hamlet of Hardington Moor and asked the way to a special hay-meadow. 'You're too late for the flowers,' they told us. 'The meadow was mown a few weeks back.' But they showed us how to find it, high up on a ridge at Coker Hill. We took in the long views, north and south.

An English Nature notice explained that our meadow, on the southern flank, was one of very few examples of the traditional, unimproved grassland of which only a tiny proportion survived the post-war intensification of agriculture. It is home to the rare oat grass and green-winged orchid and is mown in July after most of the wild flowers have seeded.

When we arrived, the cows were munching grass speckled yellow with nothing rarer than dandelions. Cattle keep down the tougher grasses and allow rarer plants to thrive in season. Looking down into the valley, we saw West Coker immediately below us, a labyrinth of narrow lanes threading between ancient stone buildings. The right-angled pattern of the 16th-century manor house stood out. Travellers who pass through the village by the overcrowded funnel of the old A30 gain no impression of the place's shape or character, but once you have looked down on its intricate plan spread out like a map, you want to explore.

We followed a steep track cut deep in the sandy hillside down into the village. Off Dibbles Lane were the schoolhouse and the old dairyhouse. The lanes were empty and silent until we turned a corner towards the manor house and heard cheerful sounds. Cream teas were being served in a cottage garden in aid of the Women's Institute.

People know about nearby East Coker, because T. S. Eliot found his ancestors' birthplace there and wrote about it. Of West Coker, some may have read that it was the home of Coker canvas, prized by seafarers when hemp and flax were local products. Our good fortune was to hear its story direct from people who live there, sitting in a garden overshadowed by the manor, enjoying home-made cream teas.

JOHN VALLINS

AN UNHEARD OF HUE AND CRY IN THE NAME OF HUNTING

March 13 2001

Lord Carter, the government whip, made a tragic plea in the House of Lords for peers to keep their speeches short. There were 69 listed to speak on fox-hunting. He said, pleading, that if they stuck to seven minutes each, 'we might even finish on the day we started'.

Fat chance. After the first four speeches they were already 38 minutes late. But, as Lord McNally said, the Lords have always been terrifically excited by 'badgers and buggery'. He meant 'badgers' to stand for animals in general, so he could have offered 'stags and sodomy' or 'foxes and fellatio'. A treat for another day, perhaps.

Lord Bassam introduced the bill sombrely, though when he alleged 'the government is neutral' the Tories erupted in a low, grumbling thunder, rather like the pounding of 200 hooves. In their view the bill is just a preliminary to locking up all morris dancers in concentration camps. (Not a bad idea, when you think about it.)

Lord Cope was about to speak for the Tories, but he couldn't, because Lord Longford thought it was his turn. 'I have an amendment tabled,' he said, angrily. Lady Jay told him to wait. He was number 58 on the list. 'Now, now!' he shouted. 'I was going to move an amendment in favour of drag hunting, which everyone agrees with. I can't wait up until 2 a.m.!' Lord Ferrers uncoiled to his full height, which takes a while, and averred, 'I have a horrible feeling that Lord Longford is right.' So they ignored him. Finally, the Tory frontbencher rose. His name is Lord Cope of Berkeley, and the Berkeley hunt rides near his seat. (The word 'berk' is derived from this, making Lord Cope a rare example of human rhyming slang.)

Things have changed in the House of Lords. People were never so rude as now. Lord Falconer nipped off for two minutes, no doubt for a pee, and was greeted on his return by loud and ironic cheers. Lord McNally got quite furious with Lord Lawson – you may recall him as Margaret Thatcher's chancellor, though to most people he is now the father of the more famous Nigella. The male Nige tried to interrupt. 'I will not give way!' yelled McNally. 'Why haven't you put your name down? If you're still here at midnight, we will be very surprised! I'm not going to play your game!'

It's not supposed to be like this in the Lords. Barking at each other is the equivalent of Mrs Bennett hurling her tea in the vicar's face. One longed for Alastair Sim to murmur, 'Girls, girls!' but they just don't have the language to cope with this kind of outbreak. Moments later, there was even an angry stir when McNally drank water.

Lord Burns, who wrote the Burns report on hunting, ruefully reflected on the way that his opinion – being killed by dogs 'seriously prejudices the welfare of the fox' – would 'pursue me for some time'. He undertook to explain what he meant by this curious circumlocution, and failed. (It had something to do with the fox feeling pain as it kicked the bucket.) Lord Longford suddenly popped up again. 'I tabled an amendment!' he shouted several times, then fell into what seemed a deep, dreamy and blameless sleep.

Baroness Castle described her own success as a countrywoman: camping and growing roses. It was a stroll down memory lane, except that memory lane has been closed due to foot and mouth. She loathes hunting. 'I couldn't do it! It makes me sick! Just to see it!' she shouted. It seemed that everyone was shouting. Some older Labour peers could not resist a frisson at this extraordinary spectacle: Barbara Castle, of all people, denouncing the practice of blood sports.

SIMON HOGGART

THE NEWS FROM GROUND ZERO: FOOT AND MOUTH IS WINNING
March 17 2001

Below the wooded hill known as Arthuret Knowes is a county council sign about the Battle of Aedderyd (AD 573). On this spot, it says, the pagans of Strathclyde were slaughtered by the Christians of Cumbria. Though the pagan king Gwenddolau had Merlin to encourage him, 80,000 humans were killed. The number seems unimaginable.

From the sign, you look across to Howend Farm, where the mass graves have been alight for the past week, sometimes blazing, sometimes smouldering. More than 5,000 pagan sheep and cattle belonging to farmer John Fisher (with just Nick Brown to encourage him) have been slaughtered by a marksman sent by the Christians at the Ministry of Agriculture. That is a tiny fraction of the animals killed in this small patch of Cumbria alone. The rest of the sheep will go in the next few days, the healthy as well as the sick: hundreds of thousands in all. The number seems unimaginable.

Howend is just outside Longtown, the small town fringing the Scottish border that constitutes Ground Zero in the war against foot and mouth, a war which the disease has been winning. Longtown (pop. 3,500; Lang-toon to the locals) used to have a mild local celebrity thanks to John Graham's amazing ironmongery. Most non-Cumbrians had never heard of the place – unless they were farmers. But Longtown also is – or was, three short weeks ago – a contender for Britain's biggest sheep market. Every Thursday up to 20,000 head of fatstock would be sold there. At this time of year, most would be hoggets: last year's hill lambs, reared on the lonely uplands of Scotland and Northumberland, destined to be killed and eaten further south. And it was here a month ago that an infected consignment arrived from Hexham and headed south, a process that silently and invisibly spread foot-and-mouth disease across much of Britain.

On Thursday, the gates to the market were shut with a rusty padlock. The pens were deserted. The town itself was not much different. Only the bar of the Graham Arms (the name Graham is everywhere here) was full, and that was because of a funeral. Longtown – static, ageing, a little melancholy at the best of times – always puts a lot of emphasis on funerals.

Longtown, however, is not just a prime source of the outbreak. It is also the very centre. Almost 10 per cent of the farms affected nationally are in this vicinity. Up the A7 towards Canonbie on the Scottish side of the border just about every farm is believed to be infected, and in the last few days the plague has been rippling out southwards towards Carlisle. Then on Thursday came the announcement that even healthy sheep would have to be 'culled' within two miles of an outbreak. Everyone round Longtown is within two miles.

Normally on a Thursday the rumours get passed round, and maybe leavened with a grain of truth, at the market cafe. This time, with the cafe shut, they just jumped from farm to farm like the disease itself. Since even Mr Brown originally thought all cattle would be slaughtered too, it was hardly surprising that the farmers were confused – and more contemptuous of London than ever. At one time, people were imagining that dogs and cats had to go.

The big talk yesterday of rebellion and shotguns seemed almost as distant as Mr Brown's blandness. There is a stoic acceptance here that there are currently three sorts of farm animals: the dead, the sick and the soon to be one or the other. The handful of farmers who have so far held off the plague listened jumpily each time the phone rang yesterday. They know the grim reaper from the Ministry of Agriculture, Fisheries and Food (MAFF) will lay his hands on their shoulders some time in the next few days.

The Great Fire of Lang-toon has been alight all week. It is a little like the burning of the Kuwaiti oil wells in the Gulf war or an Australian bushfire. Nothing like it has been seen in the English countryside since stubble-burning was banned. Unless you have worked in a crematorium, there is no analogy for the smell. It is strange, unearthly: a mix of singed rubber and old socks. On Tuesday the town stank terribly. On Wednesday it hung in the fog all day.

However, the split between farmers and their neighbours, so visible elsewhere in the countryside, is almost non-existent in Longtown. Directly or indirectly, almost everyone depends on sheep. A handful of Carlisle commuters have been attracted by the rock-bottom house prices, but only a handful. No one from the tourist trade has been shouting the odds about the damage done by farming, because there is no tourist trade worth mentioning, except from visiting sheep dealers. South of here are the Lakes; north and west are Gretna and Galloway. But hardly anyone stops in Longtown unless they are tired, confused or heading for the mart. For generations, everything here has depended on sheep farming. Within a few days there will be no sheep.

As Mr Brown made the announcement, I was with Bob Armstrong, the Longtown haulier who has been transporting animals to and from the mart since he took over his father's business in 1947. A third of his business was shut down overnight and he has been left with 26 drivers who have nothing to do; the firm is desperately trying to avoid laying them off. He also runs a few hobby-sheep in the paddock behind his house. All perfectly healthy. 'They'll have to go now,' he said phlegmatically as he digested the news. 'We had two little lambs born yesterday. Life can be cruel sometimes.' The original announcement suggested that his milk tankers, another third of the business, would also have to go. He just shrugged that off too.

Those worst affected are invisible. Every farm gate for miles around is blocked off by cones, tarpaulins, plastic netting, police tape, baler twine, anything that reinforces the Go Away message. Farmers with diseased animals lurk behind them, relying on friends to drop off supplies at the gate. John Fisher emerged briefly from his fortress at Howend and stood sentry in his flat cap and Barbour, without much purpose – but then, with no animals, he had nothing better to do. He seemed phlegmatic, too, and even smiled wryly. 'If I look upbeat, I don't feel upbeat,' he said. 'I've been having trouble sleeping.'

Mr Fisher may be one of the luckier ones: he kept up his foot-and-mouth insurance, which many others did not. Farmers keep using the same words as the TV reporters: 'devastating', 'terrible', 'heartbreaking', 'diabolical'. They are used to their animals being killed; they have become used to being sandbagged econom- ically. It is not easy for them to disentangle their true feelings: how much distress is emotion; how much is about money. Some farmers will restock and start again; those with pedigree herds will lose bloodlines that go back generations. One sometimes suspects that those who show it least, like John Fisher, may actually feel it the most.

No one in Longtown is immune, however. John Graham sits among his boxes of single screws, pull-on pipe nipples, oil-lamp parts and brass coffin nails, saying that business is worse than at any time in 30 years. He's convinced it will pass. 'People in a town like this have never expected a lot. North of Shap Fell, they can take bad times. What you've never had, you never miss.' In Lang-toon the south means the softies sitting under palm trees in Preston and Blackburn.

Everyone is taking the hit, except (so it is said) Tommy Norman, who sells the railway sleepers that go at the bottom of the funeral trenches below the coal to get the fires going. The trouble is that sheep hardly burn, especially at this time of year when they are thick with wool. 'It's like putting a woollen jumper on a fire,' explained Mr Fisher. 'It would nearly put it out. It's not like nylon.' That's why the burning takes so long. What no one can adequately explain is why the carcasses are allowed to be left before the pyre is lit, leaving the crows time to peck at them and fly off to spread the disease.

So the town shares the smoke, the pain, the grief and the grievances. But the grievances are unfocused. Is government policy too harsh or too weak? No one is certain, though they are instinctively convinced it must be one or the other. There seems no one in the area who can voice the farmers' feelings in a way that makes them both coherent and audible. The town council offices had the blinds drawn and the door locked even during its opening hours. A French community of similar size would have an elected mayor. In Longtown, there is not even a vicar.

In the absence of an incumbent, the Revd John Smith, formerly Cumbria's chief librarian and now an unpaid curate, does his best, though he lives 10 miles away. Tomorrow there will be a special session before the normal Sunday church service. They will pray by name for each of the farmers affected and ring the bell like the angelus. The church looks over to Howend, too, and if the wind is wrong the congregation might catch the smoke.

As night falls, there are patches of what seems like thick fog on the A7. But this is no fog: it's smoke. The fires light the night, as if it were Guy Fawkes or a jubilee. There is no laughter round these fires, however. Nor will there be, for some time.

MATTHEW ENGEL

AN END TO WOOLLY THINKING: COULD FOOT AND MOUTH ALLOW US TO RETHINK SHEEP FARMING?

April 4 2001

It seems insensitive to talk of silver linings when the clouds in question are winter floods and foot-and-mouth disease – but there are some, and they start in the hills and valleys which have been most affected in the past six months.

The flooding has led us to revise the way we see the role of rural river valleys. Reedbeds, water meadows, bogs, lakes and marshes seem likely to be welcomed back as natural safety valves: ideal for stopping stormwater engulfing downstream homes and high streets. More broadleaved woodland on the upland slopes can also play a positive role in flood control. About a quarter of the rain that falls on outstretched leaves and branches evaporates. The rest drips slowly to the ground and soaks into the spongy leaf mould of the woodland floor, reducing run-off, soil erosion and the risk of flooding.

So what has all this got to do with foot and mouth? The answer lies with sheep, and our treeless upland landscape can be largely blamed on them. One conservationist I know calls them 'woolly maggots', and in many landscapes that's a pretty apt description. In moderation, sheep maintain a rich mosaic of different habitats – but the days of moderation disappeared a long, long time ago. For many years, the various forms of hill-farm subsidy have tended to encourage serious overgrazing. So many sheep now roam the hills that ecological diversity is destroyed, soils erode for lack of vegetation and there isn't a hope in hell of tree seedlings surviving.

In the Welsh mountains, the Scottish glens, the Lakeland fells, the Shropshire hills and the cloughs and gulleys that run off the heather moorlands of the Dark Peak, Devon, Cornwall and the northern Pennines, the only native trees that still survive tend to be very old and inaccessible. Each blade of grass and germinating tree seedling is inevitably grazed to death. Saddest of all are the old oak woods that still survive on some fellsides and mountain slopes. Their veteran trees may well be centuries old, but there are almost never any saplings following on, no undergrowth, few woodland flowers or butterflies and hardly any songbirds. In a few exceptional cases, where a conservation charity or the Forestry Commission has invested heavily in sheep-proof fencing, you can see just how dramatically these sleeping beauties can come back to life. Keep out the sheep, and lifeless woods begin to sprout and grow and flower within a single season.

Now, due in part to foot and mouth, we may have a chance to change our approach to sheep farming. It's time to use the national flock more wisely. There is no doubt that sheep can be a powerful tool for keeping landscapes free from trees, and in some of our uplands that may well be what we want. By contrast, in the drinking-water gathering grounds we should be striving to stop soil erosion and to filter out pollution through the greater use of native broadleaved woodland. Here, it is difficult to see why we should bring the sheep back after foot and mouth.

We need to use our sheep much more creatively. With care, they can help us to restore a rich diversity of landscape, and in this task the hefted flocks are vital. These are extended families of local sheep, and they are quite extraordinary: a national treasure which may be lost if Maff continues with its policy of supporting wholesale slaughter.

Hefted flocks have inbred knowledge of their own mountain, built up over countless generations. The old 'weathers' can lead the flock to safety when the snow clouds gather. They know where the natural salt licks are; which patch of green will have the most medicinal herbs. In other words, a hefted flock is intimately tuned in to its own hereditary landscape. In any future model of sustainable upland management, these sheep must surely have a vital role to play, but definitely not in such abundance.

Hill farmers need to make a living from their flocks without resorting to the overgrazing that has wiped out so much of the subtle detail in our upland landscapes over recent years. We need to find a way of giving farmers back their dignity, by paying them for skilful land and livestock management, and even in landscapes where we favour trees instead of sheep there will still be a need for sensitive, lasting care.

CHRIS BAINES

CROFTERS TO GET RIGHT TO BUY LAND
November 29 2001

A bill to overhaul Scotland's ancient and inequitable system of land ownership and access was published yesterday – to criticism from landowners, who said the measures were nothing short of expropriation.

The Land Reform Bill is one of the most important pieces of legislation to be drawn up by the Scottish parliament. Scotland has the highest concentration of private land ownership in the world, and there has been anger at the continual buying and selling of islands and estates on the open market. The legislation unveiled yesterday gives crofters the right to buy – at independently assessed market prices – the land they live and work on at any time, and rural communities of 20 or more people first refusal on land when it goes on the market. The bill also proposes a right of access to land for recreation on condition this is exercised responsibly and with limits.

There have been some changes to the bill's draft proposals, which were published in February – most notably a crackdown on landowners who took advantage of the foot-and-mouth crisis to seal off their property. A provision allowing the temporary suspension of access rights by landowners has been removed, as has a provision allowing local authorities to exclude people from land.

The Scottish justice minister, Jim Wallace, said the bill – expected to become law by next autumn – was a landmark piece of legislation for Scotland. Landowners' representatives, however, condemned many of the bill's measures. 'This bill imposes huge penalties on landowners,' said Robert Balfour of the Scottish Landowners' Federation. 'Crofting right to buy perpetuates the nightmare scenario. This is not the familiar right to buy – like people buying their council house – and ministers should be honest enough to call it nationalisation.' The Ramblers' Association, however, welcomed the bill and said that it could make Scotland the envy of Europe.

KIRSTY SCOTT

HEDGES, REED BEDS, MEADOWS – AND MEAT DIRECT

January 30 2002

The brave new world of farming can be found among the restored hedgerows, new footpaths, reed beds and clover-rich meadows where cattle, sheep and pigs once safely grazed. On Mike and Ruth Downham's 220 acres in north Cumbria, improving the landscape naturally by spurning chemicals and encouraging wildlife goes hand in glove with rearing the finest organic animals.

This is what the government calls country stewardship, with farmers paid modestly to manage and improve land, slowly returning it to a natural state, while earning a living through a less intensive system which places a premium on high-quality stock. Rather than pushing animals through the normal wholesale outlets, the Downhams sell meat directly to hundreds of customers, fresh and in freezer packs, guaranteeing a much higher standard than conventional retail outlets.

But it is only part of the modest undertaking. After taking over Low Luckens farm at Roweltown, north of Carlisle, more than three years ago, the couple signed a 10-year 'whole farm agreement' under which they are reimbursed for the cost of creating new hedgerows, footpaths and ponds and planting trees. In addition, they are paid around £5,000 annually for managing the land. In return, people are attracted to their small visitor centre, which explains their enterprise in the context of sustainable farming. 'We came into farming later in our lives and had always been attracted to organic methods and principles,' said Mr Downham, a former paediatrician. 'It has been a tremendous, uplifting experience, seeing the land and the animals develop.'

That was until foot and mouth hit Cumbria. He is now left with only 35 cattle after the government ruled that his 200 healthy, heavily pregnant sheep, four sows and 20 piglets, had to go at the height of the epidemic last April. 'Completely needless and arbitrary,' he fumed.

Now the Downhams are at the forefront of the drive to reform an agricultural system dominated by its dependence on subsidy. Before foot and mouth struck, around a third of the industry's annual £15bn income came directly from the taxpayer. 'You're not in control with the current system and everybody has realised that for years,' said Mr Downham. Everybody, he said, apart from the National Farmers' Union. Although an NFU member, he said it would have to be dragged 'kicking and screaming' into the real world. 'They do not understand what the environment means, they don't have any concept of biodiversity or pollution and, like so many unions, they're just determined to hang on to the subsidy system which has kept them going for years.'

To break with the past, the Downhams said farmers must establish links with local and regional markets in an attempt to keep younger people on the land, create a better standard of food and – crucially – cut out the endless lorry convoys which transport produce around the country from farm to wholesaler, distribution depot and supermarket.

PETER HETHERINGTON

SCOUT'S HONOUR: ECHOES OF CLASS WARS LINGER
April 17 2002

There's a famous story about a group of Sheffield ramblers out walking on the then-forbidden mountain of Kinder Scout in the Peak District in the 1930s. They were accosted by an irate gamekeeper, who told them they were trespassing and demanded they leave. When asked why, because the ramblers said they were doing no harm, the keeper replied: 'This land belongs to my master. His ancestors fought for it.'

'Right,' replied an enterprising rambler, removing his jacket, 'then I'll fight you for it.'

The story may be apocryphal, but it sums up the deeply ingrained class struggle at the heart of the famous 'Battle of Kinder Scout', the mass trespass that took place 70 years ago next week. That event, which resulted in five young Manchester ramblers being imprisoned for up to six months for riotous assembly, is seen as the single most important milestone in the campaign for open country recreation.

The culmination of that century-old campaign for the cherished 'freedom to roam' across mountain and moorland was reached with the long-awaited passing of the Countryside and Rights of Way (CRoW) Act in December 2000. Many believe that another direct result was the creation of our 11 national parks, the first of which – significantly, the Peak District – celebrated its 50th birthday last year. Eighty-five-year-old Jimmy Jones, of Northenden, Manchester, one of the last surviving trespassers, says: 'We all supported the trespass because we were convinced that the land belonged to the people. It was in our blood.'

The battle for the ramblers' holy grail of the right to roam can be seen as a direct result of the Industrial Revolution. Workers in the dark, satanic mills of the new industrial cities of northern Britain looked out longingly at the Jerusalem of rolling moors, seeing them as the perfect recreational antidote to the grim, crowded conditions of their everyday working lives. But following the Enclosure Acts of the 18th and 19th centuries, many of the highest and wildest areas of moorland and mountains – previously common land open to all – had been acquired by landowners and were now out of bounds and private property. The owners employed burly, stick-wielding gamekeepers to patrol their estates, and ramblers without a permit were often forcibly evicted.

Frustrated by the lack of action by the official rambling movement, a group of young members of the Communist-inspired British Workers' Sports Federation, led by the late Benny Rothman, then a 20-year-old unemployed motor mechanic, embarked on a well publicised and deliberate mass trespass from Hayfield, Derbyshire, on to Kinder Scout on the fine spring morning of April 24 1932.

What happened next is now firmly part of rambling folklore. The 400 walkers met a line of some 30 keepers and a few undistinguished scuffles resulted in one temporary keeper injuring his ankle. When the trespassers returned to Hayfield, six were arrested and variously charged with public-order offences – but not, significantly, with trespass.

At the trial of the trespassers, the self-conducted defence by Rothman – who died in January this year, aged 90 – was a masterpiece of working-class rhetoric. 'We ramblers, after a hard week's work in smoky towns and cities, go out rambling for relaxation, a breath of fresh air, a little sunshine,' he told the court. 'But we find when we go out that the finest rambling country is closed to us, just because certain individuals wish to shoot for about 10 days a year.'

It was the severity of the sentences handed down to the five young defendants

– ranging from two to six months' imprisonment – which was to unite the ramblers' cause. Even the official ramblers' federations, which had been opposed to the trespass, were appalled by the sentences.

Indisputably, the mass trespass brought the access issue to a head and acted as an important catalyst to the whole national parks and countryside access campaign. But according to Kate Ashbrook, secretary of the Open Spaces Society and chair of the access committee of the Ramblers' Association (RA), much still remains to be done. 'Although a great achievement, the CRoW Act is modest,' she says. 'It gives us the right to walk on only 12 per cent of England and Wales – and even that right could be subject to all sorts of restrictions. Landowners might also succeed in diminishing this access by appealing against the provisional maps of open country currently being drawn up. Worse still, some have already taken direct action to destroy access by ploughing up open moorland in an effort to keep the land private.'

Almost 100 acres of moorland at Kirk Edge near Bradfield, South Yorkshire, were recently ploughed up by a farmer shortly after draft access maps had been drawn up under the act by the Peak District Access Forum (PDAF). The architect of the Act, environment minister Michael Meacher, reacted swiftly, ordering a 12-month moratorium on the ploughing of such land.

'Yes,' concedes John Lees, secretary of the Peak Park Moorland Owners' and Tenants' Association and a member of the forum, 'that was most unfortunate and we have been gently critical of the landowner involved.' But Lees claims that much more positive work has been done since 1932, including the successful management of voluntary access agreements covering more than 80 square miles of Peak District moorland. 'I firmly believe that the mass trespass would not happen today,' he says. 'We have learned that sensible compromise leads to a level of mutual understanding, which makes confrontations of the kind that took place in 1932 highly unlikely. Genuine ramblers never have been, and never will be, the problem. It's the odd 5 per cent minority, the ones who cause damage or let their dogs run off the lead, who give us the headaches.'

Another member of the PDAF is Terry Howard, secretary of the still active Sheffield Campaign for Access to Moorland (SCAM) and of the local RA area council. He is very aware of the political nature of the trespass and is in no doubt that, if placed in the same situation today, he would be there marching alongside the likes of Rothman and his friends. 'It highlighted the problem in a way that nothing else had before or since,' Howard says. 'The passing of the CRoW Act was a great step forward, but the access forums have still to get down to the nitty-gritty. We in SCAM are keeping a watching brief, because undoubtedly there are still problems – as the recent ploughing-up incident showed.'

The biggest private landowner in the Peak District is the Duke of Devonshire, at Chatsworth. He has always argued that ramblers and grouse shooters can peaceably coexist and is 'tremendously' in favour of access to open country. 'Although I was only 12 years old when it happened, I have always been very influenced by the mass trespass,' he says. 'I am still horrified both by the attitude of landowners at the time, who included my grandfather, the 9th duke, in not allowing people to walk in open country, and by the vicious sentences handed down to the trespassers. I would like formally to apologise for the attitude of my grandfather, who owned part of Kinder at the time, for what happened. My ambition is to depoliticise the access situation through good neighbourliness.'

For the past 20 years Kinder Scout has been in the safe hands of the National Trust, which allows free access at all times. Stephen Trotter, manager of the trust's High Peak estate, says: 'We declared that Kinder would be open country in perpetuity when we acquired the estate in 1982 – 20 years before the CRoW Act. This was seen as a fitting tribute to the place that attracted the trespassers in 1932 and inspired the wider access movement.'

Although he has admitted he is no rambler, Michael Meacher was the minister who pushed through the CRoW Act. He sees the 1932 trespass as 'a potent expression of the desire of those in nearby towns to escape poor and cramped living conditions for a few hours now and again, to enjoy the fresh air and wildness of the open moor'.

Seventy years on, the minister sees little need for confrontation – 'not just because people will be exercising a statutory right, but because the new legislation also recognises the need of those who manage the land on which others will walk'. Adapting a New Labour homily, Meacher adds: 'Walkers will have rights, but also responsibilities – to respect the countryside and its wildlife and the needs of those who depend on it for their income.' But echoes of the class wars of the 1930s still linger. As trespass veteran Jimmy Jones says: 'I always said that if the powers-that-be could can the very air that we breathe and try to sell it back to us, they would.'

ROLY SMITH

A RIGHT-OF-WAY BATTLE OVER BRITAIN'S GREEN LANES
January 8 2003

A keen wind scythes across the hills above Malham as two beefy young men attempt to haul their Range Rover out of a muddy hole, where it has sunk up to the bonnet. They try the off-roader's trick of burying the spare wheel as an anchor for the winch, but it doesn't work.

David Griffiths gives up and scans his surroundings: the pale limestone upland of the Yorkshire Dales, crossed by a great scar of ruts and tyre marks where he and other four-wheel-drivers and trail bikers come out to play. 'I can't say I'm particularly proud of this bit,' he says. 'It might be an idea to close it seasonally, but we've got a right to be here. I was born and bred in Skipton and this is my local landscape – it's not just for gentlemen like him, who want to ban us.'

The gentleman in question is Mike Bartholomew, chairman of the Yorkshire Dales Green Lanes Alliance, which aims to close routes like this to motorised traffic. He's happened upon this muddy pantomime during a Sunday walk and is watching sardonically from 20 metres away. Bartholomew fulminates about the damage. 'This argument's been won in the cities,' he says. 'No one objects to keeping cars away from fragile medieval buildings, yet these ancient routes are just as fragile and the same should apply up here.'

We're on Mastiles Lane, a partly Roman route linking Ribblesdale and Wharfedale. In 1950 one writer called it 'a green ribbon of turf between twisting white walls', but now the off-roaders have carved scars up the banks of the beck and the swathe of tyre tracks on the grass can be a hundred feet wide. Common sense tells you it's not suitable for frequent traffic of large vehicles and powerful trail bikes with studded tyres. So what's a 4x4 Range Rover doing up here in the first place?

For the answer you must enter the Alice in Wonderland world of English highway law – a tangled accumulation of statute and precedent. What it boils down to is that if you can demonstrate that a route was once used by a horse and cart, you're within your rights to take a double-decker bus down it now. 'Once a highway, always a highway' is the watchword and off-roaders dig assiduously into the archives for rights-of-way information that predates Ordnance Survey maps and the highway authority's 'definitive map' – which isn't actually definitive – on which OS maps are based. And so Gorbeck Road, a nearby green lane between Langcliffe and Malham, was recently reclassified at a public inquiry as a Byway Open to All Traffic (Boat). The off-roaders had discovered an enclosure award from 1793, which said 'there shall in perpetuity be a carriage road ...'

Brian Lewis, North Yorkshire rights of way representative of the All Wheel Drive Club, says there are about 80 green lanes in the Dales that should be classified as Boats for similar reasons. 'Only a handful have been reclassified,' he says, as he guns his four-litre Jeep Cherokee up steep stony tracks and nudges carefully through the muddy bits. 'We use about 40 of them; the others are too narrow, too wet or too cut up. What I get out of this is comradeship, a good day out with the lads, working together to get round the roads without doing any damage. I can't walk far because of arthritis, but this means I can get into the countryside and enjoy it.'

The growth in off-roading and the damage and complaint it causes means it's now among the biggest issues faced by the Yorkshire Dales National Park Authority. The authorities in the Lake District and near the Ridgeway in Berkshire have cooperated with the off-road lobby, with varying success, but here the park authority has decided to confront them. It has prompted North Yorkshire County Council (NYCC), the area's highway authority, to impose Experimental Traffic Regulation Orders (Etros) on four green lanes, including Mastiles Lane. And, for the first time, the orders are being made on the grounds of disturbance of the peace and tranquillity that is the guiding purpose of national parks.

'We've consulted on the principle and now we're consulting user groups, parish councils and others on the detailed routes,' says Graham Cressey of the NYCC. 'If it goes ahead, it will be the first time we've used orders in this way, and I assure you it will be experimental.' That assurance produces sceptical snorts from members of the off-road lobby, who think it's a dodge to produce a permanent closure without a proper public inquiry.

'We think it's a misapplication of the legislation,' says Tim Stevens, motor recreation development officer of the Land Access and Recreation Association. 'We have several ploys up our sleeve to deal with the situation,' he says. 'We're not saying what we will or won't do. But we have ideas about how to help the national park manage the situation. If they want to talk to us, they can.' Stevens argues that there are legitimate users who stick to legal routes, and 'hooligans' who use vehicles and trail bikes on footpaths and bridleways. 'We're saying: "Get us on your side and we can help sort out this problem,"' he says. 'Among other things, we can identify the hooligans because they park in the same places as us. We have a code of practice that encourages responsible use of green lanes.'

If Etros prove effective in the Dales, which is by no means certain, they might also be used in other national parks. There is provision in the Countryside and Rights of Way (Crow) Act 2000 eventually to allow Etros to be used everywhere for similar 'peace and tranquillity' reasons. The Act also introduced a fresh category into rights-of-way law called the 'restricted byway', on which vehicular traffic is banned. But there is no provision for converting a road that can be shown to be a Boat into a restricted byway.

So we are left with two determined and well-organised pressure groups fighting it out with laws rooted in the era long before the Jeep and the Range Rover.

STEPHEN COOK

COUNTRY DIARY: CLAXTON, NORFOLK

June 23 2003

As I rounded the woodland edge I spotted the foxes relaxing in a newly mown hayfield. The vixen was simply enjoying the sunshine, but her two well-grown cubs lolloped over the parallel heaps of cut grass, or occasionally came together in bouts of mock-fighting. One would collapse on to its side and look up while the other would stand victorious, front legs akimbo, head shaking as if it were worrying an old carcass. Then the roles reversed and the conqueror would become conquered. Finally the scrap fizzled out and both returned to mother, who simply looked up, blinking against the strong light. With typically maternal affection she licked one of their necks before he tired of the fuss and strode off to stalk pheasants.

A fortnight ago I stumbled on the same family sunning itself on the edge of a plantation. The spot was strewn with the remains of pheasant, red-legged partridge and at least one unfortunate shelduck, which nest in the nearby haystacks. I doubted the present stalk would result in the cub's next meal. Two cock pheasants watched it approach them and eventually they were just metres apart. One wonders what cognitive process allows the birds, which seldom seem particularly intelligent, to recognise that this particular fox presented minimal danger. The birds danced and shimmied a little at the cub's movements, then, like him, strutted off, counting the whole affair a draw. Not so the vixen. She'd picked me out against the woodland and her gaze never deviated. I slunk into the trees to try to allay her fears, but when I re-emerged the field was bare and I was sad to have disturbed the family scene.

MARK COCKER

JUDGMENT DAY: THE RESULTS OF THE GM FIELD-SCALE TRIALS
October 16 2003

On the morning of April 4 1999 a Wiltshire farmer ventured out to his field to plant a new season's crop. Several hours later, the seed was sown, the field was quiet and one of the most controversial experiments ever to be carried out in the country had begun: the government's field-scale trials of GM crops. Today, more than four years later, the results of the experiment will finally be made public.

The experiment was designed to test one simple hypothesis: that the impact of growing certain GM crops on the abundance and variety of farmland plants and creatures is no different to that of conventional varieties. If the experiment went as well as planned, the scientists behind it will today be able to say whether their hypothesis stood up to the test.

That will not be the end of the matter, however. Almost any change in farming practice is likely to have some impact on farmland flora and fauna. The tougher question, and one that will be squabbled over by opposing groups for some time yet, is whether the environmental impact of growing GM crops is really serious enough to support a ban. 'The interpretation may well differ from scientist to scientist,' says Les Firbank of the Centre for Ecology and Hydrology in Cumbria, who is leading the trials.

The field-scale trials were conceived in an atmosphere of caution and concern. By the late 1990s several GM crops had cleared many of the major regulatory hurdles required for commercial planting. The crops in question had been genetically modified to make them resistant to broad-spectrum herbicides – modern agro-chemical treatments that crush all plant life bar the GM crops.

Pressure groups had already seized GM as their latest cause and were stirring up anti-GM feeling in the wider public. But more objective groups, such as English Nature, the government's wildlife advisers, had also raised concerns. Their issue was not with GM per se. They worried that the broad-spectrum herbicides to be used with GM crops would be so effective that they would strip out all the weeds and seeds vital for the survival of farmland creatures.

If the bugs and grubs took a hit, the knock-on effects further up the food chain could be devastating. Populations of farmland birds, notably skylarks, partridges and corn buntings, had already crashed more than 50 per cent in 20 or so years, not least because better herbicides had dented their food supplies. The new broad-spectrum versions might be so effective, they feared, that the bird populations would sink down to levels from which they would never recover. 'Everything out there is competing for light and nutrients and if the farmer takes it all, there's nothing left for the birds, the beetles and the butterflies,' says Chris Pollock, who ran the steering committee for the trials.

The newly elected Labour party decided that the best thing to do was to hold things up. The crop biotech industry agreed a voluntary moratorium on growing GM crops for four years while the government set itself the task of finding out whether broad-spectrum herbicides, such as glyphosate and glufosinate ammonium really could damage the environment.

The experiment they devised was unprecedented. Each year for four years, around 70 fields up and down the country would be selected to represent the range of soil types, environmental conditions and crop-management strategies used throughout Britain. Each field would then be divided in two, with conventional crops being planted on one side and GM varieties on the other. Four GM crops were tested, namely spring and winter oilseed rape, sugar beet and maize. The farmers were told to treat the conventional crops as they would do normally, spraying whichever herbicides they favoured at the times they favoured. The GM crops were treated with broad-spectrum herbicides, according to advice given from the industry.

At key points in the crop cycle, scientists descended on the test fields to count up various species indicative of farmland biodiversity. They counted weeds and seedlings. They counted gastropods, spiders, beetles and bugs, butterflies, lacewings and bees. Beetles and other crawling insects were caught in alcohol-filled plastic cups pushed into the soil. The traps were each set for two weeks. Slugs were caught using what the scientists refer to as baited refuge traps, essentially upside-down plant-pot saucers. Other bugs were collected from weeds growing among the crops using handheld vacuum cleaner-like devices.

Despite the scale and duration of the experiment, the scientists who devised it say it will only be able to pick up a 50 per cent change in the abundance of a species. The 50 per cent figure, says Pollock, is what groups like English Nature view as a 'significant pertubation' – in short, something to be concerned about.

But what are we to make of the results? Suppose the trials reveal that slugs are down in certain fields, while spiders are up in another. How do we know if it really matters? The point emphasises the difference between what scientists call 'statistical significance' and 'biological significance'. A statistical significance will prove that the herbicides are altering the abundance of certain species. But for that change to matter, it must in turn be deemed biologically significant. In some instances, biological significance is obvious: if the results showed that skylarks might die out, for example. But there's no clear definition; the issue is open to interpretation.

'It's entirely possible to produce a statistically significant observation which has very little biological significance,' says Pollock. 'The biological significance becomes apparent not just when the results are made public, but once people have had the time to model our data to see how changes in certain species affect others.'

To go some way to addressing the point of significance, the species the scientists chose to count were those that, were they lost, could have a real impact on species higher up the food chain; in other words, they were all valuable food sources for other creatures. 'Some differences may not matter greatly in terms of overall effects on biodiversity, they may just be of academic significance if you are interested in that specific species,' says Firbank. 'But in others, a change may be more critical, because it might have a bigger effect higher up the food chain and produce the kind of effect we were worried about in the first place.'

Today, Firbank and his colleagues will give their view of how much – if at all – the impact of growing herbicide-tolerant crops matters. Their scientific papers will appear in the Royal Society's *Philosophical Transactions* journal, but people will seize the data for their own studies. Other scientists have their own models of how changes low down in the food chain affect other species and will process the data to see what they find.

Ultimately, it will fall to ACRE, the Advisory Committee on Releases to the Environment, to decide what, if anything, the results mean. Their advice will then be bundled up with the chief scientific adviser's updated science review and packed off to Margaret Beckett et al. for consideration, along with information from the GM public debate and the Cabinet Office's costs and benefits study. Then, finally, it is time for the government to work out what to do: to give some or all GM crops the green light or to say thanks, but no thanks.

IAN SAMPLE

PRIZED PONIES: THELWELL'S AWARD FOR HARNESSING ENGLAND
December 2 2003
Norman Thelwell's award from the Cartoon Art Trust for best capturing 'the English character' should really be presented by an appalling little girl on a savage fat pony. He drew the first of his pony cartoons for *Punch* as a one-off exactly 50 years ago: a little girl on a fat little pony with new horseshoes, and the blacksmith inquiring, ''Ow do they feel then?' Readers' letters poured in, and *Punch* immediately

commissioned other work. The half-century that followed produced many more ponies, eyes rolling madly, cantering through a thicket of splintered jumps, shattered tea tables and demolished picnics.

The award will be presented on Thursday to coincide with an exhibition opening today at the Mall Galleries in London. In the year of his 80th birthday, it brings together a lifetime of unmalicious playfulness. Anita O'Brien, joint curator of the exhibition, said: 'What was unique about him among late-20th-century cartoonists was his rural outlook. While his peers drew cities and technology, he drew beautifully what he loved, the countryside, fishing, animals, boats – though he did say he was only interested in horses because they were so beautiful to draw.' She pointed out that Thelwell was passionate about issues that have become intensely political – factory farming, the destruction of the landscape by ripping out hedges, pollution and quarrying. 'He was well ahead of the pack on these issues, he was drawing cartoons about them from the 1970s.'

Thelwell began far away from the village green gymkhanas of his cartoons. He was born in 1923 in a small terraced house in Birkenhead. Although the exhibition includes his striking self-portrait as an anxious 10-year-old, Thelwell was not encouraged to draw and became a junior office clerk after school. During military service in India, he started to draw Christmas cards and cartoons for an army magazine, and studied at Liverpool School of Art when he was demobbed. He sold his first cartoon to *Punch* in 1950 and became a full-time, freelance cartoonist six years later.

The exhibition includes drawings, sketches, hundreds of his exquisitely drawn cartoons and the watercolour landscapes that increasingly interest him – most of which have never been exhibited before. Many of his paintings of stormy seas, rolling fields, birds and animals will be shown with cartoon versions of near-identical scenes.

Thelwell's admirers include the Duke of Bedford, whose father was much mocked for opening his home, Woburn Abbey, to the masses. The duke's favourite cartoon is the stately-homeowner snapping: 'Some damn fool has signed the Rubens again!'

MAEV KENNEDY

CALL OF THE WILD
December 6 2003

In or around November 1932, nature writing in Britain was dealt a death-blow by Stella Gibbons. *Cold Comfort Farm*, one of the finest parodies written in English, took as its target the rural novels of Thomas Hardy, Mary Webb, the Brontë sisters and D. H. Lawrence. Mercilessly, Gibbons sought out and sent up the hallmarks of the rural genre: all those characters called Amos or Jeb, all those idiots savants, all that loam and, especially, all those gushingly naive descriptions of 'nature' and 'landscape'. Gibbons's book was such a wickedly brilliant skit it became that rare literary object: a parody that remained standing once the genre it mocked had collapsed.

Since Gibbons, it has been increasingly hard to write about 'nature' with a straight face, and to expect a serious reception in Britain. When, for instance, Alice Oswald's book-length poem *Dart*, which follows the river Dart from its source to its mouth, was read recently on Radio 4, it provoked a snidely flippant attack from A. N. Wilson. 'Thanks to Wordsworth,' Wilson sneered from his eyrie in the *Daily Telegraph* in March, 'we all have the idea that "poets" ought to be country dwellers, ought to live up lanes and use a bucket for a lavatory.' Nature writing of this sort, he continued, 'appeals to all that is gentlest and best in us, the lovers of unwrecked England'.

Wilson's caricature of writers on nature as nostalgics – steeple-climbers in flight from the high waters of modernity – has been echoed by many other critics and commentators over the past 70 years. Nature writing has been cartooned variously as a reactionary ruralism (and so tarred with the brush of Tory squireish land-love) or as sentimentalism for a prelapsarian age of at-one-with-natureness (and so tarred with the brush of woozy new-age holism). The result of this sustained hostility is that nature writing in Britain has become threatened with extinction.

The environmentalist and author Richard Mabey angrily summarised the state of things in these pages on March 18 this year. 'A tradition of celebrating our dwelling in nature,' he declared, 'a lineage that stretched from Gilbert White's Selborne and Hardy's novels to Ted Hughes' poetry and J. A. Baker's indescribable *The Peregrine*, has been replaced by a vapid and repetitive strain of guidebooks and pop-science volumes whose overriding message is that we already know all those "innermost secrets".' Vanished, in other words, is writing prepared to address sanctity in the human relationship with the natural world at a time of cultural cynicism and disconnection. Vanished is writing motivated by an interest in *duchthas*, the Gaelic word that means something like 'the sense of belonging in a place'. And vanished is writing that might help us to reacquire, even temporarily, the sense of inhabitation and attunement out of which modernity has hustled us.

Many names could be added to Mabey's list of British nature writers, among them Thomas Gray, William Cobbett, Charles Darwin, Alfred Russell Wallace, John Clare, John Ruskin, Elizabeth Gaskell (whose Mary Barton is a central work in the northern urban tradition of escape), William Morris, the drastically under-read Richard Jefferies, Gerard Manley Hopkins, Edward Carpenter, W. H. Hudson, Stephen Graham, John Cowper Powys, W. H. Auden, and – unexpectedly – Vita Sackville-West, whose long Virgilian poem *The Land* won the Hawthornden Prize in 1927, and sold more copies in her lifetime than all of Woolf's novels put together did in hers.

It is far harder, however, to come up with a list of names, comparable either in stature or in number, from the 1940s onwards. True, such an attempt would include Seamus Heaney, Geoffrey Hill and Heathcote Williams. It would mention the three landmark rural novels of the past three decades – Adam Thorpe's *Ulverton* (1992), Graham Swift's *Waterland* (1983) and Bruce Chatwin's *On The Black Hill* (1982) – and it would take in Gavin Maxwell, John Fowles's non-fiction and Ronald Blythe's bore-hole history of a single Suffolk village, *Akenfield* (1969). But it would also have to square up to the fact that nature writing has become widely perceived as the province of muddy-booted country diarists and that the majority of so-called 'literary fiction' has gone urban, with narratives of belonging giving way to new narratives of exile, displacement and alienation.

The withering away of British nature writing becomes dismayingly visible if we look across to North America. There, the tradition's tap roots also stretch back to the 19th century and to that formidable triumvirate of philosopher-naturalists Emerson, Thoreau and Muir. Unlike in Britain, however, nature writing thrived during the 20th century in America. The best-known living practitioners – Barry Lopez, Gary Snyder, Richard Nelson, Terry Tempest Williams, Annie Dillard – are treated midway between celebrities and shamans by the US literary press. Lopez's magnificent *Arctic Dreams* (1986), in many ways the founding text of contemporary nature writing in the States, was a *New York Times* bestseller and won the American Book Award; Dillard's *Pilgrim at Tinker Creek* was awarded the Pulitzer prize in 1975 and hasn't been out of print since. *Outside Magazine*, a legendary American writing venue with no counterpart in Britain, has in its 20-year history produced a cohort of exceptional writers, including Lopez, Peter Matthiessen, Alistair McLeod, Jane Smiley, Annie Proulx, Norman Maclean, Ian Frazier and John McPhee. Novelists such as T. C. Boyle, or Wallace Stegner from an earlier generation, who place environmental issues in their fiction, find a mainstream audience. American nature writing, indeed, has developed all the signs of a tradition in exceedingly good health: epiphytic sub-genres (parodies and the like), university courses devoted to its exegesis, and a resistance from its leading practitioners to being included within its boundaries.

Why, though, has all the good nature writing crossed the Atlantic? A short and short-sighted answer might be that British nature writing has been depleted because British nature has been depleted. The argument goes that suburban sprawl, increased population, the touristification of many wilderness areas, and ease of travel have produced a widespread (and, to my mind, deeply false) perception that Britain is simply all out of nature and wilderness. North America stretches from the Arctic Circle down to the Gulf of Mexico and its territory includes tundra, desert, glaciated mountain ranges and boreal forests. There are parts of North America no one has ever seen. Britain, by contrast, has no peak over 1,500 metres, no glaciers, diminishing areas of moorland, and in terms of woodland it is one of the most radically scalped of all the world's countries.

Alternatively, blame for the tradition's decline might be laid at the door of the kind of selfhood that has come to predominate in Britain: an acrid mixture of the acquisitive-materialist and the secular-humanist, which regards 'nature' as a commodity, in no way connected with human enterprise. It might also be linked with changing employment patterns, which mean that more people work further away from where they live and move more frequently. Fewer people thus experience what Lopez calls 'the complex feelings of affinity and self-assurance one feels with one's native place', and there is a diminished sense of interest in any place in particular, outside one's immediate, and often temporary, domestic sphere.

All of this sounds rather bleak. But it seems to me – contrary to what Mabey suggests – that a revival of the British tradition is under way. The vital signs are dispersed, but they are there. Interest in John Clare, for example, is growing beyond the walls of the academy: Iain Sinclair's next book will retrace Clare's footsteps during his flight from his London asylum back to his Northampton home, and Jonathan Bate's biography of Clare has just been published to general acclaim. In poetry, Oswald's *Dart* won the T. S. Eliot Prize in 2002. Fiction-wise, John McGahern's explicitly and marvellously parochial novel, *That They May Face the Rising Sun*, set by the shores of an Irish lake, was met with great critical acclaim when it appeared, also in 2002.

It is in the field of non-fiction, however, that the resurgence is most obvious. Jim Perrin, Britain's finest outdoor essayist, has won popular admiration for his funny, furious, erudite, beautiful style. Then there is Roger Deakin, whose extraordinary first book, *Waterlog*, described his 'swimmer's journey through Britain', via its lochs, rivers, bays, springs and littorals. *Waterlog* combined a subtle ecological agenda with exquisite writing about that most over-described of substances, water. After an initial print run of only 2,000 copies, it became a huge word-of-mouth success; Deakin is now working on a book about trees and wood for Hamish Hamilton.

There is also Mabey's own work, and Adam Nicolson, whose *Sea Room* (2001), about two tiny Hebridean islands, was a runaway bestseller in Scotland. And there is William Fiennes, whose prize-winning, best-selling memoir-travelogue, *The Snow Geese*, brilliantly manipulated the parallels between the annual migrations of millions of snow geese and his own conflicting desires to travel and to return home.

Why, though, should any of this matter? Literary genres come and go: why should this one in particular be grieved for or celebrated? The answer is that the disappearance of this sort of writing will only widen what Mabey calls the 'ominous and growing fault-line in the way we perceive and talk about nature' – and its reappearance might go some way towards closing this fault-line. The natural world becomes far more easily disposable if it is not imaginatively known, and a failure to include it in a literary regard can slide easily into a failure to include it in a moral regard.

When Wilson criticised Oswald's admirers ('the lovers of unwrecked England') for their nostalgia, he made the common category error of equating nostalgia and conservatism. The two are quite different. Where conservatism seeks to preserve the status quo, nostalgia laments the prevailing state of things and agitates for change. It can be a radical force, and indeed much of the best nature writing is pitilessly forward-looking, written with an eye to what will come unless certain reparations are made in the balance of our relationship with the natural world. Nature writing is an unsatisfactory term for this diverse, passionate, pluriform, essential, reviving tradition – but it is the best there is, and it serves as a banner to march beneath.

ROBERT MACFARLANE

ECO GONGS 2003

December 17 2003

- Stuffed Shirt Award for Reintroduction goes to the landowners, and others with vested interests, who have resisted so stubbornly the reintroduction of the beaver in Scotland, an important and fun addition to Britain's wildlife.
- Red Kite Award for Reintroduction goes to the Great Bustard Consortium, a coalition of amateur enthusiasts and scientists, chaired by a former policeman

and set up only in 1998, which will reintroduce the birds to Salisbury Plain in Wiltshire next year.

- Houdini Political Escapism Award goes to former environment minister Michael Meacher, for the GM farm-scale trials. Designed to get the government off the hook in its first term, the four years of scientific trials into whether GM was good for the environment turned up firm results. Having insisted that science should be paramount, the government seems to have no alternative but to say no to GM oilseed rape and beet.

- Goof Award goes to Margaret Beckett, the environment secretary, for her plan to abolish English Nature as part of sweeping reforms of how services to rural Britain are delivered, and failing to recognise the crucial role it has in defending sites of special scientific interest against crass development.

- Missed Target Award goes to English Nature, the government's statutory advisory body on nature, which is responsible for the upkeep of Britain's 4,112 sites of special scientific interest. Last week, it was revealed that more than 40 per cent are in a ropey condition – the target stipulates that 95 per cent must be in favourable condition by 2010. At this rate, it may get there by 2022. Runner-up was the British government for increasing carbon emissions through burning too much coal.

JOHN VIDAL AND PAUL BROWN

THE EYES HAVE IT AT THE WORLD'S BIGGEST GATHERING OF BIRDERS
August 18 2007

FP20813 is looking unamused. Until five minutes ago he was just a nameless, carefree woodpigeon, flying about in the middle of England. Then he flew into a net. And now he's a statistic, with a ring on his leg and his own unique number. It's for his own benefit – ringing helps conservationists understand bird populations and migration patterns better – but you wouldn't know it, looking at him. He rewards his ringer by pooing on him. 'One of the hazards of the job!' says Guy Anderson of the RSPB, cheerily. FP20813 is quickly released, 'so he doesn't get too stressed'.

Birdfare, in Oakham, by the shore of Rutland Water, is 'the biggest international birding event anywhere in the world,' according to Tim Appleton, who organises it. It's a place where bird enthusiasts come to upgrade their binoculars (a top-of-the-range Viking 20x125 pair will set you back £2,995), book birding holidays in Panama (13 days for less than £2,000 says Ana Maria Sanches, who's selling them), buy birding clothes (hats for) or just be with other bird enthusiasts. There are a lot of them in Britain. The RSPB has more than a million members. 'It's a huge lobby,' says Mr Appleton. 'Far, far greater than any political party or anything like that.' And 20,000 of them are expected at Birdfair over the three days.

The socks and sandals combination is proving popular this year. As it almost certainly did last year, and every one of the 17 years since it started. Shorts, too, and beards. It's the Bill Oddie look. He looks like Bill Oddie. She looks like Bill Oddie. He looks like Bill Oddie ... he is Bill Oddie! Surrounded by adoring fans, most of whom look like him.

'It is a bit like the Glastonbury for birders, yes,' he says. 'And actually they do usually have music too, something to do with the year's focus. I'd do one on the Birds of Minneapolis, and get Prince to come and play.'

Here Oddie is the headline act, and he's much in demand. 'It is exhausting. I never manage all three days. Trying to get to the car at the end of the day is very difficult, with everyone wanting a word.' But it must be nice to be surrounded by like-minded people? 'I don't think there are any people with minds like mine,' he says, almost sadly. He just has time to explain that the term 'twitcher' is often misused by the media. 'A twitcher is an obsessive ticker of rare species,' he says. 'It's a fascinating and not very salubrious world. I'd stick with us, the normal people.'

The generally accepted explanation for the origin of the word is that it came from a group of early twitchers who used to race about on motorcycles, like *The Wild One*, except not really, ticking off birds ('You bad, bad bird you'). When they arrived somewhere – at the north Norfolk coast, say – they would be so cold and so excited, they'd literally be twitching.

Oddie is not the only celebrity birder here. Wildlife TV personality Simon King describes Birdfair as 'the most extraordinary vanguard of all things wonderfully avian'. And the popularity of birdwatching can only be good news for the planet. 'Birds, because they're visible, because they flit about by day, and because they're quite cute, are fantastic ambassadors for the natural world as a whole. And from a conservation point of view the health of the avian world is critical to the health of the entire natural world.'

Out on Rutland Water the ospreys are not at all visible. 05 has been spotted intermittently at site B, apparently, but right now there's no sign of her. She's probably feeling binocular shy – who wouldn't be with 20,000 pairs of eyes not just looking at you, but looking at you enlarged? There's a posse of cormorants out there, a common tern, a mute swan, a deaf duck, a daft coot and a disdainful-looking heron, probably cross about the bearded invasion. FP20813 is nowhere to be seen.

SAM WOLLASTON

DISPLACEMENT THEORY: HOW MOVING HOUSE CAN CHANGE MORE THAN YOUR ADDRESS
August 20 2003

Almost a year ago, I moved house and habitat for the first time in my life. I upped sticks from the Chiltern Hills in Buckinghamshire, where I'd spent most of my life in the shadow of trees, and moved to a damp patch in Norfolk. And about time too. I'd become clotted with rootedness, a creature of habits and memories. I'd spent much of my time in woods, whose engrained sense of history and slow seasonal movements seemed to reflect my own declining mood. But now I'm in open country. The sun shines in my window and the water turns everything it touches to quicksilver.

Can landscapes shape your personality? They certainly inform it, make you more aware of your own limits and assumptions. When the first heavy rains fell on the Waveney valley last October, it felt like another kind of spring. The water seemed to be quickening the place, pulling strings, jerking earth and air (and me) back into action. The creeks and dykes along the lanes were suddenly full of raging upland bournes. Water was conspiring in every conceivable hollow, filling those it had created thousands of years ago, and opening up new possibilities as insidiously and capriciously as a Chinese whisper. Moats formed in what had looked no more than dry ditches, and lakes in dips in the road. The evening news showed the valley virtually under water and anxious friends phoned to see if we were marooned. We were fine; the house had been built 27 metres above the river level.

Once, while making a film about the limestone country of the Yorkshire Dales, our sound engineer succeeded in assembling 54 different recordings of moving water, from stalactite drip to waterfall roar. There is no such water music in Norfolk, but we do have watercolours. The farm ponds were stained yellow by sand washed out of the fields in October. Almost everything else above ground seemed to have been darkened by the wet. The trees were in silhouette, except those – split open by the gales – whose sodden gashes had turned red raw.

This is what water does to places. It gives them what ecologists call 'dynamic boundaries', makes them alert, up for change, connected. If I look at a map of this valley, I can trace a whole arterial network of water, from our little local fen, where pillows of bog pimpernel bloom within sight of Diss town, down to the Waveney itself (where there are otters occasionally), which waters the big fen at Redgrave, and fills every tributary and field dyke with meadowsweet and damselflies.

When I walk in the fen, I get the same sense of joined-upness and mobility. I think I'm getting the hang of them, learning to identify the tell-tale vegetation of the swampy bits, and end up drenched to the ankles, every time. The fens dry out one summer, and drown the encroaching woods a few winters afterwards. There is a sense – more palpable than the fable of the butterfly's wings and the Amazon storm – that when you step into the wet, something happens: a seepage opens up, a tiny patch of shade is lifted, and somewhere down the line, a slug of moisture is pressed out into the arid agricultural desert.

Most of the wetlands here have survived because they were commons. They were simply too much of a wet wilderness to be worth cultivating. Instead, burrowing here, browsing there, working out territories and livelihoods with a smidgen of give and take. The commoners were, in a sense, 'naturalised', accepting the terms of another culture, but adding some grace notes of their own.

In Norfolk's Breckland, to the west, there are shoals of small ponds, each surrounded by a miniature embankment. They're known as 'pingoes' and were created when ice boulders ('lenses') were carried south by the glaciers, lumbered to a halt and slowly melted into the sand. It is not surprising that human diggings are scarcely distinguishable, and that in the local fens there are also clusters of small pools with raised lips formed when one-time peat diggings were flooded. Water, for all its variety, is a great leveller.

This, I think, is what one can learn at the water's edge. Not the dogmatic imperatives of management and pious stewardship advocated by the new breed of conservationists, but something more pragmatic and nimble: take your chances, make the best of things, go with the flow.

RICHARD MABEY

MURKY START FOR BRITAIN'S BIGGEST WINDFARM
June 17 2005
There was no sign yesterday of Cefn Croes, Britain's biggest windfarm, which officially began supplying electricity to 42,000 homes from the wild heart of Wales. The 39

giant turbines were said to be whizzing round in the deep mists and horizontal rain covering the hills of Ceredigion, west Wales, but no one in the villages below could see or say for certain.

'Seeing nothing is gratifying,' said the author and lecturer Martin Wright, who lives a few miles away in Ystumtuen and who led (and lost) a five-year protest against the farm. On a good or perhaps bad day, Mr Wright can see from his house the 225ft turbines capable of generating 59.5MW of electricity, stretched over several miles of mountain. But from the top of nearby Plynlimon, he has a panorama of more than 300 machines in eight smaller windfarms. 'The door has been opened to the industrialisation of the Cambrian mountains,' he said yesterday.

The £50m farm, expected to produce 20 per cent of Wales's wind power, has changed ownership since the disgraced US power company Enron proposed it more than seven years ago. Wynford Emanuel, a spokesman for its present owners, Falck, yesterday admitted it was a bad day to open a windfarm. 'You can't see much at all,' he said.

But Mr Wright said the mists hid Cefn Croes's secret: the damage done to the hillside. 'When the towers first went up I thought they were not as bad as I had imagined they would be, but now I think they are worse. They've put in motorway-scale tracks across the plateau, they built a cement factory, they dug up the hillside for stone, and they have seriously disturbed the plateau,' he said.

But Mr Emanuel insisted the hillside would soon recover. 'Obviously you have to have access to the site. But in the long term, the landscape will be better for flora and fauna than before. It was previously used for intensive farming and forestry,' he said. 'The community will also benefit from more than £60,000 a year for local projects.'

Opening the windfarm, the Welsh assembly's minister for economic development and transport, Andrew Davies, said: 'Wind power is currently the only viable option to provide the bulk of our renewable energy needs, and with excellent wind resources in Wales, sensitively designed windfarms can play an important role.'

PEAK DISTRICT: WHITE AND DARK MAGIC
July 28 2007

I grew up in north Nottinghamshire, so the Peak District was where I did a lot of my early walking. For a long time I didn't really get on with the landscape: not wild enough compared with Scotland. The Cairngorms are the last great mountain-wilderness, in the old sense of the word wilderness: winds of up to 171mph, 12m-deep snowdrifts, cornices three metres long and permanent year-round snowfields. Fabulous. Arctic in winter, balmy in summer. I associated the Peaks with enforced bog-trotting – school expeditions in the rain, carrying a rucksack filled with Trangias, soaked tents and tins of baked beans.

But I'm now beginning to work out something of its attractive magic (it's the second most-visited national park in the world, after Mount Fuji). The hidden valleys of the White Peak, with their dippers and sparrowhawks. And then the big, bleak moorlands of the Dark Peak. I went up to the Dark Peak last November in search of snow hares with the photographer John Beatty: we walked in the Upper Derwent valley, and staked out a tor complex. The hares emerged at dusk, already in their white winter coats, and moved around like ghosts – dozens of them. Beautiful. Eerie.

ROBERT MACFARLANE

FLOODS: FETES, FAIRS AND SHOWS FALL FOUL OF THE WEATHER
July 28 2007

Days of coping with churned-up mud in Yorkshire have forced the cancellation of the hugely popular annual Game Fair, near Leeds, and hundreds of smaller shows, village fetes, gymkhanas and regattas have been cancelled. The tally marks a new level of misery for the battered rural economy, which has seen serious disruption since early June. Heavy rainfall began disrupting the traditional season six weeks ago, with even the Royal Agricultural Society's Royal Show, in Warwickshire, closing a day early amid scenes more like Glastonbury in a monsoon year.

The last-minute abandoning of the Game Fair at Harewood House means a loss of £50m to the regional economy, according to organisers – part in business done in the vast tented city, but more in local hotel bookings and other visitor services. The fair's chairman, Vincent Hedley Lewis, said: 'We were not defeated by foot and mouth in 2001, but the rain has defeated us this summer. Our hearts go out to all the people whose livelihood is going to be affected.'

The sodden ground and flood damage to infrastructure has forced similar decisions on major farming shows from Penrith to south Devon, in almost every case because hired fields would have turned into quagmires. Sales of everything from tractors to corn dollies apart, the collapse of the system means a disastrous interruption to networking among farmers and agricultural traders.

Richard Cuzens of the Association of Show and Agricultural Organisations said: 'Without doubt this is the most difficult show season ever.' His own New Forest show is among the victims. He said: 'We made every effort to run all three days to attempt to give beleaguered trade stands the opportunity to be commercially viable in this most difficult year. But by the last day, all the rings were turned into ploughed fields.'

Some of the most hallowed venues in the season's calendar have been affected, including Badminton, in Gloucesterhire, which features on the growing list of cancellations by members of the British Show Jumping Association (BSJA). As well as wrecking days out, the weather is threatening the programme that sorts out British competitors for international events, including, ultimately, the Beijing Olympics. Tim Stockdale of the BSJA said: 'The outdoor summer season plays an important part in assisting us to produce horses which we hope will go on to have British team success.'

Shows which are going ahead include the annual gathering at Bakewell in the Peak District, and Heckington Feast Week near Sleaford in Lincolnshire, which dates back, rain or shine, 900 years.

MARTIN WAINWRIGHT

WE NEED AN ATTENTIVENESS TO NATURE*

July 30 2007

Here's a slim book to squeeze into that last corner of the holiday suitcase. It coins a new word for a new enthusiasm – corvophile – and it's guaranteed to ensure that you never look at a crow in quite the same way again. Published this week, Mark Cocker's *Crow Country* is the latest addition to a new genre of writing. It doesn't quite fit to call it 'nature writing', because what makes these books so compelling – and important – is that they put centre stage the interconnections between nature and human beings. So Cocker doesn't just write about crows – breeding, feeding habits, patterns of flight and roosting – but the impact of his fascination with these big, raucous birds on him, his family and, in turn, the impact of humans on crows. (They've cracked the art of opening bin liners on the M4 to rifle through leftovers.) The point is that nature is no longer something to be studied from a position of scientific detachment, but an experience, a relationship in which human beings are as much part of nature as any so called wildlife.

* Mark Cocker, *Crow Country* (London: Jonathan Cape, 2007).

It was *Findings*, a book by the Scottish poet Kathleen Jamie in 2004, that first brought my attention to this genre. In her essays on Scottish landscapes, she charts her observation of a peregrine nesting in the hills above her house between loading the washing machine and looking after her children. Since then I've devoured these books – for example, Richard Mabey's *Nature Cure* or Robert Macfarlane's *The Wild Places*, published next month – which map a British landscape as rich and as full of wonder as anything we might find by catching a flight abroad, if only we are attentive enough to notice.

That is one of Cocker's central points. A long-standing ornithologist, he challenges the bird twitchers' preoccupation with scarcity by writing a whole book about one of our most common birds – and least liked, because no one claims there is anything cute about a corvid. As he writes, 'a really significant element in ascribing beauty to a thing lies not within itself but in the quality of our attention to it'. Stop for a moment to examine closely a leaf or a blade of grass, and even these commonplace things become extraordinary. We share these islands with well over a million corvids and yet we have learned to ignore them, so Cocker's task is to try and get us to look again. After his description of the spectacle of 40,000 gathered at the rookery near his home in Norfolk, it will be hard to ever treat them with dismissive contempt again.

What Cocker is doing for the corvid, Roger Deakin, in his book *Wildwood*, published last month, has done for woods and wood. He tracks the many ways he experienced them, from the wood of his pencil to the timbers of his old Suffolk home. Deakin's earlier book, *Waterlog*, in which he describes an aquatic journey around Britain swimming in ponds, lakes and rivers, became a cult hit. Deakin aptly cites Keats at the beginning of *Wildwood* to account for his quest over the past two decades (he died last year) to describe 'taking part in the experience of things'. His books reintroduce a keyboard- and screen-oriented culture to materials and the knowledge economies of water and wood, which have played such large roles in making us who we are.

Part of what makes the genre so counter-cultural is that it advocates a patient attentiveness, a kind of waiting that is so often derided as a waste of time in an age obsessed with purpose, targets and goals. One reads of Cocker spending hours with frozen fingers and toes watching out for rooks that don't arrive or driving hundreds of miles to track down elusive rookeries, pursuing a fascination that, frankly, astonishes all around him (including his own family). It's a point Cocker picks up on, and asks why is this kind of enduring enthusiasm regarded as 'weird' or 'sad' – as his teenage daughter's friends put it? Have our interests become so undemanding, easily dropped and often used towards another purpose (career, profit) that we regard someone who spends several years of his life pursuing one obscure passion as at best eccentric, at worst nutty?

The genre relates to a much broader question it links to the success of the BBC's *Springwatch* and *Autumnwatch* programmes, and the surprise series *Coast*. As globalisation seems to strip out the distinctiveness of place – Starbucks in every high street – we have a renewed fascination in this small set of islands. Just as it is easier than ever to hop on a plane and find yourself anywhere in the world, there's a counter-reaction and a new impetus to search out what's immediately around you. In part, it is perhaps driven by the increasing sense of the fragility of the natural world we need to know what we are fast losing.

There's also a backlash against a culture that is increasingly virtual; so much experience is mediated by electronic gadgets that entail sensory deprivation – of touch, of smell, of certain sounds. Meanwhile, our obsession with comfort and safety not only deprives our children of the sense of freedom inspired by outdoors, a fact we now frequently lament, but it deprives adults as well: how many of us see stars on a regular basis? Or remember the feeling of getting wet or cold? Or see the thick darkness of a night free of city street lights, or hear the call of an owl at night?

We need that attentiveness to nature to understand our humanity, and of how we fit, as just one species, into a vast reach of time and space. Cocker keeps a flint pebble in his pocket (all of these writers mention the pebbles lined up on their desks), which is 70m–90m years old. He points out that rooks followed the spread of farming from the Middle East to Europe and the clearing of woodland, so that every rook call carries the echo of a Neolithic axe.

The floods in Yorkshire last month were a sharp reminder of what happens when we don't understand the land on which we live. The sight of thousands of flooded homes made us realise what many previous generations would never have forgotten about the way in which water has to move through land. Renewing our relationship with the natural world, on which our wellbeing depends, is at the heart of this genre of writing – but it presses its case not with statistics and fear of apocalyptic scenarios of global warming, but with seduction, urging on readers an aesthetic case for the spectacular beauty that lies beyond their windscreen if they can be bothered to stop the car and get out.

It's the British equivalent in the 21st century to John Muir, the legendary writer who founded the US Sierra Club and Yosemite National Park, and who in 1901 wrote that 'thousands of tired, nerve-shaken, over-civilised people are beginning to find out that going to the mountains is going home'. We may have hills rather than mountains, but that's what summer holidays should be about – going home.

MADELEINE BUNTING

A COUNTRY DIARY: SURLINGHAM, NORFOLK
January 14 2008
The huge oak lying on its side is soft and spongy to touch. With my thumbnail I can drive right into the heartwood. In fact, it seems as much a labyrinth of beetle-gnawed cavities as it is solid fibre. Yet for once the natural insignia connoting decay and the passage of time are overshadowed by the human structure nearby. St Saviour's church was probably already a ruin when this oak was a young tree. The building's own roots go back to the early Norman period and archaeological work suggests that its construction may have been contemporaneous with the building of Norwich Cathedral. In the late Middle Ages, the village of Surlingham climbed over the hill and vanished down the other side, leaving St Saviour's alone and neglected. Eventually the round-towered St Mary's eclipsed its neighbour as the place of worship and St Saviour's was left to settle into a prolonged decline.

In the early modern period its tower collapsed. In the 19th century the roof vanished, and where the pews once stood rises a tangle of nettle, bramble and other faithful attendants of human neglect. Long sections of the flint wall have also gone and only the chancel arch soaring upwards to a roofless space gives any hint of human aspiration at the site.

Wild rabbits, which would have been almost unknown when St Saviour's was built, have riddled the stumps to the chancel wall with deep holes. Where the animals now scratch their fleas are the earliest stones ever laid at the church. I think of the medieval labourers who placed them there. I wonder what they might have done had I told them that the black flint lumps in their hands, carefully slotted into the walls layer by layer, were once sea urchins and sponges living in the warm tropical waters over this spot about 80 million years ago?

MARK COCKER

JAMIE'S FOWL SANCTIMONY

January 16 2008

The conditions of the working chicken in the UK are turning into what Americans call a hot-button issue. Jamie Oliver, in his *Fowl Dinners*, gassed a generation of boy chicks for us, like a chubby Herod. Well, it wasn't him, exactly, it was the industry. But it's such a moral grey area, isn't it, reportage? Hugh Fearnley-Whittingstall, meanwhile, rammed home the realities by creating his own intensive chicken farm, which brought him to tears at one point, at the horror of it.

Two facts stand out, beyond the grim stories of chickens being boiled alive and suffocating in vans. First, this is not new information. The traumas of battery chickens have been common knowledge for as long as people have been campaigning against fox-hunting, for as long as schoolgirls have been shopping in The Body Shop. Second, the new wave of protest hasn't put any dent in sales – the big supermarkets were apparently bracing themselves for a downturn in the market after the broadcasts of Jamie and Hugh. In fact, daily sales of chicken have slightly increased, up 7 per cent on November's figures.

So, what are we supposed to make of this? That, even knowing all we know, we are too hard-hearted and greedy to act upon it, and we find it incredibly easy to disassociate the hateful life of the creature from eating its meat? To put it even more simply, we are bad people, except those who are buying Label Anglais from the Harvey Nichols food hall at £25 a pop, who are good people.

Immediately, this riles. Yes, we all have to take responsibility for our consumer choices. But those choices are a lot more meaningful for some than for others. The difference between a three quid broiler and a £10 organic bird to someone with dependants, living on – let's not even be melodramatic and say benefits, let's say the median national income of £24,000 – is very great. To Jamie Oliver, it is no difference at all, on account of how he is loaded. And why is he loaded? Because (a) he makes quite a lot of money entertaining us by gassing boy chicks, and (b) he hoovers up that much and more again by advertising for Sainsbury's, which has been one of the driving forces behind this cheap food since mass production began.

Or, at least, this is the kind of petty-minded line of argument a person might be driven to, standing accused of cruel consumer choices. It is, frankly, obnoxious to see a rich person demanding impoverishing consumer choices from a poorer person. These chef-polemicists consider themselves outside politics, because they're being straightforward – let's eat what came out of the ground naturally, what was raised in a happy way. Let's just do as nature intended, and by gum it will be tasty, and what could possibly be political about that?

They're right, it isn't political, in that it has no consistency of ideas, indeed, doesn't even comprehend its own implications, but it encapsulates rather well what happens when rhetoric becomes unmoored from structured ideology: you get all the worst bits of the left – the proselytising, the sanctimony – and all the worst bits of the right – the I'm-all-right-Jack, the 'if you worked a bit harder, you too could afford to be me'.

The fact is, ethics that come out of your wallet are not ethics. All these catchwords that supposedly convey sensitivity to the environment, to animals, to the developing world – fair trade, organic, free range, food miles, etc. – are just new ways to buy your way into heaven, the modern equivalent of the medieval pardon. Anyone with a serious interest in this would be lobbying the legislature; arguing to tighten laws on animal cruelty. When we just preach to each other, it turns into the most undignified scramble – who can afford to be the most lovely? Well, you can, Jamie and Hugh. You've got loveliness to burn.

ZOE WILLIAMS

BROWN AND CAMERON WOO FARMERS' UNION
February 18 2008

British farmers are to be wooed by a raft of senior politicians this week as the National Farmers' Union (NFU) kicks off its centenary conference. Gordon Brown and David Cameron will be competing to see who can offer the most hope, each trying to persuade suppliers of food – and in the future, biofuels – that they are the farmer's friend.

Cameron, a known supporter of hunting and field sports, is likely to be their favourite, and his address to the conference will attack supermarkets (the farmer's bête noire) by suggesting an extension to farmers' markets, where farmers can get higher prices but food can also be sold at a discount by cutting out the middleman. Gordon Brown will be attending the NFU's dinner on Monday, where he is not expected to get such a rapturous reception, although he is likely to promise a much bigger role for farming in the age of climate change.

Hilary Benn, the environment secretary, will also address the conference where he will announce a £10m boost for a new environment-friendly system of disposing of slurry, which can pollute streams and watercourses. The process, anaerobic digestion, eats up the slurry and other waste, like chemical by-products and cardboard, and the methane produced can be used to heat farms and villages.

He will also promise more action to stop animal diseases, pointing out that Britain cannot afford the £400m bill for blue tongue and foot and mouth.

This should be good news for Peter Kendall, the NFU president. He will say Britain has a moral duty to produce more food to lighten the load on poorer countries struggling to feed their growing populations under the shadow of climate change. Kendall will demand more investment in science and research and less regulation to allow farmers 'to develop the agricultural potential of this country', but will deny he is demanding more subsidy. He will also warn that consumers must be prepared to pay higher food prices, condemning chickens sold for £2 by supermarkets using them as loss leaders. Such actions send 'completely the wrong message' about the cost of producing food to guaranteed standards, he will warn. Kendall will also say that recent farm income figures show a 'dangerously divided industry', with cereal farmers having enjoyed large improvements, while livestock farmers are still making huge losses.

The union says a future in which eastern England is given over to intensive arable production and the west to tourism and niche markets is easy to envisage but bad for farming. His remarks come as farmers get used to a huge shift in the EU's farm payments system, which is no longer predicated on food production but size of holdings. British farmers get around £2bn a year at present.

JAMES MEIKLE AND DAVID HENCKE

BIRDWATCH: SONG THRUSH

March 24 2008

Like most birders, I am often asked which bird is my favourite singer. For some, the complex jazz-musician riffs of the nightingale win the day; others prefer the deep, fruity tones of the blackbird. But for me there can be only one contender for the number one spot. My favourite is a bird that is singing outside my window as I write this piece: the humble and often overlooked song thrush.

For once, the English name of this bird is utterly apt: no other bird sings quite so persistently, or with such unalloyed joy. And although the song thrush may not be the most inventive songster, or even the most melodious, there is still something indescribably wonderful about hearing one in full voice on a chilly evening at the very start of spring.

This year, the song thrush first sang outside our bedroom window on a bright, cold day in late January. Since then he has hardly stopped: morning, noon and night he delivers an almost constant flow of sound, broken up into short phrases of two or three notes each.

In the mornings he seems to beckon me out of bed: 'Get up, get up – time to dress, time to dress …' At midday he calls us to the dinner table: 'Come and eat, come and eat …'. And as darkness falls, he seems to be encouraging the children: 'Go to bed, go to bed …' You can substitute almost any phrase you like – an excellent way, incidentally, to commit the thrush's song to memory.

I can still recall walking home from school in the late 1960s and hearing thrushes singing from almost every rooftop. Along with the lighter evenings, they were a sure sign that winter would soon be over. Sadly, in recent years not everyone has had the chance to hear this harbinger of spring. Song thrushes have suffered a major population crash – due to a combination of dry summers, modern farming methods and an over-zealous use of garden pesticides, which kill off their favourite food of slugs and snails.

Fortunately, Britain's song thrushes may finally have turned the corner, and be on the up again. Wildlife-friendly gardening, more sympathetic farming and a run of wetter summers have all given this species a helping hand, and there certainly seem to be more around this spring than there were last year. In my own neck of the woods, the bird in our front garden is competing with at least two singing out the back.

Soon, I shall take a look for the song thrush's neat, cup-shaped nest in the shrubs and bushes around our home. I remember finding one at the age of 9 or 10, and being enthralled by the clutch of four sky-blue eggs faintly spotted with black – 'little low heavens', as the poet Gerard Manley Hopkins so memorably called them.

My nest-finding skills are a little rusty nowadays, but I shall do my best to track one down, recapture the wonder of that childhood experience, and so celebrate the return of one of our most delightful birds, the song thrush.

STEPHEN MOSS

TV DINNERS: HOW TO MAKE … *SPRINGWATCH*

May 30 2008

1. You are in the kitchen, cooking (beans on toast). Inadequate, tasteless, drab. And the beans on toast aren't much better. Somewhere a world of wonder awaits. If only you were looking in the right places. Out of the window, for example.

2. The great outdoors – or your garden, as you call it. In the shrubbery, you can just make out something moving. Inquisitive, with busy whiskers, its brown furry face combines the likable character of Ratty from *Wind in the Willows* with the slight edge of menace of a ferret. It's Bill Oddie.

3. With a mix of curiosity and consternation, Kate Humble is studying something through her binoculars, muttering superlatives ranging from 'fascinating' to 'absolutely fascinating'. It's Bill Oddie again.

4. Nature's finest ingredients are laid out before you. Fish, pheasant, deer, duck. Can you eat all this, you wonder? And so organic? Resist the urge to sing, 'Goodies! Goody, goody, yum, yum.'

5. Greens are less essential. Shots of meadows, moors and mountains rarely look that good on your kitchen portable.

6. Add plenty of eggs. Eggs being hatched, eggs being laid, eggs being, er, abandoned. The mother has been disturbed – by an osprey, a fox or a lesser-spotted cameraman.

7. Kate Humble is in charge of nesting. 'Great tits!' suggests Oddie, his schoolboy enthusiasm to the fore, though they turn out to be coal tits.

8. To add sauce, finish off by watching owls having soft-focus (out-of-focus) hanky panky. You go back indoors, asking yourself: 'Filming animals having sex ... Is that legal?'

JIM SHELLEY

MR BADGER AND THE QUANGO

July 8 2008

Yesterday provided intriguing material for an examination of class in Britain today. The environment secretary, Hilary Benn, announced that after long thought he had decided not to permit the culling of badgers to stop the spread of TB among cattle. He said there was not enough evidence that it worked, and that a cull might make matters worse.

As always with the Department for Environment, Food and Rural Affairs, there was bags of new jargon to entertain us. Benn talked about the 'testing and slaughter of reactors', and 'randomised culling'. Everyone seemed to know exactly what he meant. And, as always in the Brown government, no matter how long a problem has been around it is never too late to set up a quango. This will be the Bovine

TB Partnership Group, which sounds like an organisation lonely cows join to find new friends.

But the Commons divided almost entirely along party lines: Labour MPs were pro-badger; Tories were all for slaughtering the lot and turning them into shaving brushes. The Conservatives were furious. 'A spineless abdication of responsibility,' said Geoffrey Cox. 'Disgraceful!' shouted several. Stephen O'Brien talked about Benn's 'weak and gutless' decision. Labour MPs, by contrast, rejoiced at the badgers' reprieve. Nick Palmer said the Tory attitude was always the same: 'When in doubt, kill something.' Angela Smith reckoned some farmers would be so angry they would kill them anyway. She demanded the full force of the law should be brought upon them.

I was puzzled why the Tories were so uniformly anti-badger at a time when the scientific evidence seems ambiguous at best. My theory is that it goes back to their pre-prep-school childhoods, when their parents (or nannies) read them *The Wind in the Willows* by Kenneth Grahame. If you recall, Badger is a kindly figure, whom we first meet when he welcomes the lost Mole and Ratty out of the snow into his sett, where they eat a huge meal and sit by a comforting log fire. Badger's role in the story is to stop Toad making an idiot of himself, driving cars too fast and escaping from prison. He is one of literature's great spoilsports. He would have strongly disapproved of the Bullingdon Club.

So Tories associate badgers with pursed lips and disapproval. They are, however, misreading him. Grahame was writing in 1908, when the smell of revolution was in the air. He is against Toad not because Toad is the rich owner of Toad Hall, but because he doesn't recognise that with great wealth and position comes great responsibility. Badger knows that if Toad spends his life in dissipation, the forces of the stoats and weasels will feel justified in seizing the property of the wealthy, and so destroying the class system. Badger guides the successful assault to reclaim Toad Hall, but only when he gets a (worthless) promise from Toad to reform.

So Badger was on the side of the toffs. It would be very different today. The book would have to be rewritten as if by Elmore Leonard.

'Why, come in my dear friends, you must be perished!' said Badger.

'Sorry, we're from the Bovine TB Partnership Group, and you're going to get exactly what's coming, you furry freak!' BLAM!!!

SIMON HOGGART

☙ SELECT BIBLIOGRAPHY ☙

The bibliography of the countryside is immense and the Googleography even larger. For an enjoyable initial ramble, and with warm acknowledgment, we would recommend:

Aldous, Tony *Goodbye Britain?* Sidgwick & Jackson 1975
Boston, Richard *Beer and Skittles* Collins 1976
Fitter, Richard *Wildlife in Britain* Penguin 1963
Kightly, Charles *Country Voices* Thames & Hudson 1984
Sampson, Anthony *Anatomy of Britain* 1962 and *The Changing Anatomy of Britain* 1982 Hodder
Trevelyan, G.M. *English Social History* Longmans 1942
Vale, Edmund *Curiosities of Town and Countryside* Batsford 1940

For an introduction to the contemporary countryside, the websites of Natural England, the Department for the Environment, Food and Rural Affairs, the Countryside Alliance and the Ramblers provide a wealth of information and further links. Scottish National Heritage and the Countryside Council for Wales also have useful portals.

www.naturalengland.org.uk
www.defra.gov.uk
www.countryside-alliance.org
www.ramblers.org.uk
www.ccw.gov.uk
www.snh.org.uk

⊘ INDEX ⊘